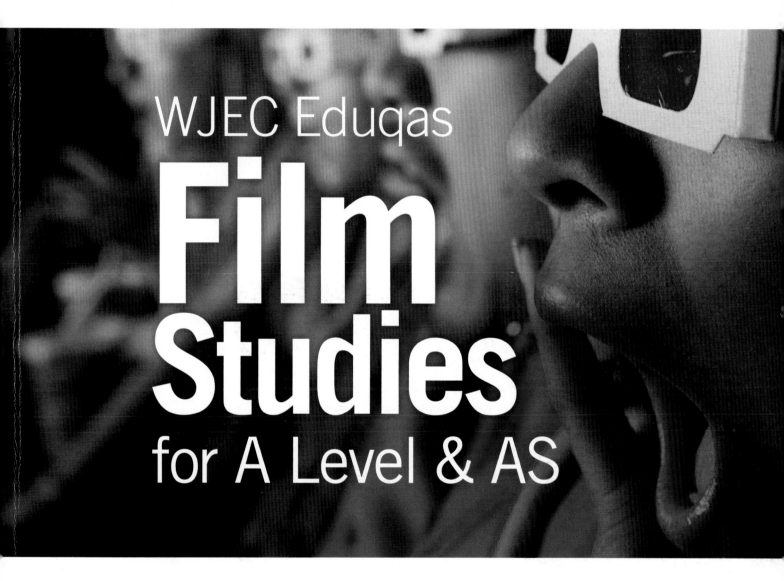

WJEC Eduqas
Film Studies
for A Level & AS

Ellen Cheshire
Mark Ramey
Jenny Stewart
Lisa Wardle
Consultant Editor: Lisa Wardle

Published in 2018 by Illuminate Publishing Ltd, PO Box 1160, Cheltenham, Gloucestershire GL50 9RW

Orders: Please visit www.illuminatepublishing.com

or email sales@illuminatepublishing.com

© 2018

The moral rights of the authors have been asserted.

All rights reserved. No part of this book may be reprinted, reproduced or utilised in any form or by any electronic, mechanical, or other means, now known or hereafter invented, including photocopying and recording, or in any information storage and retrieval system, without permission in writing from the publishers.

British Library Cataloguing-in-Publication Data

A catalogue record for this book is available from the British Library

ISBN 978-1-911208-44-0

Printed by Cambrian Printers, Aberystwyth

07.19

The publisher's policy is to use papers that are natural, renewable and recyclable products made from wood grown in sustainable forests. The logging and manufacturing processes are expected to conform to the environmental regulations of the country of origin.

Every effort has been made to contact copyright holders of material produced in this book. Great care has been taken by the authors and publisher to ensure that either formal permission has been granted for the use of copyright material reproduced, or that copyright material has been used under the provision of fair dealing guidelines in the UK – specifically that it has been used sparingly, solely for the purpose of criticism and review, and has been properly acknowledged. If notified, the publisher will be pleased to rectify any errors or omissions at the earliest opportunity.

This material has been endorsed by WJEC/Eduqas and offers high-quality support for the delivery of WJEC/Eduqas qualifications. While this material has been through a WJEC/Edquas quality assurance process, all responsibility for the content remains with the publisher.

Editor: Dawn Booth

Design and layout: Jon Fletcher

Cover design: Nigel Harriss

Cover image: Juice Images / Alamy Stock Photo

Screenshot acknowledgements

Apocalypse Now Redux, dir. Francis Ford Coppola [DVD), 1979, Miramax [2002]; Beasts of the Southern Wild, dir. Benh Zeitlin [DVD], 2012, Studiocanal [2013]; *Blade Runner – the Director's Cut*, dir. Ridley Scott [DVD], 1982, Warner [2006]; *Bonnie & Clyde*, dir. Arthur Penn [DVD], 1967, Warner [2006]; *Boyhood*, dir. Richard Linklater [DVD], 2014, Universal Pictures UK [2015]; *Casablanca*, dir. Michael Curtiz [DVD], 1942, Warner Brothers [2006]; *City of God, (Cidade De Deus)*, dir. Fernando Meirelles, co-dir. Kátia Lund [DVD], 2002, Miramax [2003]; *Daisies*, dir. Věra Chytilová, [DVD], 1966, Second Run [2009]; *Dil Se*, dir. Mani Ratnam [YouTube], 1998, YouTube music video montage; *Fish Tank*, dir. Andrea Arnold [DVD], 2009, Artificial Eye [2010]; *Frances Ha*, dir. Noah Baumbach [DVD], 2012, Metrodome Distribution [2014]; *House of Flying Daggers*, dir. Zhang Yimou [DVD], 2004, Twentieth Century Fox [2005]; *Ida*, dir. Pawel Pawlikowski, [DVD], 2013, Solopan [2014]; *Inception*, dir. Christopher Nolan [DVD], 2010, Warner Home Video [2010]; *La La Land*, dir. Damien Chazelle [DVD], 2016, Lions Gate, [2017]; *The Lady from Shanghai*, dir. Orson Welles [DVD], 1947, Sony Pictures Home Entertainment [2003]; *Life is Beautiful*, dir. Roberto Benigni [DVD], 1997, Miramax [2001]; *Michael Nyman's – Man With a Movie Camera*, dir. Dziga Vertov [DVD], 1929, BFI [2002]; *Mustang*, dir. Deniz Gamze Ergüven [DVD], 2016, Artificial Eye [2016]; *No Country for Old Men*, dir. Joel and Ethan Coen [DVD], 2007, Paramount Home Entertainment [2008]; *Nosferatu*, dir. F.W. Murnau [DVD], 1922, Masters of Cinema, Eureka [2013]; *One Flew Over the Cuckoo's Nest*, dir. Milos Forman [DVD], 1975, Warner Home Video [2002]; *Pulp Fiction*, dir. Quentin Tarantino [DVD], 1994, Lionsgate [2011]; *Saute ma ville*, dir. Chantal Akerman, [VIMEO] 1968; *Secrets and Lies*, dir. Mike Leigh [DVD], 1996, Channel 4 DVD [2015]; *Shaun of the Dead*, dir. Edgar Wright [DVD], 2004, Universal Pictures UK [2004]; *Sightseers*, dir. Ben Wheatley [DVD], 2012, Studio Canal Limited [2013]; *Stories We Tell*, dir. Sarah Polley [DVD], Curzon Film World [2013]; *Sunrise: A Song of Two Humans*, dir. F W Murnau [Blu-ray], 1927, Masters of Cinema, Eureka [2011]; *Taste of Cherry*, dir. Abbas Kiarostami [DVD], 1997, Artificial Eye [2005]; *Taxi Tehran*, dir. Jafar Panahi [DVD], 2015, New Wave Films [2016]; *The Arbor*, dir. Clio Barnard [DVD], 2010, Verve Pictures [2011]; The Cabinet of Dr Caligari, dir. Robert Wiene [Blu-ray], 1920, Masters of Cinema, Eureka [2014]; *The White Balloon*, dir. Jafar Panahi, 1995; *This is England*, dir. Shane Meadows [DVD], 2006, Studiocanal [2007]; *This is Not a Film*, dir. Jafar Panahi [DVD], 2011, Palisades Tartan [2013]; *Timecode*, dir. Mike Figgis [DVD], 2000, Optimum Home Releasing [2003]; *Trainspotting*, dir. Danny Boyle [DVD], 1996, Channel 4 [2009]; *Victoria*, dir. Sebastian Schipper [DVD], 2015, Artificial Eye [2016]; *Vivre sa vie*, dir. Jean-Luc Godard [DVD], 1962, BFI [2015]; *We Need to Talk About Kevin*, dir. Lynne Ramsay [DVD], 2011, Artificial Eye [2012]; *Wild Tales*, dir. Damián Szifron [DVD], 2014, Artificial Eye [2015]; *Winter's Bone*, dir. Debra Granik, [DVD], 2010, Artificial Eye [2011]

Photo acknowledgements

p1 Juice Images / Alamy Stock Photo; p18 Moviestore Collection Ltd / Alamy Stock Photo; p26 (2nd down) Pan's Labyrinth; p48 AF archive / Alamy Stock Photo; p49 Vertigo; p51 (top) Strangers on a Train; p51 (bottom) Vertigo; p52 Vertigo; p53 Granger Historical Picture Archive / Alamy Stock Photo; p54 cinesential.com; p58 (top right) Creative commons; p59 (top) AF archive / Alamy Stock Photo; p59 (bottom) Atlaspix / Alamy Stock Photo; p62 Everett Collection Inc / Alamy Stock Photo; p61 (middle) History of the Cinema; p64 AF archive / Alamy Stock Photo; p65 AF archive / Alamy Stock Photo; p66 (top) Under the Skin; p66 (bottom) 2001: Space Odyssey; p69 (top right) Diary of a Country Priest; p69 (middle right) The Passion of Joan of Arc; p69 (bottom right) The Virgin Spring; p69 (bottom left) Creative commons; p69 (top left) Photo 12 / Alamy Stock Photo; p71 (top) Weinstein Company; p71 (bottom) Atlaspix / Alamy Stock Photo; p72 Weinstein Company; p73 (top) Red Umbrella; p73 (bottom) Photo 12 / Alamy Stock Photo; p74 (both) Weinstein Company; p76 United Archives GmbH / Alamy Stock Photo; p77 (top) AF archive / Alamy Stock Photo; p77 (bottom) Some Like it Hot; p79 Heritage Image Partnership Ltd / Alamy Stock Photo; p80 Pictorial Press; p81 Atlaspix / Alamy Stock Photo; p82 (top) a katz / Shutterstock.com; p82 (bottom) Tinseltown / Shutterstock.com; p83 (top) Featureflash Photo Agency / Shutterstock.com; p84 (top) Empire; p87 (3 top) Creative commons; p86 (bottom) Everett Collection Inc / Alamy Stock Photo; p87 (top) Santosh Kumar - Creative commons; p87 (middle right) AF Archive / Alamy Stock Photo; p87 (bottom) Denis Makarenko / Shutterstock.com; p88 (bottom) http://www.bollywoodhungama.com/; p90 AF archive / Alamy Stock Photo; p91 (left) Granger Historical Picture Archive / Alamy Stock Photo; p91 (right) Everett Collection Inc / Alamy Stock Photo; p92 Creative commons; p98 (top left) AF archive / Alamy Stock Photo; p98 (bottom left) Pictorial Press Ltd / Alamy Stock Photo; p98 (bottom right) Gun Crazy; p100 (top) Everett Collection Historical / Alamy Stock Photo; p101 (top) Texas Hideout; p101 (bottom) ScreenProd / Photononstop / Alamy Stock Photo; p106 ScreenProd / Photononstop / Alamy Stock Photo; p107 (bottom) Granger Historical Picture Archive / Alamy Stock Photo; p109 (top) Eye-Stock / Alamy Stock Photo; p109 (bottom) Everett Collection Historical / Alamy Stock Photo; p110 (top) Keystone Pictures USA / Alamy Stock Photo; p111 (bottom) Moviestore collection Ltd / Alamy Stock Photo; p112 MARKA / Alamy Stock Photo; p113 Public domain; p114 (top) Everett Collection Inc / Alamy Stock Photo; p114 (top) Everett Collection Inc / Alamy Stock Photo; p114 (middle) AF archive / Alamy Stock Photo; p114 (bottom) Everett Collection Inc / Alamy Stock Photo; p115 Everett Collection Inc / Alamy Stock Photo; p118 Pictorial Press Ltd / Alamy Stock Photo; p119 Atlaspix / Alamy Stock Photo; p120 Pictorial Press / Alamy Stock Photo; p121 (bottom) Moviestore Collection Ltd / Alamy Stock Photo; p122 (top) CinemaScope; p125 (top) Splash News / Alamy Stock Photo; p128 (middle) Granger Historical Picture Archive / Alamy Stock Photo; p128 (top) Photo 12 / Alamy Stock Photo; p129 Public Domain / Art Institute of Chicago; p130 (top left) Creative commons; p130 (top right) Creative commons; p131 (top) ZUMA Press, Inc. / Alamy Stock Photo; p131 (bottom) ZUMA Press, Inc. / Alamy Stock Photo; p133 (bottom) Everett Collection Inc / Alamy Stock Photo; p137 La La Land Interrogation / YouTube; p142 Photo 12 / Alamy Stock Photo; p143 Pictorial Press Ltd / Alamy Stock Photo; p145 Group 13; p146 Photo 12 / Alamy Stock Photo; p147 (top) Nathan Holland; p156 (bottom) Granger Historical Picture Archive; p160 Pictorial Press Ltd / Alamy Stock Photo; p161 (left) Moviestore Collection Ltd / Alamy Stock Photo; p161 (right) Everett Collection Inc / Alamy Stock Photo; p161 (top) Courtesy BFI; p161 (bottom) Courtesy Channel 4; p161 (middle) BBC; p164 (bottom) AF Archive / Alamy Stock Photo; p165 (top) Trinity Mirror / Mirrorpix / Alamy Stock Photo; p165 (bottom) s_bukley / Shutterstock.com; p166 (bottom) S.I.N. / Alamy Stock Photo; p164 (2nd left) Pictorial Press Ltd / Alamy Stock Photo; p164 (top right) Witchfinder General; p164 (top left) The King's Speech; p164 (2nd right) Monty Python; p166 (bottom) jeremy sutton-hibbert / Alamy Stock Photo; p168 (middle right) CBW / Alamy Stock Photo; p170 (2nd top) Entertainment Pictures / Alamy Stock Photo; p175 (top) AF Archive / Alamy Stock Photo; p175 (bottom) AF Archive / Alamy Stock Photo; p179 (top) AF Archive / Alamy Stock Photo; p190 Atlaspix / Alamy Stock Photo; p192 (top) Mustang; p192 (bottom) Mustang; p193 (top) Everett Collection Inc / Alamy Stock Photo; p193 (bottom) Durgun Dernek; p194 Courtesy BFI; p206 Everett Collection Inc / Alamy Stock Photo; p208 Everett Collection Inc / Alamy Stock Photo; p210 dpa picture alliance archive / Alamy Stock Photo; p211 Granger Historical Picture Archive / Alamy Stock; Photo; p226 AF Archive / Alamy Stock Photo; p227 Everett Collection Inc / Alamy Stock Photo; p228 Creative commons; p231 Everett Collection Inc / Alamy Stock Photo; p232 (top) Koyaanisqatsi; p232 (2nd top) March of the Penguins; p232 (3rd down) Entertainment Pictures / Alamy Stock Photo; p232 (bottom) Everett collection Inc / Alamy Stock Photo; p233 (top) Everett Collection Inc / Alamy Stock Photo; p233 (bottom) Tongues Tied; p245 Moviestore Collection Ltd / Alamy Stock Photo; p246 Everett Collection Inc / Alamy Stock Photo; p250 Pictorial Press Ltd / Alamy Stock Photo; p251 Everett Collection Inc / Alamy Stock Photo; p255 (top) Everett Collection Inc / Alamy Stock Photo; p255 (bottom) Creative commons; p266 © H.C. Milner Litho Co., Public domain; p268 Everett Collection Inc / Alamy Stock Photo; p269 (bottom) iryna1 / Shutterstock.com; p270 (top) Lifestyle pictures / Alamy Stock Photo; p270 (bottom) Everett Collection Inc / Alamy Stock Photo; p271 (bottom) Everett Collection Inc / Alamy Stock Photo; p272 (bottom) The 'High Sign; p273 (top 2) One Week; p276 Cops; p276 (bottom) Everett Collection Inc / Alamy Stock Photo; p277 (top) Archive PL / Alamy Stock Photo; p280 United Archives GmbH / Alamy Stock Photo; p281 (top left) Daisies; p281 (top right) Saute ma vie; p283 Interfoto / Alamy Stock Photo; p284 (top) AF Archive / Alamy Stock Photo; p284 (bottom) Creative commons; p285 Daisies; p292 (top) Creative commons; p293 Featureflash Photo Agency / Shutterstock.com; p294 Moviestore Collection Ltd / Alamy Stock Photo; p296 Moviestore Collection Ltd / Alamy Stock Photo; p297 (middle) Moviestore Collection Ltd / Alamy Stock Photo; p298 (top) Everett Collection Inc / Alamy Stock Photo; p298 (bottom) Photo 12 / Alamy Stock Photo; p300 (top) Pictorial Press Ltd / Alamy Stock Photo; p305 (top) AF Archive / Alamy Stock Photo; p305 (bottom) Everett Collection Inc / Alamy Stock Photo; p310 AF Archive / Alamy Stock Photo; p315 La Jetee; p316 United Archives GmbH / Alamy Stock Photo; p317 Everett Collection Inc / Alamy Stock Photo; p319 The Gunfighter; p320 storyboard.com; p325 Moviestore collection Ltd / Alamy Stock Photo; AF Archive / Alamy Stock Photo; p331 2000 Days; p333 This is England; p338 AF Archive / Alamy Stock Photo; p345 Vertigo

Contents

Introduction

 Further information

These are the assessment objectives for this specification. Learners must:

AO1 demonstrate knowledge and understanding of elements of film. To achieve well in AO1 you need to show that you have a secure understanding of the core areas and specialist areas for each module. This includes using subject-specific terminology accurately such as shot types and editing techniques plus demonstrating a clear grasp of the theoretical approaches to film covered on the course such as the auteur approach or spectatorship theory.

AO2 apply knowledge and understanding of elements of film to:

- analyse and compare films, including through the use of critical approaches
- evaluate the significance of critical approaches*
- analyse and evaluate own work in relation to other professionally produced work. To achieve good marks in AO2 you need to show that you can apply your understanding of the core and specialist modules when analysing films. To do well you should use a range of examples from the films studied to back-up your points and for the Hollywood 1930–1990 module explicitly explore similarities and differences between the films. You should also be able to apply relevant theories or approaches to the analysis of films and reflect on how they improve your understanding. It is important to also be able to reflect on your own creative work and compare it with other films.

AO3 Apply knowledge and understanding of elements of film to the production of a film or screenplay. High marks here are awarded when your creative work clearly shows that you have a secure understanding of how films are constructed. Your screenplay and storyboard, or film, should use elements of film form in a coherent way and adhere to the required conventions.

* These assessment objectives apply for both the AS and A level courses with the exception of the requirement to evaluate the significance of critical approaches, which only applies to the A level qualification.

This book is designed to guide you through the WJEC Eduqas 2017 Film Studies AS and A level courses. These qualifications were designed to encourage you to explore the power and beauty of cinema by examining films from a range of eras and countries, from the mainstream to the experimental, the silent era to the contemporary. This textbook is structured to support the specification and incorporates guidance on the areas of study that can be applied to any of the set films plus in-depth case studies of at least one film for each module.

How to use this book

Part 1 offers a very detailed exploration of the core study areas:

- film form
- meaning
- response and context.

It can be used as an in-depth glossary to help you understand some of the terminology associated with Film Studies but it also includes some case studies from the specification to show you how this new knowledge can be applied. In the examination knowledge of these core areas could be tested for any film, so a clear understanding of them is crucial.

Part 2 of the book contains the detailed case studies. These sections take you through the analysis of a film, applying the core areas and the relevant specialist areas outlined by the specification. If the chapter is not on a film you are studying it will still offer relevant theoretical information and context, which can be applied to your chosen film. This part of the book also offers guidance on the production module.

The third and final part is a brief overview of study skills and revision techniques to help you get the most out of the qualification and achieve your potential.

The book includes Independent Activities (IAs) and opportunities for Stretch and Challenge (S&C). To make the most of this publication you should strive to do as many of these as possible.

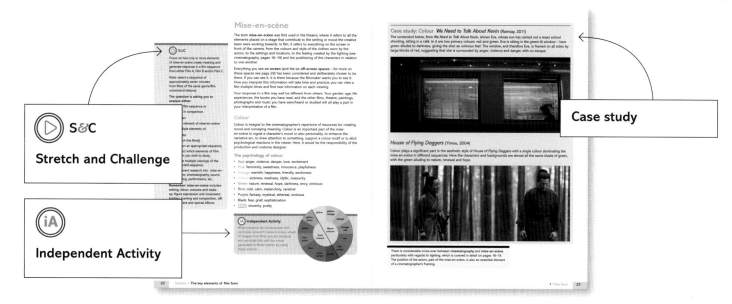

S&C

Stretch and Challenge

Independent Activity

Case study

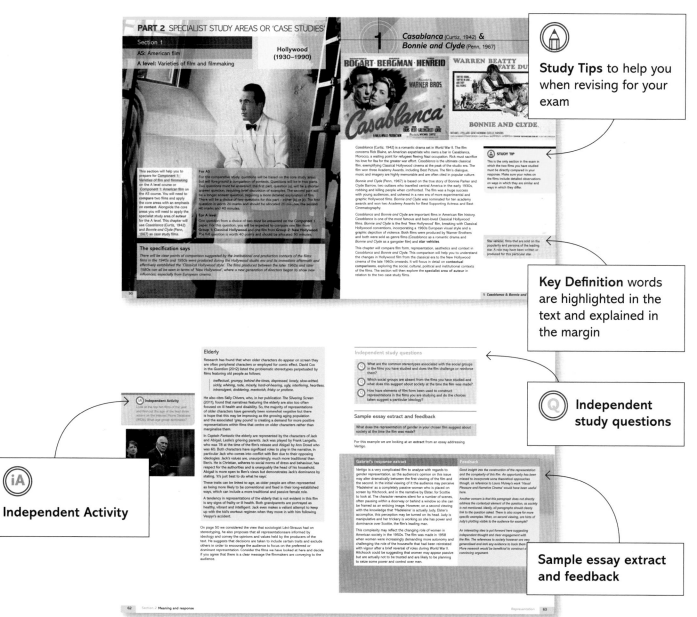

Study Tips to help you when revising for your exam

Key Definition words are highlighted in the text and explained in the margin

Independent Activity

Independent study questions

Sample essay extract and feedback

Film form

What is film form?

Film form is everything that filmmakers take into consideration when making a film. It is how the content is expressed, rather than the story itself.

By **studying**, or **reading**, a **film**, you will see what techniques filmmakers use to:

- further narrative and character
- stimulate an emotional response
- reveal further layers of meaning
- place the film within a particular genre or style.

Once you have gained an understanding of the fundamentals of **film form** you will develop your own way of studying a film. Your method may differ from other people's way of studying. You will find that a group studying the same scene will each see and interpret it differently. This is OK.

Why study film form?

A starting point for studying film is to consider all the **essential decisions** the director and key creative personnel use when planning the visual and aural elements of a film.

These elements, known as film form, are:

- cinematography
- mise-en-scène
- editing
- sound
- performance.

By examining these in close detail, you will gain further insights into the characters, narrative structure, themes and messages that you may have missed the first time you watched the film.

These elements serve to create a mood and add to the overall aesthetic of the film.

Form and meaning

Meaning, in this context, is an interpretation of the narrative based on what we see and hear (**form**). This meaning may be explicit (what the film is about, i.e. the plot) or implicit (what is lying beneath the surface).

As active film viewers, we look for the 'hidden' meanings, and studying **film form** helps us to achieve a deeper understanding of them.

Aesthetic: the style adopted by an artist (in a film's case the filmmaker) or a film movement. For example, despite the different settings of *Trainspotting* (Boyle, 1996) and *Slumdog Millionaire* (Boyle, 2009), both films share a visual look and feel, created by the director's high-energy visual style, by way of his choice of camerawork, editing and music. German Expressionism was an artistic movement that encompassed theatre, dance, architecture, painting, sculpture and film. The aesthetic shared between expressionist films included exaggeration in performance, setting, lighting and disorientating camera angles.

The director

You only have to sit through the end credits of a film to see how many people are involved in the making of it. It is not possible for a director to carry out every aspect of production. **The director is responsible for the artistic and dramatic aspects of turning a written script into a film.** The director has full control over and responsibility for the myriad of tasks required in making a film and combining them to create his or her vision.

One way of studying film is to look at the body of a work of a director. You will begin to see recurring visual styles and motifs in it. Directors with a strong **aesthetic** have become known as auteurs.

Some directors, for example Alfred Hitchcock, relish the notion of the auteur and their place within the pantheon of auteur directors; while others completely disown the auteur theory, acknowledging the input of everyone involved in the filmmaking process.

> **Production:** the period of actual shooting. As this is the most costly, as much planning is done in the pre-production process, with daily shooting schedules prepared to ensure that the material required in each location or with a group of actors is secured. Most films are shot out of sequence.

> **Auteur:** certain directors will have a strong aesthetic; you will begin to see recurring visual styles and motifs. These directors have become known as auteurs.

Case study: Film form

Film form is used to add meaning and response to a scene. The terms used here will be explored in detail in this section.

This is England (Meadows, 2006) – the party scene (00:36:42–40:16)

By analysing a scene, drawing on all its component elements, you will develop further layers of meaning. The party scene, where Combo and his friend turn up, from *This is England* signals the tipping point from the touching and warm-hearted first half to a more aggressive and bleaker second half of the film.

As we return to the party, it is clear from the first shot that the atmosphere has changed. Combo is placed in the **centre of the frame** potentially displacing Woody as the leader of the group. Combo is dressed in white, which draws the eye to him. There is no **diegetic** music; all the people have been silenced by Combo, who now dominates the conversation.

Their shared **costuming, hair styling** and **presentation** mark them as a group with a mutual connection. However, Combo and his friend Banjo's appearance, with much closer shaven hair and tattoos, is far more aggressive, indicating a more threatening presence.

Tattoos are an important part of each character's costuming. Woody and Combo both have identical crosses on their forehead, which infers a shared past. The cross appears to be Woody's only tattoo, but Combo also has a teardrop, a spider's web and a swallow, all of which are symbols associated with 'doing time' in jail.

The scene is largely filmed from **eye-level** and is **subjective**, as though we, the viewers, are sitting with them.

Combo's face is predominantly held in **close-up** to emphasise his face, which is animated with large movements around his eyes and mouth. He takes up more **physical space** than the others do, and the **midshots** show his wide hand gestures as he becomes more engrossed with his prison anecdote about a black prisoner stealing his pudding.

The others are listening, all attention is focused on him, their **body movements** are smaller and their **micro-expressions** betray many emotions, from concern (downcast eyes) to enjoyment (nodding and laughing).

When Combo uses the derogatory word 'wog', **stress** is placed on it for emphasis and the shock of its use is shown in **reaction shots**.

The tension is momentarily broken when Shaun and Smell enter the room. The camera remains at the seated eye-level and becomes a **point-of-view (POV) shot** as Combo takes in this young boy. The shot means that Smell's head and shoulders are not in shot, which amplifies how small Shaun is, as he can still be seen in full.

At first Combo is aggressive towards Shaun, before teasing and then dismissing him, to continue with his story. The introduction of plaintive **non-diegetic music** initially underscores his dialogue, and then overwhelms it, leaving just the sombre music to accompany a close-up of Combo, which seems slightly slowed down. Unable to hear what he is saying, we rely on his body movements and facial expression for meaning, and **cut-aways** to the other characters (single and grouped).

The music continues at the end of the scene into the next scene, thereby making an **aural link** that the downbeat mood has lingered to the next day.

Cinematography:
Types of shot (i)

Cinematography (the **framing** and **design of shots**) encompasses a range of processes and techniques that come together to give the film its visual look and convey messages and values.

The director will have a vision of what they want the film to look like, and during pre-production the cinematographer will make dozens of decisions in order to create this vision and reality.

The five key areas of cinematography are:
- shot types and camera angles (from which viewpoint we see the camera)
- camera movement (how the camera moves around the action)
- lighting (how the shot is lit)
- colour (how colour is used to communicate additional information)
- composition (the way people and objects are placed within the shot).

Other aspects to be considered are:
- film stock: 16mm, 35mm, 70mm, 3D, IMAX (although, today, shooting digitally is the primary method)
- aspect ratio: the standard ratios in use are 2:35:1 or 1:85:1. 2:35:1 is usually used for action/blockbusters, 1:85:1 for character-led films. 4:3 was the standard until the 1950s
- frame rate: the standard is 24 frames per second (fps), but there have been 48fps and 120fps releases.

Types of shot

Most scenes/sequences are made up of a series of shots, showing the action from different angles and points of view.

The most regularly used shot types are as follows.

Extreme long shot (ELS) or establishing shot

Filmed from a very long way away, an extreme long shot will often be a view of an exterior location. It is often used as an establishing shot to show a panoramic view of where the film is set. Such shots are the cinematographer's equivalent of a landscape painting: full of shape and hue but with little precise detail, although usually just enough to provide clues to the film's genre and setting.

Extreme long shot (ELS; *Blade Runner*, Scott, 1982)

Pre-production: the period prior to filming, where key decisions are made, including securing funding, selecting actors and creative personnel, choosing locations, building sets, designing costumes and determining the film's aesthetic, and planning the production schedule.

Cinematographer: responsible for the look of the film; in charge of the camera technique and translates the director's vision onto the screen, advising the director on camera angles, lighting and special effects.

Film stock: the type of film used to shoot the film on.

Aspect ratio: the shape of the image; this affects the composition of the shots. The first aspect ratio used was 4:3: the first number refers to the width of the screen and the second to the height. Therefore, for every 4 inches in width, there will be 3 inches height.

Frames per second (fps): the frame rate, or the speed that individual frames are projected to give the allusion of movement.

Shot: used to mean different aspects of the filmmaking process.
- For the cinematographer a **shot** is from the moment the camera starts rolling (action) to the end (cut).
- For the editor a **shot** is continuous scene or sequences between two cuts or edits.
- Refers to the process of shooting a film, e.g. 'we shot four minutes of screen time today'.
- There are different types of **shot**, which refer to the distance between the camera and the subject.

Long shot (LS)

A long shot clearly features the main character or characters, but will also offer a fair amount of background. This shot is useful for showing us who the central characters in the scene are and where it is set.

 Independent Activity

Consider the directors of the films you are studying. What do you know about their body of work? Watch some of the films again. Is their visual and aural style consistent from film to film? If so, which elements remain the same?

Long shot (LS; *Frances Ha*, Baumbach, 2012)

Medium-long shot (MLS)

A medium-long shot focuses on the main part of the characters, but probably cuts them off at the knees. It can be comfortably used to show two figures walking, talking, dancing, etc.

Medium-long shot (MLS; *Fish Tank*, Arnold, 2009)

Medium shot (MS) or midshot

A medium shot, or midshot, shows a character's upper body, arms and head. If there are two figures they will have to be quite close to each other in order to fit them both in the shot. This sort of shot therefore implies a certain intimacy between characters and between the characters and the viewers.

Medium shot (MS; *Shaun of the Dead*, Wright, 2004)

When you are assessing a shot, look at the amount of the subject you can see in it. Can you only see their eyes, their full body or are they just a distant figure? What do you learn about the characters and the setting from these different shot types?

Cinematography:
Types of shot (ii)

Two-shot

A two-shot shows two characters who are not necessarily side-by-side, but are clearly the two central characters in a scene. Their proximity and the framing of the shot are indicators of the characters' relationship. They can be placed in the foreground (FG) or the background (BG), and the **depth of field** can be adjusted to highlight and draw focus of one element of the image over another.

Two-shot (*We Need to Talk About Kevin*, Ramsay, 2011)

Medium close-up (MCU)

A medium close-up (MCU) is used to direct the viewer's attention entirely onto one character by focusing on their head and shoulders. This shot is used to deliver powerful/emotional lines of dialogue or for more nuanced facial expressions.

A medium close-up (MCU; *No Country for Old Men*, Coen Brothers, 2008)

Close-up (CU)

A close-up is perhaps the most important shot in the development of cinematography and the moment that the power is taken away from the viewer. The director is drawing attention to where they want to you focus.

This is a shot where the whole of the actor's face fills the full frame while showing their emotions, delivering key lines or simply showing their best side.

In shots that don't involve actors, close-ups give the viewer the opportunity to have a good look at one particular detail, which could be part of the unravelling of the narrative or to help create a mood.

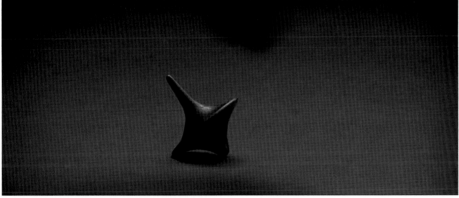

Close-ups (CUs; *Inception*, Nolan, 2010)

Extreme close-up (ECU)

Extreme close-ups (ECUs) get you almost too close to an actor, allowing the viewer into the character's intimate space to reveal detail or emotions that would go unnoticed.

Developments in macro-photography have enabled extreme close-ups of individual flecks of colour in an actor's iris or something reflected in them.

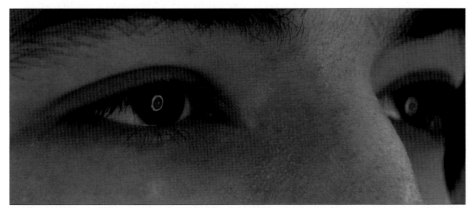

Extreme close-up (ECU; *We Need to Talk About Kevin*, Ramsay, 2011)

 Further information

Deep focus shot has a great depth of field from front to back, with the foreground, middle ground and background ALL remaining in sharp focus. The placement of objects or actors in the plane of vision allows for the manipulation of size and scale. If an object in the foreground looms larger than anything else in the frame then this is likely to be of greater importance.

We Need to Talk About Kevin (Ramsay, 2011)

The opposite is **shallow focus**, where the small depth field has one plane in focus (i.e. the foreground) and the background out of focus. The eye will be drawn to the object or actor in the foreground that is in sharp focus, rather than blurred image in the background

Inception (Nolan, 2010)

Depth of field: the distance between the nearest and furthest objects in a scene that are in sharp focus in a shot.

Cinematography:
Camera angles and perspectives

A camera angle is simply the angle from which the camera 'sees' the subject. There are several angles, all of which provide different effects.

Aerial shot

Aerial shot (*Apocalypse Now*, Coppola, 1979)

An aerial is often used as an establishing shot or at the opening of a film. It offers a bird's-eye view, swooping over a landscape. An aerial shot is designed to be impressive and is best used at the beginning of a film, before the characters and narrative have been established. If used later on, it could remind the audience they are watching a film and break the 'spell'.

Overhead shot

Overhead shot (*The Lady from Shanghai*, Welles, 1947)

This shot is literally taken from up high – looking down. Again, it is most frequently used as an establishing shot to set the scene. Although the shot begins as an overhead, it will often move down and inwards towards the characters – drawing the viewer quite literally into the story.

Eye-level shot

An eye-level shot is taken using the most natural camera angle. The eye-level chosen will usually be that of the dominant character, this helps you identify with them, as though you are seeing the world as the character sees it.

Eye-level shot (*Shaun of the Dead*, Wright, 2004)

Over-the-shoulder shot

Usually used to shoot a conversation, the camera is positioned behind one of the characters, taking in their shoulder, while filming the other.

Over-the-shoulder shot (*Fish Tank*, Arnold, 2009)

High-angle shot

A high-angle shot is usually taken from just above head-height. Using this shot is a good way of making someone look small and insignificant, simply because we are looking down on them. However, not all high-angle shots serve this purpose.

Low-angle shot

Simply by setting the camera lower than eye-level and looking up at the subject, a low-angle shot can be employed to make a character (or object) dominate the frame, making them more threatening or heroic.

Objective

With an objective camera angle you are viewing the scene through the eye of an unseen observer. The viewpoint doesn't belong to any of the characters; therefore it can be seen as impersonal.

High-angle shot (*We Need to Talk About Kevin*, Ramsay, 2011)

Low-angle shot (*City of God*, Meirelles, 2002)

Objective shot (*Fish Tank*, Arnold, 2009)

Subjective

With a subjective camera angle (also known as a **point-of-view (POV) shot**) the viewer is placed in the action either as an active participant or by trading place with a character. This is typically used when the camera replaces the viewpoint of a character looking at someone from afar. In a horror film it could indicate the killer stalking their victim, or it can be used when one character is admiring another.

Subjective or point-of-view (POV) shot (*House of Flying Daggers*, Yimou, 2004)

(iA) Independent Activity

Watch a scene from any film and note how the camera angles help shape your view of characters or spaces.

Cinematography:
Camera movements

If the angle of view in the shot is to change without there being an edit, the camera has to move. This can be done in several ways.

Fixed axis

When a camera is attached to a fixed axis it stays rooted to the spot but can turn to follow the action, as when used in:

- a **pan**: when the camera moves from left to right or vice versa. This technique is used to follow a person as they walk across a room or to swing from one part of the frame to another
- a **whip pan**: uses the same movement as a pan but at speed; however, its increased speed often blurs the image
- a **tilt** is when the camera moves its lens up or down. This type of shot may be used to look slowly upwards at a building – thereby emphasising how tall it is.

Shifting axis

When the whole camera moves it is said to have a shifting axis. This type of shot is used when the camera needs to move in a very precise direction. There are different methods for moving the camera:

- **Dolly shot:** the camera is mounted on a wheeled platform called a 'dolly', which is used to move the camera through a space in a relatively straight line. The dolly's wheels have tyres for smooth movement and it can only be used on very flat surfaces.
- **Tracking shot:** the dolly is mounted on a track, which has been laid out in a specific route through the action, and follows a subject from behind, alongside or in front.

Zoom

A zoom isn't an actual camera movement as such, but it does create the illusion of movement by starting off viewing its subject from a distance then zooming in (using a lens with a variable focus length) to look at a small part of it in much greater detail or vice versa. A **crash zoom** is the same movement but quicker.

iA Independent Activity

Select two films you are studying, and watch the opening sequences multiple times and make a note on the following elements of film form:

- the use of sound
- the use of music
- the camera angles
- the camera movement
- the pace and style of editing.

Then answer the following questions:

1. Do you think this is the work of a director with a strong aesthetic? If so, why?
2. What genre/film movement do you think this film belongs to? Why do you think this?
3. What else struck you about this opening sequence?
4. Who do you think the intended audience for this film would be?

Camera movements

Track Zoom Pan Tilt

Crane shot

A crane shot is when the camera is mounted on a crane or boom arm and is lowered, raised or swung sideways – like a vertical tracking shot. By using a crane, you can move the camera around the action from one level to another.

Originally, a camera operator would sit at the top of the crane, along with the camera. Nowadays, cameras can be controlled remotely via drones, lightweight/manoeuvrable boom arms and cranes. A camera can now travel up the outside of a wall and pass through a half-open window with very little effort, where once that would have required the building of a special wall that could be pulled apart instantly to let the camera and camera operator pass through.

Hand-held

In the early days of filmmaking when films were made on lightweight 16mm film stock, it was easy to pick up a camera and film hand-held.

The image (right) is from *Man with a Movie Camera* (Vertov, 1929) and shows how filmmakers during the silent film period could film without the restrictions that sound brought about.

With the introduction of 35mm and sound, cameras became more difficult to manoeuvre, so it wasn't until the 1950s that professional cameras were made small enough to carry that hand-held camerawork could once again be considered.

Initially, documentary filmmakers used hand-held cameras, as this created a sense of reality – it reminds the viewer of home movies that are also usually hand-held – with shaky photography, shifting focus and off-kilter framing. This style became known as **cinéma vérité**.

A camera operator holding a camera can follow the action wherever it goes, creating an immediate 'this is real-life' feel. With hand-held technology, it is possible to film in the most cramped conditions or from the most oblique angles. If you want an incredibly low-level shot, just lie on the floor with your hand-held camera and film from there.

In the late 1950s, fiction filmmakers borrowed this approach to filmmaking, including a group of young French film critics turned directors, who became known as the **French New Wave**. Their influence has had an impact on films' visual styles, particularly for more intimate 'indie' movies, such as *Frances Ha* (Baumbach, 2012).

Steadicam

The year 1975 saw the introduction of the Steadicam camera (invented by Garrett Brown). A Steadicam is a type of camera mount that uses weights and counter-balances to keep a camera level, even while hand-held. The Steadicam operator can keep the camera steady for a tracking shot, or can gently move the camera up and down, to create a floating effect, which generates a sense of unease.

Hand-held (*Man with a Movie Camera*, Vertov, 1929)

 Further information

French New Wave
In the late 1950s emerged a group of French filmmakers, many of whom were writing for French film journals including *Cahiers du Cinema*. Starved of foreign films during and immediately after World War II, when film import restrictions were lifted in the early 1950s were lifted, they absorbed themselves in films of the Hollywood Golden Age. As a consequence, their films are full of artistic references to other films. Films considered part of the French New Wave were renowned for being shot hand-held, using natural lighting on the streets. The performance style was natural, often improvised, by a youthful cast. They were concerned with how the film was shot and edited, rather than the story itself, and through their experimentations with editing and shooting they re-invented narrative techniques. The key period of this film movement was 1958–1968, and directors associated with French New Wave are François Truffaut, Jean-Luc Godard, Louis Malle and Claude Chabrol. This movement has inspired and influenced many American film directors including Quentin Tarantino, who named his production company A Band Apart after Godard's film *Bande à part* (1964).

Case study: *Victoria* (Schipper, 2015): hand-held

Victoria, a 2 hour 20 minutes German crime thriller, follows in real time, in one long take, a Spanish woman, Victoria, as she becomes embroiled in the criminal activities of a group of young German men. Director Sebastian Schipper and his small crew led by cinematographer Sturla Brandth Grøvlen filmed the same action on successive nights, before settling on one full take to use – there are no edits. This ambitious film project was only feasible with advances in digital technology and hand-held cameras.

Cinematography: Lighting (i)

When watching a film, you are usually attracted to the most brightly illuminated area of the screen. Filmmakers play on this when lighting a shot.

There are two key elements you need to consider when studying how a scene is lit and what further information you can draw from the lighting, as discussed below.

Element 1: Source

Is the cinematographer using natural **available light** or are they filling the frame with deliberately placed **artificial light**?

If they are using artificial light they will usually be employing a **three-point lighting combination**:

- Point 1: **Key light** – the brightest primary light source; the one that acts like the sun in the sky. The key light throws the dominant shadows, if there are to be any. The intensity of this light, will lead the film's lighting design.
- Point 2: **Fill light** – this will be approximately 50–75% of the key light. It is often provided by a reflector bouncing back a softened beam of key light or from a lower angle than the key light. Sometimes the shadows cast by the key light can be too dark and obscure detail – such as expressions on a human face – so the fill light softens the edges of shadows and puts back some of the detail. Using more or less key light can be an aesthetic choice known as chiaroscuro lighting, which could be low-key or high-contrast lighting.
- Point 3: **Back light** – shines from behind (and usually the side) and gives foreground objects an outline, which helps them to stand out from the background.

Most shots will be lit using a combination of the above three types of lighting.

Basic three-point lighting set-up

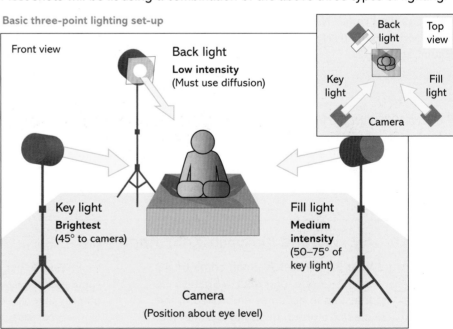

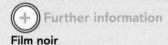
Chiaroscuro lighting: this term is borrowed from painting, and refers to the bold use of dark and light. It was a favourite for filmmakers whose work falls into film movements or styles that were filming in black and white, particularly **German Expressionism** (see pages 252–253) and **film noir**. It tends to lose its dramatic impact in colour.

An example of chiaroscuro lighting in film noir, *The Lady from Shanghai* (Welles, 1947)

⊕ Further information

Film noir

Film noirs look and feel just like their literal meaning, 'dark films', both in their narrative content and visual style. A film noir world is one of darkness, disillusionment, betrayal, pessimism and moral corruption. The plots often involve murder and the brutality of life.

The use of high contrasting black and whites and obtuse camera angles were prolific and give the films a distorted view of the world. A world of dark streets, lit intermittently by neon signs and car headlights, and the frequent lighting of cigarettes. Made during the decade following World War II, these films share strong visual motifs, narrative strands, characters and mood, and mirror concerns in the post-war America over a man's place in society and women's emancipation.

The extremes of both dark and light lighting support or develop:

- narrative themes of good versus evil
- characters' situations, e.g. a sense of peril (if well lit) and wrong-doing (if in the shade)
- a physical allusion to characters' psychological state of mind
- themes of duplicity, claustrophobia and fatalism.

When watching a scene from any film, make notes of what is illuminated and what is in the shadow. How have the filmmakers used lighting to develop the character or mood?

Element 2: Direction

The direction the light travels from source to the object it is illuminating will create different moods. Several different types are used to create distinct effects:

- **Front lighting**: tends to eliminate shadows and creates a 'flatter' image. This is the kind of lighting that is easiest to work with quickly, so is often found in low-budget or hand-held filmmaking.
- **Side lighting**: uses one strong light source on one side, which creates shadows on the opposite side. This creates mystery and intrigue: what is being hidden in the shadow?
- **Back lighting**: when the light is behind the object or person being photographed, therefore creating a silhouette. Depending on the strength of light used, this can also create a 'halo' of light around the edge of the silhouetted shape.
- **Under lighting**: when the light (or a reflector) is positioned under the object. This can throw a large shadow behind it and may have a distorting effect on the object or person.
- **Top lighting**: rarely used on its own as it just throws a light over a whole scene, with other lights filling in the details. When used in isolation, such as on a human face, the shadows fill the eye-sockets and look very menacing.

Front lighting (*Shaun of the Dead*, Wright, 2004)

Back lighting (*Blade Runner*, Scott, 1982)

Side lighting (*Blade Runner*, Scott, 1982)

Under lighting (*The Lady from Shanghai*, Welles, 1947)

Cinematography: Lighting (ii)

Cinematographers also have to consider:

- **Intensity** of the lighting. Is the lighting bright or dim? Consider the difference in lighting in a moody thriller such as *No Country for Old Men* (Coen Brothers, 2008) or a bright musical such as *La La Land* (Chazelle, 2016).
- **Quality** of the lighting. Is it hard or soft? Does it create harsh shadows or subtle shading? Hard lighting is created from multiple small light sources, whereas soft is created by larger ones.

Element 3: Colour

The cinematographer's use of colour is an important part of the film's aesthetic and is discussed further in the mise-en-scéne section on page 22.

Throwing a vivid red light, or a chilly blue, onto a scene can affect the way the viewer responds to what they see. Subtler effects are created by throwing differently coloured lights onto coloured walls or coloured costumes to indicate different times of year. Primary, muted or highly saturated colours are most effective when used to dominate a scene.

This can be done either during production or in post-production by grading.

Post-production: the work that is required to complete the film, after shooting, including the edit, sound mix, music composition, colour grading and computer-generated imagery (CGI) special effects.

Grading: colour film always needed to be graded to make sure that colours remain consistent. Like lighting, grading, affects the mood and feel of a film. Documentaries will often be 'ungraded' and appear flat and lifeless. By grading, filmmakers draw emphasis to colour themes, such as red in *Shaun of the Dead*, or visually emphasise the mood of a scene by taking out the red, to leave a scene looking blue and chilly. With digital technology it is possible to manipulate the colour palette of a scene or even a whole film.

Case study: Colour *City of God* (Meirelles, 2002)

Meirelles (director) and Charlone (cinematographer) use two different colour palettes in *City of God* (2002).

The first half of the film, told in flashback, is golden in hue (right), which indicates the heat of Brazil, as well as the nostalgia of the 'Golden Age' of life in the favelas, when the children had hope, ambition and innocence. The colour reflects their optimism and enthusiasm for life.

The film's second half is narratively darker; the bright lighting has gone and is replaced with darker browns, and greys (right). These reflect the change in fortune for the young people who are now embedded in the criminal underworld, with little opportunity for escape.

Black and white

Filming in black and white was the default format in early cinema, although from the outset filmmakers were keen to have colour in the film. Hand-colouring frame by frame or tinting entire sequences a colour to match its mood were early experiments in colour. It wasn't until the 1930s that filming in colour became viable. Colour and black and white were both in use until the early 1970s when colour dominated.

When shooting in black and white, it is not the hue of the colour that makes an impact but the brightness (how dark or light it is). For instance, to get a deep black, a very dark orange colour is most effective, rather than black itself.

Frances Ha (Baumbach, 2012)

 Independent Activity

Contemporary black and white films hark back to the glamour of the Golden Age of Hollywood or the rebellious French New Wave. But what does releasing a film in black and white mean? Is it nostalgia? A marker of a film's artiness? An aesthetic consideration? Have a look at some contemporary black and white films and read about the directors' intentions.

Cinematography: Composition

Composition is the arrangement of all the visual elements of mise-en-scène in the frame. The choice of camera angle and lighting, combined with the placement of people and objects within the setting, creates the composition of a shot.

As viewing a film is an emotional experience, the way scenes are composed will stimulate an audience's response.

The rule of thirds

The **rule of thirds** is a central premise of composition. If you divide the frame into thirds (using four lines), your main character or object should fall at the intersection of two of these lines. This will draw your eye to the main object, but leave space for further information to be communicated (see image on page 21).

Balance and symmetry

Formal or **symmetrical balanced** composition is used to depict a quiet, restful, static scene. In a two-shot, which uses formal balance, audience interest will naturally shift from one character to the other as each speaks. Having the images displayed evenly within the frame will convey a sense of calm and order.

Informal or **asymmetrical** unbalanced composition is used to challenge or attract attention. You can make a character appear more dominant by positioning them higher or lower in a frame, as well as through lighting and camera angle. Unbalanced compositions are associated with chaos and tension.

Formal or symmetrical balance
(*Wild Tales*, Szifrón, 2014)

Informal or asymmetrical balance
(*Wild Tales*, Szifrón, 2014)

Lines

Compositional lines are the contours of objects, people, props, buildings, trees, vehicles, furniture and so on, and are expressed in straight, curved, vertical, horizontal or diagonal lines.

Lines serve many purposes in visual composition. Combinations of lines may influence each other and convey different meanings. They can divide the composition, direct the viewer's eye, define shapes and lead the viewer to a particular feeling or interpretation.

The five key types of lines are:

- **Vertical lines** create a strong impression, suggesting power, strength, dignity and stability.
- **Horizontal lines** can also indicate strength but in a more restful way, leaning towards balance and harmony. In some cases they can lead to finality or a sense ending.
- **Diagonal lines** suggest a sense of action and movement. Opposing diagonal lines suggest conflict and forcefulness.
- **Organic lines** are lines found in nature. Depending on the way they are used, they can introduce feelings of chaos, complexity or beauty.

These four lines are all actual lines, the fifth doesn't visually exist at all, we merely imagine the line:

- **Implied lines** are created/implied through directional elements such as a hand gestures or the gaze between two people.

Form

Physical forms (such as people and objects) are easy to spot, but filmmakers can also create the illusion of form in the viewer's eye by grouping people or objects together to create abstract forms. This link is often made in a triangular movement, allowing the eye to move from one object to another, to create subliminal links.

A triangle pointing upwards suggests strength, stability and solidarity (imagine a mountain). This allows the eye to go from point to point in an upwards movement with ease, reinforcing positive attributes. An inverted triangle lacks stability and suggests weakness and fragility.

Physical forms (*Trainspotting*, Boyle, 1996)

Case study: Composition *Inception* (Nolan, 2010)

Both the foreground and background in the screenshot below are being used to suggest further meaning.

Dom Cobb is placed in the foreground on the far right third of the frame, leaving the remaining two-thirds for his gun, which indicates the importance and power of the weapon. The gun and Dom are positioned in a singular triangular form, which suggests that the gun is an extension of him. Your eye naturally passes from one to the other to reinforce this link. Here the triangle is pointing upwards, which implies strength, with Dom's head at the apex, showing that he is in control of the situation. By costuming Dom in white and dusting the gun with snow, a visual reference is made to the mountains that surround him, again alluding to stability and strength. The diagonal line of the gun suggests action, which, coupled with the implied line of Cobb's stare, leads to an off-screen space where further action is unfolding.

The use of the strong horizontal and vertical lines in the background reinforces the power and strength of the foreground image.

Inception (Nolan, 2010) with rule of third and compositional lines added

Mise-en-scène

The term **mise-en-scène** was first used in the theatre, where it refers to all the elements placed on a stage that contribute to the setting or mood the creative team were working towards. In film, it refers to everything on the screen in front of the camera, from the colours and style of the clothes worn by the actors, to the settings and locations, to the feeling created by the lighting (see Cinematography, pages 16–19) and the positioning of the characters in relation to one another.

Everything you see **on screen** (and the six **off-screen spaces** – for more on these spaces see page 29) has been considered and deliberately chosen to be there. If you can see it, it is there because the filmmaker wants you to see it. How you interpret this information will take time and practice; you can view a film multiple times and find new information on each viewing.

Your response to a film may well be different from others. Your gender, age, life experiences, the books you have read, and the other films, theatre, paintings, photographs and music you have seen/heard or studied will all play a part in your interpretation of a film.

Colour

Colour is integral to the cinematographer's repertoire of resources for creating mood and conveying meaning. Colour is an important part of the mise-en-scène to signal a character's mood or also personality, to enhance the narrative arc, to draw attention to something, support a colour motif or to elicit psychological reactions in the viewer. Here, it would be the responsibility of the production and costume designer.

The psychology of colour

- Red: anger, violence, danger, love, excitement
- Pink: femininity, sweetness, innocence, playfulness
- Orange: warmth, happiness, friendly, exoticness
- Yellow: sickness, madness, idyllic, insecurity
- Green: nature, renewal, hope, darkness, envy, ominous
- Blue: cold, calm, melancholy, cerebral
- Purple: fantasy, mystical, ethereal, ominous
- Black: fear, grief, sophistication
- White: sincerity, purity

S&C

Focus on how one or more elements of mise-en-scène create meaning and generate response in a film sequence from either Film A, Film B and/or Film C.

Note: select a sequence of approximately seven minutes from films of the same genre/film movement/national.

The question is asking you to analyse either:

1 one film sequence or
2 two in comparison.

And either:

1 one element of mise-en-scène
2 multiple elements of.

What to do:

1 Watch the film(s).
2 Select an appropriate sequence.
3 Select which elements of Film Form you wish to study.
4 Have multiple viewings of the selected sequence.
5 Relevant research into mise-en-scène, cinematography, sound, editing, performance, etc.

Remember: mise-en-scène includes setting, décor, costume and make-up, figure expression and movement, lighting, framing and composition, off-screen space and special effects.

iA Independent Activity

What emotions do we associate with particular colours? Create a colour wheel of images from films you are studying and annotate this with the mood generated in these scenes by using these colours.

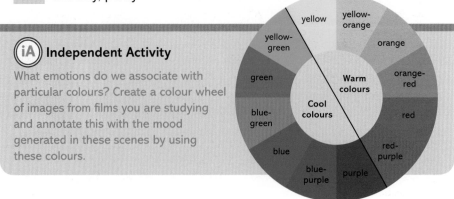

Case study: Colour *We Need to Talk About Kevin* (Ramsay, 2011)

The screenshot below, from *We Need to Talk About Kevin*, shows Eva, whose son has carried out a mass school shooting, sitting in a café. In it are two primary colours: red and green. Eva is sitting in the green-lit window – here green alludes to darkness, giving the shot an ominous feel. The window, and therefore Eva, is framed on all sides by large blocks of red, suggesting that she is surrounded by anger, violence and danger, with no escape.

House of Flying Daggers (Yimou, 2004)

Colour plays a significant part in the aesthetic style of *House of Flying Daggers* with a single colour dominating the mise-en-scène in different sequences. Here the characters and backgrounds are almost all the same shade of green, with the green alluding to nature, renewal and hope.

There is considerable cross-over between **cinematography** and **mise-en-scène**, particularly with regards to lighting, which is covered in detail on pages 16–19. The position of the actors, part of the mise-en-scène, is also an essential element of a cinematographer's framing.

Mise-en-scène:
Setting and props

Setting and props are the responsibility of the **production designer**, who helps to define and manage every visual aspect of a film.

Setting

Setting includes the location, be it an exterior, interior, a real place or a specially built set on a soundstage or on location.

However, it is not only the physical locations that form setting, but also what the time is – dawn, daylight, dusk or the dead of night.

Props

Setting props are all the items used in both interior and exterior locations. For a historical drama, attention would have to be paid to vehicles, street lighting, shop facades and background extras. For an interior scene thought would have be paid to the pictures on the wall, the books on a shelf and the items on a table. The absence of these would also be indicators to character and story.

Where props are placed and how they are used can carry additional narrative, emotional or symbolic weight.

There is some overlap between props and costumes: props that characters make use of, such as spectacles, a holstered gun, an umbrella or a wristwatch, are known as **costume props**.

(iA) Independent Activity

Create a mind-map outlining what settings or props you would expect to find in each of the following:

- a horror film
- a western
- a science fiction film.

For each genre explain what function the settings and props serve?

Case study: Setting, costume and props

Setting and **props** combined with **costume** can help develop the narrative, provoke emotional responses, offer further understanding to the characters or serve a symbolic function. Consider the two shots on the next page.

Life is Beautiful (Beningni, 1997)

The principal colour of the screenshot on the next page, from *Life is Beautiful*, is grey, giving an impression of cold, darkness and misery.

The setting is clearly a barrack in a concentration camp, with the men wearing the grey and black striped uniform synonymous with the German World War II concentration camps. The uniforms have a yellow star on them, so we know that these men are Jewish because the Nazis forced all Jews to wear the Star of David. They are all wearing their jackets, and some their hats, so we can assume that the weather is cold. The barrack is dimly lit, there is a central light fitting but, even though it is dark, it is not switched on, which suggests that these men are not worthy of such luxury. The wood structure of the bed frames looks hard and uncomfortable, and the absence of mattresses, pillows or blankets reinforces the hardship of the place and the characters' situation. There is one central dusty, empty table but there are no chairs, and there is nothing on the table, nor does it seem that any of the men have any possessions, indicating that they have been stripped of all personal identifiers.

Life is Beautiful (Beningni, 1997)

We Need to Talk About Kevin (Ramsay, 2011)

The setting in the screenshot below, from *We Need to Talk About Kevin*, is a domestic living space, filled with furniture and soft furnishings of golden browns and reds, which alludes to gold, warmth and comfort. The stripped wooden floor and throw rugs indicate an arty-affluence that is reinforced by the vinyl records, hi-fi separates and the African mask collection. The only primary colours in the room are the children's toys, suggesting that Kevin has invaded this warm golden space with his solid colourful toys. This tonal difference between the adult and child is reinforced in the costumes, with Kevin's bright blue T-shirt contrasting with Eva's pale blue one. That she is wearing white trousers to sit on the floor serves as indicator that she may not have adjusted to the role of a mother. We can see that it is a bright sunny day by the light coming through the windows, reinforced by Eva wearing linen clothes and sandals. Given that the film opens with the teenage Kevin's violent school shootout there is very little blood shown, but red props are used as a motif throughout the film to stand-in for the blood, such as the ball they are playing with in this shot.

We Need to Talk About Kevin (Ramsay, 2011)

Trainspotting (Boyle, 1996)

Daisies (Chytilová, 1965)

Pan's Labyrinth (del Toro, 2006)

Under the Skin (Glazer, 2013)

Independent Activity

Create a collage of images showing the different uses of make-up in one of your focus films. Note how make-up contributes to the construction of character and how a character's make-up alters as the narrative progresses.

Select a scene from a film. What are the different functions for the clothes one of the characters wears?

Mise-en-scène:
Costume, make-up and hair

The **costume designer** works closely with the other creative departments, particularly the production designer, to ensure that they:

- are part of the wider aesthetic vision
- develop the character
- support or contrast other characters' costumes
- are suitable for the actor's performance (physical/restrained)
- are appropriate to the setting (both time and location).

The colour of costumes and how they are worn all form part of the character and the story arc. The lighting design and whether the film is being shot in colour or black and white will influence the choice of colours.

As with setting and props, clothes the characters wear provide shortcuts to the film's genre, historical and social setting. There are certain items of clothing that are genre signifiers, such as Stetson hats in a western.

The clothes worn are not mere accessories, they are key elements in the construction of character and identity. As much care is taken in the choice of clothes in a contemporary rom-com as those set in a historical or futuristic setting.

For the purposes of mise-en-scène, make-up (including special effect make-up) and hair styling also serve as part of the costume.

There are three main uses of make-up:

- day to day, aka straight make-up or street make-up – this would be used for naturalistic performances, or used to enhance an actor's features. Additionally, this make-up may be needed to hide any blemishes, scarring, tattoos, etc.
- character or transformation make-up would employ specialist make-up alongside facial prosthetics to change a person's appearance. The materials used may include latex or silicone and could be used to make someone look older/younger, fatter or ill
- special effects (FX) make-up also uses prosthetics made of latex, foam or silicone, but these may be entire body suits and complete head/facial masks as used to create the look of the mythical creature, Pale Man, in *Pan's Labyrinth* (del Toro, 2006). Special effects make-up may also involve some CGI.

An actor may be required to wear contact lenses or false teeth in any of these three make-up uses. Their own hair may be cut, coloured or styled, or they may be required to wear a toupee, extensions or wigs.

Case study: Costume, hair and make-up
Shaun of the Dead (Wright, 2004)

The screenshot shown on the next page, from *Shaun of the Dead,* is an over-the-shoulder shot, with Shaun in the foreground. He and his junior colleagues are all wearing the same costume: black trousers, white shirt and red tie. But the styling for each reflects six different characters. Some shirts are ironed, others wrinkled. Some have the shirt neatly tucked into their trousers, while others have them bagged out or half-tucked. Some have the shirt's top button done up, others are open at the neck. Ties are loose, long or short. All these decisions offer clues to their personality and commitment to working at Foree Electric.

The colour red is used throughout the film to suggest danger, violence and blood. This scene is the beginning of the 'You've got red on you' gag, where a number of people point out that Shaun has a red ink mark on his crisp white shirt. Later this line is repeated by Ed when he is covered in blood. Red is also the colour of their work logo.

The Lady from Shanghai (Welles, 1947)

White usually stands for innocence and purity, but in many of the classic film noirs filmmakers subverted this use and costumed their manipulative femme fatales in white clothes, with platinum blonde hair. Rita Hayworth, who played Elsa, was renowned for her long red hair but with her transformation to a platinum blonde she joined Barbara Stanwyck (Phyllis Dietrichson in *Double Indemnity*, Wilder, 1944) and Lana Turner (Cora Smith in *The Postman Always Rings Twice*, Rafelson, 1946) as the wicked blonde, spinning her web around the unfortunate man. In the screenshot on the right, from *The Lady from Shanghai* (Welles, 1947), Elsa is wearing a white dress and this, coupled with the lighting, makes her stand-out from the dark background, making her appear vulnerable and overwhelmed by the setting.

Winter's Bone (Granik, 2010)

The earthy tones of the landscape in the screenshot on the right, from *Winter's Bone*, are mirrored in Ree's costumes, and those on the clothes line behind (which in this instance would be considered props). The predominant colours are brown (ruggedness), blue (cold/melancholic) and earthy reds (compassion). The one exception is Ree's winter hat, which is creamy white with a blue pattern, and is a stark contrast to the drab landscape. Her clothes are well-worn, indicating that she has no money to spend on new ones. They are practical and warm and, as she is wearing a hat, scarf, gloves, boots and thick jacket, they are appropriate for this harsh landscape and her lifestyle. They are gender neutral and she is not wearing overt make-up. The one nod to her femininity is her long, seemingly natural blonde-brown hair.

Mise-en-scène:
Staging, movement and use of off-screen space

 Independent Activity

Choose two frames from a film you are studying that feature a two-shot. Consider the way in which the position of the actors in relation to one another adds a further layer of meaning. Write 100 words on each.

Staging

How characters and objects are positioned in the frame can:

- add further meaning to their relationship to one another
- indicate their importance to the narrative
- draw attention to a particular character/object.

Case study: Staging *Shaun of the Dead* (Wright, 2004)

Consider the two screenshots below from *Shaun of the Dead*. What can we learn about the characters and their relationship to one another from the staging?

Image 1: In the foreground Liz and Shaun are sitting opposite each other, across the fairly wide table. They are placed in the lower half of the screen. In the background is Ed. He is standing, so we see more of his body, and is literally standing between them, as though his mere presence is pushing them further apart.

Image 2: Here Shaun and Ed are sitting very close together on a sofa, with their arms overlapping. This proximity to one another mirrors their friendship, which seems far closer than that of Shaun and Liz.

Movement

Rather than camera movement, in this section it is the movement of the actors that is considered. There will naturally be some cross-over with the actors' performances and this will be discussed in the Performance section.

Off-screen

When studying film we tend to focus on what is happening **on screen**, but it is important to remember that there are six **off-screen** spaces:

- to the left
- to the right
- above
- below
- behind the set
- in front of the camera.

The use of the spaces can be subtle, such as walking into frame from the right, across the frame and out of the left; or looking upwards; or for one character to point to action happening off-screen.

A more overt use is when a character **breaks the fourth wall** by addressing the audience, or looking directly into the camera, making the audience complicit in the action.

 STUDY TIP

Written assignments

1 Do not exceed the recommended length for each piece.
2 Check that you have actually answered the question asked.
3 Double-check how many films and/ or elements you are being asked to write about. It's all about the 'and/ or'!
4 Make sure you proofread them thoroughly, not just relying on the spell check.
5 Leave a day or two between completion and submission so you can re-read the assignment with a fresh pair of eyes.
6 Make sure you meet the deadline.

Case study: Off-screen space *Vivre sa vie* (Godard, 1962)

The two images below are from *Vivre sa vie*:

Image 1: Shows a more traditional use of off-screen space, with the character on screen pointing a gun at an unseen character off-screen.

Image 2: Nana is in conversation, and this fleeting breaking of the fourth wall, as she looks to the audience, is haunting, and its meaning can be interpreted in different ways. Is she looking to 'us' (the audience) for help, or is it an acknowledgement of the voyeuristic relationship between the on-screen performer and the viewer?

Editing

Editing is the process of arranging all the images in their correct order so that the narrative makes sense, the dialogue flows and you can see what you need to see, when you need to see it. Unlike the other elements of film form, **editing is unique to film**.

In this section you will gain an understanding of the conventions of continuity editing and how filmmakers experiment with editing to develop further layers of meaning.

Continuity editing

Continuity editing, or invisible editing as it is sometimes known, is the dominant editing technique in mainstream cinema. Continuity editing is designed to make the transitions between shots as seamless as possible so as not to draw attention to the film's construction, instead allowing the audience to become immersed in the narrative. The techniques outlined here are commonplace in mainstream films.

Taken altogether, the editing of shots in a scene gives the impression of an entire continuous narrative.

- An **establishing shot** is usually the point of entry into a scene, which will typically begin with a long-shot or establishing shot that establishes a location for the characters, before focusing on one or more of them and their actions.
- A **shot/reverse shot** editing pattern is used between two people in conversation. Filmed as over-the-shoulder shots, the editor will cut between the two to create the dynamism of the conversation. The camera could be focusing on either the person speaking, or the reaction of the person listening.
- An **eyeline match** is used in conversations where the two characters have been shot in close-up. To indicate that they are looking at each other, the eyeline has to match the eye height of the other character. If this doesn't match you will spot it.
- The **180° rule** is used to ensure that we understand where characters/objects are in relation to each other: the angle between any two sequential shots should not exceed 180°. Not following this is called **crossing the line**.
- The **30° rule** is a general principle that two consecutive shots should have at least a 30° variance between them. Breaking this rule is known as a **jump-cut**.
- **Cross-cutting** is the parallel editing of two or more events in an alternating pattern, for example the hero coming to the rescue/victim in trouble. Cutting between two scenes heightens interest/suspense, provides conflict and depicts contrast.
- **Match on action**: most editors prefer to cut between two shots on action, such as the actor reaching for a drink and drinking it. These two different actions and may be framed differently but the editing will make it seem as though it is a continuous movement.

Boyhood (Linklater, 2015) shot/reverse shot

Independent Activity

Watch the first five minutes of a crime/thriller made before 1970, and one made after 2000. Note every time you spot an edit. How did the editing affect the pace of the opening?

Shot transitions

Editors need to make creative decisions regarding **shot transitions** – how you move from one shot to the next. These transitions can manipulate narrative time and space, serve the film's aesthetic style, create mood, develop narrative and character, and generate further meaning.

There are several different ways of achieving these transitions, but most films use the cut, the dissolve and the fade.

Cut

A cut is a straight edit from one image to another with nothing in between. Cuts allow you to travel great distances in time and setting in an instant. Alternatively, they can show you the same action from different angles in a matter of seconds.

Fade

A fade is when the picture emerges out of, or disappears into, black or white. It is most often used at the end of a major scene or act and is the filmic equivalent to the end of a chapter in a book.

Dissolve

A dissolve is when one image overlaps another. As the scene ends you are watching 'image A'; slowly 'image B' emerges from it, until it overwhelms 'image A', which fades away completely. 'Image B' signals the start of a new scene, which could feature different characters or location. This can be particularly effective when creating a feeling of time passing, or to make a connection between two characters or a character and an object or setting.

Other transitions

The following transitions offer a more experimental approach, which can be used to develop further meaning or support a film's aesthetic.

Wipe

A wipe is the most artificial and conspicuous transition. A line travels across the screen from left to right, or vice versa, wiping out the first image and replacing it with a second. *Hulk* (Lee, 2003) uses an array of shot transitions inspired by comic-book panels. There are more subtle uses of a wipe, if something moves across the screen (such as a car) in the same direction as the wipe, at the same speed, then the wipe isn't noticed.

Match-cut

A match-cut is when the we cut from one image to something that looks similar or from one action to a similar action. The most cited example of a match-cut is in *2001: A Space Odyssey* (Kubrick, 1968), when the film opens with a prehistoric ape using a bone as a weapon, which he throws into the air and the shot cuts to a satellite (similar in shape) in space. In one edit we have been transported thousands of years into the future.

Match dissolve

A match dissolve uses the same juxtaposition of images, but dissolves between the two. At the end of the shower scene in *Psycho* (Hitchcock, 1960), we see the victim's blood running into the plughole, dissolving to the black pupil of her dead eye.

Jump-cut

A jump-cut is the result of breaking the 30° rule. This gives a scene an edgy, uneasy feeling, as though we haven't seen everything. Its use will startle the viewer, drawing attention to this action. This was a particular technique employed by Jean-Luc Godard, in *Vivre sa vie*, when Nana, hearing a sound outside, gets up and, as the camera pans across the café, there is a series of jump-cuts edited to the sound and rhythm of machine-gun fire outside.

Freeze-frame

This is where a single frame is held on screen for a period of time. It can be used throughout a film as punctuation, for emphasis, or to hold an important image or character's response in the viewer's mind. If the film ends on a freeze-frame this may leave the film open to interpretation. A freeze-frame calls attention to the filmmaking process. These can be seen in the opening sequence of *Trainspotting* (Boyle, 1996).

Editing:
Time and space

Editing is used in the organisation of time and space, both within individual sequences and throughout the film, in order to create narrative coherence. It can be used in the following ways:

- **Time** may appear in a **linear** form, where the story starts and progresses forwards until its resolution, which is known as **continuity of narrative**.

- **Near chronological order** is when the film starts in the present day, and then goes back in time to the beginning of the story and continues forwards in one long flashback until the two points meet, when it can either end or continue on. This is often used to show a character at a moment of peril, joy or anguish, with the flashback used to show how they reached this point.

- **Discontinuity of narrative** presents the story in a **non-linear** manner, which can be achieved in in a number of ways.

  - A film is **reversed** when it starts at the end narrative and works backwards to the beginning. This is complex narrative structure and is rarely used; key examples are *Memento* (Nolan, 2000) and *Irréversible* (Noé, 2003).

  - **Flashbacks** can be used to temporarily disrupt the narrative by inserting a scene from the narrative past in an otherwise linear narrative or as the overarching structure. This structure is usually used to fill in the back-story of the characters.

  - **Flashforwards**, which are also known as prolepsis, move the action from the present to the future. Flashforwards are used less often, and it may not be instantly apparent that we are being shown the future rather than the past. *Arrival* (Villeneuve, 2016) has a good example of the use of a flashforward.

  - **Dreams and fantasies** are inserted in the narrative to offer insights into a character's emotional status or to shed light on the past.

 Further information

Cinematic time and space

Films can go anywhere in time and space in a moment. Time may be compressed or expanded: sped up or slowed down; remain in the present or go forwards and backwards. Space may be shortened or stretched; moved nearer or further away; presented in a true or false perspective; or be completely remade into a setting that only exists in film time; space may be eliminated, created or presented in a manner that will help the audience comprehend. It may be real or imagined, enlarged or reduced.

Case study: Near chronological narrative structure
City of God (Meirelles, 2002)

The edit dissolve between the present and the past is on the two match-cut images of Rocket (from *City of God*), shown on the right. Using him as the central point of the flashback indicates that the narrative is being told from his perspective. These two images also reinforce the colour palette of the past and the present. As the film progresses, the colours move from the gold of the past to the blue of the present.

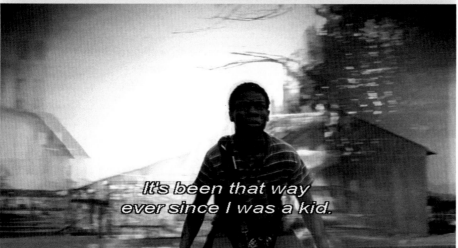

Editing:
Speed of editing

The length of each **shot**, scene and sequence will set the tone of what is happening on screen. A shot may last for a few seconds, minutes or the entire film.

A sense of urgency can be manufactured by increasing the frequency of the editing, seeing the action from various shots/angles – perhaps every few frames/seconds in a fight scene, for instance. For a more relaxed mood, scenes can last longer with less shot changes, such as a rom-com. If something is meant to be relaxing, then moving around it slowly, through occasional edits, gives the impression of wandering around in no hurry. Cutting rapidly backwards and forwards between different angles, from close-ups to long shots, all in rapid succession, reminds us of dashing about, with no time to lose or adds to the chaos of a situation.

Scenes at the beginning of a film, where we are getting to know the characters and the story is unfolding, will usually have a slower pace of editing. As the film progresses, this pace may quicken as we cut between storylines and characters.

Shot length

The average number of **shots** in a classic Hollywood film from the 1940s or 1950s would have been 150 edits. Nowadays, there are about 1,300 individual shots in an average movie. An action movie may have more than twice as many, for instance *Mad Max: Fury Road* (Miller, 2015) has roughly 3,000 shots.

One of the reasons for this change is the move to editing digitally using a non-linear editing system, making it much easier for shorter shot lengths. Before their widespread use in the 1990s, film editors would literally cut and paste the film negative – not the original shooting negative but a cutting copy.

Historically, each physical frame would have to be examined from the multiple re-takes, angles and shot types. Remember there are 24 frames for each second of screen time. That's a lot of frames.

This is why you will find that, in general, films edited on film would have less edits/longer shots. The shot length creates the pace of the film. Compare an Alfred Hitchcock film (average shot length 9.1 seconds) with a Christopher Nolan film (3.1 seconds).

Scene: may consist of one shot or a series of shots depicting a continuous event.

Sequence: a series of scenes of shots complete in itself. A sequence may occur in a single setting or several settings, i.e. a car chase. Action should match in sequence, where it continues across several consecutive shots with straight cuts – so that is depicts the event in a continuous manner.

Non-linear editing (NLE): 'is the software, computer-based editing systems we use nowadays for editing video or audio as opposed the old systems of either cutting film and/or audio tape and sticking the pieces together manually in the required order, or in video using two or more video tape machines to transfer selected shots to a recording machine.

'NLE relies on digitised material stored on the computer's hard disc or external digital storage, which means we are effectively just joining files together (in a manner of speaking). The original material is not destroyed by any of the editing actions and shots can be placed in any order with ease and rearranged if required with no degradation.' (de la Haye, Film & Video Editor/Cameraman/Photographer, 2017)

Inception (Nolan, 2010)

Case study: Speed of editing

Compare these three sequences.

We Need to Talk About Kevin
(Ramsay, 2011: 01:43:00–01:46:30)

The measured pace of the editing during the emotional conversation between Eva and Kevin is deliberately slow to mirror its importance and the length of time we have waited for this reunion. The scene builds slowly, through a series of **shot/reverse shots** culminating in a fleeting moment of intimacy as the two awkwardly embrace. This embrace is made all the more poignant because of the slow build-up to it. The editing mirrors the stillness of the cinematography, and the sparseness of the setting, costumes and make-up.

City of God (Meirelles, 2002; 00:00:14–00:04:42)

The first 2'40" comprises of fast edited **cross-cutting** between food being prepared, musicians and an escaped chicken being chased by a gang of youths with guns, led by Lil Ze. There are alternating short bursts of images comprising different **shot types** (ECU, CU, MCU and MS), and **angles** (high, low and eye-level from both humans and chickens) that are cut to the vibrant rhythms of Brazilian music. This creates a heady atmosphere of life in the favelas – a place full of energy and extremes. Out of all this confusion, the pace slows and, in the longest shot in this sequence (15"), we follow Rocket and his friend.

The scene then returns to the fast-paced cross-cutting, now between the chase and the boys, which suggests that danger and violence are just around the corner. As the two stories collide, to illustrate Lil Ze's dominance, he is seen in **slow-motion**, literally taking up more screen time. The pace of the editing slows as the youths gather at one end of the road and the police at the other, with Rocket and the chicken caught in the middle. Rocket's narration begins, the camera circles around Rocket, and we **dissolve** to a **match-cut** image of Rocket as a child (see screenshots on page 33).

Shaun of the Dead
(Wright, 2004; 00:04:04–00:04:23)

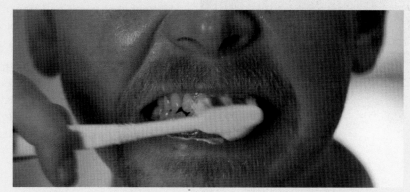

We see Shaun get up from the sofa and walk towards the door. It then cuts to a series of six **quick-cuts** (combined with **frantic-zoom ECU** cinematography) as he gets ready for work. This 4" sequence is followed by a 10" shot of him adjusting his tie and talking to Pete. This is followed by another sequence of six quick-cuts of breakfast preparation. These extreme quick-cuts are used for comic effect and form part of Edgar Wright's **aesthetic**.

Editing:
Experimental editing techniques

Montage editing and the Kuleshov effect

The **Kuleshov effect** is a film editing process, which has evolved into **montage editing**. The technique was named after the Soviet filmmaker Lev Kuleshov, who made short films in the 1910s and 1920s. He proposed that by putting or juxtaposing two images sequentially, the viewer would gain a greater understanding of the filmmaker's intent than by a single shot.

His research about how viewers process images and make meaning gained from the images presented has been widely studied by psychologists. The research had a profound influence on Soviet film directors Sergei Eisenstein and Dziga Vertov, who, at the time, were moving away from conventional narrative editing towards a new national cinema founded on the principles of **montage editing**. They used montage editing to juxtapose images to create further meaning.

Sergei Eisenstein was at the forefront of a group of **Soviet filmmakers** who took Kuleshov's research on film editing and employed it within a narrative feature film. His most widely studied montage sequence is the '**The Odessa Steps**' from *The Battleship Potemkin* (Eisenstein, 1925). In this, the continual barrage of images cut quickly together brings about emotions of confusion and helplessness. The images presented sequentially are then paired: high angles with low; close-ups with long shots; small with large. Soon it becomes unclear if we are at the top of the steps or the bottom, as we witness the helplessness and disarray of the people contrasted with the power and uniformity of the army. You can read more about Eisenstein in Part 1, Section 3 on his film *Strike* (1925).

Dziga Vertov was a documentary filmmaker who had been making films since 1919. *Man with a Movie Camera* (Vertov, 1929) has approximately **1,775 separate shots** – a new shot every few seconds. The film can be considered as part of a silent film genre known as **city symphonies**, in which a city is documented and celebrated through the poetic use of images and score. *Études sur Paris* (Sauvage, 1928) and *Berlin: Symphony of a Great City* (Ruttman, 1927) were both experimental in film form, pushing the boundaries of filmmaking, narrative and editing.

Unlike continuity editing, montage editing draws attention to the editing process by the frequent cutting between images, which can comprise of different shot types and transitions. The technique of montage (although perhaps not the political ideology) has been incorporated into mainstream cinema and is usually used to demonstrate the passing of time.

A montage sequence is used to great effect in *This is England*, where, to provide context for the film's period setting, the film opens with a montage of news footage of significant historical, political and cultural moments from the 1980s. The juxtaposition of Roland Rat and Margaret Thatcher is humorous, but also points to the extremes of the era, and perhaps even implies criticism of Margaret Thatcher.

Man with a Movie Camera (Vertov, 1929)

This is England (Meadows, 2006)

Continuous take

The continuous take is the antitheses of editing, but some filmmakers have deliberately not edited a scene, sequence or even an entire film.

The opening sequence of *A Touch of Evil* (Welles, 1958) is an elaborate 3' 30" take. *Rope* (Hitchcock, 1948) was conceived as one long continuous take, but as they were working on celluloid there were limits to the shot length, forcing Hitchcock to film ten shots of lengths varying from 4'37" to 10'06", with the edits cleverly disguised.

With the arrival of digital filming, directors were no longer tied to the limits of a film camera magazine.

The single continuous take reached its zenith with *Timecode* (Figgis, 2000): a satire on Hollywood in which four digital cameras recorded, in real time, simultaneous characters and storylines in one long 93' take. Locations were all planned ahead of time, and actors were aware of where they had to be by a certain point, but what they did on the way and conversations were largely improvised around a loose storyline. As there was to be an earthquake, all four camera operators and the actors had to 'act' the earthquake at the exact same time. The entire film was filmed 15 times on consecutive days. There are no edits between each day's takes.

There are points where two characters meet, and the action is shot from two different cameras/ angles (see bottom two images on the right).

Timecode (Figgis, 2000)

All four takes are shown simultaneously on screen. The 'editing' comes in the audio mix being raised and lowered to direct your attention from quadrant to quadrant.

Russian Ark (Sokurov, 2002) is a single 90' steadicam shot through the Hermitage Museum in Saint Petersberg. Following an unnamed narrator encountering real and fictitious people from 300 years of Russian history, 33 rooms in the museum are visited, and over 2,000 actors and three orchestras are seen. *Victoria* (Schipper, 2015) is a 260' German crime thriller shot in a single take on the streets of Berlin.

Victoria (Schipper, 2015)

Sound

For a visual medium, it is surprising how important sound, particularly music, is to a film. In this section you will gain insights into the ways in which aural elements – speech, music and noise – and the absence of it are used in relation to visuals.

Most films have music comprising an original music score from a **composer** (**non-diegetic**) and/or existing/new songs (both **diegetic** and **non-diegetic**). Music is used to set the tone, further the character/story and enhance the filmmaker's aesthetic. A **music supervisor** is responsible for bringing the two together. Sound and dialogue are recorded on location by a **sound recordist**, with further sound added during post-production by **Foley** and **additional dialogue recording (ADR) artists**. The **sound designer/sound editor** brings these components together.

Diegetic and non-diegetic sound

There are two types of soundtrack:

- **Diegetic sound** is the **vocal and ambient sound** that the characters can hear: the sounds that emanate from within the world of the narrative. This can include sounds such as footsteps when a character is walking or music when a car radio is turned on. The sounds will be those from both the on- and off-screen spaces.
- **Non-diegetic sound** is the sound that does not come from the actual world of the narrative, including accompanying music (when no-one on screen is actually seen playing or listening to music) and voice-overs.

Vocal and ambient sounds (diegetic)

The primary focus for the **sound recordist** on set or location would be to capture the actor's **dialogue** and **performance (vocal sound)**, which would be harder to reproduce later. The **ambient sounds** are recorded on location, but they are often added or enhanced in post-production.

A **Foley artist** focuses on the **ambient sounds** of objects (clinking teacups, etc.), the environment (weather, transport, etc.), human noises (footsteps, drumming fingers, etc.) and special sound effects (bones breaking, stabbing, strangling, etc.).

These sounds are usually pitched at a natural level; when a sound is exaggerated, such as a dripping tap, this is known as a **pleonastic sound**. The sound of the knife being sharpened in the opening sequence of *City of God* is pleonastic.

In an **additional dialogue recording (ADR)** session, actors will reproduce missing **vocal sounds** such as the background artistes' chatter, or those that later were deemed unsatisfactory such as a blood-curdling scream. Lead actors may have to carry out ADR work if the original recording is not of good enough quality, or changes in the edit requires new lines of dialogue or an alternative delivery of a line.

Narration (non-diegetic)

Although a voice-over narration, such as Renton's in *Trainspotting* is part of the actor's performance, as it cannot be heard by the characters this would be considered non-diegetic.

The narrator can be a character within the story, which would indicate that the story is being told from their perspective, or it can be delivered by an omnipresent narrator or storyteller in the 'Once upon a time …' tradition.

(iA) Independent Activity

Watch a trailer for four films you are studying from different countries and decades.

- How have they used diegetic and non-diegetic sound?
- Are there voice-overs? If so, how do these match the pace of the visual images used?
- What kind of music is being used, if any?
- What kind of language is used to sell the film to the audience?
- What is the relationship between the editing of the trailer and the sound?

Watch them again with the sound muted.

- What are they key images used?
- What impact did any voice-over or music have?

Consider the following:

- Are these indicative of the genre?
- What are your expectations of the film from the trailer?
- Who are the target audience for this film?

 S&C

Now have a go at storyboarding/ writing or editing your own trailer for another film you are studying.

Things to consider:

- A summary of the main elements of the story.
- Who is starring in the film.
- A tag-line for the film.
- Use persuasive language that 'sells' the film; remember that a trailer is an advert for a film.
- The soundtrack and any music that you want to include.

Narrations can be used just to draw the viewer into the world or used throughout to provide commentary on the action.

Breaking the fourth wall (non-diegetic)

Breaking the fourth wall is when a character stops interacting with the narrative/other characters, turns to the camera and talks directly to the audience. The dialogue is then non-diegetic – not part of the narrative world.

 Independent Activity

Watch Nerdwriters' short film on YouTube on how sound design enhances a scene: 'See With Your Ears: Spielberg and Sound Design.' Now watch a short scene from one of the films you are studying and make a list of all the different uses of sound and how they reinforce the action.

Case study: Sound and music *Blade Runner* (Scott, 1982)

A major part of *Blade Runner*'s impact is due to the way the film uses score and sound design to reflect the mood, setting, genre and characters' emotions, which in turn affect our emotional response.

Vangelis' score greatly contributes to the film's mood and reputation. A year earlier, with *Chariots of Fire* (Hudson, 1981) he changed the music landscape with his pioneering use of synthesisers combined with real instruments. This 'new' sound was a complete change from what had dominated film music for the previous 50 years of recorded film scores and 80+ years of film music.

Vangelis' approach was to watch edited sequences of the film and improvise, drawing on how the scenes made him feel, then developing them for the final score. This is why the music combined with the sound is so powerful, as it works on a visceral level. On occasion, the sounds are so low they are felt physically, creating tension that is only apparent when the sound ends.

At times, it is hard to tell where the non-diegetic score ends and the diegetic sounds of the narrative world begin. This is achieved by matching the qualities of the music (pitch, tone and mood) with the industrial elements of the landscape.

Opening sequence (00:00:31–00:04:45)

The film's first 2'30" contain the opening credits (black screen/mainly white text) but the soundscape is already drawing us into the narrative world.

The first sound we hear seems to be a drum roll, announcing the start of the film. This 'drum roll' continues, interspersed with music. Its blend of synth with real percussion serves as a link from the familiar scores of the past (largely orchestral) with this new sound. This non-diegetic score seems to fade in and out as the credits appear on screen. A greater sense of urgency develops over the explanation text (00:02:06), generated by an industrial sound emulating a heartbeat. Percussion is used to draw attention to key visuals, such as when the location and date appear on screen.

The first shot of the film (00:03:08) is an establishing shot of Los Angeles at night. It is now revealed that the 'drum rolls' are the diegetic sound of explosions; their sound level softer or louder depending on whether they are in the foreground or background.

Spaceships emerge from the background to foreground, their sound growing in intensity. We can hear the sound of a spaceship emerging from the off-screen space behind the camera before we see it, the sound getting softer as the spaceship disappears into the distance.

The flash and representational sound of lightning signals the start of the main music theme (00:03:29), which builds as the camera floats closer towards the skyscrapers. The music fades as we cut to an interior scene of a man in an office, then back to an extreme long shot of the office from outside, before returning to an overhead shot of the office, where a thumping non-diegetic sound mirrors the rotation of the fan. Two tannoy announcements can be heard, followed by a knock on the door, and the film's first line of dialogue: 'Come in.' Inviting both his visitor and us into this world.

Sound:
Music

Further information

Silence

Strange as it may seem, the **absence of sound and music** is also a significant part of a soundtrack. A filmmaker may use the lack of sound in the same way as they use the freeze-frame to draw attention to something or signal a change in direction or mood.

Without the music cues to guide emotions, you are left in suspense, which creates a greater tension. Silence is therefore a significant part of the horror filmmaker's use of sound, so much so that it has become a genre trope that a quiet passage will be followed by a loud noise. So, think about silence while you are studying the use of sound.

Music (diegetic and non-diegetic) helps to create further meaning for audiences. It can do this by:

- serving as the unseen narrative voice pushing us towards the appropriate emotive response, whether it be fear, longing or pride
- highlighting the character's psychological or emotional response to a situation
- creating a sense of continuity from one scene to the next (sound bridges)
- building tension and giving a sense of relief/finality.

Music also helps to indicate:

- the mood or personality of the character/scene
- location
- period setting
- a realistic setting.

There are three types of music:

- Background music (also called a film score, film music, incidental music) is written specifically for a film by one composer and used throughout the film.
- Found music is existing music such as pop songs or classical music/opera.
- Music and songs performed as part of the story.

Background music

A film score can bring all the visual elements together, and can help to add weight, meaning or power to an otherwise flat scene. Try watching a scene with the sound down and you will see how much of an impact music has in creating tension and atmosphere.

Non-diegetic background music is used to:

- define genres
- form part of the aesthetic style
- create mood
- further plot
- establish setting
- enhance action
- develop character
- offer in-jokes or knowingness.
- provide short cuts

Composers themselves disagree as to whether their work should be visible or invisible. You may not even notice that music is playing until it is gone. If it is noticeable, then this too is a form a manipulation.

The music can either enhance or reinforce the action on screen, mirroring the pace of the film created by the cinematography and editing, or it can work against such expectations, which is known as **parallel and contrapuntal sounds**.

Background music has to work immediately; there is no time to develop the mood. Some composers will use recurring themes as a recurring theme to reference the character, location or idea. These are called **leitmotifs**. Probably the most recognisable leitmotif is just the two notes (F and F sharp) used to indicate the approach of the shark in *Jaws* (Spielberg, 1975).

 S&C

Search for Neil Brand on YouTube and on the BBC Radio 4 Film Programme and you will find a number of films/ interviews with Brand analysing film scores. Watching and listening to these will give you a greater understanding of the importance of film music. Brand is also a silent film accompanist of international repute. If you are studying silent film do watch and listen to his work on that too.

Found music

Even though this is called 'found' music, considerable thought will have gone into the choice of song and how it is used within a scene. If a song is going to be used to underscore a particular piece of action (e.g. walking down a road) or to accompany a fight scene, the rights to use this would have to be cleared before filming, as the performance and the editing would be timed to the music.

A song can be used **diegetically**, such as listening to a vinyl record or by turning on a radio. The whole song may be used or just an important lyrical phrase to either support or work against a character's mood or action. Or it can be used **non-diegetically** – such as the 'Eye of the Tiger' montage training scene from *Rocky* (Avildsen, 1976).

Performed music

There are two types of performed music:

- Musical numbers that are seen within or as **part of the narrative** (a busker or nightclub act), such as the bands we see in *Boyhood* (Linklater, 2015). These are **realist** uses of performed music and can be seen across a number of film genres.
- Musical numbers that are used to express **heightened emotion**, such as the 'Another Day of Sun' in *La La Land* (Chazelle, 2016), are **anti-realist** and are usually only used in musicals.

Parallel and contrapuntal sounds

Filmgoers develop automatic responses to the combination of sounds and images. Filmmakers can either work with these expectations or against them; music is a primary tool in doing this.

Parallel sounds are sounds that go hand in hand with the images on screen: upbeat music for a comedy, sinister music for a thriller. It can also be used to mirror the life of the characters – the music in the opening sequence of *Trainspotting* appears appropriate for the characters and setting.

A **contrapuntal sound** is one that is in counterpoint the action; the mood of the sounds (often music) you are hearing does not the match what you are seeing. For example, if we see children playing, but hear an ominous sound effect or sinister music score, this could be a cue that something bad is going to happen.

Songs offer opportunities to juxtapose sound and image. In *A Clockwork Orange* (Kubrick, 1971) and *Goodfellas* (Scorsese, 1990) scenes of great violence are played out to upbeat energetic music. The music works against what we are seeing. This could be used for humour or to emphasise the characters' gleefulness and/or relaxed attitude to the violence they are perpetrating.

Synchronous and asynchronous sound

Synchronous sound is most commonly used. It simply means that the recorded sounds are exactly aligned to the image on screen, primarily so that the words people speak match their mouth movements.

Asynchronous sound is diegetic sound heard before the action that produces it is seen or sound that continues after that action is no longer on screen. This term can also refer to intentional background sounds not directly related to the image on screen.

Synchronous sounds: contribute to the realism of film as the sounds heard match the actions on screen.

Asynchronous sounds: sound effects that are not matched with a visible source of the sound on screen.

Performance: Communication (i)

In this section, you will gain an understanding of how **performance** is used to convey meaning and generate audience response.

Performance includes both individual and ensemble performances, with specific attention being paid to physical expression, vocal delivery, interaction between performers and the specificity of performance for the camera.

A film's visual and aural aesthetic, generated through the cinematography, mise-en-scène, editing and sound, will be reflected in the actors' performances. How they are placed within the frame, how they move within it and how they deliver their dialogue all add to the storytelling and look of a film.

A film's genre, whether it is a Hollywood blockbuster or an independent (indie) film, and the director's vision and working methods will impact on how the film is cast and what style of acting will be used.

Verbal and non-verbal communication

Figure, expression and movement

Film is a visual medium, and you can gain much meaning about what a character is thinking or feeling from these visual elements of performance. **Figure**, **expression** and **movement** all help to build your understanding of a character and their relationship with others. Specifically:

- **Figure**: If they are sitting still, what pose have they assumed? How do the other characters and ingredients of mise-en-scène relate to them?
- **Expression**: What thoughts or feelings does the actor's performance project?
- **Movement**: How do the actors move through the frame? Consider their speed, gracefulness or even their complete lack of coordination?

Their appearance is also relevant: are they neat or dishevelled, young or old, healthy or ill?

These are all **non-verbal communication** elements of performance, which are often more powerful than **verbal communication**, the elements used to deliver dialogue.

Body codes

Actors have a number of techniques at their disposal to help develop their character. These help to generate audience responses. Ten key communication methods (nine non-verbal and one verbal) have been identified in the table on the following page taken from Argyle, quoted in Fiske, 2010.

Figure (*Trainspotting*, Boyle, 1996)

Expression (*Vivre sa vie*, Godard, 2006)

Movement (*Fish Tank*, Arnold, 2009)

 S&C

Watch a scene from any film and consider how these ten body codes are used.

Body Codes		
1 Direct bodily context	Are characters touching each other, if so how? Combined with the positioning of characters this can reveal much about their relationship.	
2 The proximity of one character to another (or proxemics)	Are the characters close together or far apart? This will reveal how intimate (or not) these characters are and may change over the course of the film.	
3 The orientation of one to another	Are the characters turned towards or away from each other? This could reveal whether they are working together or what they feel about one another.	
4 General appearance	Are they fat, thin, tall, short? Are they well-dressed? How does their appearance compare with those around them?	
5 Head movements	How is the actor using their head to express emotion or suggest meaning? A slow side-to-side shake of the head could indicate sorrow, whereas a fast one disagreement.	
6 Facial expressions	How are these being use to reveal emotions?	
7 Eye movement or contact	Does a character look directly into the eye of another, or do they look down or up? What does this convey? How long is the eye contact held? Does the actor blink frequently or not at all? What are they trying to achieve with the eye contact?	
8 Body posture/body language	Does the way the actor walk or hold themselves, suggest a particular emotion such as pain or anger. Can you tell whether a character is confident or timid from the way they enter a room or sit? Is their body posture open or closed?	
9 Gestures (kinesics)	How does the actor use their hands? Are they still or restless? Can you tell how pleased they are to see someone from their wave?	
10 Aspects of speech (paralinguistic codes)	An actor uses a range of techniques (pace, pitch, stress, volume, pause, accents) to deliver lines of dialogue, which will develop the character and generate responses.	

Performance:
Communication (ii) and style

 S&C

Read the screenplay for a particularly dramatic scene from a film you are studying. Then watch the sequence and note how the actors' delivery of the written lines impacts upon how meaning is conveyed.

Aspects of speech

Delivering lines of dialogue draws on a range of **verbal communication** techniques such as:

- pitch • stress • tone • volume • accent • pausing.

These dramatic aspects of performance help to bring the characters to life and express the required emotion and meaning.

In real life there are certain patterns of speaking that come naturally. People vary their volume and pace, they pause and stumble over words, sentences peter out or are interrupted. If a film is striving for realism in its performance, actors will try to emulate this. Highly stylised films might require actors to fully enunciate all words, or deliver them in an exaggerated tone.

The choice of the delivery of speech will ensure that a character is well defined, believable and complements the film's overall aesthetic.

Pace or tempo

Pace, also known as **tempo**, is a basic principle of dialogue delivery. If what is being said is important the pace is generally slower so the audience can take it in. This is essential at the beginning of a film as the audience is getting to know the setting character and direction of the story. Pace will also give an indication of the character: a **fast-paced** delivery will suggest high energy or extremes of emotion. A **slow pace** suggests deep thoughts, indecision or loneliness. An **even pace** suggests control and self-confidence.

Pitch

Pitch is the relative highness or lowness of the tone of a voice, men will generally have a lower pitch than women. Therefore, if a woman has a lower pitch, they could be read as being less feminine.

Stress

Stress is used to place emphasis on key words or phrases; this can be achieved by stretching a word out, pausing or delivering the word/line with a greater force.

Volume

Volume is used for emphasis and as an indication of the emotional energy of a character or their setting.

Pauses

Surprisingly, a key aspect of dialogue delivery is when to stop speaking.

Pauses are used for a number of reasons and each will add weight to the words being spoken. The most significant reasons are:

- end of a thought
- searching for the right word
- to take a breath
- for emphasis
- being distracted
- waiting for a response
- dawning realisation.

Pauses, combined with gestures or eye movements, develop the character at each stage of the narrative and create further meaning for the audience.

Too many pauses might indicate weakness or confusion. A speech punctuated by pausing will be choppy and hard to follow.

Making pauses too long draws attention to the technique and may make the audience aware they are watching actors deliver lines of dialogue. However, it can be used effectively in an emotionally challenging scene or where there is a power dynamic between the two characters.

Accents

Accents are the most noticeable element of dialogue delivery: the one that is commented upon, celebrated or derided. An accent can be geographically, historically and class appropriate. A British costume drama set in the early 20th century would require actors to speak in a different accent than a contemporary British film. Regional accents evoke different responses, and can be used as a short cut to a character and setting. If an actor is playing a different nationality then there is considerable research needed to ensure they are geographically and historically accurate.

However, not all filmmakers want their actors to speak with a geographical or historical accent. This decision is part of the aesthetic of the film.

Performance style

There are three styles of performance and the choice of style supports the aesthetic of the film and/or its genre/setting:

- Realism (subtle): independent; social realist; docu-drama
- Classicism (naturalistic): mainstream; Hollywood
- Formalism (overt/stylistic): art film; expressionistic.

Realist

This performance style should feel authentic, the actor's technique would be barely noticed, as they are being 'themselves'. Filmmakers striving for realism seek actors that are natural on camera and may often employ non-professional actors (actors with no professional training). Our response to this style is to feel the authenticity of the performer and believe that this could be a real, recognisable world.

Improvisation and **method acting** techniques (see the following section) are often used in realist films.

Classical

This is the classic 'Hollywood' style of performance technique, which offers a surface believability. Here, characters are usually played by well-known actors who bring with them a certain set of social and moral values that audiences respond to.

Formalist

Formalist performances may be 'over-the-top', appearing arch or highly stylised. This style is rare, and films in this style would be considered 'art house' films. The rhythm and delivery of lines and/or movement are dictated by the filmmaker's aesthetic.

We Need to Talk about Kevin (Ramsay, 2011)

The Lady from Shanghai (Welles, 1947)

Performance: Improvisation and method acting

The two acting styles that can be used to creative believable characters are:

- **improvisation** and **method acting**.

Improvisation

Improvisation is seen as a tool of the director, and dictates the overriding performance style for all actors. Over a period of weeks, and in some cases even months, actors work with the director to develop their characters. The process allows the actor to inhabit that character and gain insights into what their life was like before the story being told. Doing this, they will learn how they would respond in a certain situation. This process results in a loose script outline that actors can then develop further when in production. The cinematography is often hand-held to allow the camera to follow the action, or a simple fixed shot capturing the scene as it unfolds.

Ad-libbing and **improvising** in the moment is encouraged by some filmmakers to provide a sense of authenticity and momentum.

Method acting

Method acting is seen as tool of the actor; although not all actors in the film may employ this method. Method acting developed from an earlier theatrical acting technique – the Stanislavski method – when an actor would explore the emotional inner life of the character to create a verbal and physically realist performance. This technique was brought to Hollywood in the 1950s by the Polish-born American actor and director Lee Strasberg, who developed it further, encouraging actors not to merely *play* the character but to *become* the character. The Strasberg method, or method acting as it become known, has been adopted by some of Hollywood's most well-regarded actors including Al Pacino, Robert De Niro, Hilary Swank and Daniel Day-Lewis, and has been the vehicle for many iconic film performances. Today, a method actor would attempt to replicate the experiences of their character as much as they can prior to and during the production. Method actors may also go to extreme lengths of weight gain or weight loss for a role.

 S&C

Check out Filmmaker IQ's course on `The Origins of Acting and "The Method"', which traces the origins of acting technique from early Greek theatre to the psychological approaches to performance of the 20th and 21st centuries. Do take the Final Quiz!

https://filmmakeriq.com/courses/origins-acting-method/

 STUDY TIP

Taking notes during screenings is notoriously difficult. Here are some tips

1. Just write, leaving gaps that you can fill in later.
2. Write in two columns: (A) a rough sequence of events (scenes, places, names, dialogue); (B) things of particular interest (camerawork, lighting, music, where you were moved – you can use emojis for this).

Look over your notes after the screening and check that you can read them. You might want to add to them or re-write them.

Further information

Casting is a crucial part of the filmmaking process. Consider the impact of the casting decisions made on *La La Land*. The decision to cast Emma Stone and Ryan Gosling over initial choices Emma Watson and Miles Teller had a tremendous impact. Their history of working together provided on-screen chemistry but also played into the characters' desperation, as they were slightly older and yet to achieve their dreams. Actors' physicality, their performance style and their star persona all contribute to creating character, so finding the right fit is central to creating convincing and compelling characters.

Case study: Improvisation and method acting

Secrets & Lies (Leigh, 1996, 01:11:00–01:19:28)

Mike Leigh's primary working method uses improvisation to develop his narratives and build characters.

Starring: Brenda Blethyn (Cynthia) and Marianne Jean-Baptiste (Hortense).

For the film's first hour you follow two parallel sets of characters: Cynthia's chaotic family life and Hortense's investigation to find her birth mother, which results in her calling Cynthia, her mother, and arranging to meet.

The two sit side-by-side at a table, their proximity is close but there is no body contact. The first 30" is a medium-long shot, cutting to an 8' medium shot positioned from the seat opposite. The position of the two actors means they spend much of the time looking out, not at each other, making little eye contact. They do turn to one another, but this frequently results in the other turning slightly or looking away. Indicating they are not comfortable with each other.

Cynthia's gestures are restless as she tugs on her coat and with trembling fingers smokes her cigarette, or folds her arms across her body as a form of protection. The position of the camera ensures you can see every change of expression, such as the slow realisation that she is indeed her mother. Cynthia's dialogue stumbles and falls out, punctuated by pauses.

Hortense is, in contrast, far more measured and calm. Her gestures are more controlled, using the paperwork she has brought with her to control the scene. Her line delivery is more restrained, as though controlling her emotions.

However, it is to Cynthia that we are drawn, due to her more physical performance. This is reinforced through the colours of their costumes. Cynthia is dressed in white, which draws the eye, whereas Hortense is in black.

This eight-minute scene is played out in one improvised take, which creates an emotional authenticity that is relayed to the audience through their close proximity to the action.

One Flew Over the Cuckoo's Nest
(Forman, 1975)

Starring: Jack Nicholson (McMurphy), Will Sampson (Chief Bromden), William Redfield (Harding), Sydney Lassick (Cheswick), Christopher Lloyd (Taber), Brad Dourif (Billy Bibbit), Vincent Schiavelli (Fredrickson), Danny DeVito (Martini) and Louise Fletcher (Nurse Ratched).

For the method actor, having a disability or mental illness is a challenge, which, if done well,

results in critical praise. To prepare for their roles, Jack Nicholson and his fellow co-stars spent time in an active psychiatric hospital. They attended group therapy with patients and watched electroconvulsive therapy (ECT) sessions. Many of the cast stayed in character between scenes, which is typical of a method actor. All of the actors who played patients lived in the Oregon State Hospital while in production. The cast also featured non-professional actors, including two central characters: Dr Dean Brooks, the superintendent of Oregon State Hospital, played Dr John Spivey, and Will Sampson, a Muscogee (a native North American tribe), made his acting debut as Chief Bromden.

Captain Fantastic (Ross, 2016)

The specification says

Learners study the following in relation to film as a medium of representation:

- *how film creates meaning and generates response through cinematography, mise-en-scène, editing, sound and performance (including staging and direction)*

- *how all aspects of film form including narrative contribute to the representations of cultures and societies (gender, ethnicity and age), including the ideological nature of those representations.*

Representation

How to approach representation

This aspect of the course asks you to consider how the film you are studying presents society to the audience and what messages about that society are being conveyed.

This section will define representation, explore theoretical approaches and apply them to three films:

- *Vertigo* (Hitchcock, 1958)
- *Do the Right Thing* (Lee, 1989)
- *Captain Fantastic* (Ross, 2016).

It is important to remember that representations will be shaped, in part, by the society in which the films are produced, so with the case studies in this section it could be expected that the later the film is made the more progressive the representations of social groups will be. The focuses in this section, as stated in the specification, are gender, ethnicity and age so the case studies presented here explore each of these. Remember, though, that a truly insightful examination of the representation of any of these social groups will include reference to the others. For example, in examining gender, older women are often represented very differently to young women, black women differently to Asian women, and so on.

Representation

Representation is the way the media, in your case films, represents the world to the audience. The term itself is interesting and can be read as **re**-presentation, as films, from all genres, are constructed, so reality has gone through a process of mediation before being shown to an audience.

Every filmmaker, or film studio, initially decides on the subject of their film. They choose what story they want to tell, which characters they want to include and from those characters who will be the central protagonist and what events in that character's life will be depicted. Steve Baker breaks this process down as follows:

- *Selection*: *Choosing what to represent.*
- *Organisation*: *Structuring that representation.*
- *Focus*: *Encouraging the spectator to pay more attention to certain aspects of the representation than others.* (adapted from Baker, 2011)

These decisions bring into play all aspects of film form and narrative. For example, in terms of selecting narratives, if, as is the case, most films centre on heterosexual, white male protagonists there are issues about the under-representation of minorities and women to be explored.

When it comes to organisation, structuring the narrative, the character with the most screen time is likely to be seen as the most important. The film is telling their story and attributing less importance to the more peripheral characters. With regards to focusing the audience's attention, consider the selection of specific shots; a prevalence of close-ups encourages the spectators to focus their attention on a character's emotions, while consistent use of long shots could be used to display movement and action. Certain traits in characters can be foregrounded through shot choice, thereby emphasising their significance. In mise-en-scène, decisions about staging can come into play, with a dominant, powerful character being higher in the frame than a more submissive, vulnerable one. If the former is a white man and the latter a black man then issues around the representation of racial inequality can be raised.

One way to approach looking at the representations within a film is to ask the following questions:

- Who is doing the representing?
- Who is being represented?
- What social groups are omitted from the representations?
- What messages about particular social groups are being conveyed?
- Which characters or social groups have the power in the representations?
- Do the characters adhere to stereotypes or challenge them?
- Are the characters typical of characters in films of that genre?
- What do the representations tell the audience about society at the time the film was made and/or set?
- How are elements of film form being used to construct the representations?

 Independent Activity

Choose two female characters of differing ages in any of the films you are studying and compare their representations, focusing on:

- sexuality
- costume
- role in the narrative.

Present your findings in a table.

 S&C

From one of the films you are studying, choose the lead male and female characters and work out how much screen time each one gets in the film.

Power dynamics established through staging in *Vertigo* (Hitchcock, 1958).

S&C

Find statistics on the levels of representations of women, ethnic minorities and older people and the diversity of the workforce in national cinemas other than the USA. A good starting point for the UK is the 'Education and Research' section of the BFI website.

S&C

Research Steele and Aronson's 1995 work on stereotype threat, to learn about the consequences of social groups conforming to stereotypes.

Binary opposition: when two characters or ideologies are set up against one another. It is an important concept of structuralism and can be used to structure representations and help create meaning.

Structuralism: the idea that films can best be understood through an examination of their underlying structure, including exploring how meaning is produced through binary oppositions.

Independent Activity

Consider the following groups, which are categorised by aspects of age, gender and ethnicity, and list five common stereotypes of each group:

- teenage Japanese girls
- African-American young males
- elderly Jewish women.

Consider what sources you are using to reach these conclusions and think about the power of the media in perpetuating stereotypes.

Independent Activity

Think about your family members and friendship groups; are their characteristics easily reduced to a handful of stereotypical traits? Try to list them.

Under-representation and inequality

The Media, Diversity, & Social Change Initiative at the University of Southern California (USC) has conducted extensive research into equality of representation in film. A study in July 2017 on behalf of the Annenberg Foundation (Smith et al., 2017a) analysed every speaking or named character in the top 100 fictional films at the American box office from 2007 to 2016 (excluding 2011).

In 2016, of 4,583 speaking characters examined, 68.6% were male and only 31.4% were female (Smith et al., 2017b). This could be attributed in part to the fact that the study also discovered that there are 23 male film directors to every one female. A key part of studying representation, as mentioned earlier, is considering who is doing the representing. The same study explored ethnicity and found that over 70% of characters were white. In total, only 29.2% of characters were from under-represented ethnic groups, which is significantly below the US Census (38.7%) (cited in Smith et al., 2017b).

A 2017 study by the same USC Initiative analysed 1,256 speaking or named characters in the 25 films nominated for the Academy Award for Best Picture from 2014 to 2016, to ascertain the frequency of older characters featuring in films (cited in Smith et al., 2017b). The study found that only 11.8% of these characters were 60 years of age or older and that six of the 14 films that featured an aging character contained ageist comments.

These statistics point to the fact that the film industry feels that American society values certain social groups more than others, i.e. young white males. Representation is important, as seeing your likeness reflected on screen, having role models you can identify with or feeling like your experiences are an important story to be told can contribute to increased confidence and feelings of self worth. It can also have implications on how you are perceived and consequently treated by other social groups.

Stereotyping

Stereotyping of social groups is frequently used in film as a form of shorthand. Peripheral characters in particular can be quite loosely drawn, and using stereotypes quickly and clearly creates a basic understanding of characters for audiences. Although the reasons for using stereotypes can be understood, the practice is loaded with problems as social groups are reduced to a set of typical traits that are reductive and dismissive.

Richard Dyer has written extensively about stereotyping and power (1997, 1998), and agrees that the complexity and variety of a social group is reduced to a few key characteristics through the process of stereotyping. An exaggerated version of these characteristics is then applied to everyone in the group. Stereotypes in film are generally constructed through the character's image and behaviour.

Dyer also argues that those with less power are predominantly stereotyped by those with more, which makes sense when the demographics of those working in senior roles in the film industry are considered. This leads to there being significantly fewer stereotypical representations of white middle-class men in film than of minority groups or women. Dyer argues that the use of stereotypes legitimises inequality, as stereotypes are a 'way to ensure unequal power relations are maintained'. Claude Lévi-Strauss agrees, stating that representations are deliberately placed in binary opposition to ensure the dominant culture is maintained and the minorities represented are seen as subordinate and marginalised (see, e.g., Lévi-Strauss, 1995).

Case study: The representation of gender in *Vertigo* (Hitchcock, 1958)

Hitchcock's masterpiece, *Vertigo*, is widely considered to be his best and most personal film. It was voted the greatest film of all time in *Sight & Sound* magazine's prestigious poll in 2012. Perhaps one of the reasons why the film appeals to film critics and audiences alike is that it is a film, in part, about deriving pleasure from watching, something that film fans all understand.

The narrative follows Scottie, a retired police officer, struggling with the acrophobia brought on by the traumatic death of his colleague. Scottie takes on a case that leads to him becoming obsessed with Madeleine, the wife of an old friend, and after her death desperately searching for someone to replace her. On finding a likely candidate, Judy, Scottie attempts to control her and eventually coerces her into becoming 'Madeleine'.

The film should, as all films should, be considered in context. It can perhaps be read as emblematic of men trying to re-assert their control over women in post-war America. One of the first things Scottie asks of Judy is that she not go to work but spend time with him instead, saying, 'let me take care of you'. Hitchcock's auteur status, including his level of control over his films and his cinematic preoccupation with blonde women and their ultimate destruction, are also factors that cannot be ignored when considering the representation of women in this film. Madeleine is just one of a number of women punished in Hitchcock's films at the hands of men.

One of the techniques Hitchcock uses to assert Scottie's dominance over 'Madeleine' is the power of the look. It is impossible to look at the gender roles in *Vertigo* without considering how the camera is used to position 'Madeleine' for both Scottie and the audience to enjoy looking at. In the Ernie's scene of *Vertigo* both Scottie and the audience see 'Madeleine' for the first time. There is a prevalence of shots from Scottie's point of view to establish his obsession with 'Madeleine'.

In the example shown, the shot starts as a medium close-up of Scottie and the camera follows his gaze through a zoom-out, pan and zoom-in to finally rest on 'Madeleine'. She is wearing a green dress, which vividly contrasts with its complementary colour, the sensual red of the wall behind her, so the audience's eyes, like Scottie's, are drawn to her. Only her back is shown, suggesting she is passive and unaware she is being watched. She sits opposite her husband, Gavin Elster, who has brought her there for the purpose of being looked at by Scottie. The men have the power in this scene.

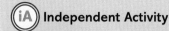

Watch Hitchcock's *Strangers on a Train* (1951) and *Psycho* (1960), and consider the representations of Miriam and Marion to establish a pattern in his representation of women. These women are both punished, what do the narratives suggest are the reasons for this?

iA Independent Activity

Independent Activity

Choose any sequence of six shots from the scenes of Scottie following 'Madeleine' before they meet and screengrab them. Annotate the images, naming the shot types and commenting on the mise-en-scène.

Eye-line match-cuts align the spectator with Scottie through most of the film, as a repetitive sequence of shots develops: a shot of Scottie looking off-screen, a shot of 'Madeleine' from his point of view, back to Scottie looking and so on. This continues for a lengthy section of the film in which 'Madeleine' appears oblivious to the fact that she is being looked at and also remains silent. She is merely there to be looked at, completely passively. The notion of women being objectified in cinema is not uncommon and has been discussed by numerous critics and academics.

In *Ways of Seeing* (2008), John Berger summarised the differences between men and women thus: 'men act and women appear'. Laura Mulvey applied this notion of the active male and the passive female to films in her 1999 essay 'Visual Pleasure and Narrative Cinema', which explores the power inherent in Scottie watching 'Madeleine' and how this transfers to the spectator. Mulvey suggests that the dominant view in cinema is masculine and women are presented for men to look at:

> *In a world ordered by sexual imbalance, pleasure in looking has been split between active/male and passive/female. The determining male gaze projects its phantasy onto the female figure, which is styled accordingly. In their traditional exhibitionist role women are simultaneously looked at and displayed, with their appearance coded for strong visual and erotic impact so that they can be said to connote to-be-looked-at-ness.*

In the stills below it is evident just how much the purpose of 'Madeleine' is, on the surface, to be looked at. She is framed like a painting in one moment and then pauses in front of Scottie for a stunning back-lit profile image. The shallow depth of field and centring of 'Madeleine' in the composition contribute to a beautiful aesthetic but also make her the focus of the gaze.

Mulvey explores how Hitchcock encourages the spectator to see the world through Scottie's eyes and adopt the 'male gaze'. She argues that,

> *Hitchcock's skillful use of identification processes and liberal use of subjective camera from the point of view of the male protagonist draw the spectators deeply into his position, making them share his uneasy gaze.*

However, Mulvey's notion is problematised when the narrative reveals that this is not in fact Madeleine being looked at, but Judy, very knowingly masquerading as Madeleine in order to deceive Scottie. Surely, then, Judy is at this point far from passive but a very active participant in a cruel entrapment. It could be argued though that during this scene the audience is no more aware of this than Scottie so they simply look at the spectacle of 'Madeleine' with him.

S&C

Read Mulvey's (1999) essay 'Visual Pleasure and Narrative Cinema' and produce a version of the final section, 'Summary', in your own words.

The representation of gender becomes arguably even more interesting after the death of 'Madeleine' when Scottie meets Judy. As Mulvey states,

> *Once he actually confronts her, his erotic drive is to break her down and force her to tell by persistent cross-questioning. Then, in the second part of the film, he re-enacts his obsessive involvement with the image he loved to watch secretly. He reconstructs Judy as Madeleine, forces her to conform in every detail to the actual physical appearance of his fetish.*

Scottie's bullying and subsequent control of Judy, and the makeover he manipulates her into having, has been read as a metaphor for how Hitchcock, and Hollywood in general, treated actresses. The film industry is one in which women in particular are expected to attain impossible levels of physical perfection.

Arguably, Hollywood has not really moved on, as demonstrated in the recent research by USC (2017), which found that women in film are significantly more likely than males to be shown in sexually revealing attire and partially or fully naked. To a worrying degree women are still in films to be looked at and a lot of a woman's value to filmmakers seems to be in her sexual appeal. The dangerous repercussions of the status of women within the film industry have become all too clear in the recent revelations about the culture of harassment and abuse endured by many. Representations are important and have a real-world impact.

The Bechdel Test

The **Bechdel Test** is a way of highlighting gender inequality in fiction. It is frequently applied to films and to pass the test the film simply has to feature at least two named female characters who talk to each other about something other than a man. It has been suggested that only approximately half of all films meet these requirements. The test draws on Mulvey's ideas to a certain extent, as it measures how active the female characters are in film. If *Vertigo* is considered in relation to this test, it fails spectacularly. The only woman Judy nearly has a conversation with is the shop assistant but Scottie puts a stop to this by taking the active, and controlling, role of deciding what Judy 'wants'.

 S&C

Consider the representation of Midge, the other significant female character in *Vertigo*. Make notes on her representation as a mother figure to Scottie, her active pursuit of him and her subsequent disappearance from the narrative. Consider too the way this representation would be altered if the alternative ending, which can be easily found online, had been retained.

 Independent Activity

Watch Stacy Smith's TED talk, 'The Data behind Hollywood's Sexism', on the internet to gain a fuller understanding of the issues facing women in the contemporary American film industry.

 S&C

Apply the Bechdel Test to all the films you are studying on this course and see if the selection surpasses the 50% mark.

Case study: The representation of ethnicity in *Do the Right Thing* (Lee, 1989)

> *Violence as a way of achieving racial justice is both impractical and immoral. It is impractical because it is a descending spiral ending in destruction for all. The old law of an eye for an eye leaves everyone blind. It is immoral because it seeks to humiliate the opponent rather than win his understanding: it seeks to annihilate rather than convert. Violence is immoral because it thrives on hatred rather than love. It destroys community and makes brotherhood impossible. It leaves society in monologue rather than dialogue. Violence ends up defeating itself. It creates bitterness in the survivors and brutality in the destroyers.*
>
> (Martin Luther King Jr, Nobel Prize Lecture, 1964)

Martin Luther King Jr (left) and Malcolm X (right)

> *I think there are plenty of good people in America, but there are also plenty of bad people in America and the bad ones are the ones who seem to have all the power and be in these positions to block things that you and I need. Because this is the situation, you and I have to preserve the right to do what is necessary to bring an end to that situation, and it doesn't mean that I advocate violence, but at the same time I am not against using violence in self-defense. I don't even call it violence when it's self-defense, I call it intelligence.*
>
> (Malcolm X, Speech to Peace Corps Workers, 1964)

The above words appear in the end credits of Spike Lee's *Do the Right Thing*, leaving the audience considering the film's ideological messages. This is a film about racial inequality and police brutality, issues still sadly very pertinent today. The film is dedicated to, among others, Eleanor Bumpurs and Edmund Perry – both African-Americans who were killed by police officers. It is a film that shows why the black community needs to fight injustice but perhaps also shows that violence can often just lead to further violence. The decision to quote both Martin Luther King Jr and Malcolm X leaves the film's final message a little more open, as these men had such different approaches in their quests for racial equality. Perhaps Spike Lee's intention was not to answer any questions but provoke further debate.

Do the Right Thing is a significant American film, considered the most important film of 1989 by respected film critics Siskel and Ebert (1989). It was nominated for Academy Awards for Best Original Screenplay and Best Supporting Actor, and won numerous awards including Best Picture and Best Director at the Chicago Film Critics Association awards in 1990. The film was part of the New Black Film Wave, marking a major shift in the representation of African-Americans in cinema. Roger Ebert argues that Lee's previous, *She's Gotta Have it* (1986), was the film that started this 'wave'. According to Ebert, black-orientated films prior to this period had either been liberal 'issue based' films or, in the 1970s, Blaxploitation films with tough, cynical protagonists. These new films were different as they, 'considered the African-American experience in its own terms, instead of filtering it through implied white values, or tailoring it for white audiences' (Ebert, 1991).

For this section the questions towards the beginning of this chapter will be used as a guide through the analysis of representation.

Who is doing the representing?

Do the Right Thing is clearly a 'Spike Lee Joint' as the posters and DVD cover proclaim. He wrote it, stars in it, directed it and produced it with his company 40 Acres and a Mule Filmworks. His production company's name could point to his agenda in filmmaking as it is a reference to the beliefs held by freed slaves that they were to be given land and a mule once released from the bonds of slavery. This choice of company name reminds the audience of the historic mistreatment of black people in America and the lies they have been told by the authorities.

Spike Lee is an important filmmaker described by Yvonne Tasker (2010) as 'the most visible symbol of a vibrant and evolving African-American film culture that extends from the mainstream to the experimental'. So, this is a significant film by a respected filmmaker but, perhaps most important of all, this is the story of a community told by someone who understands it. Lee was born into a middle-class family in Georgia but grew up in an ethnically diverse part of Brooklyn so he is, to an extent, writing of what he knows. This is crucial in representation, particularly in the representation of minority groups, as nobody is more qualified to tell a story than someone who has experienced it. This lends authenticity to the representation and prevents the dominant group controlling the depiction of those with less power.

Who is being represented?

The film features a diverse cast of characters of all ages and a range of races and ethnicities, including Koreans and Italian-Americans but predominantly African-Americans. At the core of this film is an exploration of the conflicts between these groups with animosity on all sides but this is balanced by the friendships and sense of community also depicted. There are moments of tenderness and even a begrudging respect at times between characters from different ethnic groups. Take Sal's attitude to Mookie's sister Jade as a clear example.

What social groups are omitted from the representations?

The film is dominated by working-class characters and even the relatively successful Sal is shown to have worked hard over a long period of time to build up his business. Characters from the upper/middle classes are almost absent from the representation, with the exception of the yuppie home owner, Clifton.

By only including one relatively wealthy white neighbour perhaps Lee is making a comment on tokenism. This is the casting of one minority character in a film to create the impression of equality and diversity. The character Token Black in *South Park* is a reference to this practice. It seems more likely though that Clifton's purpose in the narrative is revealed in the conversation with Buggin' Out. Clifton is asked why he wants to live in a black neighbourhood and feels the need to defend his right to be there, 'I was born in Brooklyn.' This is an inversion of a scene commonly played out by minority characters in films trying to establish that they are native to a country and thus have a right to be there.

What messages about particular social groups are being conveyed?

This is a complex question with numerous possible answers but one area that could be explored is the linking of young African-Americans with aggression, violence and relatively low socio-economic status. Despite being produced at a time in American culture when the black middle class was being represented more frequently and there were numerous black role models in the media, this film chooses to focus predominantly on characters with limited hope or aspirations. The film does not really suggest a way out for these characters but perhaps this reflects some harsh truths about society: as *Money* magazine reported in 2017 there are still, 'stark racial discrepancies across a broad range of economic indicators – from hourly pay to student debt, retirement savings to home ownership and health'.

Which characters or social groups have the power in the representations?

The film is centred on the struggle to establish who has the power and it changes through the narrative. Sal and his family initially have power within their domain as they celebrate famous Italian-Americans in framed portraits on

S&C

Watch *In the Heat of the Night* (Jewison, 1967) and *Super Fly* (Park, 1972) to broaden your knowledge of the representation of African-Americans prior to the New Black Film Wave.

S&C

Watch Lee's *She's Gotta Have it* (1986) and compare it to *Do the Right Thing*, analysing film form and the overall aesthetic alongside representation issues.

Sal and Jade

Buggin' Out confronts Clifton

Socio-economic status: an individual or group's social position in relation to others, based on education, occupation and income.

their walls and have economic power by paying Mookie and Da Mayor for their services. However, by rebelling en masse, the larger black community asserts their power. They ensure their voices are heard and direct their fury about the social injustices they have endured at Sal. But perhaps the group with the most power, ultimately, is the police, who in the film's climactic riot scene, abuse that power with horrific consequences.

Do the characters adhere to stereotypes or challenge them?

This film tackles the issue of stereotypes head on and demonstrates how negative they are with a powerful sequence of shots. Characters of different ethnicities launch a tirade of insults based on ethnic stereotypes directly at the audience by breaking the fourth wall. This is on one hand quite shocking as the language used and emphatic delivery is full of anger and hatred. On the other hand, though, it serves to illustrate just how ridiculous these insults and the views behind them are, as all the groups are directing their anger at someone different. The characters are all both perpetrators of racism and victims of it.

Da Mayor

The film also includes characters that could be seen as very stereotypical. Da Mayor arguably reflects the common African-American stereotype of the Magical Negro, Radio Raheem is the archetypal angry young black man, and what could be more stereotypical than Italian-American Pizzeria proprietors and Korean shop owners who speak little English? The question then is why Lee chose to populate Bedford-Stuyvesant with stereotypes. It could be that, in some cases, by showing us these characters who initially seem to be broadly drawn stereotypes but then revealing to us their idiosyncrasies he is encouraging the audience to see beyond the stereotype. It could also be that he is indeed using a character to represent a sector of society but doing this willfully to make a point. Maybe, if Radio Raheem represents all angry young black men then his fate makes a bigger point than just the pointless, tragic death of an individual. The manner of his death, murdered by the police and the close-up shot of his feet lifted from the ground, evoking lynching, suggest this may well be the case.

Radio Raheem

Korean shopkeepers

Are the characters typical of characters in films of that genre?

To answer this would demand that the film be placed within a genre, which is difficult as it defies simple categorisation. IMDb lists the film as both comedy and drama. It certainly, however, fits within a series of films, the aforementioned New Black Film Wave, and has characters that typify films from this movement. John Singleton's 1991 film *Boyz n the Hood* and the Hughes Brothers' *Menace II Society* of 1993 have parallels with *Do the Right Thing* in that all feature young black men living in a climate of crime, poverty and limited opportunities.

What do the representations tell the audience about society at the time the film was made and/or set?

Do the Right Thing is, in the words of *Rolling Stone*'s Gavin Edwards (2014),

> *a trenchant exploration of the racial politics of New York City at the time, from incendiary trash-talking to police violence and an ensuing riot – even extending to the graffiti on the wall reading 'TAWANA TOLD THE TRUTH'.*

Through details such as this graffiti, the dedications in the end credits to victims of police brutality and quotes from real civil rights activists, Lee is making clear statements about American society in the 1980s. He is drawing the audience's attention to social injustices and by depicting a summer's day getting hotter moment by the moment is conveying just how much the pressure is building up in society.

How are elements of film form being used to construct the representations?

This is a huge question in a film with such a diverse cast of characters but let's take Radio Raheem as an example. Radio Raheem is possibly the angriest man in the neighbourhood. He is a man of few words but the leitmotif of Public Enemy's *Fight the Power* blasting from his massive boom box on a loop speaks of his rage at the racial inequality in America and his desire to challenge this. Bill Nunn, who played Raheem, was a tall, well-built actor and his power and ability to intimidate are accentuated through the use of **low-angle shots** that emphasise his stature. His **body language is very controlled, an imposing stillness** that the audience may instinctively read hides a simmering fury. He certainly makes his presence known. With regards to **costume**, Radio Raheem's t-shirt bears the slogan 'BED-STUY DO OR DIE', which conveys his loyalty to his neighbourhood and community, a loyalty and pride that contribute to his justifiable anger.

 Independent Activity

Watch *Boyz n the Hood* and *Menace II Society* and compare the protagonists to characters from *Do the Right Thing*. Draw up a list of similarities and differences.

 Independent Activity

Research the case of Tawana Brawley and consider the range of responses to the Grand Jury decisions taken.

Leitmotif: a reoccurring piece of music that represents characters, actions or themes.

Ethnic stereotypes

In 1987, media theorist Manuel Alvarado established four key themes in the representation of ethnic minorities in the media (Alvarado & Gutch, 1987). These categories can be considered in relation to *Do the Right Thing*, a film made just two years later.

Manuel Alvarado

Exotic

Spike Lee said 'the look of the film should be bright … almost blinding Afrocentric bright!' The colour scheme of the film is dominated by orange and red hues, which are certainly bright and cleverly convey the heat of the sun as tensions rise in the community. However, this bright colour scheme also makes the setting seem almost exotic and very different to most filmic depictions of New York. Encouraging audiences to see minority characters as exotic can be problematic as it highlights their difference and positions them as the other.

Dangerous

African-American characters such as Radio Raheem and Buggin' Out often seem to be on the verge of violence as they make their anger known. However, it is arguably Sal's family and the white police officers that are more dangerous. Consider the use of the baseball bat, wielded by Sal, and Pino's dangerously racist views conveyed by his use of the N word and describing his black neighbours as animals. And, ultimately, it is a white police officer who finally snaps and takes Radio Raheem's life. Alvorado's observations, on this issue at least, are challenged by Lee.

Humorous

There is lots of humour in this film with notable examples being the Corner Men – Sweet Dick Willie, Coconut Sid and ML – who offer comic relief at regular intervals. This helps the film's climax have more power, as the audience is encouraged to enjoy this community and become invested in their wellbeing. What the film does not do, which has often been a problem in the media, is deride and belittle characters from ethnic minorities in order to get a cheap laugh. There are moments in the film when there is a danger that the Korean shopkeepers are objects of ridicule but the narrative saves this when Coconut Sid defends them from ML and the angry mob. Feeling threatened after Sal's Pizzeria is attacked, the shopkeeper shouts that he is not white, trying to align himself with the black community.

Pitied

Da Mayor certainly appears to be down on his luck, sweeping the sidewalk in front of Sal's shop for a dollar a day to feed his drinking habit. His clothes are dirty and he has the body language of a man beaten by life. His charisma and wisdom combined with his actions of charming Mother Sister and saving Eddie's life from the speeding car make him a likeable character and encourage the audience to pity his lot in life.

Spike Lee's opinion

Twenty-five years after its release, *Rolling Stone* magazine asked Lee, 'Did you have a favorite reaction to the film?' His angry and confrontational response demonstrates the power and importance of representation and the impact it has on people's opinions of other social groups:

> *I'll tell you my least favorite: the reviews of David Denby and Joe Klein saying that black people were going to riot after seeing this film. That they [black people] weren't intelligent enough to make the distinction between what's happening on screen and what happens in real life – so they would come out of theaters and riot all across America … They never really owned up to that, and when I think about it, I just get mad. Because that was just outrageous, egregious and, I think, racist. I don't remember people saying people were going to come out of theatres killing people after they watched Arnold Schwarzenegger films.* (Edwards, 2014)

Spike Lee

(iA) Independent Activity

Consider the age categories of child, adult and elderly person and create mind maps of how you might expect them to be represented. Condense your mind maps to five key adjectives for each age group.

Case study: The representation of age in *Captain Fantastic* (Ross, 2016)

Captain Fantastic centres on characters living outside of the mainstream, so it might be anticipated that they defy social expectations and challenge stereotypes – and in large sections of the film this is certainly the case. The characters range from small children to elderly grandparents, so the film is an excellent case study for looking at the representation of age.

Significant research has been done into the representation of different age groups in films. Lauzen and Dozier (2005), for example, analysed the top 100 grossing films in the USA in 2002 and found that women in their 20s and 30s are overrepresented, as are men in their 30s and 40s. This implies that women become less marketable to film audiences at a younger age than men. The research also found that both genders are under-represented from their 50s onwards, particularly women.

Children

Children in films are often vulnerable characters who need rescuing and can therefore be employed as a narrative device to evoke a powerful emotional response from some spectators. They can, however, be the characters that motivate the adult protagonists to overcome difficulties and learn life lessons. They can also be the audience's portals into fantastical worlds by being represented as free thinkers with vivid imaginations. Alternatively, they can have wisdom beyond their years or be unruly, mischievous and wild. The range of options is wide but the aforementioned are among the archetypes seen in films from all eras and from all around the world.

The teen rebel is one archetype that has been a staple of cinema certainly since the 1950s, but in *Captain Fantastic* the children are schooled in rebellion from an early age, often quoting the mantra, 'Power to the people, stick it to the man.' This leads to numerous incidents throughout the film of the children defying authorities. Examples include the elaborately choreographed shoplifting of 'Operation: Free the Food' to the mock Christian cult singing to scare off the police officer asking questions about why they are not in school.

This rebellious streak extends to family relationships; as Zaja says, 'Grandpa can't oppress us' when Ben is barred from his wife's funeral. Ultimately, this leads to the child characters having greater responsibility for their own decisions and choices than might usually be depicted in film. In the narrative's resolution it is the children who decide that they will defy both their grandparents and their father and make their own decisions about how they want to live and, more importantly, who they want to live with. It is also the children who insist on carrying out their mother's wishes in what Zaja terms, 'Mission: Rescue Dad and Mommy.' They are subverting traditional family roles and taking on the role of protecting their parents. This is anchored by Kielyr, and the rest of the children, singing 'Sweet Child O' Mine' for their mother at her cremation. The mother has become the child, cared for by her very driven, determined, decisive children.

An important section of the film to think about when considering the representation of children is the family's visit to Ben's sister, Harper. These scenes juxtapose Ben's children with Justin and Jackson, Harper's children. They have been raised in a far more conventional home by more conformist parents and have been educated in a mainstream school. The representation of Justin and Jackson is much more stereotypical of young teenagers, as they are shown to be motivated by time on games consoles, engaged in consumerism, have limited interest in education and are fairly uncommunicative. Ben's children are so unaccustomed to the typical teen pursuit of playing video games that they, with the exception of Rellian, seem almost traumatised by the violent nature of the game being played.

Adolescent

A central plot thread in this film is Bodevan's journey to manhood and independence, and the film is almost bookended with scenes highlighting this coming of age narrative. Indeed, the opening words of the film, spoken by Ben are, 'today the boy is dead and in his place is a man'. This accompanies Bodevan's killing of a deer, eating its heart and having its blood smeared on his face, the first of many rites of passage for the character in this film.

Further significant stages for Bodevan include his first, rather enthusiastic, kiss, his standing up to Ben about his college applications, shaving his head and finally his departure to Namibia, which includes another rite, Ben's gifting of the beads and the life advice.

Adult

Viggo Mortensen, who plays the father Ben, was 58 at the time of the film's release but in a film that depicts three clear generations he falls into the category adult. Ben is a complex character who at the start of the narrative is very much the head of the family exercising discipline, insisting on schedules and demanding the very best from his children. He sets targets for reading and other tasks and also controls leisure time, for example it is only when Ben gets his guitar that Bo gets his and the family have some fun together. In *Captain Fantastic* we see the burden that being a responsible adult can bring as Ben starts to question if he is doing right by his children in the absence of their mother. His concern about his own influence and power is demonstrated when he states, 'I'll ruin your lives.'

Ben may be a mature, evolved adult but the film shows you a man capable of reflecting on his actions and making changes. This can be seen in the scene when he shaves his beard, signalling a new Ben, and is anchored by his increased domesticity at the narrative's climax. The Ben who announces that the, 'school bus will be here in fifteen minutes' is a different Ben to the rigid, passionate home educator at the start of the film.

 Rite of passage: a ceremony marking an important stage in someone's life.

 S&C

Read Catherine Driscoll's 'Modernism, Cinema, Adolescence: Another History for Teen Film' (n.d.) on screeningthepast.com to gain a deeper understanding of the way teens have been represented in films historically.

S&C

Research the teen rebel archetype in films by watching:

- *Rebel without a Cause* (Ray, 1955)
- *The Outsiders* (Coppola, 1983)
- *The Breakfast Club* (Hughes, 1985).

Note the similarities between Jim Stark, Dallas Winston and John Bender.

Elderly

Research has found that when older characters do appear on screen they are often peripheral characters or employed for comic effect. David Cox in the *Guardian* (2012) listed the problematic stereotypes perpetuated by films featuring old people as follows;

> *ineffectual, grumpy, behind the times, depressed, lonely, slow-witted, sickly, whining, rude, miserly, hard-of-hearing, ugly, interfering, heartless, intransigent, doddering, mentorish, frisky or profane.*

He also cites Sally Chivers, who, in her publication *The Silvering Screen* (2011), found that narratives featuring the elderly are also too often focused on ill health and disability. So, the majority of representations of older characters have generally been somewhat negative but there is hope that this may be improving as the growing aging population and the associated 'grey pound' is creating a demand for more positive representations within films that centre on older characters rather than marginalise them.

In *Captain Fantastic* the elderly are represented by the characters of Jack and Abigail, Leslie's grieving parents. Jack was played by Frank Langella, who was 78 at the time of the film's release and Abigail by Ann Dowd who was 60. Both characters have significant roles to play in the narrative, in particular Jack who comes into conflict with Ben due to their opposing ideologies. Jack's values are, unsurprisingly, much more traditional than Ben's. He is Christian, adheres to social norms of dress and behaviour, has respect for the authorities and is unarguably the head of his household. Abigail is more open to Ben's views but demonstrates Jack's dominance by stating, 'it's just best to do what he says'.

These traits can be linked to age, as older people are often represented as being more likely to be conventional and fixed in their long-established ways, which can include a more traditional and passive female role.

A tendency in representations of the elderly that is not evident in this film is any signs of frailty or ill health. Both grandparents are portrayed as healthy, vibrant and intelligent. Jack even makes a valiant attempt to keep up with the kid's workout regimen when they move in with him following Vespyr's accident.

On page 50 we considered the view that sociologist Lévi-Straus had on stereotyping, he also proposes that all representations are informed by ideology and convey the opinions and values held by the producers of the text. He suggests that decisions are taken to include certain traits and exclude others in order to encourage the audience to focus on the preferred or dominant representation. Consider the films we have looked at here and decide if you agree that there is a clear message the filmmakers are conveying to the audience.

 Independent Activity

Look at the top ten films of the year and find out the age of the lead three actors on the Internet Movie Database (IMDb). What age group dominates?

Independent study questions

Q What are the common stereotypes associated with the social groups in the films you have studied and does the film challenge or reinforce them?

Q Which social groups are absent from the films you have studied and what does this suggest about society at the time the film was made?

Q How have elements of film form been used to construct representations in the films you are studying and do the choices taken suggest a particular ideology?

Sample essay extract and feedback

What does the representation of gender in your chosen film suggest about society at the time the film was made?

For this example we are looking at an **extract** from an essay addressing *Vertigo*.

Gabriel's response extract

Vertigo is a very complicated film to analyse with regards to gender representation, as the audience's opinion on this issue may alter dramatically between the first viewing of the film and the second. In the initial viewing of it the audience may perceive 'Madeleine' as a completely passive woman who is placed on screen by Hitchcock, and in the narrative by Elster, for Scottie to look at. The character remains silent for a number of scenes, often pausing within a doorway or behind a window so she can be framed as an enticing image. However, on a second viewing with the knowledge that 'Madeleine' is actually Judy, Elster's accomplice, this perception may be turned on its head. Judy is manipulative and her trickery is working so she has power and dominance over Scottie, the film's leading man.

This complexity may reflect the changing role of women in American society in the 1950s. The film was made in 1958 when women were increasingly demanding more autonomy and challenging the role of the housewife that had been reinstated with vigour after a brief reversal of roles during World War II. Hitchcock could be suggesting that women may appear passive but are actually not to be trusted and are likely to be planning to seize some power and control over men.

Feedback

Good insight into the construction of the representation and the complexity of this film. An opportunity has been missed to incorporate some theoretical approaches though, as reference to Laura Mulvey's work 'Visual Pleasure and Narrative Cinema' would have been useful here.

Another concern is that this paragraph does not directly address the contextual element of the question, as society is not mentioned. Ideally, all paragraphs should clearly link to the question asked. There is also scope for more specific examples. When, on second viewing, are hints of Judy's plotting visible to the audience for example?

An interesting idea is put forward here suggesting independent thought and clear engagement with the film. The references to society however are very generalised and lack any evidence to back them up. More research would be beneficial to construct a more convincing argument.

Aesthetics

Aesthetics refers to the overall style, feel and 'texture' of a film. To study aesthetics is to study film as an art form and to appreciate a film's beauty and artistic merit. A way to start thinking about the aesthetics of your chosen film is to think of as many adjectives as you can to describe the film's overall style and feel. Then consider how elements of film form, including sound, contribute to the overall style or aesthetic of the film you have just described.

The specification says

Learners study the following in relation to film as an aesthetic medium:

- *the role of mise-en-scène, cinematography, including lighting, composition and framing in creating aesthetic effects in specific film sequences*

- *the role of music and editing in conjunction with the above in creating aesthetic effects*

- *the significance of the aesthetic dimension in film including the potential conflict between spectacle and the drive towards narrative resolution in film*

- *the aesthetic qualities of specific films and the concept of film aesthetics*

- *film aesthetics, approached critically, including the relationship between film aesthetics and the auteur as well as film aesthetics and ideology.*

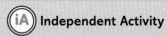 **Independent Activity**

Choose one of the films you are studying. Think of four adjectives to describe the film's aesthetic. Write a short 300-word essay explaining how two key elements of form contribute to the overall aesthetic of your chosen film.

When considering aesthetics, think about the pleasures gained from watching films. One pleasure is through the narrative. Audiences enjoy how a film answers questions and provides resolution and closure. Another pleasure is an appreciation of the art of film. Certain striking scenes may be re-watched and the overall beauty of particular shots and scenes can be appreciated. These shots and scenes may or may not have a particular narrative function but can be appreciated in their own right as memorable cinematic moments. This is the pleasure of film aesthetics.

When analysing the aesthetics of your chosen film, consider the artistic choices the filmmakers have made in their creation of the film's overall aesthetic. The director, for instance, may be known for adopting a particular style. Also, consider your film's aesthetic within its wider cultural and institutional contexts. The overall aesthetic of a film may reflect or be part of a particular cultural artistic movement, or typical of its institutional context, such as classical Hollywood cinema.

This section explores film aesthetics through analysis of three visually and aurally striking films: *Under the Skin* (Glazer, 2013), *Ida* (Pawlikowski, 2013) and *Carol* (Haynes, 2015). It focuses on each film's aesthetic style and major artistic influences on their overall aesthetic.

 Independent Activity

Choose a film you are studying which you consider to be visually striking. Find three images or screenshots which exemplify the film's aesthetic. Write a paragraph that explains why these images are particularly striking or memorable.

Case study: *Under the Skin* (Glazer, 2014)

Under the Skin is an artistic science fiction film, which features Scarlett Johansson as an alien in human form. The alien strives to understand what it means to be a human and a woman in today's world, with tragic consequences. Through its art house symbolism and understated narrative, the film explores themes such as immigration, male sexual desire and female experiences of male violence. *Under the Skin*'s aesthetic can be described as 'alien', 'eerie' and 'unsettling'. Director Jonathan Glazer wanted to direct a film that represented an alien view of the world by making the everyday seem otherworldly and strange. *Under the Skin* relies on atmosphere and style, rather than obvious scares or shocks, to create an unsettling viewing experience. Glazer holds onto images, allowing your eyes to wander around the frame and contemplate how the world appears to the alien. Your appreciation of *Under the Skin*'s unique and memorable aesthetics increases the more times you watch it, as repeat viewings uncover its themes and layers.

Under the Skin is notable for its experimental use of sound and music, which adds to the overall unsettling effect of the film. Composer Mica Levy created a score that replicated the alien's alarming and strange experience of the world. It is difficult to distinguish between the sound effects and musical track. Glazer explains his approach to the film's sound:

> For the sound, it was about capturing everything we needed, that more conventionally in a film, you wouldn't bother with. All the sonic chaos of the world that we tune out. If we stop for a second and become aware of the air-conditioning unit [points to hotel-room vent], there's clicking going on down there – we block all that out. The role of this was to use all those things and have those things somehow becoming symphonic, just bubbling away in the background. All of the things you would normally cut out of the soundtrack for being noisy would be the things we used and pushed to the foreground. (Tobias, 2014)

Artistic influences

Under the Skin's aesthetics are influenced by the films of three directors: Nicholas Roeg, Stanley Kubrick and Ken Loach.

Stanley Kubrick's bold, technical and precise visual style was a direct influence on *Under the Skin*'s highly technical visual science fiction sequences. *Under the Skin*'s unique soundtrack compares to the unsettling soundtracks in Kubrick's films *The Shining* (Kubrick, 1980) and *2001: A Space Odyssey* (Kubrick, 1968).

Nicholas Roeg directed a number of artistic and critically acclaimed films of the 1970s. *Under the Skin*'s narrative is reminiscent of Roeg's cult science fiction film *The Man Who Fell to Earth* (Roeg, 1976). Both are British science fiction films about an alien who inhabits human form and both are notable for their surreal imagery. Scarlett Johansson's costume and hairstyle is a homage to Mick Jagger's character Turner in another of Roeg's cult films, *Performance* (Roeg, 1970).

The sequences in *Under the Skin* that were shot on the streets of Glasgow are in the style of British realist auteurs such as Ken Loach. Loach's films often feature working-class characters and are shot in real city locations in a documentary style. Loach uses natural light and characters are shot as though they are being observed. *Sweet Sixteen* (Loach, 2002), for instance, was shot in the working-class areas of Greenock and Port Glasgow in Scotland.

Key sequence analysis: The opening sequences

The first shot in *Under the Skin* is of a white light, evoking birth and creation, as the alien's eye is created. The development of the eye resembles an exploding planet or star. The opening is reminiscent of the 'star gate' sequence in Kubrick's *2001: A Space Odyssey*, where mission pilot Dr Bowman races across space and encounters strange vortexes of light.

Under the Skin (Glazer, 2014)

2001: A Space Odyssey (Kubrick, 1968)

Independent Activity

Watch sequences from the following films:

- *2001: A Space Odyssey* (Kubrick, 1968)
- *Performance* (Roeg, 1970)
- *Sweet Sixteen* (Loach, 2002).

Write a short 300-word essay on how these three films compare to the overall aesthetic style of *Under the Skin*.

Independent Activity

Watch the star gate sequence from *2001: A Space Odyssey*. Write down three ways in which the opening of *Under the Skin* compares to this sequence.

Under the Skin establishes the theme of watching or 'witnessing' at the very start of the film, as we see eyes manufactured for the alien. Glazer explains how this theme of witnessing informs the film's style:

> *Everything feels witnessed. There's a* formalism *to the way the film is shot so that everything is witnessed. Even the stuff we set up needed to feel like it was witnessed. Maybe, more traditionally, you might go in on a boat with a camera, or have a diver and shoot some underwater shots of [the woman] struggling. I wanted to shoot it all like a piece of news, like you were seeing it from a rock, and it was all happening over there. I hope there's a reality to it, as a result.*
> (Tobias, 2014)

This theme of voyeurism or 'witnessing' and use of eye imagery is also evident in a memorable image from the film where the alien uses a compact mirror to put on her lipstick.

The strange musical soundscape of an odd buzzing sound merges with sounds of a human voice as the alien learns to form words. The disturbing soundscape continues over shots of the motorcycle driver riding through the rugged Scottish wilderness, making the Scottish environment seem otherworldly. For Glazer, Scotland was the ideal setting due to its sense of wilderness, as it is a less densely populated area of the British Isles. The close-up, eye-level shot of the driver in the centre of the frame as the traffic speeds by him on each side is again reminiscent of the star gate sequence in *2001: A Space Odyssey*, where flashes of bright light emanate from the centre of the frame.

Formalism: looks at a film's structure and recognises the differences between the story and how it is told through the plot. This includes a focus on the formal elements of a film.

Much of the film was shot in the streets of Glasgow. The sequences where the alien wanders through a Glasgow shopping centre are shot in a documentary, realist style. The low camera and controlled long tracking shots give the film a realism, yet also a sense of how an alien would encounter this environment where the everyday is made to appear strange.

A montage of shots depicts streets of Glasgow as seen through the window of the alien's white van. This montage represents the alien's point of view, as she witnesses men walking on the city streets, unaware that they are being watched. The shots are anchored by the unsettling soundtrack, rendering the men unfamiliar and strange. When the alien is stuck in traffic after a football match, the sounds of the crowds are muffled to further distance us from them and enable us to see and hear how the alien encounters these men.

The scenes in *Under the Skin* where the alien drives around Glasgow and interacts with various local men were shot covertly with hidden cameras. Some of the men she encounters were actors and some were real local people, unaware that they were taking part in a scene for a film. Eight cameras were implanted in the van to capture the alien interacting with her potential victims in real time. Some American audiences have commented that the thick Glaswegian accents make the world seem even more alien, as they were unable to understand what the local characters were saying. The spontaneity of the part-improvised, covertly filmed sequences contrasts with the sequences where the alien takes the victims home. In those sequences controlled tracking shots and elaborate special effects are used.

(iA) Independent Activity

Choose two sequences from *Under the Skin*: one where the alien lures a man into the van and one where the alien takes the men into her strange environment. In 100 words, state how the two sequences have different aesthetic styles. State why you think Glazer uses two different styles and what this adds to the overall experience of watching the film.

S&C

Watch two of the following Pawlikowski films:

- *From Moscow to Pietushki with Benny Yerofeyev* (1990)
- *Dostoevsky's Travels* (1991)
- *Serbian Epics* (1992)
- *Last Resort* (2000)
- *My Summer of Love* (2004).

Write a short essay of about 300 words comparing the themes and style of the two films with *Ida*.

Ida (Pawlikowski, 2013)

Case study: *Ida* (Pawlikowski, 2013)

Ida is a poetic, thoughtful and meditative art film set in Poland in 1962. The narrative concerns a young nun, who, through a journey with her aunt, discovers her name is Ida and that her parents were Jewish and murdered in the German occupation of Poland during World War II. Rather than directly explaining events, director Paweł Pawlikowski suggests what is happening through visual imagery and subtle performances. Pawlikowski's films deal with the themes of deportation and the impact of war. Many of the characters in his films are exiles or outsiders. During the 1980s and 1990s, Pawlikowski directed a number of lyrical and poetic documentaries, such as *From Moscow to Pietushki* (Pawlikowski, 1990).

Film critic Peter Bradshaw in his 2014 *Guardian* review summarises *Ida*'s aesthetic:

> *There really is a bitter, wintry cold here: it is illuminated by the stark, daylit whiteness of snow, and you can feel the chill in those barnyards and draughty churches. This film has its own kind of freezer burn.*

Ida is shot in the 4:3 ratio (a square frame), and in black and white, evoking the typical format of Polish films in the 1960s.

In *Ida*, Pawlikowski attempted 'to recapture the Poland of my childhood'. During the early 1960s, Poland was under Communist rule. It was a period of transition for Poland, as the death of Stalin, who imposed a hardline, totalitarian form of communism, led to a brief 'thaw' in Soviet-controlled Eastern European countries. This led to a slight lax in censorship and as a result aspects of Western culture seeped into Eastern Europe. Pawlikowski evokes this Poland of his childhood through the aesthetic of the film, reflecting the political climate in which the film is set. The use of jazz music reflects the influence of Western culture in Poland at this time and brings a warmth to the stark and bleak visual aesthetic of the film.

Artistic influences

Ida's aesthetic compares to the influential films of European art house auteurs Carl Dreyer, Robert Bresson and Ingmar Bergman. All three auteurs created masterpieces of art cinema that explored philosophical themes of religion, life and death, with a sparse, austere style.

Robert Bresson's contemplative films are notable for their catholic themes and minimal use of sound.

There are comparisons between the narrative and style of Bresson's *Diary of a Country Priest* (1951) and *Ida*. In *Diary of a Country Priest* the young priest does not smile and is weighed down by the enormity of his job. The film, like *Ida*, is set in a bleak winter with barren landscapes.

Carl Dreyer's *The Passion of Joan of Arc* (1928) is notable for its close-ups and use of the frame to crop faces or push characters to corners of the screen. The mise-en-scène is sparse and the overall aesthetic has a realistic yet poetic quality.

Ingmar Bergman's films are black and white meditations on God and death. In *The Virgin Spring* (1960), images of Max von Sydow chopping a tree compare to the stark, quiet images of the Polish countryside in *Ida*.

Pawlikowski was influenced by the 17th-century Dutch painter, Johannes Vermeer. Vermeer painted ordinary people in a realistic manner. He would highlight aspects of surfaces or objects through stark, chiaroscuro lighting and would often paint still, solitary women. The images of Ida in the convent are reminiscent of Vermeer's most famous painting, 'Girl with a Pearl Earring' (1665) (left).

iA Independent Activity

Watch sequences from two of the following films:

- *The Passion of Joan of Arc* (Dreyer, 1928)
- *The Virgin Spring* (Bergman, 1960)
- *Diary of a Country Priest* (Bresson, 1951).

Write a short essay of about 300 words comparing the aesthetics of the two films you watched to the overall aesthetic of *Ida*.

Diary of a Country Priest (Bresson, 1951)

The Passion of Joan of Arc (Dreyer, 1928)

The Virgin Spring (Bergman, 1960)

iA Independent Activity

Compare two stills of Ida in the convent in the opening sequence of *Ida* with Vermeer's painting, 'Girl with a Pearl Earring'.

Compare the opening sequence to the sequences later on in the film where Ida listens to the jazz band. Discuss:

- How Ida's appearance changes in the latter part of the film.
- How jazz music adds a warmth to the overall aesthetic of the film.

Key sequence analysis: The opening sequence

Ida's overall aesthetic creates a sombre mood and atmosphere, evoking Anna's life in a convent in Poland during the 1960s. The sequence has an 'austere' aesthetic, reflecting the frugal and spartan life of the convent. The static framing, along with stark black and white imagery and sparse mise-en-scène, reflects the ritualistic life at the convent and coldness of Poland. There is a contrast between life at the convent and, later, Anna's exploration of life outside the convent, where she explores Western influences such as jazz music.

The static camera, combined with figures positioned at the bottom of the frame, makes each image appear as a portrait painting. Ida is wide-eyed and innocent. The camera lingers on her and she emotes through small gestures. A feeling of sadness hangs over the characters, emphasised through them being pushed down to the bottom and side of frames, as though the weight of history is upon them. This stylistic choice also suggests that these characters are players in a much larger story, reflecting the film's personal and political narrative.

The use of minimal dialogue and only diegetic sounds, such as the clinking of spoons, add to the stark, cold atmosphere and quietness of the convent. The cuts from one static shot to another give the film a poetic and contemplative rhythm.

Paweł Pawlikowski discusses his approach to directing *Ida* in the *Guardian* online (2014):

> *In the 'financier' script for Ida, the film opened with a scene of three nuns making a scarecrow in a field and a series of generic dialogue scenes, setting up the situation and the characters. It was OK as beginnings go, but it was clear we needed something stronger. A day before filming in the monastery, I noticed our art director, Jagna Dobesz, a woman with an angelic face and character, touching up Christ's face with her brush. There was such tension and love in her face as she was doing it that I knew I had a much better scene right there in front of me.*
>
> *In fact, I had a whole sequence of scenes. This is how the sculpture of Christ, which started out as one of several props in the monastery, became the key image [...] The unexpected snow was another bonus. It gave me the idea for two graphic top shots and the quiet moment of prayer around the fountain.*
>
> *This way, pages of dialogue scenes and fluffy non-events were replaced by a series of shots that were simple, powerful and set up the tone of the whole film perfectly.*

Case study: *Carol* (Haynes, 2015)

Carol is set during the Christmas season of 1952 in New York City. The film is an emotional melodrama about a forbidden love affair between Therese, an aspiring photographer, and Carol, an older woman going through a divorce. Director Todd Haynes' films often deal with issues of identity and sexuality. His films are highly stylised and reinvent and reference cinematic styles. Haynes describes *Carol* as:

> *a low-budget film, a period film, where every detail mattered intensely to the narrative, but also to the development of character.* (*Daily Telegraph*, n.d.)

For Haynes,

> *there's a process that I go through of trying to find the visual language for the film.* (*Daily Telegraph*, n.d.)

Carol's aesthetic evokes a hazy, dream-like evocation of New York during the 1950s. When developing the film's style, Haynes put together an 'image book' that contained photographs, paintings and images from other films of New York in the 1950s. The setting of New York in the early 1950s is significant, as the city was known for its fashion, hair and beauty trends. America was emerging from wartime austerity and there was a sense of optimism with a recovering economy and consumerism. Movie stars such as Grace Kelly and Audrey Hepburn influenced fashion trends of the period. Indeed, Therese resembles a young Audrey Hepburn, while Carol has the glamour and sophistication of Grace Kelly. However, Haynes noticed that his 'image book' depicted a 'distressed, dirty, sagging city'. This evocation of New York is reflected in the film's colour palate, which consists mainly of light greens, deep pinks, gold and deep reds. Haynes also chose to shoot *Carol* on 16mm film rather than digital, to give the film a grain and further enhance the film's 'distressed' look.

Therese resembles a young Audrey Hepburn.

 Independent Activity

Create a collage of images of Audrey Hepburn and Grace Kelly alongside images of Therese and Carol in *Carol*. Note any comparisons between the film stars and characters in *Carol*.

 S&C

Choose two of the following female photojournalists who influenced the overall aesthetic of *Carol*:

- Ruth Orkin
- Esther Bubley
- Helen Levitt
- Vivian Maier.

Find three photographs taken by each photographer. Write about 200 words comparing their imagery to the look and style of *Carol*.

Carol's aesthetic develops the psychological depth of the characters. The film has a stillness, reflecting the slow pace of the development of Carol and Therese's relationship. Shots linger as characters gaze at each other through camera lenses and windows. Much direct speech was cut from the script to ensure that dialogue between the two characters was ambiguous, as Carol and Therese are not able to outwardly verbalise their feelings for one another. Instead, gestures and glances become loaded with eroticism. As spectators, we have to be attentive to small gestures and appreciate the nuance of the film's visual style. For critic Peter Bradshaw in his *Guardian* review (2015) of *Carol*:

> *The movie finds something erotic everywhere – in the surfaces, the tailoring, the furnishing and of course the cigarettes. It revives the lost art of smoking at lunch, smoking with gloves, and the exotic moue of exhaling smoke sideways, out of consideration for the person in front of you.*

Many shots in *Carol* are framed through doorways, obscured surfaces, windows or curtains, reflecting the characters' containment of their sexuality and double lives. In this respect, the film is a comment on the oppressive conservatism of 1950s America, as society disapproved of and criminalised sex outside of heterosexuality. There are several shots where Carol is partially concealed through misty windows, rain, dust and snowfall, reflecting how Therese is captivated by Carol but also distanced from her.

Artistic influences

Many street photographers of the 1950s who influenced the overall aesthetic of Carol were women. Photographers such as Ruth Orkin, Helen Levitt, Esther Bubley and Vivian Maier were photojournalists who captured life in New York during the 1950s.

Another key influence on the overall look of *Carol* is the photographer of Saul Leiter, who photographed New York in the 1950s. Haynes explained how Leiter influenced *Carol*'s aesthetic:

> *He's known for shooting through windows, for using reflection. His work is impressionistic: these exquisite frames, and then that blown colour palette, muted overall with flashes of colour.* (Leszkiewicz, 2015)

Red Umbrella (Leiter, 1958)

Director Douglas Sirk's 1950s Technicolor Hollywood melodramas are another key influence on Todd Haynes' style. Sirk used framing and mise-en-scène symbolically to critique the conformism of American society of the 1950s. He often used garish and contrasting colours, particularly deep reds. Sirk employed framing devices such as doorways and windows for characters. In Sirk's 1955 melodrama, *All that Heaven Allows*, the main character, Carey, is ostracised from middle-class society for dating her working-class gardener. Indeed, Hayne's film *Far from Heaven* (2002) is a homage to *All that Heaven Allows*. Although the colour palate of *Carol* is far more understated than Sirk's use of garish bright colours, Sirk's use of mise-en-scène and framing devices continue to influence Haynes in *Carol*, as what is unsaid is instead placed in the mise-en-scène.

All that Heaven Allows (Sirk, 1955)

 S&C

Watch the documentary *Finding Vivian Maier* (Maloof & Siskel, 2013) about the photojournalist Vivian Maier. Write three examples of how Vivian Maier compares to the character of Therese in *Carol*.

 Independent Activity

Search online for three Saul Leiter photographs of 1950s New York. Write a couple of sentences underneath each photograph explaining how each photograph influenced the overall aesthetic of *Carol*.

 Independent Activity

Watch sequences from the following melodramas directed by Douglas Sirk:

- *All that Heaven Allows* (1955)
- *Written on the Wind* (1956)
- *Imitation of Life* (1959).

List three ways in which *Carol*'s aesthetic is influenced by these melodramas.

Key sequence analysis: Therese and Carol first meet in the department store

This sequence analysis considers how the use of colour, framing and use of symbolic objects contribute to the overall aesthetic of the film.

The colours of the department store consist of pale muted greens and pinks, with splashes of vivid reds in the form of Therese's hat, the characters' lipstick, red bows and Christmas presents. The vivid reds are reminiscent of the 1950s Technicolor melodramas directed by Nicholas Ray and Douglas Sirk, where bright reds would stand out in the frame.

At the start of the scene, when Therese eats alone in the staff canteen, the camera is observational, cutting into people having conversations, reminiscent of documentary-style photojournalism. When Therese is in the store working in the toy department, a slow panning shot reveals cabinets of dolls in glass. The dolls are 'trapped' in the department, which reflects Therese and Carol's world. Notice how Therese is in the bottom of the frame behind the cabinets, one of many framing devices where characters are obscured through glass and frame.

When Therese first sees Carol in the store, the camera views Carol from a distance, and shoppers walk into the foreground of the frame, beginning the recurrent visual motif of Therese's obscured view of Carol, distancing her and simultaneously eroticising her. The scene is all shot in static shots until Carol walks away, after which Haynes employs slow tracking shots into Therese and then Carol walking away. These tracking shots build up the emotional impact of their meeting.

The attraction between the two characters is evoked through subtle glances and gestures, rather than what is said. The slow tracking shots then cut to a close-up of Carol's leather gloves. The gloves function both symbolically to represent Carol's sensuality and sophistication, and as a narrative device, as the gloves provide an excuse for Therese to contact Carol. The camera cuts to a shot of Therese at the end of her shift, the camera seemingly paced inside her locker. This is one of many framing devices, as Therese appears boxed in, confined to societal norms. Again, the camera lingers, allowing us to read Therese's gestures as she appears visibly moved by her subtly erotic attraction to Carol; one she can never outwardly express in 1950s America.

Independent study questions

For each question, refer to one or two key sequences.

> **Q** Discuss how your chosen film's aesthetic helps convey the overall meaning of the film.

> **Q** How do mise-en-scène and sound contribute to the overall aesthetic of your chosen film?

> **Q** Who are the key artistic influences on the filmmakers of your chosen film and how do these artistic influences contribute to the overall aesthetic of the film?

> **Q** Explore how aesthetics are created in your chosen film.

Sample essay extract and feedback

> Who are the key artistic influences on the filmmakers of your chosen film? How do these artistic influences contribute to the overall aesthetic of the film?

For this example, we are looking at an **extract** from an essay addressing *Carol*.

Alesha's response extract	Feedback
A key influence on *Carol*'s overall aesthetic is the photographers who documented New York in the 1950s. Photographer Saul Leiter would often shoot through reflections, giving his photographs a misty, impressionistic feel. His colour photographs consisted of muted colours with splashes of red. Haynes adopts this aesthetic in *Carol*, as many shots are framed through windows and Carol is often obscured through snowfall, rain and mist. This reflects how Therese sees Carol as she eroticises her, yet is also distanced from her. The colour palate of muted pastel colours also reflects Leiter's photographs and presents what Haynes' describes as a 'distressed' New York. We see this in the department store scene where flashes of red can be seen in each frame, evoking the sense of Christmastime in New York City.	*Alesha demonstrates an understanding of how Leiter's photographs influenced the style of* Carol. *Alesha provides a specific example from the film to illustrate her point. She links her next point about the influence of Sirk's melodramas. Again, Alesha uses a key sequence with some detailed analysis to illustrate her points. Overall, Alesha is able to use her contextual understanding of the film's key artistic influences to inform her analysis.*
The use of flashes of red and symbolic mise-en-scène is influenced by the films of Douglas Sirk. Sirk's 1950s melodramas were full of contrasting colours and symbolic meanings. Like *Carol*, the characters in Sirk's films were often ostracised from society. Sirk would use framing devices such as doorways and mirrors to show characters trapped in their situation. Haynes adopts this style in *Carol*. In the department store scene, Therese is first glimpsed from behind a cabinet that frames her. Later, when she opens her locker, the scene is shot seemingly from inside the locker, which creates a frame around her. This is used symbolically to reflect how Therese must keep her feelings for Carol contained.	

Social, cultural and political contexts

Studying social contexts

To study films within their social contexts is to examine how films may reflect the dominant attitudes and beliefs of the society in which they are produced. When studying contexts, it is therefore important to consider *when* a film was made, *where* it was made and *who* made it. Some films may engage directly with social issues. Filmmakers may set out to deliberately challenge dominant attitudes and beliefs of the time, through representations, messages and values.

When placing films within their social contexts, consider the following questions:

- What were the dominant social attitudes towards gender and ethnicity at the time the film was made?
- How does your chosen film reflect the society in which it was produced?

The specification encourages you to consider the debates films raise about ethnicity and gender, where relevant.

Case study: Studying the social contexts of *Some Like It Hot* (Wilder, 1959)

Some Like It Hot is a Hollywood comedy film about two musicians who disguise themselves as women and join an all-female touring band to escape a group of mobsters. The film raises interesting debates about gender, with its themes of gender identity and cross-dressing. Today, at a time when gender norms and binaries are being increasingly challenged, *Some Like It Hot* can be seen as progressive for its time, as the characters of Joe and Jerry play with gender roles by assuming female identities.

To a certain extent, *Some Like It Hot* challenges the gender norms of 1950s America. Film critic David Thomson argues that *Some Like It Hot* was a radical film for the period. The film's famous final line of dialogue, 'Nobody's perfect', challenges heterosexual norms, as Osgood does not care that Daphne is a man – he has fallen in love with the person irrespective of gender. While the line is played for laughs, when watching today, in an era of discussions about trans rights and visibility, the film and its final sequence take on a new resonance.

1950s America and *Some Like It Hot*

*Some Like It Ho*t was produced in 1959 and set in the late 1920s, a period in American history known as the jazz age. The film looks back nostalgically on this period of speakeasies, gangsters, flapper girls and jazz – a period of liberation and fun in comparison to the conservative 1950s. However, by 1959 attitudes in American society were slowly starting to change, with increasing permissiveness.

MGM test screened *Some Like It Hot* to two very different audiences. Their responses reveal changing societal attitudes in late-1950s America. The first screening was to a middle-aged audience in a small American town. They responded with silence and one audience member was reported to have even walked out of the cinema. MGM then screened the film to a younger audience of college students who loved it and laughed throughout.

Young people's responses to *Some Like It Hot* reflect changes in American society during the 1950s, as they had developed their own distinct identity and culture from that of their parents. They began to question the traditional values of their parents' generation. Filmmakers increasingly targeted young people as they had more leisure time and money to spend on movie-going.

Censorship and *Some Like It Hot*

Marilyn Monroe's overt sexuality and suggestive costumes reflect more open attitudes towards sex and sexuality, paving the way for the more explicit films of the 1960s.

Although Marilyn Monroe is still subject to the male gaze, *Some Like It Hot* moves beyond simply representing women as objects of heterosexual male desire. By dressing as women, Joe/Josephine and Jerry/Daphne realise what it is like to be objectified. They question their roles as 'men' and gain a greater sensitivity towards women. This is evident in the sequence where Jerry/Daphne explains to Joe that Osgood has made unwanted sexual advances towards him/her: 'Dirty old man … I just got pinched in the elevator.'

(iA) Independent Activity

American society in the 1950s was gradually becoming more permissive. A permissive society has more liberal values and increasing sexual freedoms. Write down examples from *Some Like It Hot* that reflect a more permissive American society.

(iA) Independent Activity

Give more examples from the film of where Joe and Jerry understand what it is like to be a woman. How does their new-found understanding of what it is like to be a woman differ to their attitudes earlier in the film before their transformation?

Some Like It Hot was released at a time when the Production Code, which provided moral guidelines for filmmakers to adhere to, was in force.

Some Like It Hot defies the rules of the code in the following ways:

- unmarried characters in sexual relationships
- hints at homosexuality with male characters flirting with cross-dressing males
- characters seen drinking and gambling at a time of prohibition
- Marilyn Monroe's revealing outfits
- sexual jokes and innuendos.

Director Billy Wilder refused to submit copies of the script for *Some Like It Hot* to the Production Code Administration Office. As a result, *Some Like It Hot* was released without approval from the censors and received a 'condemned' rating. The Catholic National Legion of Decency accused the film of being 'outright smut' and 'seriously offensive to Christian and traditional standards of morality and decency'.

The release and popularity of films that defied the code's guidelines, such as *Some Like It Hot* and Alfred Hitchcock's *Psycho* in 1960, demonstrated how the code had become increasingly outdated.

Independent study questions

 How far does your chosen film reflect societal attitudes to gender and/or ethnicity at the time it was made?

 To what extent does your chosen film challenge the dominant attitudes of the society in which it was made?

How to approach cultural contexts

Studying cultural contexts

To study a film within its cultural context is to explore the relationships between a film and the culture in which it was produced. Placing a film within its broader cultural contexts enables you to understand the significance of the film as a work of art. The film you are studying may be typical of broader artistic modes or styles during the time of the film's production.

You may consider how certain filmmakers developed a particular film style and/or aesthetic. For instance, European filmmakers who came to work for Hollywood studios during the 1920s onwards contributed to the classical Hollywood style. Films from particular cultures outside the USA may have distinct styles that differ from Hollywood cinema. These styles may be in deliberate opposition to Hollywood or develop out of the artistic and cultural norms of that particular culture. Some filmmakers many be influenced by other film cultures outside of their own culture. For instance, Quentin Tarantino adopted the style and structure of European New Wave films in *Pulp Fiction* through non-linear narratives and long takes.

Case study: Studying the cultural contexts of *Strike* (Eisenstein, 1925)

Strike is a political propaganda film that raises awareness of class struggle and advocates unity, promoting the ideology of the ruling Communist party. *Strike* is also the first major Soviet Montage film with a unique cinematic style. The film is based on a series of factory strikes that took place in Russia in 1903, concerning factory workers striking for better wages and treatment. The workers are eventually suppressed by the capitalist factory owners and their spies.

Soviet Montage

Soviet Montage was a key movement in Russian filmmaking from 1924–1930. Russia's leader and founder of the Russian Communist Party, Vladmir Lenin, considered cinema to be the most important of the arts and a powerful tool in educating the masses. From 1921–1924, Lenin's New Economic Policy allowed for limited private investment to help boost the Russian economy. This helped the growth of the Russian film industry and the flourishing of Soviet Montage.

Soviet Montage was developed by key filmmakers and theorists, including, Sergei Eisenstein, Lev Kuleshov, Dziga Vertov and Vsevolod Pudovkin. These filmmakers made revolutionary films that depicted the upheavals leading to the Bolshevik Revolution of 1917. They attempted to make films that would appeal to the masses and constructed a new language of cinema called montage. In montage films, meaning is derived from the juxtaposition of images.

Juxtaposition: the positioning of two shots, characters or scenes in a sequence to encourage the audience to compare and contrast them.

Sergei Eisenstein and 'Collision' Montage

The Soviet Montage directors developed the theory of montage through a series of publications, such as Eisenstein's 'The Montage of Attractions' (1937). As the majority of Russians were illiterate, Russian Montage directors considered the creation of meaning through visual imagery and rapidly edited juxtaposing images to be of prime importance.

All the Soviet Montage directors had a slightly different approach to and interpretation of montage. For Eisenstein, editing could create powerful effects through the juxtaposition or 'collision' of shots. As meanings are created in the minds of the spectator through collision, Eisenstein considered montage to be a powerful propaganda tool and an alternative to the continuity editing that was typical of Hollywood cinema.

 S&C

Watch a film by Lev Kuleshov, Dziga Vertov or Vsevolod Pudovkin. List five aspects of film style that are similar to Eisenstein's work and five that differ.

Strike as a Soviet Montage film

In Soviet Montage films, characters may appear as stock types who represent particular social classes in Russian society. Characters or 'types' were often performed by non-professional actors. This was known as **typage**. In *Strike*, workers are depicted as a collective unit, upholding the Communist values of people working together for the state. The mass or collective as heroes contrasts with Hollywood cinema, typified by one main hero played by an individual star.

Soviet Montage films contain repeated images or motifs. Animals and the fate of animals is a recurring motif in *Strike*. Rural life in Russia is represented as an idyll through happy and free animals such as a kitten and a duckling. All the spies in *Strike* are coded as animals that reflect their characters, such as the Bulldog, the Fox and the Owl. Images of a particular animal cross-fade into the character whose physical attributes resemble the animal.

Strike is most famous for the use of montage in the slaughterhouse sequence. The film cuts between long shots of the suppression of the workers by the army and cattle being slaughtered, followed by a long shot of the defeated workers' lifeless bodies strewn across a field. Through montage, the spectator is invited to make the connection between the civilians and the cow, and liken the treatment of cattle to that of the workers.

Strike's cultural influence

Strike was not a commercial success upon its initial release in Russia. The film may have been too ahead of its time and too experimental for popular tastes. However, *Strike* was rediscovered by film buffs in the 1960s and is now considered to be a work of art. Soviet Montage has since influenced filmmakers in Hollywood such as Alfred Hitchcock and Francis Ford Coppola.

 S&C

Take ten photographs of a place you know that could be used to create a montage. The images should be well selected to reveal something to the audience about this place.

 S&C

Research where the influence of Soviet Montage can be seen in the films of Alfred Hitchcock. Find screen grabs to illustrate this.

Independent study questions

 What were the key artistic and creative trends at the time of your film's production?

 What are the artistic influences on the filmmakers of your chosen film?

 To what extent is your chosen film typical of the style of films from its country of origin?

How to approach political contexts

When placing your chosen film within its political contexts, consider what political movements, issues or events were taking place at the time of the film's production. Some films may engage directly with political issues, while others may hide political messages in a film's subtext. Some filmmakers may set out to make a political point or explore political issues. Other films, such as *Selma* (DuVernay, 2014), may use past events to comment on current political issues.

Consider also any political pressures filmmakers may face. Films made within restrictive or repressive regimes may be subject to strict censorship. In these circumstances, filmmakers may use metaphors or allegory as a way to discuss forbidden political issues. For instance, in *Daises* (Chytilová, 1966) the two female protagonists, playful behaviour and disrespect of rules can be read as a condemnation of Communist Czechoslovakia.

As with social and cultural contexts, you should consider *when* the film was made, *where* it was made and any possible political motivations of the filmmakers.

Case study: Studying the political contexts of *Selma*

(DuVernay, 2014)

Selma concerns the struggles black people in America faced to gain voting rights. The film focuses on events leading up to three planned marches that led to the Voting Rights Act of 1965. *Selma* was released in the USA on 9 January 2015, then re-released in the USA on 20 March 2015, on the 50th anniversary of the Voting Rights march from Selma to Montgomery.

A key sequence in *Selma* is the depiction of the brutal events of 'Bloody Sunday' at Edmund Pettus Bridge on 7 March 1965, where black protestors were violently attacked by troopers on the orders of County Sherriff Jim Clarke. Events are told from the perspective of civil rights leader Dr Martin Luther King Jr, who campaigned for racial equality through peaceful resistance.

Selma, Ferguson and Black Lives Matter

Many critics have read *Selma* as a comment on the ongoing struggle for racial equality, particularly after the events that took place in Ferguson, Missouri. On 9 August 2015, an unarmed black teenager, Michael Brown, was shot dead by a white police officer in Ferguson. Brown's body was left

iA Independent Activity

Choose one film you are studying on your Film Studies course. Research the film's political context based on the following questions:

1. Does your chosen film contain any implicit or explicit political messages? If so, what are these messages and how are they conveyed in the film?

2. Research key political issues and events taking place at the time of your chosen film's production. How have these issues and events impacted on the film's narrative, representations and audience response?

iA Independent Activity

Research the events of 'Bloody Sunday' at Edmund Pettus Bridge on 7 March 1965. Look for newspaper headlines and documentary accounts. Compare and contrast the representations of events in your found news material with the sequences in Selma which recreate these events. Answer the following questions:

1. How does Selma offer a more emotional depiction of events? Who do we empathise with and why?

2. To what extent does Selma offer a historically accurate representation of events? Are any incidents omitted or added for dramatic effect?

(iA) Independent Activity

Analyse the sequence in *Selma* where protestors first attempt to march across the Edmund Pettus Bridge. Consider how cinematography, mise-en-scène, editing and sound position the audience on the side of the protestors. How does the representation of the protestors contrast to the representation of the troopers? What point is Ava DuVernay making here about police brutality in America? Summarise all this in 500 words.

Ava DuVernay

unattended in the street for over four hours. Local people, mainly young, black and working-class, took to the streets of Ferguson to protest police brutality. Ferguson's demographic is 65% low-income black, while the police force is predominantly white. The protests gathered momentum and soon further protests sprang up in other American cities, which even sparked solidarity protests in other cities around the world. As a result of Ferguson and other incidents of unarmed black people being shot by white officers, political, grassroots movements such as Black Lives Matter gained international recognition and continue to protest against racial violence worldwide. Although the events of Ferguson took place after the production of *Selma*, the film gained a particular resonance in light of these events.

For the *Los Angeles Times* (Silberman, 2015), *Selma* 'carries important lessons for people in contemporary political movements', particularly Black Lives Matter (BLM), arguing that BLM can learn lessons about the importance of leadership in movements for political change. The *LA Times* argued that:

> *Selma* shows that bottom-up grassroots work and top-down strategic leadership are not inherently in opposition – and that when deployed wisely, they are indeed profoundly complementary.

Selma's closing song, 'Glory' (by John Legend and Common, 2015), sung by John Stephens and Lonnie Lynn, explicitly connects important events in the struggles for racial equality with present-day America. It reminds us that the struggle is ongoing and there is still work to be done:

> Justice is juxtapositionin' us; Justice for all just ain't specific enough … That's why Rosa sat on the bus, That's why we walk through Ferguson with our hands up.

Ava DuVernay as a political filmmaker

The director of *Selma*, Ava DuVernay, was the first black female director to be nominated for an Academy Award for best picture in 2015. For DuVernay, filmmaking is political activism:

> *This is a tool. These are seen around the world. Films last forever. And so I really feel like to not say something is to miss the point in so many ways.* (Mays, 2014)

DuVernay founded the African-American Film Festival Releasing Movement (AFFRM) to distribute films representing African-American experiences. In *Selma*, DuVernay draws upon her documentary background by using real, archival footage of protestors attempting to cross the Edmund Pettus Bridge. Her recent acclaimed documentary film, *13th* (2016), contextualises the high number of black Americans in prisons in a wider legacy of racism in the USA.

Independent study questions

 How far does your chosen film engage with political issues and events?

 What major political movements or events were taking place at the time of your film's production? To what extent have these events shaped the film text?

Institutional, financial and technological contexts

How to approach institutional contexts

To gain a deeper understanding of a film, it is important to explore the institutional contexts under which it was produced, distributed and exhibited. The films you are studying may be indicative of a significant moment in film history, or part of a wider film movement or industry.

Key areas to investigate when considering a film's institutional context are:

- **Financial**:
  - How was the film financed?
  - How much money did it make at the box office?
  - What was its return on investment?
  - What was the budget for marketing the film?
  - How was the film distributed?
- **Technology**:
  - What technological advancements were prevalent when the film was in production?
  - Was it made during the silent film period? Before or after stable colour technology?
  - Was it shot on film or digitally?
  - Was it edited before or after non-linear editing?

In this section we will be using the British film *The Arbor* (Barnard, 2010) and the Indian film *Dil Se* (Ratnam, 1998) as case studies.

Clio Barnard

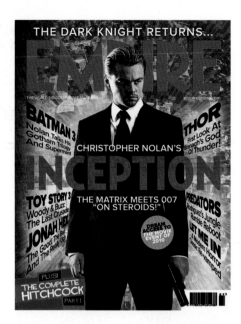

Financial contexts

Film production, for the most part, is an industry based on commercial values; films are produced to make a profit. The budget of the film will affect all decisions from locations chosen to equipment used, from casting choices to distribution.

A big-budget studio film such as Warner Brother's 2010 *Inception* (Nolan; estimated production budget $160 million) has a greater chance of being seen than a low-budget independent film such as 2010's *Winter's Bone* (Granik; $2 milion). It is estimated that a studio can spend up to $100 million marketing and distributing its films. Studio blockbusters are far likelier to hire high-profile actors who will bring in an audience and be attractive to chat shows, and newspaper and magazine feature writers. These films will also be supported by large advertising campaigns, all leading audiences to see the film on the opening weekend, which is deemed crucial in judging the success or failure of a film.

A low-budget independent film will not be able to compete in saturating the media through publicity and advertising. As budgets are smaller, filmmakers usually have greater creative freedom, and can be more innovative in their film form. There will be a reliance on less well-known actors, rather than film stars, and non-professional actors may be used to add authenticity. Independent films will have a more limited theatrical release, often showing at 'art house' cinemas or on streaming services rather than at a multiplex cinema.

Technological contexts

The history of film production has been marked by key technological developments from the first use of a close-up to the use of remote control drone cameras. From the outset, filmmakers experimented with using colour, by hand tinting each frame; technology now allows for entire films to be graded digitally. The arrival of stable, synchronised sound systems in the late 1920s transformed the way in which films were produced and exhibited.

For the first 100+ years of filmmaking, film (initially 16mm and later 35mm) was the preferred method of filming and distribution. Since the 2000s, the development of high-end digital cameras has transformed the film industry. The savings in cost and efficiency combined with the quality of digital film reached a point where it is now the dominant method of filming. Filming on 35mm film is expensive and logistically complex, but still in use by some directors.

The development in digital technology has also had an impact on the way in which films are edited and distributed.

Case study: *The Arbor* (Barnard, 2010)

The Arbor is a British Independent film directed by artist and filmmaker Clio Barnard; its blend of documentary and fiction mark it as experimental.

The Arbor traces the life of British playwright Andrea Dunbar (1961–1990), who grew up on Brafferton Arbor on Buttershaw Council Estate in Bradford. She began writing her first play, 'The Arbor', when she was 15, and it was performed at the Royal Court Theatre when she was 19. Her second play, 'Rita, Sue and Bob Too', was made into a film in 1987, directed by Alan Clarke. She died of brain haemorrhage when she was 29.

⊕ Further information

The budget for marketing *Inception* was $100 million, and the first teaser trailer, depicting the crucial spinning top, was released in August 2009, a year before the film's release. In December 2009 a website was launched, which was an online game that once completed revealed the poster. Two months before release in May 2010 was the first official trailer. These more unusual marketing elements were targeted at what they perceived to be their core audience male 16–30 year olds. This was complemented by more traditional elements such as magazine features, chat shows, premieres and a print poster campaign. However, the scale of the some of the posters was staggering.

The production and marketing budget was approximately $260 million, and the film made close to $830 million worldwide. Leonardo DiCaprio was on a 'first-dollar gross' deal, meaning that, as of July 2017, it is estimated that he had made close to $60 million for the movie with a combination of up-front fee and a percentage of tickets sold/home entertainment sales. (Source: www.statisticbrain.com)

Financial

Typical of many independent films, the film was developed over an extended period. Barnard combined making the film with her teaching commitments at the University of Kent and her video art projects.

The film's opening credits list Artangel Trust, the UK Film Council/National Lottery, Jerwood Charitable Trust, Arts Council England and More4 as producing partners, who are discussed below.

Barnard was one of four artists selected as part of Artangel's 2006 Open Call for art-project proposals. Artangel was founded in 1991 by Michael Morris and James Lingwood. It is a charitable organisation that commissions and produces new works from contemporary artists using different types of media. In 1999, it held the first Open Call and developed two projects. The 2006 Open Call was a more ambitious £1 million initiative between Artangel and the Jerwood Charitable Foundation, in association with Channel 4 and Arts Council England. As the £1 million was to be divided between four art projects, further funding for *The Arbor* had to be sourced.

In 2008–2009 the UK Film Council provided £25,000 of funding towards the production of the film, through its Development Fund and a further £128,885 in 2009–2010 under its New Cinema strand.

The UK Film Council was set up to develop and support the film industry in 2000, with funding available for emerging filmmakers, those working outside the mainstream and for commercial cinema. It closed in 2011; however, during its ten years of operation, it distributed more than £160 million of lottery money to over 900 films. Many of its functions have transferred to the BFI Film Fund, which provides funding for feature film development and production, including international co-productions and completion funding.

In 2009, Barnard received an Arts and Humanities Research Council (AHRC) Research Leave Award, which allowed her time away from the university to further research and develop *The Arbor*.

Verve Pictures, a specialist in distributing independent films in cinemas and on DVD, received a £4,000 grant from the UK Film Council to support the film's release and distribute it in the UK. Over 75% of Verve Pictures' releases are from first-time directors. *The Arbor* premiered at the Tribeca Film Festival in April 2010, where Barnard won the Best New Documentary Filmmaker prize. It was screened as part of the BFI London Film Festival in October 2010, where it won the Best British Newcomer & Most Original Debut award.

The film opened in the UK in October 2010 and was seen by approximately 8,000 people in UK cinemas. As part of it distribution strategy it featured in 80 festivals internationally, winning ten national and international film awards, including Best Debut Director at the British Independent Film Awards 2010, Best Cinema Documentary at The Griersons 2011 and the Guardian First Film award.

The film was released on DVD in March 2011 and 169,000 watched the Film4 television broadcast in December 2011. *The Arbor* also reached an international audience through theatrical, broadcast and DVD release. From March–May 2011, it was available as an in-flight film showing on all Virgin Atlantic international routes, making it available to approximately 1.5 million passengers.

The development of streaming services such as Curzon Home Cinema, BFI player and Amazon Prime offers greater viewing choice, particularly for

Actor Kathryn Pogson lip-synching to Pamela Dunbar interview.

 S&C

You have inherited some money and with it you want to establish a UK-based film production company. But you want to research your competitors in the industry.

To do this, you need to:

1 Find the names of at least four UK-based production companies

2 Find out the last four films each company has made.

3 What year were they released?

4 Who directed them?

5 Were there any other production companies involved in financing the films?

6 What were the films' budgets?

7 How much money did the films make at the UK/US box office?

8 How were they received by the press? Find a quote that you could use on the poster.

Once you've researched these points (and any others that you feel would be of use), decide whether opening a production company in the UK is a viable use of your money. What kind of films seem to be most popular?

Re-enactment of play; Jimi Mistry (Yousaf) and Natalie Gavin (Andrea Dunbar)

Andrea Dunbar archive footage

Cinéma vérité: a style of documentary filmmaking, also called observational cinema.

independent and/or experimental films such as *The Arbor*. The BFI, through its regional Film Hubs, provides funding and support for cinemas who wish to programme films from outside the mainstream.

According to boxofficemojo.com, the theatrical box office for the film was $21,620 (UK), $104,562 (international), with a total worldwide gross of $126,182 (approximately £95,000), so less than the film's production budget. The film was therefore a critical success but not a commercial success.

Technological

Clio Barnard studied Fine Art, before developing video art projects in which she investigated the relationship between fictional film language and documentary. She explored this tension in *The Arbor* where she challenged notions of what a documentary film is. Here she carried out interviews with the friends and family of the playwright Andrea Dunbar (the subject of the film), but rather than using the documentary footage she used their words as the audio screenplay, employing actors to portray these real people from Dunbar's life, but rather than the actors speaking they lip-synched to the original recordings. The 'to camera' interviews are combined with archive footage, dramatised sequences and re-enactments of Dunbar's plays.

In keeping with the gritty realism of the film, and the blurring of documentary and fiction film, it is filmed in part as a standard documentary with the actors speaking to camera, in domestic settings. The dramatised sequences are filmed in a cinéma vérité style, which seamlessly blends with the archive footage. It was filmed using a Red One 4k digital camera.

A complex technological element of the production was the incorporation of the lip-synching, as Barnard explains:

> *There were two editing stages, one for the audio and then one after the shoot. The process was to edit the audio interviews into roughly the shape* [The Arbor] *ended up being. In between, I storyboarded the film. The actors took the recordings away, and really went into it. Technically, it was very challenging for them.* (Smith, 2011)

The Arbor benefited from a significant change in cinematic distribution in the UK that emerged in 2005, with the launch of the 'digital film network'. The installation of high-definition projectors and computer servers did away with the distribution of cumbersome and expensive 35mm films. Films could be screened via a digital cinema package (DCP), a collection of digital files that could be distributed in physical form or increasingly via an upload. The distributor can encrypt the DCP with key delivery messages (KDMs), ensuring that only authorised users can 'activate' the DCP. This technology allowed for greater saturation of big-budget films, meaning they could be shown in more than one multiplex cinema as well as making it more economical for independent distributors to release films.

Conclusion

The support Barnard received from Artangel, Jerwood, UK Film Council, More4, Arts Council of England and the AHRC meant that she was able to experiment with film form and genre. The film may not have recouped its costs at the box office, but the critical acclaim ensured that Barnard's next feature film, *The Selfish Giant* (2013), would secure more funding and be eagerly anticipated by audiences and critics, and receive attention from film festivals and award ceremonies. Her third feature film, *Dark River*, was released in 2017.

Case study: *Dil Se* (Ratnam, 1998)

Dil Se was Mani Ratnam's 15th film as director, he also served as writer for most of his films. His first film, *Pallavi Anu Pallavi* (1983), an Indian Kannada-language film, was a moderate box office success. Its multiple awards at the Karnataka State Film Awards marked him as a director to watch. Over the next decade he continued to make films in Tamil, which were gaining a huge following in the Tamil-speaking pockets of India.

Hindi is the official language of India (English being the other official language) and is spoken by nearly 425 million people as a first language and by around 120 million as a second language. With this in mind, Ratnam dubbed his 1993 Tamil-film *Roja* into Hindi. Its subject matter was highly controversial: a romantic film about terrorism in the Kashmir region. For Hindi audiences, used to the conventions of Bollywood cinema, Ratnam's realist approach was refreshing and it became a major hit.

Dil Se was the third in his trilogy of controversial, gritty, realist films. Its political and socially controversial blend of romance and thriller mark it as a film outside the Bollywood film industry. However, it still employs key characteristics of Bollywood cinema: namely, the use of big stars, exotic locations, special effects, and spectacular song and dance numbers.

Mani Ratnam

India has 22 official languages: Assamese, Bengali, Bodo, Dogri, Gujarati, Hindi, Kannada, Kashmiri, Konkani, Maithili, Malayalam, Manipuri, Marathi, Nepali, Oriya, Punjabi, Sanskrit, Santhali, Sindhi, Tamil, Telugu and Urdu. Hindi and English are used for official purposes.

Dil Se (Ratnam, 1998)

Financial

A report produced in September 2016 by Deloitte states that,

> The Indian Film Industry is the largest in the world in terms of the number of films it produced with 1,500–2,000 films produced every year in more than 20 languages. In terms of revenue, the industry has gross box office realisations of $2.1 billion which is expected to reach $3.7 billion by 2020. (page 9)

The report continues,

> The Indian film industry is dominated by Bollywood, the Hindi film industry, contributing 43% of the revenue, while regional films [in the other 19 languages] contribute the remaining 50% [with 7% international cinema]. (page 9)

To capitalise on this and to widen its appeal at the box office, *Dil Se* was produced in both Tamil and Hindi. Tamil language films account for 19% of the box office – the second highest after Hindi.

Dil Se was popular in the Tamil region of South India, where audiences are supportive of Ratnam, but elsewhere it came under criticism,

Shah Rukh Khan arriving at a film premiere in 2012 with his wife, film producer Gauri Khan. Shah Rukh Khan, known as the 'King of Bollywood' or 'King Khan' is one of the most successful film stars in the world. He began acting in television in 1988, before moving into film in 1992, he has since made over 80 movies, and won many film acting awards.

Shah Rukh Khan

> *... the biggest problem is that* Dil Se *takes itself too seriously ... after a while, it all becomes a bit of a bore.* (Chopra, 1998)

The film did well internationally, particularly in the UK where it became the first Indian film to enter the top ten, when it grossed over £224,636 in its first week. Its sensitive handling of political material and the casting of Bollywood's reigning heart-throb Shah Rukh Khan made it a firm favourite with British Bollywood cinemagoers. It would go on to gross £537,930 in the UK and $975,000 in the USA.

Despite its limited success at the box office on its release, *Dil Se*'s use of realism with Bollywood elements proved popular at international film festivals. It won the Netpac award (Ex-Aqueo) at the 1999 Berlin International Film Festival and picked up two National Film Awards (India) and six Filmfare Awards (India).

Technological

Key to Bollywood cinema's success are the lavish song and dance numbers integrated into the film, regardless of their genre. These songs are not performed by the actors but by professional 'playback' singers, who are of equal importance as the actors on screen. Sukhwinder Singh, the playback singer for the film's star, Shah Rukh Khan, is one of Bollywood's leading artistes, who won two awards for his work on *Dil Se*. Audiences are aware that the star on screen is not the singer, and there is no attempt to mix the sound to match the distance the actors are from the camera.

It was reported that the soundtrack for *Dil Se* had 100,000 pre-sales in the UK, and was so popular that the soundtrack was recorded in a number of languages including Hindi, Tamil, Malayalam and Punjabi.

Conclusion

Ratnam has continued to make films in Tamil and Hindi, and although he has never reached the successful height of *La Ardilla Roja* (Medem, 1993) he is still a significant director in Indian cinema.

In 2002 the government of India honoured Ratnam with Padma Shri, India's fourth highest civilian award, granted in recognition of his distinguished contribution to the arts. Former Indian President, K.R. Narayanan, presented him with the award at a ceremony in New Delhi. In 2015, he was honoured with the Sun Mark Lifetime Achievement Award at the Bagri Foundation London Indian Film Festival for his 'esteemed contribution to international cinema'.

Sukhwinder Singh

Independent study questions

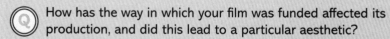

Q How has the way in which your film was funded affected its production, and did this lead to a particular aesthetic?

Q Has your chosen film been shaped by any historical and ongoing technological developments in film production? If so, how?

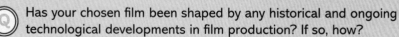

Q To what extent did your film rely on film festivals, awards, reviews and advertising to reach its audience?

Sample essay extracts and feedback

To what extent does your chosen film challenge the dominant attitudes of the society in which it was made?

For this example, we are looking at **extracts** from an essay addressing **social contexts** of *Some Like It Hot*.

Ali's response extract	Feedback
Some Like It Hot was produced in the late 1950s, an era considered to be conservative in its attitudes towards gender and sex. It is an era we associate with images of women as housewives and men as the 'breadwinners'. Hollywood typically represented men and women in traditional gender roles. However, by 1959 attitudes were beginning to shift. The film is more explicit in its portrayal of sex and gender than earlier Hollywood films. Characters have relationships outside of marriage and Marilyn Monroe displays an overt sexuality. The film was condemned by the Production Code administrators, suggesting that the enforcers of the Production Code, mainly older men, were out of touch with a changing society.	*Ali demonstrates an awareness of the society in which Some Like It Hot was produced. Ali provides examples from the film to illustrate their point. However, Ali could provide more detailed, specific examples.*
The film's ending challenges dominant gender, as Osgood does not care that Daphne is in fact a man. This, however, is presented as a joke. The film also represents traditional notions of femininity as Marilyn Monroe is presented as a sex object. This is evident in the scene where she sings 'I Wanna be Loved by You'. Monroe is presented as a spectacle to be admired. Her outfit is revealing and the lighting is cleverly used to suggest nudity, as her shoulders and face are brightly lit but the lighting obscures her breasts. Her blonde hair, feminine voice and curves are typical of images of beauty for 1950s women. In order to be women, Jo and Daphne also conform to dominant notions of femininity through their clothes (skirts and high heels) and high-pitched voices.	*Ali is aware of how the film challenges gender norms yet is also a product of the society in which it was produced. Detailed examples from the film are provided to illustrate their points. Ali's example of the use of lighting and costume links textual analysis within wider contexts of women presented as sex objects.*
The audience response to *Some Like It Hot* upon its release reflects societal attitudes of the time. When the film was screened to an older, more traditional audience, they disliked it and one audience member even walked out. However, younger university students loved the film and the film went on to be a huge success. This response suggests that attitudes were shifting for young people as society was becoming slowly more permissive in attitudes to sex and gender.	*Ali uses their knowledge of how the film was received by audiences very well to demonstrate how American society was changing in the late 1950s.*

PART 2 SPECIALIST STUDY AREAS OR 'CASE STUDIES'

Section 1

AS: American film

A level: Varieties of film and filmmaking

Hollywood (1930–1990)

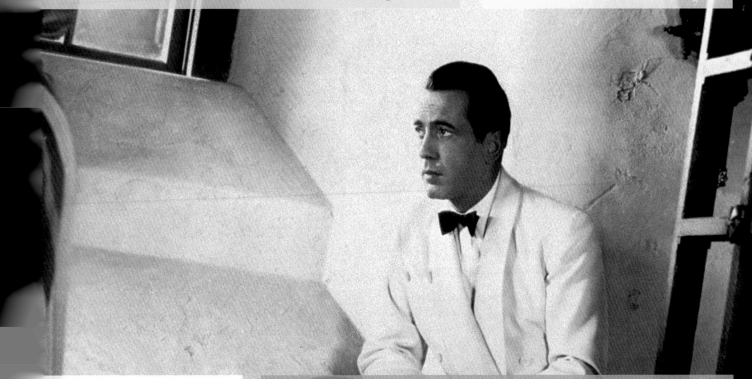

This section will help you to prepare for Component 1: Varieties of film and filmmaking on the A level course or Component 1: American film on the AS course. You will need to **compare** two films and apply the core areas with an emphasis on **context**. Alongside the core areas you will need to apply the specialist study area of **auteur** for the A level. This chapter will use *Casablanca* (Curtiz, 1942) and *Bonnie and Clyde* (Penn, 1967) as case study films.

For AS

For the comparative study, questions will be based on the core study areas but will foreground a comparison of contexts. Questions will be in two parts. Two questions must be answered: the first part, question (a), will be a shorter answer question, requiring brief discussion of examples. The second part will be a longer answer question, requiring a more detailed exploration of film. There will be a choice of two questions for this part – either (b) or (c). The first question is worth 20 marks and should be allocated 20 minutes, the second 40 marks and 40 minutes.

For A level

One question from a choice of two must be answered on the Component 1 paper. For this question, you will be expected to compare one film from **Group 1: Classical Hollywood** and one film from **Group 2: New Hollywood**. The full question is worth 40 points and should be allocated 50 minutes.

The specification says

There will be clear points of comparison suggested by the institutional and production contexts of the films: films in the 1940s and 1950s were produced during the Hollywood studio era and its immediate aftermath and effectively established the 'Classical Hollywood style'. The films produced between the later 1960s and later 1980s can all be seen in terms of 'New Hollywood', where a new generation of directors began to show new influences, especially from European cinema.

1 *Casablanca* (Curtiz, 1942) & *Bonnie and Clyde* (Penn, 1967)

Casablanca (Curtiz, 1942) is a romantic drama set in World War II. The film concerns Rick Blaine, an American expatriate who owns a bar in Casablanca, Morocco, a waiting point for refugees fleeing Nazi occupation. Rick must sacrifice his love for Ilsa for the greater war effort. *Casablanca* is the ultimate classical film, exemplifying Classical Hollywood cinema at the peak of the studio era. The film won three Academy Awards, including Best Picture. The film's dialogue, music and imagery are highly memorable and are often cited in popular culture.

Bonnie and Clyde (Penn, 1967) is based on the true story of Bonnie Parker and Clyde Barrow, two outlaws who travelled central USA in the early 1930s, robbing and killing people when confronted. The film was a huge success with young audiences, and ushered in a new era of more experimental and graphic Hollywood films. *Bonnie and Clyde* was nominated for ten academy awards and won two Academy Awards for Best Supporting Actress and Best Cinematography.

Casablanca and *Bonnie and Clyde* are important films in American film history. *Casablanca* is one of the most famous and best-loved Classical Hollywood films. *Bonnie and Clyde* is the first 'New Hollywood' film, breaking with Classical Hollywood conventions, incorporating a 1960s European visual style and a graphic depiction of violence. Both films were produced by Warner Brothers and both were sold as genre films (*Casablanca* as a romantic drama and *Bonnie and Clyde* as a gangster film) and **star vehicles**.

This chapter will compare film form, representation, aesthetics and context in *Casablanca* and *Bonnie and Clyde*. This comparison will help you to understand the changes in Hollywood film from the classical era to the New Hollywood cinema of the late 1960s onwards. It will focus in detail on **contextual comparisons**, exploring the social, cultural, political and institutional contexts of the films. The section will then explore the **specialist area of auteur** in relation to the two case study films.

 STUDY TIP

This is the only section in the exam in which the two films you have studied must be directly compared in your response. Make sure your notes on the films include detailed observations on ways in which they are similar and ways in which they differ.

Star vehicle: films that are sold on the popularity and persona of the leading star. A role may have been written or produced for this particular star.

Classical Hollywood Films

The studio system

From the 1920s to the 1950s, Hollywood was dominated by eight large studios:

- The Big Five (MGM, Warner, Paramount, RKO and Fox) produced and distributed films and owned their own theatre chains.
- The Little Three (Universal, Columbia and United Artists) produced and distributed films but did not own theatre chains.

These eight major studios controlled the distribution of 95% of films shown in the USA.

Commercial feature films were produced on studio lots, with producers, directors, technicians and stars all working under contract. Each studio developed a particular house style, determined mainly by its chief executives. According to the director Billy Wilder:

> *Studios had faces then. They had their own style. They could bring you blindfolded into a movie house and you opened it and looked up and you knew.* (Haney, 2005, page 11)

Studio production reached its peak in the 1940s, as successful studios efficiently produced mass entertainment films and cinema attendances were at their highest.

After World War II, Hollywood studios went into a steady decline. In May 1948, the US Supreme Court ruled that the major Hollywood studios must end 'block booking' – the process of selling multiple films as units to theatres, preventing independent studios getting their own films into cinemas. This resulted in the breakdown of **vertically integrated** studios and the rise of independent studios in the 1950s and 1960s. In the 1950s, cinema attendance also declined due to changes in leisure pursuits, including the growing popularity of television in the home.

New Hollywood

The 1950s and early 1960s was a period of decline in Hollywood, marked by expensive flops, such as the Cinemascope film *The Conqueror* (Powell, 1956), and declining audiences. However, a new generation of filmmakers came to prominence in the mid to late 1960s and, freed from the constraints of a studio system, produced fresh new films for younger audiences. These new directors and films revived Hollywood cinema and audience attendance increased.

New Hollywood is a critical term that can refer to the more experimental Hollywood films produced in the late 1960s. There have been various incarnations of New Hollywood, including more experimental films of the late 1980s such as Spike Lee's *Do the Right Thing* (1989). This chapter focuses on the first incarnation of New Hollywood films produced in the late 1960s and 1970s.

In New Hollywood films it is the director, rather than the studio, who has the key authorial role. These were cine-literate directors who had a knowledge and interest in European films they saw in arts and independent cinemas, and older Hollywood films they watched in the cinema and on television. Many

(iA) Independent Activity

Research the statistics of cinema attendance in the USA from the 1940s to the 1970s. Present the statistics as a graph.

What trends do you notice in cinema attendances?

When are there periods of decline and what might account for these?

Vertical integration: when a company controls the different stages of a product's process or construction. During the studio era, the Big Five Hollywood studios were vertically integrated, as they controlled production, distribution and exhibition.

 S&C

Read Douglas Gomery's chapter 'Hollywood as Industry', in John Hill and Pamela Gibson (eds), *The Oxford Guide to Film Studies* (1998) for a detailed summary of the Hollywood studio system. Summarise the key points in 200 words.

of these directors learned filmmaking as film obsessives or 'buffs', often with backgrounds in film schools, film criticism and acting. As the studio system was in decline, they were less bound by institutional styles and open to experimentation.

However, the New Hollywood films were not a complete departure from Classical Hollywood films. Many were still produced by major studios. Studios did not reject the star system and instead were keen to exploit the personalities of new film stars such as Warren Beatty, Dustin Hoffman and Robert Redford. In this era, stars were also auteurs, often with a level of creative control in their films.

Applying the core areas of study to *Casablanca* and *Bonnie and Clyde*

Film form in Classical Hollywood films

The Classical Hollywood style developed during the later 1910s and 1920s, and was solidified in the 1930s. It is typified by a set of conventions and guidelines which we still see in Hollywood films today. These conventions were flexible, as filmmakers experimented and changes in technology enabled new stylistic innovations.

Overall, Classical Hollywood films follow these unwritten rules or conventions:

- The narratives are 'a chain of events in cause and effect relationship' (Bordwell & Thompson, 2012).
- They were shot in a controlled environment, often on the studio lot, yet are made to appear believable and realistic.
- They have invisible or continuity editing.
- There is one main plot with a limited number of sub-plots.

This formula was incredibly successful, as film scholar Kristin Thompson explains in *Storytelling in the New Hollywood* (1999):

> *Hollywood's success was based on telling stories clearly, vividly, entertainingly. The techniques of continuity editing, set design, and lighting that were developed during this era were designed not only to provide attractive images but also to guide audience attention to salient narrative events from moment to moment.* (page 1)

John Belton summarises the purpose of style in classical Hollywood films in *Classical Hollywood Cinema: Style* (2008) as:

> *Elements of style serve to shape the narrative [...] They draw attention to, underline, and point out what it is that the audience needs to see or hear in order to read or understand the scene.* (page 47)

Film scholars Bordwell, Staiger and Thompson in *The Classical Hollywood Cinema*, describe the typical guidelines for a shooting a sequence in the classical Hollywood style:

- The scene should first establish the time, place and relevant characters.
- Location might be indicated with an exterior shot of the location.
- Characters then take over the narration.

 Independent Activity

Watch one or more of the following New Hollywood films:

- *The Graduate* (Nichols, 1967): a ground-breaking sophisticated comedy about a young graduate, Ben, who is seduced by an older woman, Mrs Robinson. The film deals with themes of alienation and questions the values of American society.

- *Point Blank* (Boorman, 1967): a disorientating, surreal neo-noir crime film about the nature of memory and trauma.

- *The Swimmer* (Perry, 1968): a surreal story about a man who decides to swim home via swimming pools in his upper-class neighbourhood. During this journey he shifts from being an affluent executive to a broken-down outcast.

To what extent do these films differ from Classical Hollywood films in form, representations and ideology? Present these differences in a table and include at least three points for each.

 Independent Activity

Write a 400-word essay based on the following question:

> To what extent has film form in Hollywood cinema changed since the classical era?

Refer to the contemporary Hollywood films you have studied to help you answer the question.

- The scene should reveal character's spatial positions (where they are located within the space and their states of mind).
- The establishing shots should indicate where everyone is located.
- Once location and characters are established, characters then act out their goals.
- The classical scene ends with a step towards the goal and/or a character's reaction to a new piece of information. (adapted from Bordwell et al., 1988)

Film form in a scene from *Casablanca*

Let's apply Bordwell, Staiger and Thompson's guidelines to the sequence in *Casablanca* where we are first introduced to Rick. In terms of its formal elements, the sequence is a 'typical' classical Hollywood scene:

1

1 Long, establishing, exterior shot. This is a typical way to begin a scene in a classical Hollywood film. The shot establishes place (Rick's Bar, Casablanca) and time of day (night time).

2 Close-up. This shot draws attention to 'Rick's Café American', further establishing place. As Humphrey Bogart is the star of the film, the audience would assume that Bogart is Rick.

3 Interior long shot. The camera pans around the interior of Rick's bar to establish the space inside it and convey atmosphere. We see conversations between patrons, revealing their spatial positions and giving us an indication of the types of people who frequent Rick's bar. Notice how the filmmakers do not reveal Rick straight away. This builds a sense of anticipation for the audience.

2

3

(iA) Independent Activity

Chose one short sequence from a Classical Hollywood film produced between 1930 and 1960. Pause each shot and note the purpose of each shot. Is your chosen sequence shot in the classical Hollywood style? If so, note which conventions are followed and why.

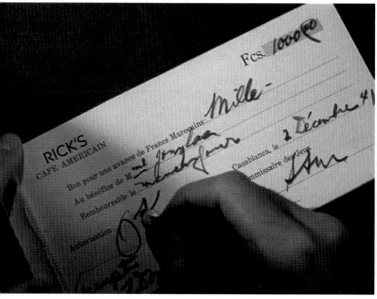 

4   5

4 Close-up. This shot gives important information establishing the specific date. The cheque is dated 2 December 1941. These are the days leading up to the attack on Pearl Harbor on 7 December 1941, the event that led America to enter World War II.

5 Medium long shot. The shot reveals Rick and key character information. We see his actions (playing chess), his facial expression and some of his surroundings (we know Rick is located in the same bar). This shot gives us an indication of Rick's psychological state. Rick is a loner. He plays chess alone and drinks alone. He looks cynical and weary. The low-key lighting emphasises his cynicism.

6 and 7 Characters are now acting out their goals. These shots illustrate the typical way to shoot two characters having a conversation. Notice the use of shot/reverse-shot and the 180-degree rule. We can easily follow the characters' conversations, their reactions and spatial positioning.

6   7

Film form in *Bonnie and Clyde*

Now we shall compare and contrast the opening of *Bonnie and Clyde* with *Casablanca*, to consider the extent to which the film breaks the conventions of classical Hollywood style.

French New Wave: a movement in French cinema of the late 1950s and early 1960s. Directors, such as Jacques Demy, Agnes Varda, Alain Resnais, Claude Chabrol, Jean-Luc Godard and Francois Truffaut, created stylish, energetic and self-conscious films. French New Wave films were typified by on-location shooting, naturalistic acting and ambiguous or unresolved endings. While New Wave directors were inspired by Hollywood auteurs such as Hitchcock, they often broke the rules of Classical Hollywood films. For instance, in *Breathless* (1959, Godard) the opening scene lacks an establishing shot and a conversation scene breaks the 180-degree rule.

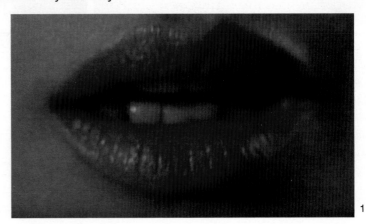

1 The first shot in *Bonnie and Clyde* after the credits is an extreme close-up of Bonnie's lips. This is a direct contrast to the opening establishing long shots in Classical Hollywood films. Here, the film uses experimental devices from **French New Wave** films, where scenes may begin by deliberately omitting the conventional long establishing shot.

2 The camera pans out to reveal Bonnie's face, followed by a series of medium close-ups of Bonnie naked and restless in her bedroom. The camera is positioned to show that Bonnie is naked, yet does not actually reveal anything. Notice how there is still no full establishing long shot of Bonnie's surroundings, as the focus is on Bonnie's character. Notice also how the bed frame is in the foreground of the shot, suggesting that Bonnie is feeling trapped in her situation.

▶ S&C

Watch the French New Wave film *Breathless* (Godard, 1960). Make a list of key moments where the film deliberately break the rules of classical Hollywood filmmaking. Then discuss the ways in which *Breathless* influenced the visual style of *Bonnie and Clyde*.

3 The camera is now placed outside of the bedroom, looking in on Bonnie who is looking outside. The editing so far creates a clear continuity and utilises shot/reverse-shot as used in *Casablanca*. Notice how we see Clyde in a high-angle long shot, from Bonnie's point of view.

3

4 The camera cuts closer to Clyde as he responds to Bonnie's call of 'Hey boy, what you doin' with my mama's car?' Notice the use of shot-reverse-shots and medium shots to enable the audience to focus on the characters' interactions and locate characters' spatial positioning and surroundings.

4

From analysing this sequence, it is evident that *Bonnie and Clyde* breaks some of the conventions of the Classical Hollywood style and narrative, yet is not a complete departure from classical Hollywood. The scene incorporates the style of French New Wave films by lacking establishing shots; however, it still uses conventional devices such as shot/reverse-shot.

Compare *Bonnie and Clyde* with *Gun Crazy*. Compare and contrast two key sequences from *Bonnie and Clyde* and *Gun Crazy*, noting the similarities and differences between the two films.

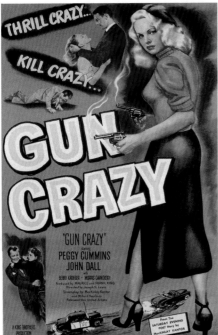

The narrative structure of *Bonnie and Clyde* is conventional, with a chain of events in cause and effect relationship and a linear narrative with a clear beginning, middle and end. The film does not end as abruptly as some experimental French New Wave films. There is a sense of closure as Bonnie and Clyde are ultimately punished for their crimes through their violent deaths.

There is a direct relationship between Hollywood films of the classical era, the French New Wave and New Hollywood films. French New Wave director Truffaut adored the classical Hollywood film noir *Gun Crazy* (Lewis, 1950) so he screened it for screenwriters Robert Benton and David Newman when they were developing the story for *Bonnie and Clyde*.

Warner Brothers publicised *Bonnie and Clyde* as a genre film and star vehicle, typical of a Hollywood studio film. The poster for *Bonnie and Clyde* has similarities to the poster for *Gun Crazy*.

Gun Crazy (Lewis, 1950)

Cinematography

Casablanca

The lighting in *Casablanca* plays an important role in the overall mood and aesthetic of the film. It conveys characters' psychological states and unspoken emotions, heightening the spectators' emotional response.

Classical Hollywood films conventionally used **three-point lighting**, consisting of a back light, a fill light and a key light. **Low-key lighting**, however, is where the fill light is removed, creating shadows and a mysterious, doom-laden atmosphere. The use of shadows conveys a sense of entrapment, as people who were trying to flee Nazi persecution are stuck in Casablanca. A searchlight surveys the area at night, conveying a sense of uncertainty and threat. Notice how the light invades the safety of Rick's bar, casting light and creating shadows as it moves.

Low-key lighting conveys a war-torn world and characters' inner conflicts. When Rick sits in his bar after a chance meeting with Ilsa, the searchlight casts light and shadow, reflecting his despair. The low-key lighting used to convey Rick's turmoil contrasts to Laszlo, who is brightly lit, reflecting his heroic nature and certainty about his commitment to the war.

Female stars were often lit with a soft light to make their eyes sparkle and accentuate their femininity and glamour. Ilsa is often shot in this manner, conveying her tenderness and sadness. When Ilsa visits Rick while he is alone in his bar, she is at first bathed in light, reflecting her innocence, while Rick sits in the shadows, conveying his self-pity.

 Independent Activity

Analyse the use of lighting in this shot of Captain Renault in the doorway and Rick in shadow.

What type of lighting is used here and to what effect?

Depression era photography of Walker Evans

Bonnie and Clyde

Bonnie and Clyde alternates between realistic cinematography and more expressionistic devices. Arthur Penn was inspired by the photography of Walker Evans, an American photographer famous for his Depression-era photographs of farming families living in poverty.

For some scenes, *Bonnie and Clyde* adopts a naturalistic, high-key lighting style. This is evident in the final shootout scene, which makes the violence seem more realistic and vivid. At other times, the film adopts a more hazy, dream-like style. Watch the sequence where Bonnie is reunited with her family. This scene was shot through a windscreen to give it a dream-like quality. Notice how the lighting and use of a filter make the scene seem like a fantasy, suggesting how different Bonnie's life would be if she had stayed with her family.

Mise-en-scène

Casablanca

Casablanca takes place in exotic and romantic locations, yet these places become sites of danger and threat. Most of the action is contained in Rick's bar, a place of safety for refugees fleeing the war; yet it also acts as a prison, as characters are often stuck inside. Paris is a city with romantic connotations, and is used here for the flashback sequence when Rick and Ilsa fall in love. However, the romance and safety of Paris are again undercut as the Germans occupy France. Paris now becomes a place of danger.

Although *Casablanca* is set in Morocco, it was filmed on the Warner's studio lot in Hollywood. This is typical of production of the studio era, as elaborate sets could be built and dismantled easily. Lighting and mise-en-scène were also much easier to control in a studio.

Casablanca's final sequence in the airport hangar is an excellent example of how set design and clever use of props create the illusion that the scene is shot in a real location. A cardboard cut-out of the aeroplane was used in the background and the mechanics seen in the distance were very small actors. This use of miniatures in the background with key characters in the foreground creates a forced perspective. The scene also uses fog, a common device in Warner's films to convey atmosphere and disguise the set.

Bonnie and Clyde

In *Bonnie and Clyde*, the use of real Texas locations contrasts with the controlled studio shooting in Classical Hollywood films. The dusty roads and unpredictable weather give the film an energy and realism. This use of exterior locations was inspired by French New Wave films, for which French directors took their cameras out onto the streets of Paris.

In *Bonnie and Clyde*, mise-en-scène evokes the poverty of the Depression era and barrenness of the Texan landscape. The mise-en-scène also subverts some of the conventions of the traditional gangster film. Classical Hollywood gangster films were often set in big cities with night-time shootouts. *Bonnie and Clyde*, however, is set in rural Texas and the key action sequences take place in daylight.

Objects are used symbolically in *Bonnie and Clyde* to connote Bonnie and Clyde's sexual relationship, as it was still unusual to see explicitly sexual scenes in Hollywood films in 1967. In one sequence, Bonnie handles the barrel of Clyde's gun, suggesting that they are now in a sexual relationship.

Bonnie's costumes give her a stylish, cool demeanour, inspired by 1930s Hollywood stars such as Marlene Dietrich. Bonnie's beret is also a homage to the character of Annie in *Gun Crazy* and female characters in French New Wave films. Her costumes inspired fashion trends, as black berets, bobbed hair and maxi skirts became all the rage.

According to the costume designer *for Bonnie and Clyde*, Theadora Van Runkle,

> *Dull colours … were ruled out – the styles had to be palatable by Hollywood standards. The stars were, after all, two very good-looking people who had no particular desire to resemble physically the real Bonnie and Clyde.* (Young, C., 2013)

(iA) Independent Activity

Find images online of the following:

- Publicity stills of Faye Dunaway as Bonnie.
- Female Hollywood stars of the 1930s, including Marlene Dietrich.
- Female characters in French New Wave films, such as *Breathless* (Godard, 1960) and *A Woman is a Woman* (Godard, 1961).

Create a montage of the images and write 200 words comparing Bonnie's look to 1930s female stars and female characters in French New Wave films.

Editing

Casablanca

Casablanca is edited in the classical continuity style. The editing disguises transitions from shot to shot, making the film appear as a seamless flow of images. Our attention is not drawn to the edits, thus they appear 'invisible'. In *Casablanca*, the pace of editing is fairly rapid, reflecting the urgency of the situation as the war develops and characters are desperate to gain exit visas.

Casablanca's opening montage is typical of the classical Hollywood use of montage as exposition. A voice-over narration anchors a series of dissolves of ships sailing and people on the move. The opening montage borrows from the documentary genre. It serves to contextualise the story and grounds the film in the realities of war.

Stories are not always edited or conveyed in a linear fashion in Hollywood films, as flashbacks are commonplace. The flashback to Rick's memories in Paris are typical of the Classical Hollywood approach to editing flashbacks, as the camera zooms in slowly on Rick, then dissolves out of focus. The film dissolves into an image of Paris that slowly comes into focus, a conventional device used to signal a flashback in a Hollywood film.

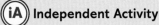

Independent Activity

Watch the opening montage sequence in *Casablanca* and the final sequences in *Bonnie and Clyde*. Write 200 words comparing and contrasting the use of editing in these sequences.

Canted angle: when the frame is deliberately slanted to one side. This is often to portray an intoxicated or unbalanced character or to help convey a sense of unease or disorientation.

Bonnie and Clyde

The editing in *Bonnie and Clyde* is deliberately stylised and draws attention to itself, a contrast to the 'invisible' editing of classical Hollywood films.

The final sequence of *Bonnie and Clyde* is where the stylish use of editing comes to the fore. The shots leading up to the shootout utilise cross-cutting and fast editing effectively. Quick-cuts juxtaposing the long shot of the birds flying away, to the quick close-ups of Bonnie and Clyde's panicked faces as they realise their fate, was, for film critic Pauline Kael (1967), 'a stunning example of the art of editing'.

The final shootout is a montage comprising of 51 shots (around one shot per second). Clyde's death is edited in slow motion, as Penn envisaged Clyde's death to be like a ballet. This contrasts to the sudden death of Bonnie, which evokes shock. Notice how the final shot of the sequence is framed through bullet-shot glass at a **canted angle**, a contrast to the usual long shots that ended Classical Hollywood films.

Arthur Penn's description of the editing style in *Bonnie and Clyde* demonstrates new approaches to film editing:

> *I was not interested in continuity of action. I was interested in the idea of appetite – I had to establish the appetite of this woman for anything that would replace the tedium of her life. So that's how we developed it from that close up on her mouth. And that set the tone for the whole film. With the editing, we wanted nervous bursts of energy, a way of showing how Bonnie felt. It was a metaphoric visual style.* (Friedman, 2000, page 106)

Sound

Casablanca

Classical Hollywood films such as *Casablanca* use incidental, non-diegetic music to heighten drama and provoke an emotional response during key dramatic moments. However, in *Bonnie and Clyde* some sequences lack incidental music, which makes the film seem more realistic.

The entire score for *Casablanca* was based on the song 'As Time Goes By', a romantic and nostalgic song that appears in key moments throughout the film to remind the spectator of Rick and Ilsa's love. Composer Max Steiner based the score for *Casablanca* on this popular Broadway song. Different versions of the song can be heard throughout the film. Sam plays 'As Time Goes By' on the piano in the bar. Here the sound is diegetic and integral to the narrative, as Rick at first does not allow Sam to play the song because it invokes painful memories of his lost love. However, later on Rick asks Sam to play the song once Ilsa has come back into his life. An orchestral, non-diegetic version of the song is heard over the Paris flashback, evoking Rick and Ilsa's romance.

 Independent Activity

Watch the opening credit sequence of *Casablanca*. Note how the non-diegetic orchestral score is used to evoke the following:

1 A sense of place – consider how the music evokes the exotic location.
2 Different genres.
3 Dramatic tension.

Casablanca is best known for its quotable dialogue. The witty, snappy dialogue is typical of Warner Brothers' films starring Humphrey Bogart. The dialogue cleverly intertwines the personal and public narrative, as lines such as, 'I stick my neck out for nobody', reflect Rick's isolationist stance and America's attitude to the war before the invasion of Pearl Harbor. However, at the end of the film Rick says, 'it doesn't take much to see that the problems of three little people don't amount to a hill of beans in this crazy world', indicating the wider sacrifices that Americans had to make in the war effort.

Diegetic music in *Casablanca* is also used to reflect particular nations and their role in the war. The scene where the French and Germans sing their anthems is a particularly emotional moment in the film, one that would have resonated with audiences watching at the time. The German soldiers confidently sing their patriotic anthem *Die Wacht am Rhein* (*Guard on the Rhein*), a popular song in Germany that rivalled the national anthem. This represents German power over the refugees in the bar trying to escape Nazi persecution. Victor Laszlo walks over to the band and demands they play the French national anthem *La Marseillaise*, a moment that reflects Laszlo's heroism and defiance. The band look to Rick for approval and his nod of approval is a key turning point for his character, as Rick is now choosing a side in the war effort. The singing of *La Marseillaise* in front of the Germans becomes an act of resistance against Nazi rule. Notice how the entire bar joins in and the sound of voices joining in becomes louder. The camera cuts to a close-up of the French character Yvonne with tears streaking down her face as she sings the anthem, an emotional moment reflecting the sacrifice people made to resist Nazi rule.

Bonnie and Clyde

While music in *Casablanca* parallels action on screen, at times the musical soundtrack in *Bonnie and Clyde* is contradictory to the violence on screen. The bluegrass song 'Foggy Mountain Breakdown' adds a light, comic tone to some crime sequences. The use of bluegrass also evokes the period of the Great Depression and the Deep South locations. Warner Brothers released a soundtrack album for the film in March 1968, as bluegrass music was in fashion as a result of the film's popularity.

Bonnie and Clyde's unique sound is due mainly to the work of the film's editor, Dede Allen, whose background was in sound editing. Her work is notable for the use of sound bridges, beginning the sound from the next scene while the previous scene is playing, which she employs in *Bonnie and Clyde*. Allen was an innovator in the use of sound bridges, which are now commonplace in Hollywood films.

Heightened diegetic sound is used in *Bonnie and Clyde* to shock the spectator. Film scholar Jay Beck explains this heightened use of sound in one sequence in *Designing Sound: Audiovisual Aesthetics in 1970s American Cinema* (2016):

> *The escalation of violence is met with an elevation of both soundtrack volume and the visceral quality of the gunshots and other acoustic effects. The extreme loudness of the gunshots, heard when Clyde is showing Bonnie how to shoot, undercuts the light atmosphere of the narrative moment.* (page 41)

Performance

Casablanca

In *Casablanca*, Humphrey Bogart brings a psychological realism to his depiction of Rick. We can infer Rick's troubled state of mind through Bogart's facial expressions. Bogart's acting style was considered to be 'natural' for the period. Other actors on the set of *Casablanca* believed that he brought his own personal unhappiness to his performance. Bogart's performance in *Casablanca* was also a continuation of the world-weary, 'tough guy' persona he had developed in previous Warner Brothers films such as *The Maltese Falcon* (Huston, 1941).

Ingrid Bergman's performance as Ilsa conveys the inner turmoil and conflict Ilsa faces. Like Bogart, Bergman's performance style was 'natural'. Bergman conveys emotion through her eyes, which convey her fear and sadness. Professor David Smit in *Ingrid Bergman: The Life, Career and Public Image* (2012) describes Bergman's distinctive performance skills, praising:

> *her ability to display adoration and devotion (the skills we associate with her stardom) but also her ability to project hidden emotions in quick facial shifts, her emotional range revealed in scenes of breakdown and emotional release, and her ability to sustain that range through long takes.* (page 155)

Watch Bergman's performance closely in the climactic airport hangar sequences. Notice how her eyes convey her sadness at having to sacrifice her love for Rick and how her performance is heightened by a soft gauze filter and lighting.

 Independent Activity

According to David Smit in *Ingrid Bergman: The Life, Career and Public Image*, the scene in *Casablanca* where Ilsa confronts Rick in his room near the end of the film best exemplifies Bergman's ability to display adoration and devotion. Watch this scene carefully, focusing on Bergman's performance. Write down how Bergman displays adoration and devotion through facial expression and body movement.

▶ **S&C**

Find the screenplay for *Casablanca*. Look at the scene towards the end of the screenplay where Rick and Ilsa sacrifice their love and part company. Now compare the scene in the screenplay with the scene in the film. What do Humphrey Bogart and Ingrid Bergman contribute to the scene through performance that is not stated in the screenplay?

Bonnie and Clyde

The performance style of Faye Dunaway and Warren Beatty in *Bonnie and Clyde* is more self-conscious than the performance styles in *Casablanca*, reflecting changes in acting styles in New Hollywood films. Film scholar Jack Shadoian in *Dreams and Dead Ends: The American Gangster Film* (2003) describes the performance styles of the actors in *Bonnie and Clyde*:

> ... the performances drift towards the comic, the inadequate, the designedly awkward. The actors project a strain, an inauthenticity, as though they are newly graduated from acting school. They seem alienated from their roles. This, perhaps, is part of Penn's desire ... to suggest the nervousness, insecurity and non-integrated personalities of his characters. (page 249)

Warren Beatty plays Clyde with a boyish charm. He often smiles with glee when talking about his past exploits. Beatty evokes the real Clyde Barrow in his performance, as he walks with a limp. Faye Dunaway as Bonnie embodies screenwriters' Benton and Newman's description of Bonnie in their original treatment for the film:

> a kind of strange and touching vision: a pretty girl who was both tough and vulnerable, who was both Texas and universal, who wrote poetry and shot policemen, who loved life and courted death. (Goldstein, 1998, page 132)

 Independent Activity

Watch the opening sequence of *Bonnie and Clyde*. Write down examples of how Bonnie's non-verbal communication connotes her boredom and frustration. How do her mannerisms change when Clyde offers her the opportunity of excitement and escape?

Aesthetics

Casablanca

Casablanca combines the aesthetics of film noir, expressionism, melodrama and documentary. The aesthetics depict a sense of romantic longing, as smoky bars, exotic locations, the foggy runway and wartime costume all contribute to the film's classic look.

The overall aesthetic also stems from Warners' 1940s 'house style', with low-key lighting, and a combination of a downbeat style found in Warners' detective films and a nostalgic romanticism typical of their melodramas. The film's aesthetic also reflects film scholar Dana Pollen's argument that *Casablanca* is typical of a more modern, tough-minded Hollywood cinema of the 1940s (cited in Geiger & Rutsky, 2013: 363).

 Independent Activity

Analyse the memorable still on the left from *Casablanca*. How does it reflect the overall aesthetic of the film? Consider the use of lighting, costume and location.

 Independent Activity

Watch the film *Mildred Pierce* (Curtiz, 1945), another Warner Brothers film also directed by Michael Curtiz. Do you notice any similarities with *Casablanca* in the overall aesthetic of the film?

Bonnie and Clyde

Bonnie and Clyde's overall aesthetic is an amalgamation of French New Wave films and a homage to Classical Hollywood films. The use of ironic music, fast motion, slow motion and extreme close-ups illustrates how *Bonnie and Clyde* merged the aesthetics of New Wave filmmaking with Hollywood cinema. The colours used in *Bonnie and Clyde* reflect the barren farmlands of Texas during the Great Depression, with various shades of yellow, brown, gold and green.

Representations

Age

Casablanca

In *Casablanca* Rick is an older leading character. Humphrey Bogart was aged 42 when he played Rick. It is necessary to the narrative that Rick is a middle-aged character. When we are first introduced to Rick, he is world-weary and cynical, a man who has loved and lost. We learn about Rick's past – in 1936 he fought on the side of the loyalists in Spain and lived in Europe for some years. The Rick we see in the flashback sequence is a happier, younger and lighter Rick than the cynical middle-aged Rick. Rick's transformation at the end of the film to a man willing to make personal sacrifices for his country reflects how American people should be willing to undergo change. Ilsa is portrayed as a much younger, more innocent character than Rick. Ingrid Bergman was aged 27 when she played Ilsa. Her innocence is often conveyed in the film by soft lighting, making her look angelic.

Bonnie and Clyde

In *Bonnie and Clyde* the main characters reflect the growing countercultural movement in the USA during the late 1960s. The counterculture refers to a period when many young people were questioning the old, established order and norms. The feminist movement grew, as women questioned the traditional roles of housewife and mother. Attitudes towards sex loosened, reflected in more explicit sexual context in films. This countercultural attitude is reflected in the sequence where Bonnie kisses lawman Frank Hamer in a picture to send to the press. Here Penn wanted to reflect countercultural kids who had contempt for authority. For film scholar Lester D. Friedman (1998),

> *Bonnie and Clyde came to represent a stark depiction of contemporary dissent in opposition to a repressive American system of rules and regulations.* (page 30)

Gender

Casablanca

Casablanca conforms to traditional gender norms of the 1940s. Rick's masculinity, defined by toughness and cynicism, is typical of 'tough-guy' characters in Warner's detective films. Ilsa conforms to traditional notions of femininity, as she is represented as being innocent and emotional. She often functions as an object of the male gaze and is lit in a manner that accentuates her beauty. It is Rick who has the most agency in the film. Rick makes the decision to sacrifice his love for the greater good. The narrative is also told through the perspective of the male character, Rick, and we often view Ilsa from Rick's perspective. In one sense, Ilsa functions mainly as a narrative device in Rick's transformation.

Bonnie and Clyde

To a certain extent, *Bonnie and Clyde* subverts traditional gender roles. Clyde contrasts with the traditionally masculine character of Rick in *Casablanca*. Bonnie is an overtly sexual woman in need of excitement and danger, yet the film suggests that Clyde is not a strong enough man for her, and indeed he may not even be sexually attracted to her. Clyde is impotent, as hinted at in the dialogue when he says, 'I aint much of a loverboy'. Beatty's portrayal of Clyde reflects a new kind of male star that emerged in New Hollywood films, one that was self-doubting and playing against generic expectations. This contrasts with the self-assured, confident personas of male stars in classical Hollywood films.

Classic Hollywood gangster films focus on the male hero, with women in supporting roles as the wife or moll. In *Bonnie and Clyde*, the female character is given an equal role and one of power and agency. This representation of Bonnie as a strong woman reflects the civil rights movement as **second wave feminism** came to the fore. Bonnie is introduced first in the opening sequence and we see Clyde from her point of view, an inversion of the male gaze. However, it is Bonnie whose body is on display in the opening sequences as she conforms to conventional notions of female beauty.

Women in the late 1960s march for equality.

(iA) Independent Activity

Watch the trailers for Bogart's earlier Warner Brothers' films *The Maltese Falcon* (Huston, 1941) and *High Sierra* (Walsh, 1941). Consider how *Casablanca* develops Bogart's persona and representation of a traditional, 'tough guy' masculinity.

Second wave feminism: a period of feminist activity that began in the USA in the early 1960s and continued to the early 1980s.

(iA) Independent Activity

Describe the character traits of the main female and male lead characters in *Casablanca* and *Bonnie and Clyde*. Write a list of the similarities and differences between Bonnie and Ilsa, and Clyde and Rick. Argue in one paragraph how far *Bonnie and Clyde* is a departure from traditional gender roles of the classical Hollywood era.

Ethnicity

Casablanca

Casablanca has a multicultural cast, mainly from Western nations. Although the film is set in Morocco, native Moroccans are relegated to the background. The main characters in *Casablanca* reflect their nation's role in the war: Rick represents America, Laszlo represents French resistance fighters, and Ilsa, a Norwegian, represents European women whose personal lives have been devastated by Nazi occupation and the war. Supporting cast members were made up of immigrant actors. The studio's publicity department boasted that:

> *The cast and crew of the production represent so many different nationalities that the set is the most cosmopolitan spot in Southern California.* (Isenberg, 2017)

For some critics, the character of Sam was quite progressive for a Hollywood film of the 1940s. Usually, black characters were relegated to the roles of maids and butlers, and were often crude stereotypes. Although Sam has a supporting role and is at the servitude of while characters, he is portrayed with dignity, and is Rick's confidant and friend, as well as an entertainer.

Bonnie and Clyde

In *Bonnie and Clyde*, the leading characters represent poor southern whites hit by the grinding poverty of the Great Depression. Black characters appear in the background and are not given lines of dialogue or any substantial role in the narrative. Film scholar David Laderman in *Driving Visions: Exploring the Road Movie* argues that

> *we would expect some substantial interaction between our outlaw couple and the victims of institutionalized racism [black people]. Instead their appearance feels rather contrived, mostly as token, passive spectators to the picaresque adventures of our attractive white anti-heroes.* (page 65)

Political, social and cultural contexts

Political contexts

Casablanca

For film scholar Thomas Schatz, *Casablanca* is 'an anthem of America's commitment to the war' (1998, page 317). To fully understand *Casablanca*, it is therefore important to have some knowledge of the political events of the time, as they are integral to the film's plot.

Casablanca, Morocco, was a French Colony and became a holding place for refugees escaping Nazi rule while attempting to get exit visas to Lisbon, Portugal. As a result, a black market in forged visas sprang up. These refugees were a mixture of political refugees, members of underground movements and escapees from German concentration camps. Jack Warner, president of Warner Brothers, heard about these refugee stories and together with associate producer Hal. B. Wallis came up with the idea for *Casablanca*.

Rick is the embodiment of the USA's initial reluctance to enter the war.

Rick's transformation, from a self-serving character who tries to stay neutral, to a character willing to make sacrifices for the greater good, reflects the USA's entry into World War II. Here, Rick's personal relationship with Ilsa is intertwined with the political narrative. Rick's willingness to sacrifice his love for Ilsa sends the message to ordinary Americans that sacrifice is necessary as the USA must support the allied war effort to defeat the evils of fascism.

At first, Captain Renault represents the Vichy government, in power in France between 1940 and 1944, in French-controlled Morocco. The Vichy government was loyal to the Nazis after surrendering to them, which many French people saw as a betrayal. In the film's final sequences, Renault pours a glass of Vichy water, discards the bottle into the bin, which he then kicks over, symbolising his rejection of the Vichy government and Nazi regime, and willingness to stand side-by-side with Rick.

 Independent Activity

Analyse the final sequences of *Casablanca* and note how the film's political messages are conveyed through formal elements, including dialogue.

The character of Victor Laszlo is a symbol of the resistance movement. The resistance was composed of people who, under Nazi oppression, helped the allies at great risk to their own safety. Laszlo is devoted to resisting Nazi rule and willing to sacrifice himself to ensure Ilsa's safe passage out of Casablanca. In this sense, he is the true hero of the film.

The dates when *Casablanca* is set are important for understanding the political context of the film. The plot starts on Tuesday 2 December 1941 and takes place over four days. The film ends with Rick sacrificing his love for Ilsa on Friday 5 December 1941. On Sunday 7 December 1941, the Japanese navy launched a military strike against a US Naval base at Pearl Harbor, Hawaii. The bombing of Pearl Harbor led to US entry into World War II.

Bonnie and Clyde

While *Casablanca* was produced at a time when the nation was uniting for the war effort, *Bonnie and Clyde* was produced during a period of discord in the USA. Political events in America in the late 1960s influence *Bonnie and Clyde* indirectly. Rather than uniting the nation, the Vietnam War divided America, as many young people opposed the war. The 1960s was a decade characterised by violent events including: the Vietnam War; the battle for Civil Rights; and the assassinations of Dr Martin Luther King and Robert Kennedy.

The Vietnam War influenced the way Arthur Penn made the film, with images of graphic violence. Penn stated that people needed to view guns as terrifying instruments.

The graphic violence in the film's final sequences is politically significant, reflecting a mood of pessimism after a summer of riots and the rising death-toll in the Vietnam War. In the film's final sequence, Clyde has a gunshot to the head, a reference to the 1963 assassination of President John F. Kennedy.

Social contexts

Casablanca

Casablanca was released in the USA on 23 January 1943, and was an instant commercial and critical success. *Casablanca* was released at the same time as the British Prime Minister Winston Churchill and American President Franklin D. Roosevelt were attending a summit in Casablanca. This conference was headline news and as such gave Warner Brothers plenty of free publicity, increasing the film's popularity.

Casablanca was produced for a mass audience at a time when cinema-going was the key leisure activity.

Bonnie and Clyde

Faye Dunaway and Warren Beatty attend the premiere of *Bonnie and Clyde* in Paris, France.

While Hal B. Wallis at Warner was intricately involved in all aspects of the production of *Casablanca*, the executives at Warner Brothers did not approve of *Bonnie and Clyde* and initially only gave the film a short release in cinemas. However, the film gained popularity and upon its second release in theatres it became a huge hit.

In contrast to *Casablanca*, *Bonnie and Clyde* was produced during a period of declining profits and fragmented audiences.

Rather than appeal to a mass audience, *Bonnie and Clyde* targeted the baby boomer generation. The boomers referred to young people who were born just after World War II. They were known as a more rebellious generation, and many were anti-establishment and questioned the values of their parents' generation. Between 1964 and 1972, this generation developed a countercultural movement and campaigned for racial and gender equality and an end to the Vietnam War. In the late 1960s, these boomers were now teenagers and young adults who were more receptive to more experimental foreign films. As director Arthur Penn noted,

> *young people understood this movie instantly. They saw Bonnie and Clyde as rebels like themselves. It was a movie that spoke to a generation in a way none of us had really expected.* (cited in Anastasia & Macnow, 2011)

As a result of the release of films such as *Bonnie and Clyde* and *The Graduate*, audience attendance in the USA rose significantly. In the UK, however, *Bonnie and Clyde* garnered a mixed response. The *Daily Mail* published young people's responses to the film. It reported that half the young people watching the film enjoyed it, while the other half thought the film was immoral.

Cultural contexts

Casablanca

Casablanca's cultural contexts are intertwined with its social and political contexts, as World War II had a profound effect on American society and reignited the war genre. Many Hollywood films were produced to help boost morale, with patriotic films in which ordinary people came together for the common good. In 1942, agencies in the Office of War Information were established to ensure that films contributed to national morale. These agencies reviewed film scripts and produced educational films. Many American filmmakers such as Frank Capra and John Ford were enlisted into the forces and made documentary and propaganda films.

Casablanca inspired numerous homages and parodies, including the Woody Allen film *Play It Again Sam* (1972), whose main character identifies with Rick in *Casablanca*. More recently, *La La Land* (Chazelle, 2016) references *Casablanca* both visually and in its narrative. The final scenes in *La La Land*, where Sebastian encounters Mia in his jazz club, reworks Rick's chance meeting with Ilsa in Rick's bar in *Casablanca*.

La La Land

Bonnie and Clyde

Bonnie and Clyde's scriptwriters, Robert Benton and David Newton, were both fans of the French New Wave and were inspired by the unconventional relationship between the two characters Patricia and Michel in French New Wave film, *À bout de souffle* (*Breathless*) (Godard, 1960). Bonnie's poem, in *Bonnie and Clyde*, copies the exchange of letters between the characters of Jim and Catherine in the New Wave film *Jules et Jim* (Truffaut, 1962).

 S&C

Watch French New Wave film *Jules et Jim* (Truffaut, 1962). Compare the letters exchanged between Jules and Jim and Bonnie's poem in *Bonnie and Clyde*.

Scriptwriters Benton and Newman originally wanted French New Wave director François Truffaut to direct *Bonnie and Clyde*. Although Truffaut liked the script, complications with finances meant he was unable to direct the film. It was star and producer Warren Beatty who said, 'You've already written a French New Wave film. What you need is a good American director' and brought Arthur Penn on board.

Bonnie and Clyde deals with the theme of celebrity, as the film was produced in an age of mass media, where celebrity images were circulated on television and in newspapers and magazines. Bonnie and Clyde were both portrayed in the media as self-publicists. Benton and Newman were influenced by the character of Michel in *À bout de souffle* (*Breathless*), who reads newspaper accounts of his actions.

It was *Time* magazine that, in 1967, heralded in the New Hollywood cinema, putting *Bonnie and Clyde* on the cover with the headline 'The New Cinema: Violence … Sex … Art'.

Institutional contexts

Casablanca

Casablanca is a hybrid of two popular genres produced at Warner Brothers: the film noir and the melodrama. All the key talent who produced the film were on contract at Warner Brothers, including the director, producer and cinematographer (discussed in detail in the auteur section of this chapter), as well as popular actors in major and minor roles.

Bonnie and Clyde reflects the move away from studio control. One of the reasons the film was shot on location in Texas was that executives at Warner Brothers were unable to interfere with the making of the film. Studio head Jack Warner did not like the film when he saw it, calling it 'the longest two hours and ten minutes I ever spent'. Jack Warner sold his share in Warner Brothers a few weeks later, signalling the end of the studio moguls.

Casablanca contains no explicit references to sex and its use of language may seem tame compared with films today. This was because *Casablanca* was produced at a time when the Production Code was in force. The Production Code was a set of moral guidelines, most rigidly applied from 1934 to 1954, which were voluntarily adopted by Hollywood studios as a way to prevent the government from banning or censoring films. The original code was devised under the leadership of Will Hays, president of the Motion Picture Producers and Distributors of America (MPPDA) from 1922 to 1945, and it is therefore sometimes known as the Hays Code.

The code set out a series of rules designed to ensure that films upheld moral standards and 'correct standards of life'. Film scripts were scrutinised by the Production Code Administration (PCA) office. Filmmakers developed clever devices to suggest adult content through careful editing and use of innuendo.

Bonnie and Clyde

Bonnie and Clyde was produced at a time when the PCA was seen as increasingly stuffy and outdated. The explicit scenes of nudity and violence in the film reflect resistance to the PCA. Indeed, just one year after the film's release in 1968, the PCA was disbanded and replaced with a ratings system that is still in use today.

Specialist study area: auteur

The term auteur is the French word for 'author'. The French New Wave critics and filmmakers of the 1950s were keen to establish film as an art form, therefore it was important to ascribe an 'artist' or author to the work of art. These French critics credited certain Hollywood directors of the studio era as auteurs, including Alfred Hitchcock, Orson Welles, Howard Hawks and John Ford. For French critics, these directors were particularly impressive due to their unusual degree of control over their films while working in a studio system.

In 1962, American critic Andrew Sarris expanded the idea of the auteur theory for American audiences in his essay 'Notes on the Auteur Theory'. For Sarris:

> *Over a group of films, a director must exhibit certain recurrent characteristics of style, which serve as his signature.*
> (cited on *The End of Cinema*, 2013)

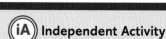

Independent Activity

Research the Production Code in more detail. List the rules Hays put in place.

State how *Casablanca* adheres to the Production Code. Then list the ways in which *Bonnie and Clyde* defies the code.

Director Alfred Hitchcock at work

Sarris also argued that a director must accomplish a high technical competence with a personal style in terms of a film's overall look, feel or meaning.

Later in the 1960s, critics began to question the focus on the director as auteur, as the theory did not always account for the collaborative nature of commercial filmmaking, and the importance of key figures such as the producer and scriptwriter.

However, the notion that the director can be an auteur has not been entirely dismissed. Some directors in Hollywood still have a high degree of control over their films and key trademarks can be established over their body of work. Consider, for instance, the films of Quentin Tarantino and Tim Burton. Also consider their regular collaborations with key personnel; the style of Tarantino's films can be partly ascribed to editor Sally Menke, who, until her death in 2010, edited all his key films. Composer Danny Elfman frequently collaborates with Tim Burton and his notable compositions contribute to the overall aesthetic of Burton's films.

Today, the notion of the auteur is used loosely and expands beyond the director to recognise the collaborative nature of filmmaking, including the influence and contribution of key personnel and talents such as the star, cinematographers and editors. Even studios during the studio era can be given auteur status, as each studio developed a distinct 'house style'.

The specification defines auteur as:

> any contributor who has had an impact on the film. This could be director, star, composer, cinematographer or institution for example.

For your chosen film, consider the contributions of key talent on the film and how key talents leave their 'trademark' on the film.

Applying auteur study to *Casablanca* and *Bonnie and Clyde*

Casablanca

Casablanca is a good example of collaborative filmmaking within a studio system. The film combines the talents of the producer, director, scriptwriters, stars, composers and cinematographer. Chris Tookey (2009) noted that *Casablanca* was

> proof that great films are often made not by auteurs but by collaboration between craftsmen, at uncomfortable speed, within an authoritarian studio system.

Consider the input and trademarks of some of the following key talent on *Casablanca*:

Executive Producer: Jack Warner

Jack Warner entered the film business with his three brothers, Harry, Albert and Samuel, in the early 1900s. By 1923, Warner Brothers was a fully incorporated film company. Jack was critical of the Nazi regime and became fully committed to the war effort. Warners made more films about the war than any other studio. Jack Warner was known as a tough and committed executive producer. Along with his brothers, Jack Warner developed the studio's distinct style.

 Independent Activity

Choose one of the following directors who the French New Wave critics considered to be auteurs working in a Hollywood studio system:

- Alfred Hitchcock
- Orson Welles
- John Ford
- Howard Hawks.

Research the director's work (there are plenty of websites available on each director).

Define the director's distinct style in less than 50 words. Which films are considered to be the director's 'masterpieces'?

Jack Warner

Hal B. Wallis

Michael Curtiz

Arthur Edeson

Max Steiner

Producer: Hal B. Wallis

Wallis was responsible for putting together the budgets and recruiting actors, directors and personnel for each film he produced at Warners. It was Wallis who developed the idea for *Casablanca* by buying the film rights for an unproduced play, *Everybody Comes to Ricks*, for $20,000. He then assigned scriptwriters Julius and Philip Epstein to adapt the play for the screen. He closely supervised the production and editing of *Casablanca*, chose the actors and the director, Michael Curtiz, and even wrote the film's famous final line of dialogue, 'Louis, I think this is the beginning of a beautiful friendship.'

Director: Michael Curtiz

Curtiz was an Austrian émigré who was based at Warners for most of his career. He directed over 100 films for them, including some of their biggest hits. Curtiz was a highly regarded, efficient and accomplished commercial director who could turn his hand to different genres.

Here are just three notable films directed by Curtiz at Warners:

- *The Adventures of Robin Hood* (1938) – an expensive Technicolor swashbuckler.
- *Angels with Dirty Faces* (1938) – a classic gangster film starring James Cagney.
- *Mildred Pierce* (1945) – a film noir melodrama starring Joan Crawford.

Although Curtiz is not usually considered an auteur in the same sense as Hitchcock and Welles, film scholar Sidney Rosenzweig identifies Curtiz' style as:

> *high crane shots to establish a story's environment; unusual camera angles and complex compositions in which characters are often framed by physical objects; much camera movement; subjective shots, in which the camera becomes the character's eye; and high contrast lighting with pools of shadows.* (cited in Leonard, 2014, page 85)

Cinematographer: Arthur Edeson

Arthur Edeson was an acclaimed Hollywood cinematographer. He was contracted to Warners fairly late in his career, from 1936 to 1947. Edeson was adept at the two dominant aesthetics of film: realism and expressionism. His expressionist style can be seen in the cinematography of the classic films *All Quiet on the Western Front* (Milesone, 1930) and *Frankenstein* (Whale, 1931). Edeson was the cinematographer on an earlier Warner Brothers film starring Humphrey Bogart, *The Maltese Falcon* (1941). It is considered by many film critics to be the first film noir, renowned for its low-key lighting and use of shadows. In *Casablanca*, Edeson utilises the expressionistic low-key noir style.

Composer: Max Steiner

Max Steiner was a Vienna-born composer who created Hollywood film scores for over 300 films from the 1930s to the 1960s. He is often referred to as the Godfather of film music. Steiner was influenced by German and Austrian composers and symphonies, particularly Wagner's use of leitmotifs. Steiner created dramatic, memorable scores that matched the themes and characters on the screen. He was able to perfectly synchronise music to the action on screen (a technique known as 'mickey mousing'). The musical scores Steiner composed for over the credits of films were highly dramatic and set the tone for the whole film.

Bonnie and Clyde

New Hollywood films ushered in a new era of auteurs, as power shifted from major studios to young directors and stars. Many key auteurs emerged in American cinema of the late 1960s and continued in the 1970s. Directors such as Woody Allen, Martin Scorsese, Brian De Palma and Robert Altman all made critically acclaimed films during this period.

Screenwriters: David Newman and Robert Benton

Newman and Benton were frequent collaborators. They were both film fans and wrote *Bonnie and Clyde*, their first ever film script, in the style of a French New Wave film.

Director: Arthur Penn

From the 1950s to the 1970s, Arthur Penn directed some of the key artistic films of American cinema. According to the director Paul Schrader,

> *Arthur Penn brought the sensibility of '60s European art films to American movies. He paved the way for the new generation of American directors who came out of film schools.* (Blake, 2010)

Penn favoured on-location shooting with small production teams. Many of his films reveal a fascination with American myths and culture, classic American genres and feature characters who are 'outsiders'.

The following are three of Penn's most critically acclaimed films:
- *The Left Handed Gun* (1958) – Penn's directorial debut, re-telling the story of Billy the Kid.
- *Mickey One* (1965) – a surreal film influenced by the French New Wave.
- *Night Moves* (1975) – a neo-noir that reflects the cynicism of mid-1970s America.

Editor: Dede Allen

Allen pioneered the use of jump-cuts and audio overlaps in Hollywood cinema. She often worked in New York and was given relative freedom when editing films. Indeed, her style became known as the 'New York School of Editing'. Allen trained a number of editors in her style. For Allen,

> [The 1960s] *was a very rich period for New York. There was a vitality and an independence in being away from the studios.* (LoBrutto, 1991 page 78)

Producer and lead actor: Warren Beatty

Beatty was only 29 years old when he produced and acted in *Bonnie and Clyde*. According to Robert Benton, Warren Beatty was a key influence on the film. It was Beatty who hired Newman and Benton, selected most of the cast and oversaw the script development. Beatty's involvement reflects the trend in New Hollywood of star-auteurs. Other key stars of the period, including Robert Redford and Jack Nicholson, directed and produced films.

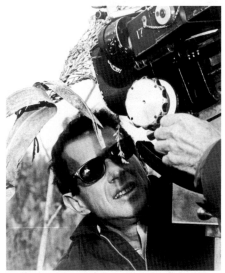

Arthur Penn

 Independent Activity

Watch two Arthur Penn films produced between 1958 and 1975. Note any similarities in the films' visual styles, structures and themes to *Bonnie and Clyde*.

 Independent Activity

Consider three key talents' input on *Casablanca* and three on *Bonnie and Clyde*. Make a list of where each key talent's trademark is most evident in each film.

Independent study questions

(Q) How do your two Hollywood films reflect their different social, cultural and political contexts?

(Q) To what extent is the director the auteur of your two Hollywood films?

(Q) What were the factors that led to a period of experimentation in Hollywood films in the late 1960s?

(Q) How are your two chosen Hollywood films' visual style shaped by their production and institutional contexts?

(Q) To what extent do your two chosen Hollywood films reflect attitudes to gender within American society at the time they were made?

(Q) How far do your two chosen Hollywood films engage directly with political issues or events?

(Q) To what extent were New Hollywood films a break from Classical Hollywood films?

Sample essay extract and feedback

How far do your two chosen Hollywood films engage directly with political issues or events? Compare your chosen Classical Hollywood film and New Hollywood film and refer to key sequences to illustrate your points.

For this example, we are looking at **extracts** from essays addressing *Casablanca* and *Bonnie and Clyde*.

Alex's response extract

The character of Rick (Humphrey Bogart) in *Casablanca* is the personification of US foreign policy and America's changing attitudes to the war. When we first meet Rick in his bar, he is presented as a solitary figure. This is illustrated through the mise-en-scène, as he plays chess alone and the low-key lighting that reflects his cynicism. His isolationist stance is reflected in his dialogue, 'I stick my neck out for nobody'.

The sequence where characters sing their national anthems in Rick's bar directly engages with the defiance of the resistance to Nazi rule. Rick's small gesture of a nod to the band to allow them to play 'La Marseillaise', the French anthem, is a turning point for Rick as he is now involved in the war effort. When the anthem is being sung, the camera cuts to a close-up on French character Yvonne, with tears streaming down her face. This close-up reflects the sacrifice and impact of Nazi occupation on the French people.

Feedback

Alex answers the question with detailed reference to the film. He uses film language and links specific sequences to the film's wider political contexts.

Alex discusses this sequence in relation to Casablanca's political messages. He refers to the sequence in detail with use of film language.

Alex has a good understanding of the emotional impact of 'La Marseillaise' and the significance of the song.

To a certain extent, *Casablanca* can be viewed as a propaganda film masquerading as entertainment. During the war, studios engaged with the war effort and films were seen as a way to boost morale, with patriotic messages of ordinary Americans coming together for the war effort. Indeed, Warners in particular were committed to the war effort, as studio head Jack Warner was anti-Nazi. *Casablanca* reflects the ethos of the studios and Warners at the time. In the final sequence of *Casablanca*, Rick fully commits to the war effort and puts himself at personal risk to ensure Laszlo and Ilsa's safe passage out of Morocco. This is emphasised in the dialogue 'This is the beginning of a beautiful friendship', as Rick joins forces with Renault. Renault's abandonment of the Vichy government who supported the Nazi occupation of France is depicted symbolically through the mise-en-scène, as Renault throws a bottle of Vichy water in the bin and kicks it.

Alex applies contextual knowledge. He is able to discuss Casablanca *within its broader institutional context.*

Alex provides good detail from the film to illustrate his points and demonstrates how mise-en-scène is used symbolically to convey political messages.

Political events and issues also affected the messages and style of *Bonnie and Clyde*. The final sequence is a graphic depiction of violence, made possible, according to Arthur Penn, because people were so used to seeing violent images of the Vietnam War on the television news. Clyde is also shot in the back of the head, with realistic special effects and use of vivid red to heighten the scene. This is a reference to the assassination of President Kennedy. However, many audience members may not have gotten these references; therefore political references in *Bonnie and Clyde* are more covert than the overt references in *Casablanca*.

Alex contrasts Bonnie and Clyde *with* Casablanca *well here. He links contextual knowledge well with specific examples from* Bonnie and Clyde. *Alex is aware that spectators read films in different ways, as not all audiences at the time would pick up on indirect political references.*

The characters of *Bonnie and Clyde* reflect the new counterculture movements, as young people in the US questioned the established order and defied authority. This is evident in the sequence where Bonnie kisses a law enforcement officer, an anti-authoritarian statement.

Overall, *Casablanca* directly engages with political issues, as the film deals with the events and fates of nations leading up to the invasion of Pearl Harbor on 7 December 1942. In contrast, *Bonnie and Clyde* indirectly refers to political events of the 1960s such as the Vietnam War in the film's overall style and themes.

Alex provides a valid concluding statement, comparing and contrasting the two films.

Overall, Alex's extracts use detailed examples to illustrate key points and demonstrate a good understanding of the political messages of the films.

This chapter will help you prepare for Component 1: Varieties of film and filmmaking on the A level course. Alongside the core areas of study you will need to apply the specialist study areas of **spectatorship** and **ideology**. This section will use *La La Land* (Chazelle, 2016) as a case study.

For A level

One question from a choice of two must be answered on the Component 1 paper. For this question you would be expected to write about one film from Group 1: Mainstream film and one from Group 2: Contemporary independent film with no expectation that the films be compared in your response. The full question is worth 40 points and should be allocated 50 minutes.

The specification says

La La Land is a throwback to an earlier era of Hollywood filmmaking as well as an original, highly stylised take on the musical romance – a love story involving a musician and an aspiring actress.

La La Land (2016) built on Damien Chazelle's success with *Whiplash* (2014) and like that film has the niche culture of jazz at its core. This film is arguably unusual for a contemporary mainstream American film, as the genre, a musical, harks back to Hollywood's golden age. The film's style boldly incorporates an eclectic mix of homage and expressionistic moments into its more conventional romantic narrative. Still, as a heterosexual romance, the film does in some ways typify contemporary Hollywood output. The film also had a reasonably large budget, two established, attractive, young stars and explored the populist theme of the American dream – factors that help place it in the mainstream.

This section will explore the film's form and aesthetic in detail, consider the representations featured, investigate the film's context, introduce the concept of spectatorship and apply a feminist approach to considering the film's key ideological messages.

Contemporary Hollywood

The US media is often perceived as an industry ruled by six dominant entertainment conglomerates, which have film as just one of their areas of production. These are, according to Business Insider UK (Lutz, 2012):

- CBS
- News-Corp
- Disney
- Viacom
- GE
- Time Warner.

From 1983 to the present day, a series of mergers and takeovers took place that created these six conglomerates from 50 smaller companies. The era of New Hollywood, where production, at least, was diversified to include many independent companies, is well and truly over. These **conglomerates** are arguably both vertically and horizontally integrated, that is they own production houses, distribution companies and cinema chains, plus publishing

> Conglomerate: a company that owns and controls a diverse range of other businesses.

houses, record companies and television stations, along with other concerns. This enables them to produce, distribute and exhibit their own products and gain additional profit from merchandising and soundtrack releases among other streams of revenue. However, this still marks a shift from the monopolies of the golden age of Hollywood. The main difference is the autonomy of the 'creatives' as writers, directors, stars and other filmmaking personnel is no longer routinely tied to one company and locked into long-term contracts.

If you examine the top ten box office successes of 2016 you will see that these global concerns are responsible for the films with the biggest budgets and the highest grosses. The biggest success story of 2016, the year *La La Land* was released, was the $200 million production *Rogue One: A Star Wars Story*, which took over $530 million at the US box office alone, according to boxofficemojo.com (2016a). This would have been added to substantially by worldwide sales and merchandising, making a tremendous profit for Disney and the other major production companies and distributors involved.

However, *La La Land* was produced for just $30 million by Summit Entertainment, a subsidiary of Lionsgate, which also acted as the US and UK distributor for the film. Lionsgate had previously distributed very successful franchises such as *Saw* and *The Hunger Games*. The question arises, then, is this inventive musical really a product of mainstream Hollywood at all? It owes nothing to the conglomerates that dominate the industry and is instead fundamentally a passion project from a relatively new filmmaker. The story of how the film was produced sheds some light on this.

Institutional context

Matt Mueller at ScreenDaily.com (2016) provides great insight into how *La La Land* came to be produced in the article 'How Damien Chazelle Made "*La La Land*" for just $30m'. He writes of how Chazelle and composer Hurwitz, college roommates from Harvard, wrote the script and the score for this film, before 2014's *Whiplash*. The latter was a phenomenal success for a $3.3 million indie film. Its success was even more astonishing as it featured no major stars and had an unconventional theme – jazz drumming. It took the typical independent film route from short to feature via the festival circuit with the help of smaller companies Bold Films, Blumhouse Productions and Right of Way Films, and went on to be a commercial and critical success. It took over $13 million at the US box office and won three Oscars and the Grand Jury prize at the Sundance Film Festival. Chazelle explains,

> *I made* Whiplash *in order to make* La La Land, *so as soon as the doors opened even an inch, we were charging right in with this script.*
> (Mueller, 2016)

In 2010 Chazelle pitched *La La Land* to New York indie film producers Fred Berger and Jordan Horowitz. They admired the ambition and determination to try and produce a film that was, according to Berger, 'essentially impossible in the mould of Hollywood financing' (Mueller, 2016). This suggests that the film was considered a risky proposition for a mainstream production, as the musical genre does not have a secure and established audience in the present day.

However, the script was optioned in 2011 by Focus Features, a subsidiary of NBC Universal (Comcast), songs were written and pre-production started. Unfortunately, Focus Features pulled out of the project at this stage, clearing the way for Lionsgate to step in following Chazelle's triumph with *Whiplash* in 2014. According to boxofficemojo.com (2016b), in 2016 Lionsgate's revenue

Whiplash (Chazelle, 2014)

of $665 million gave it a 5.8% share of the US box office, so *La La Land* was certainly produced and distributed by a major Hollywood studio. The film was shot in just 42 days on location in Los Angeles and Lionsgate gave Chazelle and his team the artistic freedom to make the film they wanted. In some ways, this nostalgic genre film had the backing of a big studio not dissimilar to films produced in Hollywood's golden age. In addition, Chazelle had similar levels of autonomy as directors in New Hollywood. He is an auteur, ex-film student director and shot the film on location, both of which were common characteristics of New Hollywood films. *La La Land* was, in effect, afforded the best of both worlds.

Social, cultural and political context

It has been argued that *La La Land* was released at a time in which America was craving escapism. The musical genre is by nature far removed from reality. Musicals are often vibrantly coloured and include distracting song and dance numbers and themes of romance. Movie musicals reached the height of their popularity in the 1940s, when audiences flocked to the cinemas to escape the all too real tragedies of a world at war. *La La Land* is certainly nostalgic, looking back fondly to the early days of jazz in its score and themes, and to the golden age of Hollywood and 1960s European cinema in its **intertextual** references to classic musicals. This would prove to be very appealing to an America looking to the past with affection.

Geoff Nelson's (2017) article on pastemagazine.com reported on a poll taken just before Trump's election in 2016. The poll found that 52% of all Americans felt life was better in the 1950s, and 72% of Trump voters believed this was true. Cas Mudde at *Newsweek* (2016) calls this a politics of nostalgia and argues that the UK is similarly affected:

> From Nigel Farage's 'We want our country back' in the British EU referendum to Donald Trump's 'Make America Great Again' in the US presidential elections, the emphasis was on a glorious past, sold as the blueprint of a magnificent future.

An alternative perspective on why the film's release was perfectly timed is that cinemagoers were hoping to escape from the turbulence, fear and instability of Trump's America. The title of John Patterson's (2017) review of the film in the *Guardian* certainly suggests this:

> La La Land: *Why this Magical Musical Will Transport You From Trump-World.*

Either way, in 2016 a lot of potential moviegoers were looking at the past with affection.

It is often reported that *La La Land* pays homage to, or borrows from, numerous classic musicals but it is worth noting that the film's more recent cultural context also points to some contemporary trends and possible inspirations.

Since 2010, a number of Best Picture winners and nominees at the Academy Awards have traits in common with *La La Land*. Consider 2011's winner *The Artist* (Hazanavicius, 2011), which harks back to the era of silent film in its themes and use of black and white cinematography, or 2014's winner *Birdman* (Iñárritu, 2014), which has a soundtrack dominated by jazz drumming. *Birdman* also has stylistic similarities with *La La Land* in its use of long takes, a trait

 Independent Activity

Read the film's 'Production Notes' online for detailed insight into the making of the film and insight into the key personnel (Summit Entertainment, 2016).

Intertextual: the practice of one media text paying homage to or referencing another. An example would be Sebastian in *La La Land* swinging around a lamppost like Gene Kelly's character Don in *Singin' in the Rain* (Kelly & Donen, 1952).

S&C

Read and summarise Cas Mudde's (2016) *Newsweek* article 'Can We Stop the Politics of Nostalgia that Have Dominated 2016?' on Newsweek.com.

The Artist (Hazanavicius, 2011)

also shared with Best Picture nominee *Gravity* (Cuarón, 2013). These films are bucking the trend as 'the average shot length of English language films has declined from about 12 seconds in 1930 to about 2.5 seconds today' according to James Cutting, a psychologist at Cornell University, in an interview with Greg Miller (2014).

Although Chazelle conceived of *La La Land* before these films were released, aspects of their style may have had some influence on the final film.

Film form in mainstream cinema

Just as Classical Hollywood largely adhered to linear narratives and continuity editing and New Hollywood sought to break out of these rigid structures and incorporate art film techniques inspired by European filmmakers, there is a range of techniques and styles favoured by contemporary American mainstream filmmakers. The **tentpole** releases of most of the conglomerates of contemporary Hollywood in recent years have been **high-concept**, fast-paced, large budget spectacles, often in the fantasy or action genres, with broad family appeal. Contemporary Hollywood invests heavily in production, special effects and marketing to maximise the chance of garnering massive profits. This can lead to an over-reliance on genre films and very few risks being taken.

When considering film form, it could be argued that contemporary Hollywood films can no longer be analysed in isolation from their intertextual references and that the way that audiences consume media – absorbing special features, repeating viewings and the variety of formats available – will impact upon their responses.

Cinematography

The film is shot in widescreen and is presented in the 2:55:1 CinemaScope ratio: a popular form between 1953 and 1967 but rarely used today. This contributes to the nostalgia of the film and is set up from the film's titles, which start with a boxy black and white Summit logo before the screen visibly widens to reveal the famous CinemaScope logo in glorious colour.

Maintaining the nostalgia, Chazelle and the film's cinematographer, Linus Sandgren, filmed the musical numbers in a style that pays tribute to musicals from Hollywood's golden age. The song and dance scenes are designed to look like they are filmed in single takes, as this is how such scenes would have been filmed on the vast soundstages of classical Hollywood. To achieve this on more difficult location shoots, Sandgren utilised numerous ambitious and innovative techniques, but eventually he had to incorporate some cuts. These were cleverly hidden with whip pans to create the illusion of a single shot. The film's opening sequence, 'Another Day of Sun', is a clear example of the complexity of this shoot, as it involved the EZ-Pass ramp, which links two of Los Angeles' major freeways, being closed for the whole of a busy August weekend. This demonstrates the ambition and scale of a contemporary Hollywood mainstream production, as location shoots of this nature would not be viable for low-budget, independent filmmakers.

The complexity of the camera movements in the film's musical sequences, a variety of panning and tracking shots, take the audience right into the action and make the film more immersive. The audience are invited to be part of the dance. In an interview with IndieWire, Sandgren told Chris O'Falt (2017a) that the music had a huge impact on the film's cinematography:

(▷) **S&C**

Watch *The Artist* and consider the parallels the narrative has with *La La Land*.

Tentpole: a movie with a massive budget deemed by the studio to carry less financial risk. It will be marketed heavily and given an extended saturation release. Its revenue is intended to help financially support the other films released by the studio.

High concept: films centred on a relatively simple scenario that can be easily pitched with a succinctly stated premise.

> *the camera and its movement really were like an instrument working with music and actors dancing.*

The 'dance' of the cameras on this production, stopping and starting and pushing into the action on the beat, adds a rhythm to the sequences that makes some cuts, often used to give a scene pace and tempo, unnecessary.

Another example of complex cinematography is the 'Someone in the Crowd' musical number, where Mia is persuaded to go to a Hollywood party by her flatmates. The camera follows the women dancing, first separately and then in unison. The shoot was proving to be difficult, so a wall with a double archway was built between rooms allowing Mia to go through one archway and the camera through the other. This is another aspect of creative cinematography made possible through a reasonably large budget.

Outside the immersive long take musical sequences, the film has more realistic scenes where the narrative follows the fluctuations in Sebastian's and Mia's careers and relationship. These sections are generally filmed in a more conventional way but lighting is frequently used to draw the spectator's attention to a particular character and black out the rest of the scene. Sandgren told IndieWire (O'Falt, 2017a) that to create this intimacy,

> *we move in and spot them up, which was also a metaphor for their dreams of being in the spotlight and performing.*

 S&C

Read '*La La Land*'s Many References to Classic Movies: A Guide' by Aisha Harris (2016) on slate.com then watch the song and dance numbers from at least two of the films she references. Compare the cinematography of them to the opening scene of *La La Land*.

 Independent Activity

Read Chris O'Falt's (2017a) 'How *La La Land* Cinematographer Linus Sandgren Taught His Cameras to Dance' on IndieWire.com for a more detailed analysis of the film's cinematography.

Mise-en-scène

The backdrop of Los Angeles is crucial to this film and is one of the allusions of the film's title. *La La Land* is a nickname given to Hollywood that conveys its appeal to dreamers, those aspiring to stardom and immortality. The film includes iconic locations such as the Griffith Observatory, which featured in Nicholas Ray's 1955 film *Rebel Without a Cause*, and the famous 'You are the Star' mural, featuring numerous instantly recognisable faces from Hollywood's golden age, painted by Thomas Suriya in 1983. These visual references evoke Hollywood's rich and glamorous history and reward spectators' prior knowledge of film culture.

If the images of LA featured in the film are examined closely, an eclectic mix of old and new is seen, offering the city an almost timeless quality that reflects some of the themes of the film. Sebastian is a character looking back fondly to the early days of jazz, and this nostalgia is reflected in the car he drives and the clothes he wears. He drives a 1982 Buick Rivera and he is styled after the character Roland in Jacques Demy's 1961 film *Lola*. Mia, however, has one foot in the past, seen by her huge Ingrid Bergman poster and wardrobe inspired by the costumes of Bergman, Judy Garland and Ginger Rogers, but is moving with the times, driving a Prius, which Sebastian implies is driven by most people in modern LA.

 Independent Activity

Consider the image of Mia below, juxtaposed with that of Bergman. What does it suggest about her character at this point in the narrative?

 S&C

Read Julie Miller's (2017a) article for *Vanity Fair*, 'Emma Stone and Ryan Gosling's *La La Land* Costumes Were Inspired by These Old Hollywood Stars', and create a collage of images of the stars she references and the lead characters in *La La Land* to compare their looks.

Independent Activity

Read 'Never Shined So Brightly: The Use of Color in *La La Land*' by Zosha Millman (2017) on filmschoolrejects.com for an interpretation of the use of colour in the film.

Use of colour in *La La Land* is an aspect of the mise-en-scène that has been written about extensively and, from the film's vibrant opening sequence featuring dancers sporting simple costumes with blocks of bright colour, it is easy to see why it has attracted attention.

Numerous locations in the film were repainted or dramatically lit to create a stimulating, colourful, unreal world. Part of the reason for this was to make the transitions between the colourful musical sequences and scenes of everyday life less jarring. Mary Zophres, the film's costume designer, spoke to the *Los Angeles Times* about the film's expressionistic use of colour:

> *There's this arc in the movie and it has to peak at the planetarium and it comes down from there after they have their dating montage. So the color sort of gets removed because it's an expression of their romantic emotion in the film – it dissipates until [Mia, Emma Stone's character] is literally wearing black and white at her one-woman show.* (Ordona, 2017)

Editing

Tom Cross, the film's editor, and Chazelle had a very experimental approach to putting the film together, and the editing process was consequently lengthy and involved. The finished film has two distinct editing styles: dreamlike musical sequences consisting of extended takes with limited cuts; and the more realistic everyday life scenes comprising shorter takes with a much faster-paced edit. Striking the balance between these two styles was the greatest challenge for the filmmakers. Chazelle told Chris O'Falt (2017b) on IndieWire that,

> La La Land *is trying to straddle two different tones and find a happy medium.*

He explains further,

> *the musical scenes are like breaths, the movie exhales and becomes wider, so sometimes you want to build up a certain amount of claustrophobia especially in the realistic section of the movie.*

Two useful scenes to compare when considering the film's editing are the opening freeway sequence and the dinner scene. The opening demonstrates how spectacular and immersive the long take can be. The sequence works to establish the film as a musical from the outset and as Cross told the *Hollywood Reporter,*

> *the final touch was when we put the title of the film on the last downbeat of the musical number, so it kind of separated that number from the rest of the movie in a way that felt like an overture.* (Giardina, 2016)

Tom Cross

(iA) Independent Activity

Choose two three-minute sequences from the film: one musical number and a more realistic sequence. Compare the editing.

Overtures, pieces of music used at the beginning of films to set the tone, are a staple of musicals with notable examples being *South Pacific* (Logan, 1958), *West Side Story* (Wise & Robbins, 1961) and *Sweet Charity* (Fosse, 1969). So, as well as establishing a location, introducing our protagonists and setting the film's mood, the overture places the film in a long line of classic films in the musical genre.

S&C

Listen to the podcast featuring Chazelle and the film's editor Tom Cross discussing their process and make notes about it. The podcast is available on IndieWire (O'Falt, 2017b).

The dinner scene, in contrast, illustrates perfectly how faster cuts can help ramp up the tension and convey to the audience the conflict arising in the relationship. The editing technique used was referred to by Chazelle as 'a staccato cutting pattern' (O'Falt, 2017b) that incorporated a series of short take close-ups creating a claustrophobic stilted atmosphere. As the conversation becomes more strained, the camera moves in from over-the-shoulder shots, with them both in the frame, to close-ups isolating them from each other and capturing their escalating emotions. The only cutaway in the scene, the record reaching the end, could be read as symbolic of their relationship declining. The diegetic music from the record stopping, leaving silence, contributes to this heightening of tension.

Sound

As stated earlier, Chazelle worked closely with Justin Wurwitz, the score composer, from the film's inception. They previously collaborated on Chazelle's earlier films, jazz musical *Guy and Madeline on a Park Bench* (2009) and *Whiplash*. Their biggest challenge in creating the multifaceted soundtrack for the film was creating music that sounded timeless enough to evoke the classic musical but also captured wide-ranging emotions, as the film is about complex characters experiencing love, heartbreak, joy and disappointment.

The music and lyrics reveal an awful lot about the characters. Sebastian is seen performing a range of different musical styles, from the jazz he loves to banal 1980s pop covers. Ryan Gosling spent three months learning to play piano for the role, his quest for authenticity was not dissimilar to Sebastian's jazz preservationist ideals. The range of music he has to play contributes to the film's love affair with the past as the traditional music is celebrated and commercial pop derided. Consider Mia's dance at the 1980s party and the dancers who take to the stage at The Messengers' concert as evidence of this.

This could be read as a précis of the film's core ideology: those who take risks in pursuit of their dreams should be commended and rewarded.

iA **Independent Activity**

Listen to the film's soundtrack and consider the lyrics of the songs 'City of Stars' and 'Someone in the Crowd'. Note what they bring to your understanding of the characters.

Mia's performances equally contribute to the film's messages as the song 'Audition (The Fools who Dream)' includes the lyrics,

> Here's to the ones who dream,
> Foolish as they may seem,
> Here's to the hearts that ache,
> Here's to the mess we make.

This could be read as a précis of the film's core ideology, those who take risks in pursuit of their dreams should be commended and rewarded. The music is not the only aspect of sound required to make the film feel like an authentic classic Hollywood musical. Sound editor Ai-Ling Lee explained to Deadline that,

> *in the duet scene, when Mia and Sebastian were dancing … we had [choreographer] Mandy Moore come in with her dancer to redo the dance feet … we tried many different kinds of shoes and surfaces to get the classic Fred and Ginger sound.* (Grobar, 2017)

iA **Independent Activity**

Read Matt Grobar's (2017) article 'From "Boogie Nights" to "Mean Streets"' to discover more about the process of recording sound for *La La Land*.

Performance

The lead roles in *La La Land* presented an extra challenge for casting as the actors had to be able to sing and dance, and, as Chazelle told *Variety*,

> *those worlds don't overlap as much as they used to.* (McNary, 2017)

Chazelle also wanted the singing to be conversational:

> *It had to feel like singing but not singing. We were working on that all the way into the last days of mix.* (McNary, 2017)

Crazy, Stupid Love (Ficarra & Requa, 2011)

To Have and Have Not (Hawks, 1944)

 S&C

Watch Mia's first audition sequence and note how the cinematography encourages the audience to focus on aspects of performance. List the techniques used.

 Independent Activity

Watch two scenes of Sebastian playing piano or keyboard, one of him playing the jazz he loves and another of him playing commercial pop music. Make notes on body language and facial expression, and how these convey the character's feelings in these scenes.

 S&C

Watch and take notes from the *Vanity Fair* video 'La La Land's Choreographer Explains the Freeway Dance Scene' available on YouTube.

Achieving this is key to the performances in the film feeling naturalistic and authentic within the highly artificial genre of a musical. Part of the verisimilitude comes from the genuine palpable connection and affection between the lead actors. Emma Stone and Ryan Gosling appear on screen together for a third time in this film, having co-starred in *Crazy, Stupid, Love* (Ficarra & Requa, 2011) and *Gangster Squad* (Fleischer, 2013). Producer Fred Berger stated to ScreenDaily that,

> *no degree of masterful craftsmanship can create the emotion and chemistry that Ryan and Emma bring. They're legitimately the beating heart of the movie.* (Mueller, 2016)

This on-screen chemistry between stars is an indefinable yet powerful pull to audiences and has been since the heyday of Hollywood when fans would flock to see Bogart and Bacall or Tracy and Hepburn sizzle on screen.

Emma Stone won the Academy Award and Screen Actors Guild award for Best Actress for her role in *La La Land*; in both ceremonies the clip used to demonstrate her skill is the sequence in which Sebastian turns up at her family home to persuade her to go back to LA and audition for the film role that launches her career. Analysis of this sequence points to some of her strengths as an actress, as Stone's extraordinarily expressive face and large eyes display emotion clearly. Another useful sequence for exploring this is Mia's first audition scene in the film.

As a musical, the range of performance is more varied than in films from other genres. Alongside acting, time should be spent considering the styles of dance seen and the genres of the music performed and how these impact on delivery.

Aesthetics

As explored earlier, a crucial part of *La La Land*'s aesthetic is its combination of old and new. Chazelle told ScreenDaily:

> *I wanted to see what would happen if I pasted these MGM musicals onto a modern landscape with modern characters going through a life where the dreams don't always match up to the old movies.* (Mueller, 2016)

One key inspiration was Jacques Demy, whose 1964 film *The Umbrellas of Cherbourg* was described by Chazelle as the 'most perfect in form that I know' (DW, 2017). This was just one of the films screened by Chazelle for the cast and crew to help convey his desired aesthetic, others included Hollywood classics *Top Hat* (Sandrich, 1935) and *Singin' in the Rain*.

Alongside film, art was an influence on the overall look of *La La Land*. In the *New York Times* article 'LA Transcendental: How *La La Land* Chases the Sublime', Mekado Murphy (2016) comments on the film's lighting saying of the Griffith Observatory scenes that,

> *Chazelle captured both the building and the city in a painterly way, calling to mind the art of Edward Hopper.*

This observation is extended by Dave Calhoun in *Time Out* (2016), applying it to the film as a whole and incorporating a reference to the director of *The Umbrellas of Cherbourg* (Demy, 1996),

> *The look of Los Angeles in* La La Land *could be called Demy meets Edward Hopper: all pastels, soft light, twilight and street lamps.*

Chazelle describes the processes used to achieve this aesthetic in the *New York Times* (Murphy, 2016) speaking of the decision to,

> *use real LA, do things in-camera without digital effects, but try to find those moments where real life looks as fake as possible.*

 Independent Activity

Read Julie Miller's article for *Vanity Fair*, 'The Clever Tricks that Made *La La Land* Look Technicolor and Timeless' (2017b), to gain insight into the film's production design, a key part of its aesthetic.

 S&C

Read the complete *New York Times* article 'LA Transcendental: How *La La Land* Chases the Sublime' by Mekado Murphy (2016) and use the films and artists referenced to create a mood board for *La La Land*.

 Independent Activity

Find three frames from the film that have a similar tone and atmosphere to Hopper's painting 'Nighthawks' (below). List the techniques used to create this mood.

Edward Hopper, 'Nighthawks' (1942)

Billy Stevenson (2017), on the Senses of Cinema website, points to other inspirations suggesting the shots used in the film,

> resemble the kind of hyper-cinematic stylisation pioneered by artists like Jeff Wall and Gregory Crewdson.

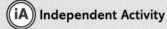

Independent Activity

Consider the images on the right and note the similarities and differences in composition, use of colour, lighting and tone.

Gregory Crewsdon, 'Untitled' (2004)

Jeff Wall, 'The Pine on the Corner' (1990)

Frame from *La La Land*

There is a notable section of the film, the epilogue, with a very different expressionistic aesthetic when the spectator is shown what might have occurred if the couple had travelled to Paris together. These sequences evoke films such as *An American in Paris* (Minelli, 1951) and break from the relative realism seen earlier in the film by using imaginative theatrical sets and inventive techniques.

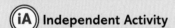

Independent Activity

Re-watch the epilogue and examine in particular the images on the right and below. Consider them in relation to the aesthetic of the rest of the film. What impact do you think the combination of such different styles has on your response to the narrative?

Sound contributes to a film's overall aesthetic and Chazelle had a clear concept of how he wanted the city of LA to sound. He gave the sound editors film references of *Mean Streets* (Scorsese, 1973) and *Boogie Nights* (Anderson, 1997) to inspire them to capture the bustling ambient sounds of a major city.

Representations

Contemporary Hollywood still has a long way to go with regards to the depiction of diverse social groups as explored in the Representation section of this book. To summarise,

> *White, straight, able-bodied men remain the norm on screen in film.* (USC, 2017)

This is particularly pertinent for this module as the films considered in the USC research that provided these findings were from the mainstream. In fact, *La La Land* was one of the films analysed. A lack of diversity among those behind the camera is a contributing factor to this problem, which is still persisting in contemporary Hollywood. In 2014, film producer and writer Stephen Follows discovered that:

> *Women make up only 23% of crew members on the 2,000 highest grossing films of the past 20 years.*

Age

The ages of the two lead characters in *La La Land* are relevant to the narrative in that they are both experiencing something of a crisis with regards to their careers, which could exacerbated by their ages. Mia, the barista who wants to be a movie star, and Sebastian, the jazz purist who wants to run his own club but can't hold down a steady job, are torn between their dreams and the reality of making a living. Mia confronts this when trying to talk her way out of returning to LA for the audition that launches her career, 'you change your dreams and then you grow up'.

She responds to Sebastian's accusations that she is a baby by saying, 'I'm not a baby, I'm trying to grow up.' This notion of 'growing up' and facing reality is central to the film and can be seen again in their argument over dinner about Sebastian's commitments with The Messengers. He says, 'this is what you wanted from me' and clarifies, 'to be in a band to have a steady job'. He tries to justify his decision to sacrifice his artistic integrity in favour of a steady income by stating, 'it's time to grow up'.

The ages of the characters and their stages in life changed from the original screenplay and initial casting of Emma Watson and Miles Teller as the leads. As Matt Mueller wrote in Screen-Daily (2016):

> *Mia became a struggling actress rather than someone just off the bus, while Sebastian acquired a more jaded perspective as a musician attempting to keep bitterness at bay.*

Casting slightly older actors contributes a little more urgency to the characters' dreams and ambitions that shapes the film's narrative.

(iA) Independent Activity

Choose a scene set in a busy city street from *La La Land*, *Mean Streets* and *Boogie Nights*, and compare the sounds used to convey the pace and atmosphere of an urban location.

Emma Watson

Miles Teller

Gender

Critics of the gender representation in this film have suggested that Mia is quite a passive character and that her key decisions and actions are motivated by Sebastian. There is certainly evidence to support this perspective on the film, as it is Sebastian that comes to find Mia at work after their first meeting and he is instrumental in persuading her to put on her one-woman show, and he attends the audition that launches her career. Mia is also shown as an audience member at many of Sebastian's performances, passively watching him actively performing.

The counter-argument to this is that Mia leads this narrative as the audience is placed with her for the first few scenes and it is arguably Mia who achieves the most success by the end. This argument is explored in more depth later in this section, when a feminist ideological reading of the film is offered.

Sebastian's sense of masculinity is a key feature of the film and his insecurity about it motivates some of the decisions he makes. It can be seen in the brief standoff he has with Bill, his employer at the restaurant, which sees Sebastian capitulate as he soon realises that he has no power in the negotiation because he needs the job. The following dialogue reveals how much Sebastian needs to cling to a sense of autonomy:

> SEBASTIAN
> I thought in this town it worked on a sort of one for you, one for me type system. How about two for you one for me? How about all for you and none for me? That's perfect yes.
>
> BILL
> Great, ok mutual decision then.
>
> SEBASTIAN
> Right, made by me.
>
> BILL
> Right, and I sign off on it
>
> SEBASTIAN
> Whatever, tell yourself what you wanna know.

The staging in this scene contributes to the sense of power imbalance, as Sebastian is seated throughout and Bill stands over him.

The scene is echoed later at the party where Sebastian and Mia meet, as he says of the singer in his 1980s cover band, 'he doesn't tell me what to do'. Mia replies, 'he just told you what to do', to which he rather pathetically argues, 'I know I let him'. In these examples Sebastian's sense of emasculation is used largely for comic effect but it has more serious implications in the narrative when it becomes clear that he takes the sell-out job that compromises his artistic integrity, playing keyboard for The Messengers, to satisfy the traditionally masculine breadwinner role that he mistakenly thinks Mia wants him to adopt.

Ethnicity

A more problematic aspect of the nostalgic appeal of the film, explored earlier in the political context section, is, according to some critics, its under-representation of characters from ethnic minority groups. Samuel Earle (2017) on Jacobinmag.com explores this trend for looking to the past as follows:

> Throughout the advanced capitalist world and beyond, a xenophobic, nostalgic nationalism is taking shape. A flock of old and new leaders are rising up, declaring that our best days are behind us and that they are the most qualified to build a better yesterday. Forget about the future, they say, the past is now the place to be – but not everyone is invited.

He reiterates this later in the article stating,

> To turn back the clock, others must be turned out.

The others, in some criticisms of *La La Land*, are the significant African-American and Hispanic populations of Los Angeles that it has been claimed are under-represented in the film. The film's opening sequence includes a diverse cast and minority characters can be seen throughout the film but these are predominantly peripheral characters who play no real role in the narrative.

The only major role for a black actor is John Legend's role as Keith, the lead singer of The Messengers. His portrayal could also elicit some criticism as he is shown to have sold out the authentic soul of jazz music, undeniably music of black origin, to play commercially successful pop music instead. It is left to the white male lead, Sebastian, to try and save pure jazz.

S&C

Read Billy Stevenson's (2017) article 'From Los Angeles to *La La Land*: Mapping Whiteness in the Wake of Cinema' on sensesofcinema.com to explore these ideas in more depth.

Independent Activity

Read the 'Establishing Shots: *La La Land*' (n.d.) article about the film's opening sequence, on the Lensflare Theory website, for further insight into both film form and the debates around the film's representations of LA's ethnic diversity.

S&C

Summarise the chapter on spectatorship in Jill Nelmes' *Introduction to Film Studies* (2011) in 500 words or less.

Independent Activity

After watching your focus film all the way through once, uninterrupted, note the memorable moments or scenes and consider which character you identified with the most at those moments. Then re-watch the film paying particular attention to your memorable scenes and analyse the techniques the filmmaker used to create an impact on spectators and encourage them to identify with a particular character.

S&C

Construct a diagram with the film at the centre. On one side list the techniques a filmmaker may use to try and elicit a particular response. On the opposite side list the factors about individual spectators which may impact upon their response.

The jazz club scenes do feature a lot of black performers and black people dancing in the crowd but invariably the camera and the lighting direct the audience's attention to our leads, Sebastian and Mia, thereby marginalising those of other ethnicities.

Spectatorship

For both the AS and A-level exams spectatorship is a specialist subject area for contemporary American film. Spectatorship is the study of how individuals view and respond to films, and includes an examination of how the film positions members of the audience – what point of view a spectator is encouraged to assume.

Active versus passive spectators

Debates around the issue of spectatorship have historically centred on a relatively simple question. Are film audiences a homogenous mass who all respond identically to the narratives and spectacles provided for them by the film industry or are they made up of individual spectators who play a role in determining their own responses to the texts they choose to consume? Active spectatorship theory suggests each spectator is different, so there are as many different responses to a film as there are viewers.

A useful way to think about spectatorship is to see the interpretation of a film as a dynamic interaction between the text and the audience. The filmmakers use aspects of narrative and film form to construct a story, which is often loaded with meanings they hope to communicate to the person watching. The spectator plays their role by bringing to this interaction their own ideologies formed by their past experiences and their own perspectives shaped in part by demographic factors.

Reasons for uniformity or diversity of responses

Film form

Early models of communication such as the **magic bullet theory** and the **hypodermic needle model** suggested that a largely passive mass audience unquestioningly accepted the content of, among other forms of communication, propaganda films and Hollywood movies (Davis & Baron, 1981). These models explored the capacity of Hollywood films to use escapist narratives to distract the population from social problems such as poverty and inequality. This is an interesting area of thought when the popularity of *La La Land* in a modern world facing numerous conflicts and injustices is considered.

The concept of the mass audience with a unified response has since been challenged but it can still be argued that filmmakers employ all aspects of film form to **encourage** a particular response from their audience. Soaring orchestral scores are used to try and provoke emotion, close-up shots selected to encourage identification and a rapid edit used to ramp up tension and suspense. All consideration of film form should include close attention to what impact the filmmaker is intending to have on the spectator.

Narrative

Decisions about how to tell the story and how to construct the narrative have a tremendous impact on audience response. Incorporating binary oppositions encourages the spectator to take a side and feel invested, using archetypes can lead the audience to have certain expectations of characters and create enigma in the film's opening scenes can draw an audience in to seek the answers to their questions.

Also worth consideration is whether the narrative structure and style encourages spectators to become lost in the story or instead reminds them that they are watching a film. In relation to *La La Land*, Anna Leszkiewicz in the *New Statesman* (2017) said,

> La La Land*'s own audience can never fully escape the fact that they are watching a movie: though it is undoubtedly immersive, the experience of watching a La Land is too referential and self-consciously cinematic to transport its audience out of their seats into another specific place.*

The film's intertextuality may encourage spectators to become less emotionally involved in the narrative as they instead focus on spotting the references to art and classic films.

 Independent Activity

Select three very different key sequences from the contemporary Hollywood film you are studying, ideally an emotional scene, a scene in which tension is created and an expository scene. For each scene consider how film form is being used to encourage a specific response and focus from the audience.

 S&C

Research or revisit at least two of the narrative theories listed below and apply them to your contemporary Hollywood film. How might the film's narrative structure impact upon a spectator's response to the film?

- Syd Field's three-act plot structure (1979)
- Vladimir Propp's character functions (1928)
- Tzvetan Todorov's model of narrative (1966)
- Lévi-Strauss' binary oppositions (1995).

 Independent Activity

Consider whether the film you are studying is truly immersive and if not note the narrative techniques that remind the spectators they are watching a film. These may include, among other things, manipulations of time, direct address or generic **tropes**.

Tropes: recurring or significant themes.

 S&C

Research the following terms and think of a film you have seen that uses the technique. What impact does it have on your response to the narrative?

- Distanciation
- Self-reflexivity
- Focalisation
- Subjectivation

Viewing context

Films are created with the intention that they will be seen on a large screen as part of an audience and indeed this used to be the only way films could be viewed. A spectator's response would be impacted upon by the reactions of fellow audience members, laughing at funny moments or screaming at jump scares. The large image makes the film more spectacular and immersive, and in contemporary cinemas the surround sound places the spectator at the heart of the action. Technology such as 3D and IMAX arguably heighten this immersion further and mainstream US films are often seen in these formats. Perhaps most importantly though, when viewing a film at the cinema that is all the spectator is doing, they have dedicated that time to getting lost in the on-screen world.

Compare this to watching a film on a laptop while chatting with friends on social media. The film may be paused repeatedly, breaking up the narrative, and the spectator may be distracted and miss important plot points or emotional scenes. The context in which a film is viewed will undeniably have an impact on the spectator's response to it.

Demographic factors

Demographic factors that may impact upon spectator response include:

- gender
- age
- ethnicity
- socio-economic background
- sexuality.

Established earlier, big-budget productions aimed to appeal to as large a cross-section of the population as possible in order to secure a huge audience and thus maximise profit. To increase the chance of achieving this broad appeal, extensive audience research is conducted, including pre-production surveys and focus groups, and, post-production, test screenings. Feedback from test screenings can lead to scenes being re-edited or in some instances rewritten and reshot. The people invited to test screenings are from diverse social groups to give insight into which demographics the film is likely to be most successful with. This helps the production companies and distributors know where and when to screen the film and who to target their expensive marketing campaigns at. This suggests that demographic factors play a significant role in determining a spectator's response. This could be largely due to identification, as people often find it easier to relate to people more like themselves.

Preferred, negotiated, oppositional readings and *La La Land*

Films are generally produced for mass consumption, particularly mainstream Hollywood films which tend to have high budgets and therefore require large audiences to generate a substantial revenue to cover costs. As established earlier, however, not every spectator will respond to these films in the same way. This can be considered by applying Stuart Hall's encoding/decoding model (Hall, 1973). This model explains that when creating a media text, in this case a film, the producers encode a range of meanings – place messages within the narrative. Some of this is done deliberately as they have a concept of the morals or ideologies they want the film to convey. Some is less deliberate as filmmakers, like anyone else, have subconscious beliefs and attitudes that seep into their work. These beliefs have often been shaped by the society in which the film is made, which is why the study of context is so crucial. The spectator's role is then to decode the text and decide what the filmmaker is trying to impress upon them.

Hall argued that there are three ways of reading and decoding texts:

- **Dominant reading**: when spectators take away the meaning from the film that the filmmakers intended and accept what they have been shown relatively passively.
- **Negotiated meaning**: when viewers negotiate the film's perspectives or ideas, agreeing with some of the film's messages but not all of them.
- **Oppositional reading**: when the spectator understands the film's messages but rejects them.

Applying Hall's theories is arguably easier when a media text other than a film is analysed: adverts have clear, preferred readings as they want the viewer to buy the product; newspaper columns often use persuasive language to argue a very clear viewpoint on an issue. Films, however, are often more complex, offering multiple interpretations.

Applying Hall's ideas to *La La Land* could, however, work as follows:

- The preferred reading is that the film is a romantic exploration of the transformative power of love and the American dream, and the spectator leaves the cinema impressed by the film's artistry and is emotionally uplifted.
- A negotiated reading could be that the spectator is moved by the characters achieving their dreams but finds their relationship unconvincing or unbalanced and therefore problematic.
- An oppositional reading could include a spectator finding Sebastian's obsessions with jazz regressive and self-indulgent rather than inspiring and charming.

In general, contemporary Hollywood output, in particular the high-concept blockbusters that dominate the box office, tend to have very clear preferred readings. These films are less likely to use narrative devices such as open endings or characters with ambiguous motivations that encourage the spectator to challenge the message or seek an alternative reading.

Ideology and *La La Land*

For the A level exam, ideology is a specialist subject area for contemporary American film. Ideology involves the main messages and values conveyed by a film, which are often revealed through the behaviour or beliefs of the main character.

Mainstream cinema often presents dominant ideologies, whereas alternative or independent films are more likely to challenge the prevailing ideologies.

We might therefore anticipate that as a mainstream Hollywood film *La La Land* would present to the audience the dominant ideologies of contemporary American society. The narrative will probably reveal a world dominated by white middle-class men, with women and minority characters playing secondary, supporting roles. Heterosexual love will dominate and a successful life would be one focused on finding fulfillment through gainful employment, happy relationships and the traditional family unit.

 S&C

Produce an example of a preferred, negotiated and oppositional reading of another film you have studied on this course.

 Independent Activity

Watch the *Saturday Night Live* sketch, 'La La Land Interrogation' on YouTube and consider what readings the characters are demonstrating.

An argument could be made that the film does just that. Sebastian's vocation is explored and he achieves his dream of owning his own jazz club. Mia also secures a successful career, ends the narrative in a happy relationship and completes the family unit with a child.

Linked to this is another dominant ideology frequently seen in films: the notion of the American Dream. This is the idea that with hard work anyone in America can secure success and happiness and achieve their goals, even if their aspirations are very ambitious. Central to this ideology is the notion of equality of opportunity. *La La Land* is a film about dreamers and it could be argued that Sebastian and Mia achieve their dreams through perseverance and hard work.

There are of course alternative ways of looking at the film and a specific ideological approach that can be considered in relation to *La La Land* is a feminist one.

The exam board's *Guidance for Teaching* suggests a number of ways in which a feminist ideological approach to film can be taken:

A By looking at an avowedly feminist filmmaker who attempts to make a film that embodies any of the central tenets of feminist thought.

B The approach adopted by feminist scholars in 'recuperating' or 're-validating' the women's picture, the family melodrama or the musical as films enjoyed by female audiences which also reveal important ideas about women's lives and their struggles within patriarchy.

C The approach by feminist scholars in studying genres and films by male directors which have been assumed to be targeting men and to expose the contradictions in their underlying ideologies.

D The approach by some feminist scholars which focused on theory itself and produced specific theoretical insights such as Laura Mulvey's in relation to the 'male gaze'.

E Something as simple as the ideas or subversions that contemporary female filmmakers bring to their films. (WJEC, 2017a)

A number of these approaches could be useful in taking an alternative look at *La La Land*.

A feminist interpretation of *La La Land*

As expressed in the gender section of this chapter, some critics of *La La Land* express frustration at the representation of gender in the film, as Sebastian plays a pivotal role in Mia achieving success by helping her overcome her doubts and insecurities. He also fails to attend the performance of her one-woman show, despite the fact that she is seen on numerous occasions in the film supporting him from the audience. These interpretations suggest that the film plays into the problematic concept of men being active and driving the narrative, while women are passive and in need of guidance and motivation.

However, one way of applying a feminist ideological approach to the film is a consideration of the techniques Chazelle employs to place Mia at the centre of this film's narrative rather that Sebastian. This starts from the film's opening few scenes where, after a fleeting glimpse of a grumpy Sebastian caught in traffic on the freeway, the camera and consequently the spectator stay with Mia

iA **Independent Activity**

Watch three films made by female directors and consider how they represent women.

for the first few scenes. Sebastian does not reappear for 17 minutes, by which time the spectator has discovered a lot about Mia's ambitions and dreams, experienced the failed audition with her, and is therefore encouraged to care about her and feel invested in her wellbeing.

Anna Leszkiewitz (2017) certainly sees Mia as the film's focus and has an interesting perspective on the scenes of Mia watching Sebastian perform. She argues that these scenes,

> don't actually focus on Seb, nor do they form deep explorations of his career ambitions – they are important to us as an audience **because** Mia is watching. We rarely see him perform if not through her gaze, and we see her emotionally develop through her evolving reactions to his music.

Aside from the angry glare Sebastian shoots Mia in the road rage of the film's opening moments, the audience is predominantly placed with Mia and look at him through her eyes.

The first scene of Sebastian playing piano in the restaurant is a complex but interesting example of the gaze: a core topic in feminist film theory. It could *almost* be interpreted as a reversal of the Ernie's scene in *Vertigo* (Hitchcock, 1958) explored in the Representation section but Chazelle makes a significant change. The audience sees Mia watching the piano player and *expect* that through an eyeline match we will then see what she is looking at: Sebastian. If at this point the audience was shown Sebastian playing piano it would suggest he is there to be looked at and she is the controller of the gaze, and thus Mulvey's notion of the male gaze would be subverted. What actually happens, though, is a non-linear cut to Sebastian in his car, allowing the spectator to be brought up to date with his side of the story. Only after the spectator has caught up with Sebastian do the two narratives, and characters, finally meet at the restaurant, where we see each of them looking towards the other: there is then an equality to the gaze.

Leszkiewitz (2017) also compellingly argues that,

> the film's most fantastical scenes are all her [Mia's] projections, her imaginative response to what she hears. We repeatedly see Mia writing, auditioning, and performing without Seb present – and the film's opening and closing scenes are all shot through her eyes. For me, this is Mia's film, the story of her ambitions realised.

 S&C

Research and summarise at least three of the following challenges to, or developments of, Mulvey's ideas of the male gaze as outlined in *Visual Pleasure and Narrative Cinema* (2009):

- Kaplan and Silverman's argument that both male and female spectators can adopt the gaze.
- de Lauretis' idea that female spectators engage in 'double identification' relating to both the active and passive characters.
- Stacey's argument that spectators don't always adopt the role expected of their gender.
- Neale's consideration of gay spectators and the positions they may take.
- Dyer's exploration of how men are objectified in cinema too.
- Mulvey's own 'Afterthoughts on 'Visual Pleasure and Narrative Cinema'.

Independent Activity

Re-watch the fantasy sequence at the close of the film and consider Sebastian's role in Mia's ideas of what could have been.

Mia certainly does achieve her ambitions and the American Dream, as she becomes a credible actress and star, appears to be in a loving relationship and has a family. Sebastian, on the other hand, in always looking backwards, has realised his ideas for a successful jazz club but ends the film looking forlorn and alone as Mia disappears into the night with her new partner.

Conclusion

La La Land is an intriguing case study that offers insight into how mainstream Hollywood films tend to reflect the dominant ideologies of the society in which they are produced. The film, however, invites numerous interpretations as some of the narrative devices employed leave aspects of the story open and diverse spectator positions possible. In the film's 'Production Notes' (Summit Entertainment, 2016) Chazelle said that,

> *La La Land is about passion – it's about passion for art and passion for love … La La Land is something you feel.*

However, as spectatorship theory demonstrates, everyone watching this film will feel something different.

Independent study questions

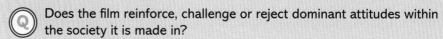 What are the main messages and values of the film?

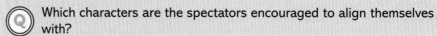 Does the film reinforce, challenge or reject dominant attitudes within the society it is made in?

Q Which characters are the spectators encouraged to align themselves with?

Q What is the preferred reading of your focus film?

Q What is an oppositional reading of your focus film?

Sample essay extract and feedback

How far do your chosen films' concluding scenes confirm their key messages and values?

For this example we are looking at an **extract** from an essay addressing one sequence from *La La Land*.

Max's response extract	Feedback
In the closing scene of *La La Land* one of the film's key messages, that living in the past is less positive than looking to the future, is partly confirmed. The use of cinematography and editing combined encourage the spectator to consider Seb's situation as the film ends.	*Max has clearly identified the sequence he is focusing on and is very quickly addressing the question by referring to one of the film's key messages. There is also an indication that the 'How far' aspect of the question is going to be addressed.*
One of the ways this is achieved is through the editor's choice of final shot in the film. Mia leaves the retro-styled club that arguably represents the past but the spectator, via the camera, stays there with Seb. They witness the change in his facial expression after her departure through a long-held close-up shot. His brave smile fades and he is left looking bereft. Gosling's subtle performance in this sequence is very influential in encouraging the spectator to empathise with him and witness his sadness. This moment suggests that by focusing on jazz traditions and history Seb has let a positive future escape his grasp.	*This paragraph successfully covers a range of film form demonstrating a breadth of understanding and the analysis stays focused on the question.*
The music in this scene is a further aspect of film form that is employed to anchor the film's message. Instead of hearing the jazz that Seb nods to his band to start playing, the spectator hears a rather magical choral refrain that leads into the film's end credits. This is hard to interpret as hearing the jazz may have been read as a positive indication that Seb is happy doing what he loves and has made the right choice to stay in the past but the music chosen is romantic and emotive. It could be interpreted as a reflection on the love he has lost and is remembering on seeing Mia or as it is somewhat uplifting, an indication that he is going to be OK.	*Max presents a balanced argument by including analysis of film form that quite clearly encourages spectators to understand the key messages and aspects that are more ambiguous.*
How spectators respond to this may be impacted upon by their own frames of reference. For some the music will evoke the happy ending of a typical Hollywood musical, whereas other more cynical spectators may read it as ironic. Spectators may disagree on whether Seb has made the right choice and this may be in part due to their response to this key piece of music.	*Bringing in the role the spectator plays in deciphering the film's messages is useful as it stops the essay from making simplistic assumptions.*

This section will help you prepare for Component 1: Varieties of film and filmmaking on the A level course or Component 1: American film on the AS course. Alongside the core areas of study you will need to apply the specialist study area of **spectatorship** for the AS *and* A level and **ideology** for the A level. This chapter will use *Beasts of the Southern Wild* (Zeitlin, 2012) as a case study.

For AS

Two questions must be answered from a choice of three in section B of the Component 1 paper. For these questions you would be expected to write about one American independent film. The first compulsory question is worth 10 marks and should be allocated ten minutes, the second 20 mark question is from a choice of two and you should allow 20 minutes.

For A level

One question from a choice of two must be answered on the Component 1 paper. For this question you would be expected to write about one film from Group 1: **Mainstream film** and one from Group 2: **Contemporary independent film** with no expectation that the films be compared in your response. The full question is worth 40 points and should be allocated 50 minutes.

The specification says

The independent American films characteristically explore non-mainstream cinema subjects and tend to adopt stylistic features associated with lower budget production.

3 *Beasts of the Southern Wild* (Zeitlin, 2012)

Beasts of the Southern Wild (Zeitlin, 2012) centres on a young girl named Hushpuppy and her life in the Louisiana bayou before and after a catastrophic flood. Reviews of the film praise Zeitlin for his imaginative vision, and the film's themes and aesthetic are certainly highly original, surely a key aim of any filmmaker working in the contemporary American independent film industry.

However, in many ways the film is also typical of the output of this sphere of film production. The film is low budget, arguably targets a niche audience and was financed outside of the six major Hollywood studios. It was marketed largely through word of mouth, critical acclaim and publicity generated by film festival success and award wins.

This section will explore the film's 'indie' credentials as a way of looking at the contemporary American independent film scene, examine the film's unusual style and representation of idiosyncratic characters and investigate further the concept of spectatorship introduced in the previous chapter. The section will conclude with a brief analysis of the film from an ideological perspective.

American independent films

Bob Rosen, one of the founding board members of the non-profit organisation that is now called Film Independent, suggested four criteria for what makes a film independent. He suggested that independent films should be 'risk-taking in content and style', express a 'personal vision', be backed by 'non-Hollywood financing' and demonstrate the 'valuation of art over money' (Ortner, 2012).

Beasts of the Southern Wild certainly meets these criteria. The film combines the subgenre of magic realism with the emotive topic of the fate of the dispossessed poor after a natural disaster. This could be considered to have restricted appeal to mainstream audiences and therefore convey willingness to risk-take on the part of the filmmakers.

This could account for the film initially having a limited release, playing on only four screens across the USA. The film was unquestionably the result of a personal vision and passion project for Zeitlin – the film having started life as a one-act play written by his friend Lucy Alibar.

In terms of financing, *Beasts of the Southern Wild* was produced outside Hollywood by Court 13 for just $1.8 million and funded primarily by the not-for-profit foundation Cinereach. The film went on to take a worldwide gross of over $21 million and was therefore a commercial success. However, profit was not the motivating factor for the production company. The desire to tell this story was what motivated Zeitlin and Court 13, as he stated in *Smithsonian Magazine*,

> *I wanted to celebrate people living on the precipice of destruction, hanging onto and fighting for their homes.* (Lidz, 2012)

Court 13 is an arts collective that was formed far from Hollywood at Wesleyan University in Connecticut, USA. Its mission is shaped around the idea of representing outsiders and embracing the challenges that working outside the system brings. Court 13 member and producer of *Beasts of the Southern Wild*, Michael Gottwald, said,

> *Court 13 is more of an idea than an organization. We're dedicated to making films as a community about communities on the edge of the world. Limitations are motivating forces for us. We love to bust through challenges.* (Lidz, 2012)

This ethos is recognised in reviews of the film; as Steven Rea (2012) said,

> Beasts of the Southern Wild *is like outsider art: patched together with found materials, conjured up by untrained artists (the actors), and evocative of a truly American attitude of eccentricity, boldness, transcendence.*

The term 'outsider art' was created by art critic Roger Cardinal to describe art created outside the boundaries of official culture, so the term works perfectly for this film and the independent film scene in general.

Beasts of the Southern Wild is also a typical 'indie' film, as it challenges mainstream Hollywood conventions by foregrounding an exploration of character over a focus on action and entertainment. It also forgoes the stereotypical Hollywood happy ending which ties up all the loose ends for an open conclusion that, although hopeful, is steeped in sadness and loss.

Institutional context

The Independent Film & Television Alliance (n.d.a) states that independent companies produce at least 500 films per year, constituting more than 70% of film production in the USA. *Beasts of the Southern Wild* was released in 2012, a year in which independent box office takings in the USA amounted to $4.5 billion: 41.7% of the total box office for the year. From 2000 to 2011 the historical average percentage of the US market attributed to 'indie' films is 35%. This statistic is particularly impressive when you consider that America went through a major recession in 2007, so independent filmmakers will have had to fight hard to get their projects funded in a risk-averse financial climate.

Role of film festivals and awards

Film festivals played a significant role both in bringing *Beasts of the Southern Wild* to the screen and in publicising it to a wider audience, typical of numerous contemporary independent films.

Independent filmmakers often launch their careers by directing short films and Benh Zeitlin is no exception. One of his early films, a stop-motion animation entitled *Egg* won Best Animation Short at the 2005 Slamdance Film Festival in Utah. In 2008 he made his first short live action film, *Glory at Sea*, inspired partly by Hurricane Katrina. It was conceived as a five-minute film with a month-long shoot and a budget of $5,000 but became a 25-minute film that took 18 months to produce and cost $100,000. The film premiered at the 2008 South by Southwest Festival in Austin and went on to win the Wholphin award there and numerous other awards at festivals that year. With each festival win came publicity and credibility for Zeitlin as a new director to watch out for.

The Sundance Institute and its influential film festival played a significant role in Zeitlin's career as he was selected for the prestigious Sundance Institute Directors Lab Program, which annually supports just eight projects. It is a non-profit organisation founded by Robert Redford. The Sundance Institute website (2018) says of its lab programme:

> *The Sundance Institute Feature Film Program (FFP) advances original storytelling from distinctive voices by supporting independent filmmakers from development through distribution of their feature projects. The program was established over 30 years ago, responding to the shared conviction that independent film has the ability to catalyze far-reaching artistic and cultural impact. Through Labs, mentorship, grants, and year-round customized strategic support, we are committed to fostering self-expression, risk-taking, collaboration, and community. The program has championed the unique visions of a next generation of feature filmmakers from around the world, and has become an international model for supporting artists.*

This makes clear that the values and mission of this organisation embody the ethos of independent films, with creativity and originality being a clear focus.

Having worked on *Beasts of the Southern Wild* in the Sundance Directors Lab, Zeitlin was eligible to apply for financial support from the Sundance Institute, as the organisation provides over $400,000 in financial support to Feature Film Program Alumni each year. The Sundance Institute/NHK Award, which includes a $10,000 cash prize, was awarded to Benh Zeitlin and Lucy Alibar in 2010.

The Sundance Festival's role in securing the film an audience was crucial. The film premiered at the festival to a standing ovation and received predominantly positive press. The film has a rating of 'Universal acclaim' and a metascore of 86 on Metacritic, a website that aggregates reviews from leading critics. In total, *Beasts of the Southern Wild* has won 74 awards including the Grand Jury Prize at the Sundance Film Festival and the Camera d'Or in Cannes. This has generated positive publicity for the film and led to the film getting a much wider release, with it being screened at 318 cinemas at the height of its popularity.

Award nominations, even without the win, have a huge impact on a film's success and *Beasts of the Southern Wild* was nominated for four awards including Best Picture and Best Director at the 85th Academy Awards in 2013.

 S&C

Watch Zeitlin's short film *Glory at Sea*, which is available online and make notes under the headings of film form:

- cinematography
- mise-en-scène
- sound
- editing
- performance.

Repeat this process for *Beasts of the Southern Wild* then use your lists to compare the films.

Glory at Sea (Zeitlin, 2008)

 S&C

Research the Directors Lab Program and watch other films it has helped bring to the screen. How do these films compare with Beasts of the Wild?

The Oscar nominees were announced on 10 January 2013 and the impact of this on the box office takings of the film was startling. The weekend of 18 January saw a rise of over 2,000% in takings from the previous weekend and the film was screened on 71 American cinema screens that weekend having only been on four screens the preceding week. The television broadcast of the 2013 awards ceremony had 40.4 million viewers, so acted as great promotion for the film. As Keith Simanton of IMDb points out about the ceremony, the film being lauded by a famous star acts as, 'a super great trailer being played in everyone's home across their TV screens' (Allen, 2015).

Role of major studios in distribution

Marketing films is a costly part of the distribution process, with conservative estimates suggesting that the marketing budget should be 50% of the overall budget and others suggesting that for independent films this should be up to three times the film's production costs. A route commonly used by independent filmmakers is to secure a distribution deal with one of the major US studios which, according to the Independent Film & Television Alliance, 'have gradually become more marketing and distribution specialists in the US marketplace than production entities' (2013). *Beasts of the Southern Wild* was distributed by Fox Searchlight Pictures, the 'independent' arm of the conglomerate Fox, for its theatrical release in the USA. The benefit of an independent film securing a theatrical release is not only to allow audiences to see the film on the big screen and collect box office revenue, but also to encourage critics to review the film in the press. Fox Searchlight Pictures used a counterprogramming strategy to try and maximise revenue from *Beasts of the Southern Wild*. The film was released in the summer, traditionally the season of major blockbusters, to attract audiences that would find a more alternative film appealing. The benefits of having an established major studio take care of distribution is that it will have years of experience, significant resources and global reach. Fox Searchlight Pictures is part of 20th Century Fox Film, one of the 'world's largest producers and distributors of motion pictures' (21st Century Fox, 2016) with over ten thousand staff and offices all around the world. 20th Century Fox Home Entertainment then released the blu-ray and DVD in the USA, taking over $11 million.

(iA) Independent Activity

Analyse the poster below. How are the distributors trying to appear to an art house audience?

Social, cultural and political context

Hurricane Katrina and Black Lives Matter

Beasts of the Southern Wild does not directly reference Hurricane Katrina but it is easy to see why audiences and critics alike often mention the film and the disaster in the same breath. As Stephen Rea states in *The Inquirer* (2012),

> The specter of Hurricane Katrina and its aftermath hovers over the story – if not literally, then metaphorically.

The film does focus on the impact of a natural disaster on a community comprised predominantly of the demographics worst hit by Hurricane Katrina. Zeitlin maintains, however, that he did not intend the film to be a political one and stated,

> I feel very strongly about environmental issues but I wanted even people who don't believe in global warming to sit down and watch it. (Rea, 2012)

Hurricane Katrina struck the Gulf Coast of the USA in August 2005, bringing winds of up to 140 miles per hour. The storm devastated the communities affected and its aftermath was catastrophic as immense flooding occurred due to breaches in the levees – the embankments built to avoid such floods. Hundreds of thousands of people were displaced from their homes and estimates suggest more than $100 billion in damage had been caused. More than 1,800 people across seven states were killed, with the city of New Orleans being particularly affected. Eighty percent of the city was submerged under 20 feet of water at the height of the hurricane. People of colour, the elderly and the poor were disproportionately affected by the destruction and loss of life.

The government's slow and ineffective response to the disaster provoked a lot of criticism and protest. This response has since been investigated by the Federal Emergency Management Agency's internal watchdog, which concluded that the criticism was largely deserved. Some argue that the government may have responded differently if the demographic of those affected by the storm had been different. As Jamelle Bouie explained on Slate.com (2015),

> to black Americans this wasn't an equal opportunity disaster. To them, it was confirmation of America's indifference to black life.

Rapper Kanye West famously made this point to a large television audience at NBC Universal's 'A Concert for Hurricane Relief' in 2005 by criticising the president saying, 'George Bush doesn't care about black people.'

There are moments in *Beasts of the Southern Wild* that echo images from news coverage of Hurricane Katrina. Jamelle Bouie (2015) asserts that,

> Black collective memory of Hurricane Katrina … informs the present movement against police violence, 'Black Lives Matter'.

The film's messages and values certainly resonate in a world where social inequality continues to be a huge problem and campaigns such as 'Black Lives Matter' are still very much needed.

Film form in independent films

Independent filmmakers often have greater creative freedom than mainstream filmmakers, as the financial risks they are taking are smaller. It is therefore much more difficult to summarise the conventions of independent films than mainstream Hollywood films, as by nature, 'indies' tend to be about doing things differently – defying conventions. They can therefore be more easily defined by what they are not. They are not as likely as mainstream productions to be genre films and they are less likely to follow a traditional narrative structure. *Beasts of the Southern Wild* is definitely a drama but it is also classed in the fantasy and adventure categories by IMDb and incorporates aspects of magic realism as mentioned earlier. In terms of narrative, the film is conventional in that it is predominantly linear but the Elysian Fields scenes could be read as real or figments of Hushpuppy's imagination. This openness to various interpretations is characteristic of independent films, which generally encourage the audience to explore their own responses to the narratives more freely.

Independent films are more likely than mainstream films to break the 'rules' of film form. The filmmaker may choose a shot from an unusual perspective or use mise-en-scène with greater symbolic meaning. They might structure a scene in a less formulaic way by foregoing an establishing shot or making greater use of contrapuntal sound to challenge the spectator.

 S&C

Watch Spike Lee's 2006 documentary on Hurricane Katrina, *When the Levees Broke: A Requiem in Four Acts*, to gain greater insight into the disaster. Collect screengrabs from the documentary footage and compare them to similar shots from *Beasts of the Southern Wild*. Use these to assess the impact televised images of the storm and its aftermath had on the film's overall aesthetic.

 Independent Activity

Read and summarise Jamelle Bouie's (2015) article 'Where Black Lives Matter Began' to gain a fuller understanding of the impact the government's response to the storm had on racial politics in the USA. The article can be found online.

Independent Activity

Does your understanding of the film's social and political context impact upon your response to Wink and Hushpuppy resisting the intervention of the authorities? Respond to this question in 100 words or less.

Independent Activity

Choose three contemporary American independent films and three contemporary mainstream films and analyse the opening scene of each. Write a short essay on how these films use the elements of film form differently.

However, film audiences generally do have a set of expectations from independent film. According to Grant (2007), academic David Bordwell has argued that 'art cinema itself is a genre, with its own distinct conventions' (page 1), and maybe the same can be said of independent films in general. Sherry B. Ortner (2012), of the University of California, reflects on these typical traits, arguing that,

> *One of the striking features of contemporary independent films is a pervasive darkness – of mood, of tone, of look, of story.*

This can be explored in relation to *Beasts of the Southern Wild*.

Cinematography

There is certainly a 'darkness' to some of the key themes of the film: disaster, poverty and loss. The settings, including makeshift, water damaged and mud-stained homes, reflect this. *Beasts of the Southern Wild* was predominantly shot on 16mm film to give the shots a grainy quality that reflects this grittiness of the Bathtub location. Director of photography on the film, Ben Richardson, set the film's cinematography apart from mainstream cinema, stating:

> *In contemporary blockbuster movies where every single black and white level is perfect in every single shot, it can kill the realism to me. When you're creating a world that is so removed from reality, the idea of controlling it and keeping it neat seemed entirely wrong. We wanted to shy away from shiny, sparkly visuals and keep the photography grounded.* (ARRI News, 2017)

The film was principally shot using an Easyrig, which, according to Nofilmschool.com (Hardy, 2015),

> *isn't going to provide silky smooth motion like a Steadicam … nor is it going to resemble traditional hand-held footage. It falls somewhere between the two, which produces a type of movement that mirrors the movement of the body when the camera operator is walking around.*

This lends documentary-style realism to a lot of the footage and also places the spectator in the action, creating immersion. One useful example is the firework scene where the camera operator takes the audience running through the location with the characters. Benh Zeitlin explained his approach to cinematography to *Filmmaker Magazine* (Anderson, 2013) thus,

> I would direct the cameraman like an actor. Rather than giving technical directions, he had to perform like a documentary cameraman … He had to be reacting to the world in the same way that Hushpuppy did.

This use of the camera to echo Hushpuppy's responses and the prevalence of shots either of her or from her perspective helps to keep her at the centre of the narrative and encourages spectators to align themselves with her. The opening scene demonstrates this clearly as the audience, with Hushpuppy, are down with the animals.

Zeitlin also makes great use of close-ups, combined with shallow depth of field, to focus the spectator's attention on one character blurring out any distractions in the shot. These techniques encourage the spectator to consider what a character may be thinking or feeling at a specific moment, thus foregrounding the psychology of a character, as is typical in independent films.

Mise-en-scène

Realism was prioritised when selecting the mise-en-scène for most of the film and is characteristic of a lot of independent cinema. The filming location of Isle de Jean Charles in South Louisiana, USA is severely affected by land loss, so conveys the sense of peril and emergency very authentically. The BP oil spill occurred just as filming commenced, so the filmmakers had additional challenges to overcome, which contributed to the film's theme of communities surviving disasters.

 S&C

Create a storyboard using the first ten shots of the film to help you understand the way the camera is being used. For each shot identify the shot type, camera movement and shot duration, and note the impact that shot may have on the spectator.

Local artists and boat builders constructed the homes and other structures in the film to reflect the lifestyles of the inhabitants of the Bathtub. Zeitlin described Court 13's process to the BFI and it helps to explain why the sets look so organic and authentic:

> We'd tell [the set builders] the story – that when the character Wink first moved to the Bathtub he lived on the ground but then the floods started coming he had to raise his house up. As he couldn't go to the store he would have built the house and raised it up with materials he could find. Then someone from our production actually went and lived life in that way and built 'his' house themselves. (Stevens, 2015)

The aurochs, an extinct species of wild cattle, are a less realistic but key metaphorical aspect of the film's mise-en-scène, and were inspired by cave drawings Zeitlin encountered on a visit to France. As Zeitlin told the French Association of Directors of Photography (AFC; Most, 2013):

> They were the mark our ancestors made before going extinct. The aurochs were always the building blocks of the film: it is the predator versus their prey, maybe a metaphor about the fearlessness in Louisiana because it tests them.

One of the most profound moments in the film is when Hushpuppy finally encounters the aurochs she has been fearing throughout the narrative and boldly stands up to them. The character directions in the screenplay state, 'Hushpuppy raises her chin in confident defiance' and 'the aurochs lowers her head with respect'. This body language conveys Hushpuppy's strength of character and fearlessness. Her simple line at this point,

> You're my friend, kind of

suggests that she realises that the fear and challenges she has faced, represented by these extinct creatures, have been instrumental in helping her develop strength of character. The resilience and resolve that she developed in the face of adversity enabled her to cope with Wink's death and look to the future with optimism.

The aurochs certainly depart from visual realism but arguably help the spectator to visualise and engage with Hushpuppy's vivid imagination.

Editing

Hushpuppy was prioritised in the edit by ensuring that the majority of shots included her or were from her point of view. Zeitlin told *Sight & Sound* magazine:

> *Hushpuppy was always the centre of the film and its point of view. But it wasn't until we watched all the footage and started cutting that we realised that we couldn't sneak some information in that she didn't know about. The minute you stepped out of her head the emotional tension lagged ... it was important that her subjectivity be absolute.*
> (Stevens, 2015)

The film is, for the most part, linear and follows a fairly conventional narrative structure for an independent film. This allows the audience to experience Wink's decline, from his appearance in a hospital gown approximately 14 minutes into the film to his eventual death, alongside Hushpuppy. Her naivety and youth, combined with the narrative clues foreshadowing Wink's death, could even encourage a spectator to feel they have a better sense of what is coming than Hushpuppy and feel anxious about the loss she is to face.

Wink's flashback of meeting Hushpuppy's mother is arguably lent greater power by being the only such scene in an otherwise linear film. Throughout the narrative Wink appears to be a character firmly placed in the present:

pragmatic, hedonistic and living hand to mouth. To see him reminisce about meeting Hushpuppy's mother in such a romanticised, surreal flashback reveals a softer, more vulnerable side of his character.

 Independent Activity

Watch Wink's memories of Hushpuppy's mother approximately 34 minutes into the film and consider all aspects of film form. What is seen and, crucially, what remains unseen? What do these choices suggest about Wink and what do you learn about Hushpuppy's mother? Note down your responses.

Sound

The music of *Beasts of the Southern Wild* is frequently praised in reviews of the film, and orchestras have performed the score to audiences worldwide including events in London, New York and New Orleans. Benh Zeitlin co-wrote the film's Cajun and folk music score with Dan Romer. Music plays a significant role in conveying the atmosphere and life in the Bathtub. Zeitlin said,

> *jazz-funeral culture is a huge part of the celebration sequence at the start of the film that defines the town. A funeral in New Orleans begins with these tragic dirges but then transforms into a celebratory, joyous party.* (Stevens, 2015)

This sequence, and this music, is crucial in conveying the positive aspects of living in a vulnerable place at a challenging time. The sense of fun, community, of appreciating life and the world is palpable.

Another key aspect of film sound in *Beasts of the Southern Wild* is Hushpuppy's voice-over. From the film's opening moments and throughout, this helps to convey her isolation as well as giving the spectator insight into how she perceives the world. She has nobody else to talk to so is sharing her story with the audience.

Hushpuppy's accent and **dialect** are important factors to consider when analysing the use of sound in this film. This example from the film's opening scene demonstrates this:

```
All the time, everywhere,
everything's organs be beatin' and
squirtin' and talkin' to each other
in ways I can't understand. Mosta
the time they probably just sayin'
'I'm hungry,' or 'I gotta poop,'
but sometimes they talkin' in
codes.
```

Her use of language may be considered endearing and childlike by some spectators and encourage them to feel protective of her. Others, however, may

 Independent Activity

Watch the celebration sequence approximately five minutes into the film with no sound and then re-watch it with the music on. Note the impact the score has on how you respond to the scene. Try playing a different piece of music over the scene too and see what impact this has on your response.

Dialect: a form of language that is peculiar to a region or social group.

iA **Independent Activity**

Find three examples of the heartbeat in the film and write 50 words on each, exploring how the sound is being used and what meanings are being conveyed by its use.

struggle to fully understand what she is trying to communicate and it could have a distancing effect.

An important feature of the soundtrack of this film is the recurring use of a heartbeat. The dialogue above is preceded by this character direction,

> Hushpuppy grabs a baby chick and puts it to her ear.
> A TINY HEARTBEAT. She listens with focused wonder and intensity.

The audience hear the heartbeat with Hushpuppy and her response conveys how important and magical she thinks this is. The heartbeat in the film represents life but also Hushpuppy's desire to connect with another. This makes the use of this sound later in the film in relation to Wink profoundly moving.

Performance

The film was cast with non-professional actors who were able to bring their own experiences and stories to the film. Dwight Henry, whose role as Wink was his first acting job, was a local baker who had experienced Hurricane Katrina. His comments on this experience, given to cnn.com (Ayers, 2012), help explain why he was so convincing as Wink:

> *A lot of people refused to leave. We're not just going to walk away from these things. I'm one. I stood back, I was in neck-high water and got stranded down there and had to run for higher ground, trying to stay back and protect the things I loved the most. I understand a lot of what the people in that movie, who live on that island, what they go through.*

Quvenzhané Wallis was cast as Hushpuppy and Amy Biancolli (2012) writes of her performance:

> *it isn't one. It's a fact. Onscreen she simply is, a being as elemental, incontestable and strong as the advancing aurochs.*

iA **Independent Activity**

A useful scene to examine for performance is approximately 51 minutes into the film when Hushpuppy and Wink are in their home after the flood: fighting, drinking, arm-wrestling and at the scene's conclusion falling asleep together. Make notes on how their complex relationship is portrayed in this scene and how aspects of film form are used to convey meaning.

iA **Independent Activity**

Choose the two sequences from the film that you feel portray Hushpuppy at her strongest and at her most vulnerable. Make notes on her facial expressions, body language and movements in these scenes and compare them.

Wallis is compelling and naturalistic, and arguably this is because she had not been trained to act so is just *being* Hushpuppy. Zeitlin incorporated aspects of Wallis' personality and world-view into Hushpuppy. Her body language in the film balances defiance and power with vulnerability and fear. It is understandable with this range that, at the age of nine, she became the youngest ever nominee for the Academy Award for Best Actress.

Aesthetics

Richard Corliss in *Time* magazine (2012) said the film,

> *speaks in words and images of a clarity and vision nearly unique in today's independent cinema.*

This originality is tied to the film's aesthetic, as the artistic choices made in terms of the look, rhythm and music offer a sensory spectacle. The audience is taken to a world rarely seen on a cinema screen.

iA **Independent Activity**

How is the movement, positioning and body language of the actors within the space used to convey meaning in the Elysian Fields scene? Note down your response.

Some of the most memorable moments in this film are not tied to the narrative but stand on their own as moments of beauty. The use of twinkling lights and the muted soulful singing in the Elysian Fields scene are not required to propel the narrative forwards but create a strangely beautiful but disconcerting environment.

 S&C

Select five frames from the film and annotate them, focusing not on what they convey about the characters or contribute to the narrative but instead highlighting how they use visual elements such as contrast, colour, lines, framing, tone, lighting, negative space, pattern and balance/imbalance.

 Independent Activity

Do you think the film's strong aesthetic contributes to the meanings being conveyed? Write down at least three examples of the aesthetic anchoring the meaning.

 Independent Activity

Look up definitions of stereotypes and archetypes. How do the terms differ?

Representations

Independent films tend to be, as mentioned earlier, more focused on character development and exploration than spectacle and action. As such, characters in indies are less likely to be archetypes or stereotypes and more likely to be well-drawn, complex representations of individuals. The inhabitants of the Bathtub are a close community and share ideologies but they are diverse in terms of age and ethnicity.

Age

Although there is a range of ages represented in *Beasts of the Southern Wild*, the clearest comparison is between Wink and Hushpuppy. Wink as the elder, the parent, would stereotypically be expected to display the wisdom acquired with age. He certainly has authority and a high status in his community, and is regarded as a leader at times. An example of this is his role in blowing up the levee. He gives instructions to his friends and contributes to the plan's success, when others have failed. Interestingly, the young Hushpuppy also plays a pivotal role by following Wink's directions. This is a key dynamic between them, as throughout the narrative Wink prioritises teaching Hushpuppy how to survive, particularly when he realises how unwell he really is. A clear example of this is the fish-catching scene. Hushpuppy's respect for her father's knowledge is demonstrated by her use of 'Daddy says' or 'Daddy always saying' in her voice-over. She is being shaped by his views and ideologies. Miss Bathsheba is another adult whose authority and wisdom help form Hushpuppy's view of the world. It is the aurochs, which the teacher speaks of and shows her tattoos of, that come to dominate Hushpuppy's imagination and represent her fears.

Children, and arguably girls in particular, are typically represented as physically and emotionally vulnerable. Hushpuppy challenges many of these stereotypes, as she is relatively independent, has her own brand of wisdom and copes admirably in traumatic situations. The voice-over at the film's conclusion demonstrates Hushpuppy's insight into life as she states:

> I see that I'm a little piece of a big, big
> universe, and that makes things right.

Her ability to be so positive in such harrowing circumstances conveys a resilience and strength of character beyond her years and as the film ends she is depicted as a leader of her community. The final words of the screenplay confirm this intention:

> Hushpuppy leads them forward, into the future.

Gender

The film was made in 2012 and set in the then present, so this and the fact that contemporary independent films often feature progressive gender representations would lead audiences to anticipate a narrative that avoids gender stereotyping. Wink, however, clearly holds the belief that strength and the ability to cope in adverse conditions are masculine characteristics, as Hushpuppy is encouraged to toughen up by being more like a man. This is demonstrated through Wink challenging her to arm wrestle, and through encouraging her by praising her in masculine terms, 'Hushpuppy you the man' and 'You're gonna be the king of the Bathtub' being two clear examples.

Wink also highlights Hushpuppy's gender as a means of criticising her for showing emotion or fear. When she speaks of her anxiety about his health he says, 'That's just a side effect of being a stupid little girl.'

This could also contribute to why Hushpuppy's clothing through most of the film is primarily practical and fairly androgynous. In the opening scene her clothing is described in the screenplay as, 'boys' underpants and a child-sized wife-beater [vest]'. In the hospital she is washed, dressed and re-styled by the staff in a more stereotypically feminine way and her discomfort is apparent through her more inhibited body language.

Ethnicity

Ben Kenigsberg, writing in *Time Out Chicago* (2012), had some serious concerns about the representations in *Beasts of the Southern Wild*, pointing out that in the Bathtub,

> *every day is a holiday, and the largely black residents are depicted as alcoholics, inattentive parents or fools who accidentally set fire to their homes.*

The film's representations of ethnicity do sometimes edge towards some disturbing stereotypes, with the inhabitants of the Bathtub being shown as poor, dirty and even animalistic at times. These representations are apparent from the opening moments of the film when Hushpuppy plays with dirt before being fed herself alongside the animals, as Wink shouts, 'share with the dogs'.

However, the film arguably represents a community within which ethnicity is irrelevant. The characters face the same challenges and live similar lives regardless of race.

(iA) Independent Activity

Read bell hooks' (2012) article 'No Love in the Wild' to gain fascinating insight into some of the issues critics of the film have with its representations of race, gender and class.

Spectatorship

For both the AS and A level exams spectatorship is a specialist subject area for contemporary independent film. Theories of spectatorship were explored in the previous section but can be examined in relation to *Beasts of the Southern Wild*.

It has been argued that independent films are more challenging for audiences as they are more open to interpretation and invite a wider range of responses. This supports the notion of the active spectator.

Roger Ebert, one of the world's most celebrated and revered film critics, said (2013),

> *I've always felt that movies are an emotional medium … We become voyeurs. We become people who are absorbed into the story, if the story is working. And it's an emotional experience.*

Emotionally engaging the spectator is a key aspect of spectatorship studies and the emotional impact of this film was certainly crucial to Zeitlin. He suggested to *Filmmaker Magazine* that authenticity is central to achieving this:

> *I think Court 13 is about living the story, about trying to create the actual feeling that you are trying to shoot on set. You want to shoot a party, you have a party. You want to shoot a flood, you go to a flood. Its trying to get the real thing on camera and emotionally too. There is a lot of slight-of-hand acting using real performances and real emotions.*
> (Anderson, 2013)

Numerous studies have been conducted into the emotional impact of films on the spectator, and theories broadly fall into two categories:

- The **identification view** allows that spectators may engage with a film to the point that they are able to imagine themselves in the character's situation and truly empathise with that individual. This can be referred to as imaginative identification.
- The **assimilation view** posits that real identification is rare and spectators instead tend to experience sympathy or antipathy. The spectator is an external observer viewing the characters from the outside.

It has also been argued that spectators feel very different emotions to those experienced by characters and this is referred to as the **asymmetry of emotional response**. Using Wink's death scene as an example, you might argue that the spectator feels grief just like Hushpuppy. It is unlikely, however, that you would feel grief on the same level as her. Zeitlin worked hard to keep Hushpuppy at the film's centre. For many spectators, this may result in their emotional response being dominated by protective concern for Hushpuppy's wellbeing rather than grief for the loss of Wink.

Most theories of the active spectator, as discussed in the previous chapter, share the notion that the spectator plays a role in interpreting a film and people will have diverse responses to any scene. A theory that challenges this, and places the spectator in a passive role, is the idea of **emotional contagion**. As Coplan (2006) says, this has been defined by psychologists Elaine Hatfield, John Cacioppo and Richard Rapson as,

> *the tendency to automatically mimic and synchronize expressions, vocalizations, postures, and movements with those of another person, and, consequently, to converge emotionally.*

 Independent Activity

Consider your own emotional response to this film. Make notes under two headings:

- 'Techniques used that helped me relate to Hushpuppy' and
- 'Factors that prevented me from relating to Hushpuppy'.

 STUDY TIP

When writing about your own response to the film it is advisable to write about the range of different feelings provoked. It is also useful to broaden your vocabulary of terms for different emotions. Spend some time looking up synonyms of the more common ones and try to incorporate them into your analysis.

According to Coplan (2006, page 29), Carl Plantinga argues that filmmakers try to exploit this tendency by constructing 'scenes of empathy' to encourage spectators to 'catch' the emotion the onscreen character is feeling. A scene of empathy typically features shots of long duration, with shallow depth of field, which take the spectator increasingly close to the protagonist's face. To maximise the chances of the spectator experiencing emotional contagion the narrative will generally slow in pace for these scenes.

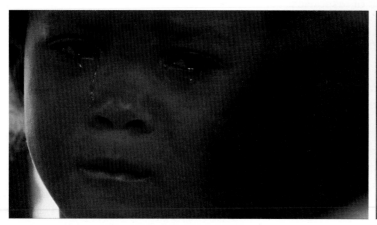 

Zeitlin certainly utilises these techniques to make Wink's death a scene of empathy. He employs long takes, shallow depths of field and a series of close-ups of both characters.

The use of Hushpuppy's voice-over is also crucial in encouraging identification, as we have privileged insight into her thoughts throughout the film.

It could be argued that the magical realist aspects of the narrative such as the aurochs and the ice caps disrupt the realism of this film and prevent the spectator becoming fully immersed. The incorporation of these aspects of Hushpuppy's imaginary world could conversely take the spectator closer to the protagonist as the spectator *sees* how Hushpuppy is feeling.

Ideology

For the A-level exam, ideology is also a specialist subject area for contemporary American independent film. Ideology was defined in the previous chapter but a specific ideological approach that can be considered in relation to *Beasts of the Southern Wild* is a Marxist one.

The film director, Eisenstein, one of the key proponents of Marxist film theory, argued that,

> *American capitalism finds its sharpest and most expressive reflection in the American cinema.* (Hauke, 2013)

However, independent films are intended to challenge the hegemony of Hollywood, so it might be anticipated that this not be the case with *Beasts of the Southern Wild*.

Marxist film theorists assert that Hollywood's traditional narrative structures should be challenged, and filmmakers should avoid dictating the spectator's response and allow them to interpret the film in their own way. Deep focus is advocated to allow spectators to choose what element of the frame to give their attention to. Zeitlin certainly does not adhere to this principal as he favours shallow focus to direct the audience's attention to specific characters in particular moments.

The fact that this character is more often than not Hushpuppy would also not adhere to another Marxist filmmakers' principle: the goal of creating narratives that prioritise the community over the individual. *Beasts of the Southern Wild* unquestionably celebrates the close-knit Bathtub community and suggests some equality through scenes of communal eating, teamwork and close friendships. Wink even goes so far as to suggest one of his drunken friends could step into his parenting role if their plan to blow up the levee goes awry,

> Boss, anything go wrong, Walrus is Daddy.

Heavily industrialised America

However, Hushpuppy's centrality to the narrative means that even though the film ends on a group shot this really is her story and in the closing moments, through her position at the front and centre of the grouping, she is shown as a leader.

Marxist theorists tend to applaud films that contextualise and analyse hierarchical relationships. This film certainly does this. Capitalism, industrialisation, wealth and material possessions are not celebrated. Instead, community, nature and strength of character are praised. *Beasts of the Southern Wild* asserts that this community possesses things lacking in the industrialised world. Hushpuppy states,

> Daddy always saying, that up in the dry world, they got none of what we got.

Social class is a key representation in the film and the Bathtub is portrayed as a community where few work, income is low and living standards are compromised. The division between social classes can also be seen in the film with the inhabitants of the bayou being set up in opposition to the people from the rest of America, on 'the dry side'. Blame for this division is clearly levelled at more privileged Americans,

> They built the wall that cuts us off.

The more natural environment of the Bathtub

This statement may resonate particularly strongly in contemporary America and the social divisions exploited by President Trump in his campaign.

The film cheers the underdog throughout, as the audience is encouraged to share the joy of these characters surviving in the most challenging of situations. A clear example is the negative portrayal of the heavy-handed authorities trying to evict the vulnerable Wink and the young Hushpuppy very forcefully.

The film explores concepts central to Marxist film theory, but perhaps structurally Zeitlin leads the spectator a little too firmly towards a preferred reading and places too much emphasis on the individual.

 Independent Activity

Consider how the US authorities are represented in the film and summarise what this suggests about the film's overall ideology in 200 words or less.

Conclusion

Zeitlin's goal was to:

> take some of the language of artistic, lyrical film, but to have the heart of it be wisdom and big questions and simple ideas and universal themes. I think that is one of the reasons why people see it as not an art film that's trying to push you away, but one that is trying to draw you in. And it's about things everyone goes through. (Anderson, 2013)

By combining an unusual premise, memorable and unique characters, and a distinctive aesthetic, Court 13 has produced a truly original independent film. Its success is testament to the quality of the filmmaking and the fact that spectators can usually relate to some of the characters' experiences.

Independent study questions

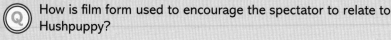 How is film form used to encourage the spectator to relate to Hushpuppy?

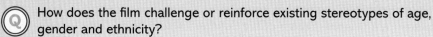 How does the film challenge or reinforce existing stereotypes of age, gender and ethnicity?

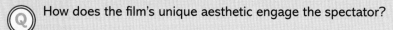 How does the film's unique aesthetic engage the spectator?

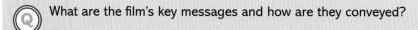 What are the film's key messages and how are they conveyed?

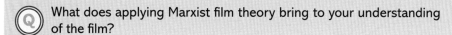 What does applying Marxist film theory bring to your understanding of the film?

Sample essay extract and feedback

> How far do your chosen films demonstrate the importance of elements of film form in influencing spectator response? Refer in detail to at least one sequence from each film.

For this example we are looking at an **extract** from an essay addressing *Beasts of the Southern Wild*.

Rosa's response extract

According to the identification view on spectatorship a key way to influence the response of the spectator is to encourage them to identify with the character on screen. Spectators are helped to imagine themselves in the character's situation and truly empathise with them. This can be referred to as imaginative identification. The first four minutes of *Beasts of the Southern Wild* see Zeitlin engaging numerous techniques to allow spectators to imagine Hushpuppy's experience.

Among these is cinematography and Ben Richardson, the cinematographer, uses the camera to place the spectator alongside Hushpuppy and see the world through her eyes. The opening scene incorporates a number of close-up shots of Hushpuppy, including the first time we see her which shows a fragile bird being held by Hushpuppy who's looking rather lost on a mud pile. This could be interpreted as a visual metaphor, representing Hushpuppy's own isolation. The camera then tilts up to Hushpuppy's face and her care for nature and her sensitivity are visible through the use of close-ups. The camera is placed very low and, as Hushpuppy is small and seated on the floor, it places the spectator with her, arguably encouraging identification.

In this scene, and throughout the film, camera movements are very free as an Easyrig was used. This lends a documentary style to the footage and combined with the use of grainy 16mm film, creates realism that encourages the spectator to believe in the world being witnessed. Add to this the context of Hurricane Katrina and other similar natural disasters and it's easy to see why this film can have a profound emotional impact. Spectators are likely to respond more strongly to something that feels real.

Sound is used effectively in this sequence to try and influence spectator response. The quiet non-diegetic score sounds like a music box and evokes childhood. This combines with Hushpuppy's childlike voice over to help spectators grasp her innocence and vulnerability. Using a voice-over also takes the spectator closer to Hushpuppy as her thoughts and feelings can be expressed verbally. However, Hushpuppy has a strong accent and uses local dialect, which may alienate some spectators as her meaning is not always clear. Wink's dialogue, spoken in harsh tones, includes comments like, 'Get out of the way' and 'Share it with the dogs'. This sets up a binary opposition between these two characters and encourages the spectator to align themselves with Hushpuppy from the outset.

Feedback

Rosa has effectively incorporated a theoretical approach into her response, demonstrating a wider understanding of spectatorship.

Rosa identifies the film and extract studied very clearly, which is helpful for the examiner and suggests a solid understanding of the film.

Rosa offers a detailed analysis of a specific shot using terminology effectively. This demonstrates a high level of understanding of cinematography.

Phrases such as, 'this could be interpreted as' are useful in showing an understanding that spectatorship is complex and not everyone will respond the same.

Rosa contextualises the film effectively, showing she understands the role context plays in impacting on audience response.

Using the word 'influence' here takes the essay back to the question and helps Rosa's response stay targeted and direct.

In her comments on Hushpuppy's accent and use of dialect Rosa demonstrates a strong ability to analyse, effectively looking at the impact of the voice-over from differing perspectives.

Section 1

A level: Varieties of film and filmmaking

British film since 1995

This part will help you to navigate the A level **Component 1: Varieties of film and filmmaking** by offering guidance on **Section C: British film since 1995**. This is a two-film study and this section will focus on *Trainspotting* (Boyle, 1996) and *Sightseers* (Wheatley, 2012). Aside from the core areas of study, students must also focus on specialist study areas: ideology and narrative for A level, just narrative for AS. This includes critical approaches to narrative for AS and critical approaches to narrative and ideology for A level.

For AS

You answer two questions and must refer to both your chosen films in both answers. The first compulsory question should be allocated 20 minutes. The second question is selected from a choice of two and you should allow 40 minutes. These questions may test an understanding of critical approaches to narrative.

For A level

You answer one question from a choice of two and must refer to both your chosen films. You should spend 50 minutes on your response. These questions may test an understanding of critical approaches to narrative or ideology.

The specification says

Trainspotting … raise[s] questions about different kinds of social and national identities.

Sightseers combine[s] horror and comedy …

4 *Trainspotting* (Boyle, 1996) & *Sightseers* (Wheatley, 2012)

Trainspotting is in many ways the defining British film of the 1990s. Many of its energetic cast and crew have now become household names (people such as Danny Boyle and Ewan McGregor); it spawned a sequel, *T2 Trainspotting* in 2017 and a huge variety of youth-oriented merchandising, not least the cult source novel by Scottish writer Irvine Welsh. *Trainspotting* may sound geeky but it is anything but … it was and still remains 'cool'. Its cinematic charisma earmarked the film for controversy, as its subject matter is, at least on the surface, about heroin addiction in a working-class community in Edinburgh.

Sightseers, on the other hand, represents the relatively mainstream calling-card of the new star director of alternative British filmmaking, Ben Wheatley. Since his film debut, *Down Terrace* in 2009, Wheatley has produced a body of provocative work that has been referred to by Lowenstein (2016) as, 'the cinema of disorientation'. *Sightseers,* his third and arguably most accessible film, is an off-beat road trip following a murderous couple on a caravan holiday around the UK.

Trainspotting and *Sightseers* are therefore insights into two poles of UK-based filmmaking. *Trainspotting*, as already noted, is a cult phenomenon, something that defined a zeitgeist and still has resonance. *Sightseers* represents a more down-beat, low-budget approach to genre realism, a homely horror infused with black humour and off-beat observations. Both films, however, are the work of UK auteurs and their collaborators.

 S&C

Watch *Shallow Grave* (Boyle, 1994) and note the thematic similarities with *Trainspotting* and compare how the films use aspects of film form.

 Independent Activity

Read the novel *Trainspotting* (Welsh, 1994), or at least the first page, and contrast it with the opening of the film. What differences do you notice and why do you think those changes were made?

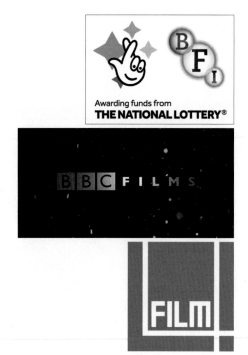

(iA) Independent Activity

Look at the *BFI Statistical Yearbook* online. It's full of brilliant information and it's free.

British film

Given the dominance of Hollywood in our culture, the UK film industry and its success stories are often overlooked. The *BFI Statistical Yearbook* is a superb online resource, detailing the contemporary state of the industry, recording in the 2017 edition that the top 100 films released in UK cinemas during 2016 earned 92% of the box office. The majority of these films were either USA produced or UK produced with USA studio backing. The box office share of such USA products is now on average 85%.

The top 20 box office earners in 2016 accounted for just over 50% of all takings and the list of their production/distribution companies reads like a Hollywood studio roll-call: Walt Disney released the year's top earning film *Rogue One: A Star Wars Story* along with *The Jungle Book, Finding Dory, Captain America: Civil War, Zootropolis, Doctor Strange* and, finally, *Moana*. Warner Brothers released three films, 20th Century Fox five and Universal three. Of these 20 films, 17 earned over £20 million at the box office. To put that into context, of the top 20 UK films at the 2016 UK box office only one, *Absolutely Fabulous: The Movie* (Fletcher, 2016) earned double figures at £16.1 million and even that was distributed by 20th Century Fox and partially funded by Fox Searchlight Pictures, which is the independent film arm of 20th Century Fox.

Hollywood is still king in the UK, as it is in many regions around the world. But that isn't to say that the UK doesn't have a vibrant and historic film industry. It absolutely does but it is largely always overshadowed by the financial power and long reach of the Hollywood majors.

In terms of being a market for film product the UK remains the third biggest market in the world, after the USA and China, generating over $1.2 billion annually and in terms of the UK film industry as a whole it is very buoyant, contributing over £4.3 billion of gross domestic product in 2014. In 2015 the BFI noted there were 6,800 film production companies in the UK and 2,700 post-production companies, 420 film distributors and 230 film exhibitors. The majority of these are, however, small, with turnovers of less than £250,000 per annum.

The UK has a film industry that is clearly thriving but does not have the financial weight and scale of Hollywood.

Historically, there have been some standout achievements by UK-based production companies some of which have tried to adopt the classic Hollywood model of vertical integration. A good example would be the UK studio Rank (1937–1996), which announced its ambitions with the construction of a studio facility called Pinewood and took control of the Odeon cinema circuit. Remembered fondly for the films it made largely in the 1940s and 1950s, Rank's legacy exists at Pinewood which is still very much a fully operational production facility, famous for hosting the Bond films; there is even an 007 stage. The Pinewood Group not only oversees productions at Pinewood but also at another great UK studio: Shepperton.

In conjunction with these two great studio facilities, the UK also boasts an incredible array of technical and creative talent. British actors are renowned for their theatrical craft, with great thespians such as Dame Judi Dench and Sir Ian McKellen adding gravitas to Hollywood products such as the *Bond* and *X-Men* franchises. Newer faces on the scene such as Ewan McGregor (*Star Wars*) and even more recently in the *Star Wars* franchise, John Boyega, Daisy Ridley and Felicity Jones, illustrate the depth of UK acting talent.

There are also the writers, such as the creators of source material, including J.K. Rowling (the *Harry Potter* franchise) or Ian Fleming (the *Bond* franchise).

Technically, the UK is blessed with a vast reservoir of great talent. Ranging into the past we find directors such as Sir Alfred Hitchcock, Sir Charles Chaplin and Sir David Lean, and more recently Sir Ridley Scott, Ken Loach and, of course, Danny Boyle. But, equally, supporting these directorial legends there is a host of screenwriters, cinematographers, production designers, sound recordists and so on. It is not insignificant that Hitchcock, the UK's preeminent director of international and academic renown (he's in the specification in the Classical Hollywood section with his famous and much lauded film *Vertigo*) cited his wife Alma Reville as his greatest and most trusted critic. She too was a film professional, forging a successful career as an editor and screenwriter.

Other notable successes in the UK worth investigating are Hammer Studios and their famous horror cycle of low-budget shockers that found an international market in the late 1950s and 1960s; Ealing Studios and their whimsical, anti-authoritarian comedies of the 1940s and 1950s, and more recently the amazing back catalogue of Film4 (1998 to date) and Channel 4 films (1982 to 1998). Both companies are offshoots of the TV company Channel 4 and have helped fund some of the most significant films of both UK and global culture over the last 40 years – not least *Trainspotting* and *Sightseers*.

Independent Activity

Look at the back catalogue of films from Film4. How many do you know? Do you think the studio has a house style?

The use of money generated by the television industry to help make UK film products is perhaps the significant difference between UK and USA industries. In the UK major players such as Film4 and BBC Films help attract other production partners through the co-production model, thus securing funding without access to Hollywood cash. Another way of establishing an adequate production budget includes by securing some financial support from the BFI (British Film Institute). At present it operates a number of financial schemes to aid UK filmmakers, which are in turn funded by the National Lottery and some government grants. To successfully apply for these schemes requires the film production company to submit a form called the Cultural Content Test and so prove that the proposed film will have a high proportion of cultural signifiers such as talent, crew, locations and story matter. It is on this basis that the BFI funds. Franchises such as *Bond*, *Potter* and the *Star Wars* films are often included in the BFI measure of UK films because of their use of UK talent, source materials and production bases. However, because they are also major USA studio co-productions they do not qualify for BFI financial support, despite passing the Cultural Content Test.

Independent Activity

Research the Cultural Content Test and apply the criteria to *Trainspotting* and *Sightseers*.

Regional film bodies also exist and provide further revenue sources for cash-strapped UK producers and there are, of course, private investment and European partners. But, at the end of the day, in comparison to mainstream USA blockbuster budgets, the UK is a cottage industry. In the UK a high-end film may cost up to approximately £10 million/$11 million. Recent UK success stories such as *Slumdog Millionaire* (Boyle, 2008), *The King's Speech* (Hooper, 2010) and *The Woman in Black* (Watkins, 2012) were all made for this amount of money. However, the majority of films made in the UK are made on small micro budgets. Ben Wheatley made his first film *Down Terrace* (2009) for £30,000 and *A Field in England* (2013) for £300,000. Such figures are, by Hollywood's standards, very low; an average star-driven studio comedy such as *Zoolander 2* (Stiller, 2016) cost over $50 million and blockbuster franchise films such as *Logan* (Mangold, 2017) cost $97 million and *Dunkirk* (Nolan, 2017) cost $100 million. *Batman v Superman: Dawn of Justice* (Snyder, 2016) cost around $250 million to make.

Independent Activity

Check out the trailers and statistics on the websites of the **British Council** and the **British Film Commission**.

Again, to try and put all this into perspective, the two relatively successful and critically lauded UK films that we are studying in this section were both combined made for less than $5 million/£3 million (*Trainspotting* £1.5 million and *Sightseers* apocryphally under $2 million/£1.3 million).

Due to the difficulty of taking on Hollywood at what it does best (mainstream genres, franchises, star vehicles, high production budgets, an emphasis on spectacle) the UK tends to specialise on other types of films such as:

Heritage: UK history and historic locations, perhaps with a royal flavour or World War II and possibly with source material from Shakespeare, Jane Austen or Charles Dickens.

Horror: a relatively low-budget genre and something the UK has pioneered in terms of literature and the sub-genre of gothic horror.

Social realist: tough 'kitchen-sink dramas' usually about working-class life; aiming to expose social inequality or issues.

Comedy: also achievable with a low budget with plenty of opportunity to spin-off from the success of TV situation comedies and with a predilection for 'black' or 'quirky' humour.

It should be clear from this list that *Trainspotting* and *Sightseers* share a social realist pedigree mingled with black comedy and, in *Sightseers'* case, horror. Other UK films already mentioned in this section can easily be placed in one or more of these reductive but still useful categories. However, art films, which are the traditional preserve of the truly independent low-budget filmmaker, don't fit this schema. I challenge anyone to generically place Wheatley's unashamed art house masterpiece *A Field in England*: IMDb has a go with 'Drama, History and Horror'.

Fashion is a fickle cultural phenomenon and film fashion no less so. On occasion, UK film has triumphed on the public stage ('The British are coming!', Colin Welland on receiving a Best Original Screenplay Oscar in 1982 for *Chariots of Fire*), receiving plaudits at high-profile global events such as the Oscars and sometimes even scoring colossal revenues at the global box office, but such days are rare. That said, when things do work well, then we can talk about UK film and fashion in one breath and two, now sadly historic, periods come to mind: the Swinging 60s and the 1990s.

The Swinging 60s

The Swinging 60s, a journalistic euphemism for a largely London-based youth market phenomenon, focused on all aspects of youth culture. Underpinning the movement was intolerance of the older authoritarian generation and a desire for more personal freedom. Against this emotional and cultural backdrop occurred a sexual revolution fuelled by the availability of the contraceptive pill, relaxed dress codes and campaigns to empower marginalised groups such as women, the working classes, black people, students and non-heterosexuals.

Many of the films from this period have dated badly but one film that still stands the test of time and which can in some sense be seen as a forerunner of *Trainspotting* is The Beatles' first feature, *A Hard Day's Night* (Lester, 1964). The film is brash, vibrant, cheeky and unashamedly constructed around a binary of positive youth versus decrepit old age. Just over 30 years later, a generation on and *Trainspotting* became part of a new cultural explosion.

The 1990s

The 1990s was a cultural watershed for all the arts. Aside from the music scene (rave, indie and Brit-pop) and a new political direction (the promise of Tony Blair's New Labour ending decades of Thatcherite rule) there was the

Young British Artists movement typified by such creatives as Damien Hirst and Tracey Emin. This interest in the arts was reflected in UK film output which, consciously or not, captured some of the energy of the 'Cool Britannia' tag in commercially successful films such as: *Four Weddings and a Funeral* (Newell, 1994), *The Full Monty* (Cattaneo, 1997) and *Lock, Stock and Two Smoking Barrels* (Ritchie, 1998). The mid-1990s was buzzing and Geri Halliwell's dress in the design of the Union flag was the symbol of this new brash confidence. Perhaps the similarities between the 1960s and the 1990s start to fall away on close inspection but *Trainspotting* undoubtedly fed into, as well as feeding off, a positive youth experience. This era was more Generation Extra than Generation X, which had been typified by the band Nirvana and the young people who were apathetic and aimless, nick-named slackers, of the early 1990s. How else can we explain Renton's cheery grin as he heads into central London with a bag of cash, no longer a junkie, bouncing along to the thumping bassline of 'Born Slippy' by Underworld, the soundtrack of a generation of ravers … 'Lager! Lager! Lager! Mega, Mega white thing.'

The institutional contexts of *Trainspotting*

The film was made by **Channel 4 Films**. This company was renamed in 2006 as Film4 Productions and Film4 is the name of the company's TV film channel. Film4 Productions is still a pivotal producer of films in the UK. Their back-catalogue, stretching back to 1982, is also a catalogue of UK cultural attitudes and interests. Their films' subject matter is often controversial and leftfield although they have been behind relatively mainstream successes too, not least *Trainspotting* which for a £1.5 million budget generated £48 million worldwide on its release.

Danny Boyle is one of Britain's highest profile filmmakers, a director in television and film as well as a producer. His film work includes the worldwide smash hit *Slumdog Millionaire* (2009) for which he won, as director, one of its eight Oscars. In making his first feature film, *Shallow Grave* (1995), Boyle put together a team of actors and filmmakers some of whom would go on to make *Trainspotting*. The two films share: director, cinematographer, editor, writer, producer, production company, UK distributor and actors Ewan McGregor, Peter Mullan and Keith Allen. The latter appears in both films as the same drug dealer and *Trainspotting* acts as the prequel to his character's eventual death in *Shallow Grave*. Boyle's status as a national arts icon was cemented when he successfully directed the staging of the 2012 Olympics.

The social/political/cultural contexts of *Trainspotting*

In the early 1990s the UK faced a divisive time due to a recession and an increasing dislike of the Conservative government that had been in power since 1979. The National Lottery was launched along with Sky and Channel 5, and the Channel Tunnel opened. Two infamous criminal cases led to moral panics. Firstly, in 1995 Leah Betts, a young teenager, died in an incident connected to ecstasy use and news coverage of this tragic death contributed to the moral panic surrounding the new rave culture. Secondly, in 1993 Jamie Bulger, a young toddler, was brutally murdered by two young boys, leading to fears over the malign influence of violence on film. Also during this period a huge Poll Tax

 S&C

Research Generation X and the preceding generations: the Baby Boomers and before them the Veterans. What generation do you belong to or identify with?

Danny Boyle

 Independent Activity

Look at Danny Boyle's amazingly staged opening ceremony of the 2012 Olympics and consider how it represents Britain.

Independent Activity

Research the Poll Tax and in particular responses to its introduction in Scotland.

 Independent Activity

Look at the Bulger case. It is heart-breaking but it led to an amendment of the Video Recordings Act in 1994 and impacted on the making and reception of certain kinds of films such as horror.

 Independent Activity

Look at the opening of *Fight Club*. It is a perfect example of Generation X's malaise and self-loathing.

 Independent Activity

Listen to Blur and Oasis and other 1990s pop/rock bands. Compare and contrast them with the anger of early 1990s USA grunge bands like Nirvana.

riot occurred in London and sporadic rioting continued to flare up in working-class urban areas around the country. By 1996, however, there were signs of a new dawn contributed to by the feel good success of the English football team at the European Championships and the mainstream arrival of the effervescent Spice Girls. The high tempo introduction to *Trainspotting* is then in some ways a reflection of this period: energised and upbeat. The music of Iggy Pop's 1970s anthemic song 'Lust for Life' erupts on screen as we see Renton and Spud, running from security guards in well-heeled Edinburgh. Renton's narration of Welsh's iconic and nihilistic 'Choose life' monologue also sets the tone for the film's iconoclasm.

At the end of the film Renton leaves Begbie, Spud and Sick Boy, and runs off with the money received from a drug deal. The feeling created by the film's dénouement is optimistic. Renton has quit heroin and is going straight. He's leaving his violent, nihilistic, wastrel friends behind and is moving on – literally crossing a bridge (Waterloo Bridge) to a new life that he's chosen. 'I'm going straight and choosing life …' he happily tells us in a voice-over as the dance music of Underworld ushers in a positive and energised vision of the future.

The generation that was sired by the baby boomers and went on to make punk and then slacker rock, as typified by bands such as Nirvana, was called **Generation X**. This generation found some purpose in rave culture and lost some of its existential angst but in the mid-1990s there was still plenty of disillusionment with contemporary culture and the diseased capitalist dream. In the USA this feeling of generational malaise was evidenced by the riots at Woodstock 99 and in films such as *Fight Club* (Fincher, 1999). This mood of alienation and disillusionment is also evidenced in *Trainspotting* until its end.

The film heavily features **British music culture in the 1990s**. It takes the audience on a journey through contemporary musical culture moving from punk to anthemic rave: starting with Iggy Pop's 'Lust for Life', a song from 1977, and ending with 'Born Slippy' by Underworld from 1996. The 1990s saw an explosion of creativity, particularly in the UK, which was labelled by journalists 'Cool Britannia'; the dance scene, Brit-pop bands like Blur and Oasis and even pop creations like the Spice Girls gave Britain, for a time, a musical sense of positivity and energy. This is very much mirrored in the film's closing sequence with its high-powered percussive beat.

The film is the first of a number of **Irvine Welsh** adaptations. *Trainspotting* is based on his book of the same name, which was published to acclaim in 1994. Other adaptations have been: *Acid House* (McGuigan, 1998); *Filth* (Baird, 2013); and *T2: Trainspotting* (Boyle, 2017). The screenplay effectively captures a number of features from the source novel such as: a focus on Renton; Aids; drug abuse, in particular heroin; violence; and low-level criminality. Some characters get more novel time than screen time and it is perhaps significant that some of the ones edited out in the adaptation are black or female. That said, the film and novel are arguably largely about the male experience of living in the working-class Edinburgh suburb of Leith and Renton's posse of male friends do form the focal point of the novel, as they do eventually the film.

Reading the book is strongly advised, not least because the unavoidable sheen of glamour that the film possesses is very much missing; in the novel the main characters are all seriously flawed and damaged, yet Begbie and Sick Boy in particular are even more detestable.

The film form of *Trainspotting*

The film largely follows a linear pattern and is very much focused on the viewpoint of Renton, whose voice-over and close-up intro and outro the film. In the intro, however, he is suspended in time, literally in a freeze-frame, staring provocatively at the audience. Later he walks towards the audience but becomes unfocused. A possible reading of these two cinematic devices is that in the former Renton is trapped and in the latter he is free but at a cost to his own identity.

There are a number of jump-cuts and montages in the film, along with dream sequences (Renton's cold turkey) and fantasy sequences (Renton's OD and the toilet-diving escapade) but generally the film progresses in a linear fashion. The passing of time is partly communicated through music, starting with Iggy Pop in the 1970s and ending with mid-1990s dance from Underworld.

Interiors such as bars, pubs, cafés, squalid shooting galleries, flats, bedrooms and so on form the bulk of the film's settings, but when Renton does step out of his Edinburgh suburb of Leith he appears ill at ease. His visit to the Highlands with Tommy, Spud and Sick Boy is the clearest example of this. Renton's escape to London reflects his attempted maturation but he ends up swapping his childish bedroom with train wallpaper for a grotty bed-sit, funded by renting expensive flats to yuppies. Only in the final scene of the film, as he advances towards the audience, does he exude confidence in his environment. Although significantly he is in transit at this point and unfocused, having double-crossed his so-called friends and made it rich with cash made from a drug deal.

Cinematography

The images below offer the recurring aesthetic of very low-level, worm's-eye view framing that communicates a sense of a life with limited perspectives and ambition. Renton is literally 'low life' and his world is just one step up from the gutter.

Above we see the first of a number of Renton's overdose POVs, having surreally sunk into the fleshy carpet and lost touch with reality. A doctor revives Renton with adrenalin. The irony of Lou Reed's song 'Perfect Day' underscores this visual nightmare. The combined effect of these POV shots is to situate Renton at his literally lowest point, close to death. The images both pacify and objectify him as well as placing us in his rapidly dying body.

The film terminates in London, which is depicted as a land of questionable opportunity but undoubted cultural pull. This is referenced below in a homage to The Beatles' famous Abbey Road photo. It is also a reference to the notion of a Swinging 60s reborn for the mid-1990s.

Mise-en-scène

The shabby brown tones and drab minimalism of a dilapidated drug den are perfectly communicated through set design, costume and colour palate. However, this is not evidence of social realism but rather hyperrealism or a heightened realism. Thus, the colour-coordinated cubes of working-class life serve as symbols of a banal and packaged individualism rather than depictions of a grim social reality. These cells hide their contents from us and their conformist normality reflects something Renton is escaping from.

Editing

RENTON — SICK BOY — BEGBIE

SPUD — TOMMY

These title sequence freeze-frames serve to give the main characters in the film an immediate iconic status. Aside from foregrounding the notion of football as attractive and presenting the protagonists as an embattled team, the sequence also serves to introduce the key symbolic ideas of their characterisations: Renton as a cynical gremlin; Sick Boy, cool and argumentative; Begbie as violent and sadistic; Spud as a fool; and Tommy as the embattled honest straight.

Jump-cutting is another intriguing editing technique used throughout Spud's awkward, hyperactive interview. Here the edit works alongside the sparse mise-en-scène and claustrophobic set to create a comic effect. The juxtaposition of the interviewers' static body language and stern faces plus the absurdity of the space, with its awkward distance between Spud and them, all makes for comedy but is heightened by the abruptness of the jump-cuts and Spud's winning manner.

Sound

Music

The music in the film is chronological in its appearance and often has some narrative importance in terms of commentating on scenes rather than merely accompanying them. Thus 'Lust for Life' introduces Iggy Pop (an idol of Tommy's who is referred to in the film a number of times) as well as augmenting Renton's 'Chose life' monologue. The drug-induced haze of Lou Reed's 'Perfect Day' also acts as a counterpoint to Renton's far from perfect OD. 'Born Slippy', the anthem that concludes the film, ushers in mainstream rave culture and energises a nation.

Renton's voice-over

Throughout the film Renton narrates and his acerbic, cynical, foul-mouthed and resigned delivery perfectly captures the 'exhaustion' of Generation X. His escape from a dead-beat life of remorseless drug abuse and empty friendships is suggested by his sense of epiphany at the end of the film. Here he chooses life even though it is the life he has been previously criticising. Behind his euphoric smile, as he crosses the bridge in London to literally a new life, the spectator can't help but feel that Renton may be still deluding himself.

 S&C

Listen to Iggy Pop's song 'Nightclubbing' which also is heard in the film. How does it convey a sense of drugged inertia and disorientation?

Independent Activity

Find evidence of other Scottish stereotypes in film.

Independent Activity

Look at the first and most famous example of surreal short film making, *Un Chien Andalou* (1929) written by Dali and Buñuel (who was also the director), to gain an understanding of surrealism.

Performance (A level only)

The delivery of the voice-over has already been discussed but there are other, perhaps more subtle areas of the various performances on offer worth discussing.

Firstly, it is interesting to see how each of the main characters is defined through both mise-en-scène and through their performance. Renton is a smirking cynic and his final treachery is therefore not unexpected. Indeed, he has already messed up Tommy's life with the infamous 'video swap'. His relationships are paper thin and it is only towards clueless Spud and perhaps Tommy that he exhibits any compassion. With Sick Boy there is a sense of parity, they are after all best friends, but by the same argument their friendship is not deep. They are in some sense copies of each other: cool and rebellious types out for their own ends. Renton's only successful love making is with a teenage schoolgirl and on the whole he exists in a bubble of his own making: a narcotic, solipsistic world not unlike the 'carpet grave' into which he disappears when he ODs. His relationship with his parents is awkward: a sense of failure and disappointment overlaying their disgust at his addiction. But ultimately McGregor plays Renton as a likable, articulate and cheeky bestial gremlin. What prevents the audience from despising Renton is his boyish charm and the fact that we are positioned in the narrative to follow his journey. Thus, Sick Boy, despite his intellectual posturing, entrepreneurial nature and cool pop cultural asides, is somehow more of a despicable character.

Spud is, as we have already noted, aimless and amiable. His character acts as comic relief and incidents involving him are the comic high points of the film. The terrible faeces-covered sheet incident at his girlfriend's parents and his speed-assisted job interview are all played for laughs involving broad physical humour or verbal delivery. Generally, Spud is depicted as the moral core of the group, a happy-go-lucky buffoon but someone who wouldn't hurt a fly. This is achieved through his shambling gait, inarticulate speech and hapless behaviour.

In direct contrast to these three characters we have Begbie. Played by Robert Carlyle as a firecracker of a character: incendiary, explosive and indiscriminately aggressive. Carlyle makes Begbie strut like a bantam fighting cock, chest puffed out, short sharp hand movements, fierce verbal delivery full of expletives. The final scene where he is incandescent with rage reflects his defining feature. He is feared and despised. He is a bully and a sociopath, and when we laugh at his antics it is largely out of shock at his brazen nerve. Significantly, Begbie is a heavy drinker, a trait linking him to a stereotypical aspect of Scottish culture, so his scorn for hard drug use is presented as hypocritical.

Aesthetics

Surrealism and hallucination

The hyper-realism of the set design and cinematography is also enhanced by sequences that are clearly reflective of Renton's deranged mind. They are surreal in that they have a dream-like quality but more accurately they have the taint of nightmare, most obviously in the 'baby on the ceiling' hallucination of an addict enduring 'cold turkey' and the rescue of morphine suppositories from 'the Worst Toilet in Scotland'. Renton is forever disappearing and escaping. The nightmares only really become inescapable when he fights his addiction.

Humour

The film is permeated with an ironic tone; this is not a social realist film and that is of course why so many people took offence. The characterisations and dialogue are witty, as well as the situations the characters find themselves in, such as the surrealism of 'the worst toilet in Scotland'; the schadenfreude of Renton and Sick Boy shooting a thug's dog in the park; and the social embarrassment of stealing and playing of Tommy's sex tape. Strictly speaking the use of humour is not an obvious link to a film's aesthetics but the use of symbolism and surrealism are aesthetic choices and the fact that they are often used for a humourous rather than an estranging effect gives them credence in this section.

S&C

Choose a comic scene from the film and explain how the humour is achieved.

Representations

The following representations are illustrative of the binary categories at work in the film. However, the most controversial representation is that of drug use and drug culture. Even now it is hard not getting charmed by Renton and Sick Boy's smart patter, their cool 'heroin chic', and the trendy music and stylistics of the film itself. For some critics and viewers at least the film is too soft on drugs: one dead baby and Tommy's death from Aids being deemed not weighty enough for the catastrophe of heroin addiction in working-class areas of urban Scotland.

S&C

Research the Aids epidemic and how it helped define an era as well as how it fuelled homophobia.

Age

Age is represented through the nihilism of the Generation X experience, most vividly evidenced through the death of Allison's and Sick Boy's baby: they are unable, it seems, to successfully give life to a new generation. A contrasting generational representation occurs through the schoolgirl, Diane. Here is someone who is more in control of her own destiny and sexuality (unlike Renton).

Renton's parents and Spud's mum are sympathetically presented, somewhat in contrast to the norm of social realist, kitchen-sink dramas where the older generation is often portrayed as out of touch and spirit crushing. Renton is not running from his mum and dad but rather himself. Indeed, they offer a loving vision of humanity, largely devoid from the rest of the film's self-interested and venal characterisations.

Gender

Gender representation is largely male focused but both Tommy and Spud's girlfriends get screen time as does Sick Boy's girlfriend, Allison (another heroin addict) and Renton's on/off schoolgirl lover, Diane. However, these characters are largely love interests to the main protagonists and the film has little interest in them. Diane is the most empowered but the issue of her being perhaps under the legal age of consent creates numerous problems for the analyst as well as Renton. Renton's monologue in the London club towards the end of the film suggests that gender equality will become the norm: 'One thousand years from now there will be no guys and no girls.' The fact that Begbie discovers this, to his horror, with a transgender lover is a fitting commentary on his ultra-macho sexual redundancy.

Independent Activity

What other films create and challenge notions of a Gaelic identity?

 Independent Activity

Create a checklist of the suggested areas to cover in the study of narrative by the exam board and make notes on each section from each British film you study.

 Further information

Critical approaches to narrative

Formalism

This approach examines a film's structure and recognises the differences between the story and plot. An example provided in the exam board's Guidance for Teaching is as follows,

'Speidel (Nelmes, 2007) uses the example of "Bambi", in which the story and the plot are the same, charting a character's (Bambi's) life story from birth to death. The narrative follows the same order, chronologically. *We Need to Talk About Kevin* is, similarly, the story of Kevin from birth to adulthood. However, the non-linear narrative structure of events, seen from Kevin's mother Eva (Swinton)'s point of view provides a very different experience for audiences.' The films explored for this module, *Sightseers* and *Trainspotting*, are both predominantly linear but use fantasy or dream sequences that take the spectator on a surreal journey away from the central plot. These elaborations provide story detail by offering character insight and stylistic interest for the spectator.

Ethnicity

The film is largely filmed from a white male Scottish perspective and most screen time is devoted to 20-something Renton. Interestingly, the source novel does feature a black supporting character. Celtic ethnicity is, however, notably represented and Tommy's trip with Spud, Renton and Sick Boy to the Highlands leaves them all underwhelmed. It is as if even Tommy, the physically most stereotypical Scot, has become severed from his ethnic origins. If the film is about forging an identity and standing on your own two feet without crutches, then, for Tommy, the loss of his girlfriend and his sense of Gaelic identity could in part explain his descent into heroin addiction.

Narrative

In terms of narrative the exam board's Notes for Guidance suggest studying the following:

* Representation of time
* Use of narration/voice-over
* How dialogue propels the narrative
* Creation of drama or action
* Character development – heroes and villains, ambiguity
* Character alignment and identification
* How narratives present an ideological viewpoint
* Enigma codes
* Generic narratives and formulas
* Binary oppositions

The narrative construction of *Trainspotting* is largely linear and absolutely anchors our focus on the film's main protagonist, Renton. This is achieved through his voice-over starting the film and the first freeze-frame image introducing us to him in close-up. The plot absolutely follows Renton and there are very few scenes where he isn't present. He starts and ends the film, and it is his journey that the audience is primarily encouraged to follow. The film is, however, also an ensemble film (as evidenced by the marketing) and so we also do find out about main subsidiary characters such as Spud, Begbie and Sick Boy.

Critical approaches to narrative – formalism and structuralism

A formalist conception of narrative distinguishes between plot and story, and certainly *Trainspotting* matches this conception. The plot concerns the structuring of story information, effectively the order of events as presented in screen time; story is the world of the material that extends beyond plot, it is what we infer, rather than what we see.

We enter the story of Renton's life quite a long way into his descent into heroin addiction, and only hints from his parents and friends paint a backdrop of his life that precedes the first plot point: his escape from the security guards.

In terms of structuralist theory, there are clear binary opposites at work in the film. Binary opposites in narrative highlight the principal of conflict giving power and drive to the plotted material. Spud and Begbie are polar opposites. Sick Boy and Renton are evil twins. Drug users and non-drug users seem to exist in uneasy company with each other. Work and leisure do not seem to mix and no one seems able or willing to do conventional work. In the novel, Sick Boy becomes a pimp and Begbie a hardened burglar and thief. There are other binaries at work in terms of class, age, gender, region and nation, all referenced earlier.

Genre is a less obvious tool to use in this case but certainly films that concern drug abuse rarely end in such an upbeat, feel good manner as *Trainspotting*. Usually, the genre conventions require a sacrifice for the criminality displayed, but in *Trainspotting* only Tommy and the baby die and they are both innocents. Perhaps that is the overarching ideological message behind the film: drugs kill innocence. For just that reason Renton's escape can thus be read as a rebirth.

In terms of specific narrative techniques used in the film, the obvious conceit is that of using a voice-over to familiarise and engage the audience with the film's central protagonist: Renton. Our alignment with Renton makes the subsequent narrative that plays out engaging enough to stick with. Interestingly, the source novel is voiced by many of the characters, not only Renton, so the accumulation of their awful lives makes the novel a far harder read (psychologically not aesthetically) than the film.

In terms of cause and effect there are no enigmas left unsolved other than the exact character arcs of all the main cast: *T2 Trainspotting* was conceived in part to answer those broader questions. The use of a flashback to kick-start the film is an effective means of creating discontinuity in the narrative flow but the audience only realise this has happened later in the film.

From the sections covered above it should be clear that all aspects of film form, such as mise-en-scène, etc., have been used in this film to develop character insights and give sub-textual information to critical plot points.

Ideology

Ideology is a complex notion but in essence it is a belief that permeates a social group. Such beliefs can be relatively harmless or deeply pernicious. The following ideologies reflect commonly held beliefs at the time and reflect the tensions that a film can bring into the social discourse.

Aids

Aside from the Archie Gemmill goal, the one time we see a TV show in the film is when it's a fake game show hosted by Dale Winton about Aids, which haunts Renton's drug withdrawal hallucinations. The graffiti outside Tommy's flat ('Aids, Junky, Scum') also references the hostility faced by Aids sufferers and the tale told to Renton of Tommy's death by a friend is far from empathetic. Renton tests negative for Aids:

> It seems however I really am the luckiest guy in the world, several years of addiction right in the middle of an epidemic, surrounded by the living, but not me, I'm negative …

Aids was clearly a social problem and it still is a pressing problem for addicts who share needles.

Addiction and drugs

On the right we see Renton infantilised by his addiction. Returned to his parental home and the room he had as a kid, perhaps from this old nest he will be reborn. However, controversial and graphic detail of heroin use suggests that it is also a very pleasurable 'high' and in the opening sequence we see Spud high and happy.

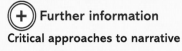

Further information

Critical approaches to narrative

Structuralism

This approach focuses on the binary oppositions used to structure a narrative. Binary oppositions are ideas or concepts that appear to oppose each other. They feature heavily in films as they help create tension and can provoke engagement as spectators enjoy taking a side. Analysing a narrative by looking at these oppositions can be a useful way to examine the film's key messages and themes. The exam board's Guidance for Teaching offers a useful example stating, 'in "Under the Skin", there are many binary oppositions at work, the most obvious being Alien V Human. However, there is no clearly delineated Good V Evil trajectory, which one may commonly associate with a Sci-Fi film about humans and an alien serial killer (Scarlett Johansson). This leads to an interesting audience response as we are often left in the position of feeling more empathy towards the alien than her victims.'

So the oppositions used in structuring films can be much more complicated than just two completely opposing forces clearly representing good and evil. Consider Renton, the hero of *Trainspotting*, a character with a questionable moral compass whose actions have such a terrible impact on Tommy. If he is one side of a binary opposition, what is he placed in opposition to? At times it seems that heroin is his nemesis and the film is structured around his battle with this. However, it could also be argued that his friendship group is his real opposition.

Sexuality

Renton says,

> *The world is changing, music is changing, drugs are changing, even men and women are changing. One thousand years from now there will be no guys and no girls ... It sounds great to me ... We're heterosexual by default not by decision. It's just a question about who you fancy.*

Aside from this very contemporary and liberal view on gender difference and sexuality, the film contains some nudity – male as well as female – and some positive representations of empowered and sexually active women. The sexually active schoolgirl, Diane, who Renton meets at a club, is perhaps the most shocking representation.

However, the film is partly about the absence of sexuality, as, aside from Tommy, none of the main characters have regular girlfriends because heroin is their lover. When Tommy loses his girlfriend he soon becomes an addict too.

Scotland and England

Above we can see Tommy attempting to lead Spud, Sick Boy and Renton on a refreshing walk in the great outdoors: a stereotype of Scottish nature and its rugged outdoor appeal. Renton rebels, 'It's shite being Scottish!' They all get back on the train and return to the city where in the next scene they are all back on the heroin, sadly soon followed by Tommy.

Later in the film Renton decides 'to find something new'. Leaving heroin and Scotland behind he heads to London, introduced with an upbeat dance track and a highly ironic montage of the tourist stereotype that is our capitol with Big Ben, red buses and cockneys.

The mediated reality of Scotland and England is a far cry from the actual truth. In the scene following this cheesy montage of London we see Renton as a rental agent letting out overpriced city appartments.

Drug films

Trainspotting can be seen as part of a cycle of films about drugs which have come out of Hollywood and the UK. They are usually films that also reflect on problems of generational conflict and youth alienation. A US film that shares *Trainspotting*'s

 S&C

Look at the drugs awareness website, TalktoFrank, and research the effects of heroin addiction. How honestly has the film portrayed these effects?

 S&C

Visit the Scottish tourist board's website, Visit Scotland. How far does its vision of Scotland contrast with that of *Trainspotting*?

critique of culture and heroin addiction would be *Requiem for a Dream* (Aronofsky, 2000). This film shows the dark effect of heroin addiction in a technically stylish way while also confounding simplistic notions of drug addiction: one of the main characters is a middle-aged woman addicted to diet pills.

Youth underclass movie cycle

Trainspotting is also a film about an underclass and so, despite its hyper-realism rather than social realism, and despite its irony and heavy use of non-diegetic music, it can still can be seen as a film that helps audiences understand social groups often ignored and sidelined by conventional film. Thus, *Trainspotting* could be read alongside working-class youth films from the UK such as *Kidulthood* (Huda, 2006), *This is England* (Meadows, 2007) and *Attack the Block* (Cornish, 2011), and from overseas *La Haine* (Kassovitz, France, 1995) and *City of God* (Meirelles, Brazil, 2002).

Summary

Trainspotting remains an era-defining film and is one of the most successful UK films of the 1990s. Aside from its ability to talk to a generation and capture the zeitgeist, it remains (despite the huge critical and financial success of 2009s *Slumdog Millionaire*) Danny Boyle's defining film. Its vibrant soundtrack, its aspirational new stars (Ewan McGregor most famously), its wit, its controversial representation of Scotland and its energetically edited, beautifully shot material led to some criticism for its perceived glamorisation of a drug-fuelled lifestyle. True or not, the marketing for the film certainly communicated to its audience a sense of cool, featuring iconic portrait mid-long shots of the main characters as well as trumpeting the arrival of a new wave of UK cinema.

Trainspotting affords us many opportunities to apply an ideologically critical approach not least from the broad perspectives of politics and feminism. A political approach would involve applying various political ideologies to the text. For example, the anti-materialistic and anti-consumerist stance of Renton in his 'choose life' monologue clearly presents him as a character who does not feel enfranchised by the opportunities given to him in a Liberal Democracy such as the UK. Renton is a disenfranchised nihilist and as such his political views are paper thin and without partisan allegiance. He is angry and disillusioned and pointedly apolitical.

Conversely, a feminist critical approach yields more insights. A feminist perspective would note the literal sidelining of the protagonists' girlfriends in the opening montage of the football match. Here, the young women are acting the thankless task of 'supporters' and that is largely their role throughout the film. As such, the film tends to operate within a fairly traditional patriarchal structure: the main protagonists are all male who activate the plot and women play a largely passive supporting role. However, Diane's character is arguably a female representation that challenges this hegemonic view. Diane is very much in control. She makes decisions and initiates action, not least by sleeping with Renton. That she is still a schoolgirl and deceiving her liberal middle-class parents turns her act of empowerment into something more questionable and troubling; not least from the very illegality of the sex act with Renton, something she cunningly reminds him of. Diane is therefore powerful but, like many of the characters in *Trainspotting*, even she is flawed.

 S&C

Watch *Requiem for a Dream* and consider the techniques used to convey the effects of drug abuse; however, beware, it is a very powerful and shocking film. How does it compare with *Trainspotting*?

The institutional and production contexts of *Sightseers*

Sightseers began life as a series of short comedy improvisations by writers and comic actors, Alice Lowe and Steve Oram. They further developed their characters over a number of years, finding dark humour in the idea of a murderous couple going on a caravanning holiday in the Midlands and north of England. Political theorist, Hannah Arendt's concept of the 'banality of evil' is thus given an amusing tweak leading some commentators to reverse the idea and, in terms of *Sightseers*' mise-en-scène at least, note the 'evil of banality'. In a BFI interview in 2014 Lowe noted:

> *We wanted to take the stereotype of British tourism, which has this extremely polite veneer, and do something that confounded that.*
> (O'Callaghan, 2014)

Oram and Lowe then worked up their characters into a short teaser film directed by Paul King who had directed the very 'off-the-wall' TV comedy show *The Mighty Boosh*. Initially, no TV broadcaster was interested in the 'very dark material' but the teaser impressed Edgar Wright (UK auteur famous for *Shaun of the Dead* (2004), *Hot Fuzz* (2007) and the TV sit-com *Spaced*) who went on to receive an executive producer credit for the film. Wright had contacts at the independent TV and film production company, Big Talk Productions, which had made the majority of his films and TV work. He passed the material to Wheatley and Rook Films (Wheatley's production company) intuiting correctly that Wheatley was the perfect director to helm Oram and Lowe's cinematic vision. Wheatley too was impressed, as he'd just made *Kill List* and was looking for something comic to cleanse his directorial palette. In the 2014 BFI interview cited above he commented:

> *I knew I wanted to do a comedy after Kill List – something that might make people laugh as opposed to unhappy! I fancied doing something that was fast and loose, and the prospect of working with comedians who had an improvisation background appealed. In terms of the script, I liked that Chris's character was quite anarchic and breaking out from his constraints, and that with encouragement Tina goes even further. I was also drawn to the sweeter rom-com elements of the story.*

Budgets remain hard to track down but in 2012 David Gritten in the *Daily Telegraph* noted it was £1.2 million. The film, despite hugely positive reviews and a Cannes Film Festival premiere, didn't sustain itself at the box office (as of September 2017 IMDb has a figure of just over $1 million in the domestic market and the same again for overseas sales). However, the film has generated a cult audience and found life on DVD and beyond. In many ways the film is a textbook example of low-budget UK film funding, with money coming from Film4 and the BFI. The subject matter is 'quirky' and the treatment something of a hybrid combining horror, comedy and social realism. The star of the film, as one strapline on a DVD suggests, is its production provenance rather than its largely unknown cast:

> *From the acclaimed director of* Kill List *and the producers of* Shaun of the Dead.

Its 15 certificate was also designed to maximise an audience, with *Kill List* and *Down Terrace* both garnering the badge of out and out horror, 18. The film also continued Wheatley's involvement with his wife, creative partner and business partner, Amy Jump, who received a screenwriting credit and helped edit the film.

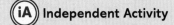

Independent Activity

Look at the websites for Big Talk Productions and Rook Films. What links them?

Independent Activity

Look at the rest of Wheatley's work. But be careful as some of the material is very strong and the overall effect of his films (certainly his first two films) can be very disconcerting.

The social/political/cultural contexts of *Sightseers*

The focus of the film is the 'psychologies' of the main characters and the landscape and spaces through which they travel. This is something that really upsets Chris when he meets people who are on paper 'better than him' such as the middle-class caravanning couple and the National Trust member. With the latter character Chris is also angered by the man's supposed sense of entitlement, as he went to a public school. Chris, in particular, sees himself as something of an avenging class and eco-warrior but there is little or any ideology to back up his own prejudices. Tina also shows little political awareness.

Culturally the film has more relevance, as its heavy irony and hybridity could be said to illustrate yet another strand of postmodernity. Certainly, Wheatley's career seems at home with postmodern attitudes to genre, narrative and character.

Historically and socially Chris and Tina exist in an early 21st-century context but they are not connected to the contemporary world. One obvious instance of this is when Tina writes Chris a love note after an argument, using a huge pencil. It's a visual gag but its also acts as further evidence of Tina's estrangement from the present. Their love of knitting, a dated form of recreation, further isolates them from the contemporary world and is something also played-up on in terms of one of the film's tagline:

> *Killers have never been this close-knit.*

They are both emotionally stunted humans, unable to liberate themselves, but both are desperately seeking liberation. In many ways Chris and Tina are postmodern entities, cut off from reality by their rootless, backwards looking nostalgia.

A more pertinent social analysis can be found in the avowed feminism of the film. Lowe's character, Tina, steps out from the controlling shadows of Chris and her mother to, at least for a short time, become her own person. We will investigate this idea further in the later sections on 'Representation' and 'Ideology'.

In terms of further political, cultural and social contexts, both Chris and Tina, as noted above, exist in a disconnected relationship with their world and one interpretation of this representation could be that the modern world is disconnected too. Tina cannot communicate with her mum. Chris feels he needs a muse to create. Chris's writing, when briefly glimpsed, is that of a child: incoherent and scribbled. And despite all the signposts on their road trip they seem lost in life. This sense of disconnection makes an astute social and political critique oblique at best.

Tina, it could be argued, is so infantile and inward focused in terms of her love of Poppy and domesticity that she cannot engage politically. Murder, not democracy, is her chosen method for political transformation. Chris, on the other hand, has some vague political sense of class-consciousness and eco-activism, but his ideologies are as much expressions of his attempt to give meaning to his unhappy life, as they are authentic expressions of political awareness.

Once again, then, Chris and Tina can be read as metaphors for the heart of a contemporary England: vapid, empty, and seething with repressed anger and resentment. Their alienation is fuelled by a crushing sense of low self-esteem, finding themselves disconnected from a shabby and loveless modern world. Indeed, they and the film (and England) are always looking back to a happier past (museums, National Trust properties and old ruins loom large in the film).

'Show me your world, Chris', Tina urges Chris as they embark on their journey. Smiling with worldly pride Chris informs her, 'I thought we could start with the Crich Tram Museum.'

The film form of *Sightseers*

Realism is the dominant form of this film. Indeed, the opening exchanges between Tina and her mum and then Chris are social realist in style: hand-held single camera in naturalistic locations. This is Wheatley's aesthetic combined with an experimental streak that has something in common with the French New Wave's relaxed and often ground-breaking treatment of the form: a further example (aside from those techniques mentioned above) could be the use of jump-cuts.

In terms of the narrative flow the film is largely linear, although we do get a flashback to the death of Tina's dog and there are two dream sequences: one from each of the main characters' perspectives. Tina's dream is the first and also acts as a montage of Chris's second murder, reflecting her awareness and acceptance of his psychotic nature. Chris's dream suggests a possible outcome for Tina (arrest by the police) and reflects his growing unease with Tina's emergent empowerment. Aside from these non-linear flourishes, the film adopts the road trip trope of travel and arrival and departure. Only at the end do we have a cliff-hanger ending of sorts, as Chris literally exits the frame and the film by jumping off a bridge to his death while Tina remains standing at the bridge head.

Cinematography

There are some wonderfully filmed scenes of natural beauty to complement the realist, low-budget shooting style favoured by Wheatley. Laurie Rose has been director of photography on all Wheatley's films to date and must take a lot of credit for some of the most memorable images in *Sightseers*.

In the screenshot above, we first meet Tina and her mum. Mum is groaning in pain and Tina is hidden by the barrier of a door. Visually this medium two-shot symbolises their dysfunctional relationship. Verbally the inability for at least Tina to communicate with her domineering mother is further echoed by her insistent repetition of the word 'mum' (eight times) falling on deaf-ears. Mum's pain is due to the death of their dog Poppy, who we have already seen in photographs in the opening credit sequence. Mum explains that Poppy was her only friend, to which Tina replies that she is her mother's friend too. Mum's response is dismissive and barbed: 'You're not a friend; you're just a relative.'

In the next scene we understand that Tina is 34, she's met someone (Chris) and is planning a holiday. Her mum sees this as a threat and taunts Tina that she is actually running away from her guilt at accidentally killing Poppy. Tina's mum picking up Poppy's leash further condemns Tina and is also symbolic of her own entrapment as if she were her mother's pet.

The shot above is the final close-up, two-shot of lovers Chris and Tina. Filmed in slow-motion and accompanied by Frankie Goes to Hollywood's 1980s classic, 'The Power of Love', Tina and Chris watch their caravan burn and unsettle the spectator by breaking the fourth wall. Having dispensed with her rival to Chris's affections and reignited their passions, the couple are, it seems, destined to literally go out in blaze of glory by leaping to their deaths in a romantic double suicide.

In the final shot of the film, above, Chris has jumped to his death and Tina is left standing on Ribblehead Viaduct. Now alone, she is in complete charge of her own destiny, a process she has been building towards, no matter how psychotically, throughout the film.

In conclusion, the cinematography, which is eye-catching and loaded with interpretative meaning, seems to act on two levels. Firstly, there is the dour realism of the earlier scenes with their hand-held aesthetic and then there is the more symbolic and surreal quality of the latter half of the film with its dream sequences and enigmatic dénouement.

Mise-en-scène

Much of the film's dark humour derives from its juxtaposition of murder with real scenes of natural beauty and more quirky tourist sites like the Crich Tram Museum and Pencil Museum. Even the weaponisation of the caravan, itself an item of quaint fun for many, is loaded with dark humour.

Above we can see the first proper close-up two-shot with Tina and Chris. They are in Tina's dated and unfashionable bed together separated by a teddy bear that symbolises Tina's immaturity and probable virginity. In this scene we learn that Tina was unhappy as a child and that she hates the room and would be quite happy if it were destroyed. It is a familiar domestic space but in Wheatley's hands it becomes a source of psychological misery and repressed violence. Tina's red pillow speaks of a reservoir of psychic fury, which Chris will soon unwittingly unleash. They both confess to being unhappy at school. Chris notes he was 'invisible' and didn't like having ginger hair. They are both clearly outsiders, something further emphasised by their bland, anachronistic dress codes.

Later in the film (see shot below) their infantilism is further echoed through the use of playgrounds to represent their alienation from the adult world.

The use of footwear in the above shot is an effective way to crisply illustrate the varied goals and self-identity of Chris and Tina. The rugged walking boots communicate the fundamental aspirations of Chris the manly adventurer. Indeed, later in the film he tells Tina that,

> Mobility [is] the key to personal opportunity ... I want to be captain of my own fate.

In his mind they are on an 'erotic odyssey'. Tina, on the other hand, wears feminine pink slippers, which serve to identify her as the old-fashioned maternal homemaker.

The film includes a montage depicting the harmonious relationship Chris and Tina have now developed. This part of the film represents their romantic peak, alone together in a desolate landscape but one which, like in the extreme long shot above, is littered with death. The carcass of an animal in the foreground of this deep focus shot provides a grim counterpoint to romantic views of nature.

Chris is disappointed with Tina for 'going off schedule' and murdering the bride and he is also attracted to Martin and his lifestyle. Martin's prototype invention, the Carapod, is attractive to Chris's sense of wanderlust and self-containment. It is a more rugged and solitary form of the caravan he currently possesses. Tina goes to the Pencil Museum alone, while Martin and Chris play around with the Carapod. Even the dog they steal, Banjo, which they rename Poppy, rejects Tina. This is Tina's low point and significantly it is now that she makes contact with her mother again.

Tina writes Chris a love note in the shot above, which is incongruous and childish, dwarfed by the huge pencil 'the big Scribbler' which she has just bought for £24.00. The film cuts between her alone at the Pencil Museum and Chris enjoying himself with Martin.

In conclusion, as with cinematography above, we can see the use of mise-en-scène operating on many levels but most clearly in terms of both realism and symbolism.

Editing

The editing is quick paced, at times reflecting Wheatley's love of short films and his origins in the world of viral filmmaking and advertising. Consequently, scenes are not generally held for long. He likes to use slow motion in places (the first four death scenes use slow-mo) and complex montages to music, but he doesn't usually do cut-aways between scenes unless for atmosphere. He edits all his work and his wife Amy Jump and his business partner and collaborator Robin Hill are also credited with the editing of *Sightseers*.

The film's first significant montage cuts between three planes of action all taking place early in the morning: Chris stalking Ian on the moors; Janice making breakfast and Tina tossing and turning in her sleep. The two darkly humorous shots below match actions on a cut: Ian's murder with a rock and Janice breaking an egg for breakfast.

 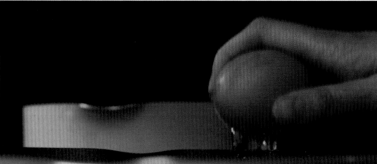

In the screenshot on the right we see a presentiment of Tina's possible destiny and her inevitable arrest. Montages traditionally are used to condense time, so this shot, appearing as it does so very briefly, may simply act as a precognitive flash forwards. However, it may also represent a more literal image of Chris's wish fulfilment as he wants rid of Tina.

Sound

Sightseers uses a number of off-beat and leftfield songs not least in the montage sequences. A recurring tune is Hot Fudge's eerie cover of 'The Season of the Witch' by 1960s folk musician Donovan. Earlier, when the couple start their journey, Soft Cell's obviously symbolic 'Tainted Love' pointedly accompanies them as they escape Tina's mum in their caravan. The impact of these choices is to serve both as a direct commentary on the narrative and to further alienate the present by conjoining it with a retrospective soundscape.

In the third murder, a stanza from the patriotic poem/song 'Jerusalem' by William Blake and read by John Hurt, provides an ironic undercurrent to Chris murdering the walker. Ironic, of course, because 'Jerusalem' is seen as a quintessentially patriotic anthem to England and its use here underscores the poverty of that notion. The murder is the first witnessed by Tina, Chris having confessed to killing Ian the day before. She is now utterly complicit in the killing spree, agreeing a bit later to not tell and also musing that she herself had never really thought about killing innocent people. This scene is the turning point for Tina's descent into murderous psychosis. The poem ends abruptly with the words 'dark, satanic' and then the soundtrack cuts to the diegetic crunch of the rambler's head being smashed against an ancient stone (part of the Kimberley Stone Circle), thus omitting the concluding world 'mills'. The effect is startling for the spectator but the shock soon evaporates as Chris then says, 'Report that to the National Trust mate!'

Performance (A level only)

The characters derive from improvised performances created by Oram and Lowe over a number of years. Wheatley has a reputation for encouraging adlibs and improvisation, so the three are a perfect meld. To aide their scriptwriting Lowe and Oram took a caravan holiday together and tried to infuse their characters with a plausible level of realism. This is certainly evident in their lovemaking, which is treated in a haphazard and un-explicit manner. An interesting contrast could be the murderous young lovers in *Natural Born Killers* (Stone, 1995), who sport their rock star looks with an unabashed sense of cool charm, and whose love is consummated with passion. Chris and Tina are attracted to one another but this soon wanes and the sensuality of their love is parodied in Tina's home-knitted lingerie set.

 Independent Activity

Read the poem 'Jerusalem'. What poem would you use to create a patriotic sequence?

Aesthetics

The most significant aesthetic device at work in this film is the realism of its settings and locations, and an improvised set of performances. The 'banality of evil' is given a twist and becomes 'the evil of the banal' (a subtle but revealing reversal). Thus, in Hannah Arendt's original use of the phrase to describe the humdrum inhumanity of the perpetrators of the holocaust, we find caravanning, knitting, cardigans, the Midlands, tourist sites and so on all having an equally perverse part to play in mass murder but now as cause rather than effect. The decision to not stage the deaths as conventional 'horror' murders and preserve a 15 certificate also means that there is little explicit gore and that most of the victims are all murdered outside in daylight; all bar the bride-to-be who dies at night.

Representations

Critic, Neil Young, writing for the website Jigsaw Lounge (2013), noted that,

> *Sightseers joins classics like the* Wicker Man *and* Witchfinder General *as horror-inflected by unnerving explorations of Britain's wilder, more remote landscapes, lending an ominous cast to even the most picturesque of landscapes.*

This review is spot on. The film takes us to a number of off-kilter tourist sites imbuing them with a sense of menace, the very germ of 'incongruous humour' that acted as the originating premise for Oram's and Lowe's banal monsters.

Age

Tina and Chris are still children – adults who have never grown up. They are even depicted playing on swings in playgrounds. Tina, however, has yet to leave the maternal bosom and is very much a prisoner in her home. The opening words of 'Mum!' repeated endlessly to deaf ears speaks volumes about their dysfunctional and uneven relationship. Chris is Tina's escape. 'Show me your world', she says to him full of hope and expectation when they eventually take off in the caravan. Chris's limited horizons are, however, evidenced by their first stop at the Crich Tram Museum, where Chris's dark side is unleashed. The man he kills – a litterbug who rudely resists Chris's remonstrations – can be read as the juvenile presence in this scene and Chris as the stern patriarch and lawmaker. That Chris, in a fit of rage, runs his caravan over the man, serves to both weaponise the homely vehicle as well as detach Chris from any dawning maturity.

Tina's mum is presented as a repressive and monstrous force, venal and deceitful in her efforts to make her daughter return to her and to punish her daughter for her accidental killing of their much loved dog, Poppy. 'Murderer!' she accuses Tina, in a moment of ironic precognition, for that is, of course, what Tina will soon become.

Tina's mum is also very much a stereotype of the bitter, insular and neurotic elderly woman. Presumably she is widowed, although no pictures of her husband are evident. Her relationship with Tina is clearly one that lacks any warmth and tenderness (the opening exchange, for example) and equally she seems happy to infantilise Tina to keep her with her at home, much as a pet. The fixation they both have on pasta sauce reflects Tina's insecurities, which manifest themselves on the most basic level of food and which mum clearly encourages as a means to further infantilise Tina.

Independent Activity

Watch the original *Wicker Man* and the *Witchfinder General* and compare them with *Kill List*.

It's worth hypothesising that if *Sightseers* were *Down Terrace* (Wheatley's first feature) then surely Tina would have murdered her mum with a cricket bat and then put on the kettle for a nice cup of tea. As it is, Tina only needs Chris to liberate her.

Otherwise, the majority of characters that Chris and Tina encounter are of the same age as themselves: mid-30s to 40s. An interesting example of psychic-slippage, whereby wish-fulfillment spills into real life, involves Tina and Chris pretending to be Janice and Ian when they meet a nice older couple at Fountains Abbey. Janice and Ian, with their bigger model of caravan, Ian's professional status as a published author, and Janice's role as homemaker and surrogate mummy of Banjo (Poppy) are the kind of people Tina and Chris wish they were. The film, however, depicts them as cold and superior, and later in the film Chris notes that why he killed Ian was Ian's 'smug complacency'. This also links to class and throws light onto Chris's inferred working-class origins.

Gender

By far the most interesting aspect of the film is its treatment of gender. Tina is at first in awe of Chris. He is a writer and she is his muse. Chris does just that and inadvertently unleashes Tina's murderous impulses. However, he loses control of her. The sexual abandon of their early relationship becomes more clinical and Tina's lovingly homemade knitted lingerie fails to ignite Chris's fading ardour. He accuses Tina of being chaotic in her murdering, thus playing on the stereotype of the cool calculating killer (Chris) and the emotional hothead (Tina). In fact, the very opposite applies.

Chris kills the litterbug at the tram museum and the walker at the stone circle in an unpremeditated rage supposedly justified by his sense of self as firstly an eco-warrior and then as a class-avenger. Only the writer is murdered on the moorland hill with a more measured sense of brutality. Tina kills the bride and the jogger and the cyclist in his Carapod on sudden whims of anger but she is not so different from Chris despite his own delusions of psychopathic grandeur. Thus, their gender stereotypes are subverted whereby he is no less or no more rational than her. Indeed, a raw and desperate emotionality dominates both their lives and as the murders stack up it is only Tina who in the end shows a level of thought and off-kilter reasoning.

Ethnicity

There are no ethnic representations in the film other than those identifying as white British Midlanders. The impact of this choice is, however, intriguing as suggested above, whereby the Midlands is a paradigm for England itself: literally the beating heart of our country. That this heartland is presented as an all-white preserve (despite the multiculturalism and ethnic diversity of the region) is clearly an intended under-representation to emphasise Chris and Tina's monotonous, reactive and backwards looking life.

Narrative

The narrative is largely linear, as mentioned above. The film very much follows the tropes of both rom-coms and horror films in that the plot moves around brutal killings enacted by both characters and the impact of those deaths on the couple's relationship. As we can see in the box below, Tina's final killing matches Chris's tally of three and in some sense unites them again as the cyclist Chris had befriended was inadvertently coming between them.

> **Death 1**: Litterbug; Crich Tram Museum; impulsive; caravan used as weapon by Chris.
>
> **Death 2**: Middle-class caravan owner and writer – Ian; caravan park; premeditated; Chris stalks and bludgeons victim; Tina dreams of Chris and unconsciously suspects.
>
> **Death 3**: Middle-class rambler; impulsively bludgeoned by Chris; Tina complicit.
>
> **Death 4**: Bride to be; restaurant; impulsively pushed to her death by Tina; Chris outraged.
>
> **Death 5**: Jogger; on the road; Tina impulsively runs him over while driving; Chris outraged.
>
> **Death 6**: Cyclist – Martin; desolate valley; Tina impulsively pushes him over a cliff in his 'Carapod'; Chris outraged and then forgiving when he realises Tina is 'a force of nature'.
>
> **Death 7**: Chris; suicide; Ribblehead Viaduct; Tina is liberated.

Critical approaches to narrative – formalism and structuralism

A formalist conception of narrative distinguishes between plot and story, and certainly *Sightseers* matches this conception. The story begins with Tina and Chris's life when they are in their 30s and you only really get glimpses of the fairly dull and miserable lives they must have both led. Chris remains the bigger enigma and his statement that he brought an older girlfriend to a certain spot in the countryside is eerily loaded, as if he may have buried her there. At least with Tina we meet her mum, see her home and bedroom, and see some of her back story presented to us in a flashback: the tragic and cruelly funny death of poor Poppy the family's beloved pet dog, skewered by knitting needles.

In terms of structuralist theory there are clear binary opposites at work in the film, as discussed previously. Men and women form a natural cleavage point as well as class. The latter is most keenly felt by Chris, with his aspirations and insecure sense of class consciousness: two of his victims are most definitely middle-class and educated men with a kind of (to use Chris's words) 'sense of entitlement'.

Genre is an obvious tool to use in this film. The film is a psychodrama and a love story. An odd hybrid but not unique as films such as *Bonnie and Clyde* (Penn, 1967) and *Natural Born Killers* (Stone, 1994) testify. However, it is a narrative convention of such genre films (effectively subgenres of the crime and horror families) that the key protagonist must die and effectively atone for their crimes. This, it could be argued, is the ideological underpinning of such films: you can't get away with it and if you transgress you will be punished.

In terms of specific narrative techniques used in the film, the obvious conceit is that of aligning our sympathies with Tina very early on. Her sheepish interactions with her clearly mentally unstable and invalid mother create an enormous empathy for her and her sense of confinement and lack of emotional warmth. Chris is very much, on this reading, the knight in shining armour rescuing her from a wicked witch's enchantments.

In terms of cause and effect there are some enigmas left unsolved. The use of a flashback and two dream sequences creates some discontinuity in the narrative flow and the question of Tina's fate is never really resolved. Will she jump later or will the police arrest her like we witnessed in Chris's dream. Tina's future remains uncertain at the end of the film but what is clear is that she has dispensed with Chris. Tina represents a princess that no longer needs her knight, so she is more of an active rather than passive protagonist.

From the sections covered above it should be clear too that all aspects of film form, such as mise-en-scène, etc., have been used in this film to develop character insights and give sub-textual information to critical plot points.

Ideology

The film does not satirise contemporary lifestyles as *Trainspotting* does but contents itself with a study of the psychologies of Tina and Chris. Equally, the film is not really a satire of caravanning as one may suppose. Indeed, Wheatley was at a pains not to depict the pastime as ludicrous. The caravan itself acts as a metaphor for the paradox of Tina and Chris's claustrophobic and yet outward-bound relationship. In one early shot we see Chris in his walking boots and Tina in her slippers and thus the caravan is both Chris's means of transport and Tina's home. Its use as a weapon, by both of them, perfectly symbolises their deranged viewpoints and shared psychologies.

Ideologically a feminist approach yields the most mileage for analysis as suggested above. In such a reading of the film the narrative focus concerns Tina (not Chris) and the character arc follows her quest for liberation (not his). That she is driven to the murder (in the first instance) of a young bride and that her gaoler is her mother suggest that the film does not present a simplistic male/female binary. However, the story is ultimately Tina's and we applaud (despite ourselves) her decision not to die with Chris. Despite being a homicidal maniac she becomes a figure of female empowerment and we are cleverly encouraged to cheer her achievement.

 S&C

Research notions of the monstrous feminine, the final girl and abjection in feminist film theory. Do they apply to Tina?

Further guidance on ideological approaches

The exam board's Notes for Guidance helpfully define political or feminist ideological approaches and offer suggestions on how they should be applied.

A political approach

> *All films are rooted in some kind of political reality and posit some kind of political position, either explicitly or implicitly. For example, a film may focus on poverty and the lives of people living on the margins of society. A starting point would be to ask whether these lives are represented sympathetically.*

A feminist approach

This could be taught by looking at feminist filmmakers, feminist academics and feminist analyses of patriarchal genres (such as Barbara Creed's writings about the horror genre) and their re-appropriation of so-called 'women's pictures' such as romantic-comedies and musicals.

> *In some assessments of these sections, learners will be required to analyse the usefulness of applying a critical approach. The implication is that the film was viewed somewhat innocently before being critically interrogated. As a result of this interrogation the student is able to claim greater understanding and insight into the film's complexities.*

Applying an ideological critical approach

The film is a beautifully observed dark comedy of manners, reminding some commentators of films such as *Kind Hearts and Coronets* (Hamer, 1949) that have a murderous protagonist and a high body count with victims all dispatched in ingenious and tongue-in-cheek ways. Certainly, the humour in the film derives largely from its violent set pieces and their incongruous settings. However, the English landscape, the caravan as a road trip device and the central pairing of two odd-ball but romantically involved killers all give the film its quirky character.

Sightseers affords us many opportunities to apply an ideological critical approach not least from the broad perspectives of politics and feminism. A political approach would involve applying various political ideologies to the text. Thus, a broadly conservative approach would see the film as deeply problematic as it seems to align our sympathies with psychotic murderers and doesn't really dole out the justice they evidently deserve. Equally, a liberal sensibility would find it hard to develop empathy with Chris and Tina. As with *Trainspotting*, Chris and Tina largely exist in their own bubble, a depoliticised haze of internalised resentments. Chris is the more political of the two with his awareness of class 'entitlement' and his distrust of middle-class institutions such as the *Daily Mail* and the National Trust. However, his class struggle is really only a product of his social inadequacies and a sense of profound personal failure. His murderous acts are not political despite his attempted justifications of them in terms of environmentalism or working-class rage.

Feminism yields more interesting results. As we have seen, Tina is in some ways empowered by her psychotic holiday with Chris. Indeed, although the film starts in fairly traditional patriarchal territory with Chris holding his clipboard and itinerary, Tina soon outgrows her knight in shining armour and becomes his femme fatale. Chris's dream sequence details this well as we see him in a knight's helmet, screaming as a vampiric Tina drains the blood of a victim. At the end of the film Tina is the last one standing and it is she who rejects Chris's suicidal overtures. Once she had escaped her mum's oppression, Tina's warped psyche properly blossoms: producing a Venus Fly Trap rather than the sweet fragrant flowers of her much loved potpourri.

The film remains one of Wheatley's most accessible films and carries all the hallmarks of his work but equally it is not penned by himself or his wife, Amy Jump, so care must be taken with an overt auteur judgement.

However, the film's wit, its improvised realism, the violence, its low-budget treatment and finally its more exuberant and experimental montages all give it an identity which is unmistakably that of Ben Wheatley.

Sample essay extract and feedback

How useful has an ideological critical approach been in understanding the narrative resolution of your chosen films?

For this example we are looking at an **extract** from an essay addressing *Trainspotting* and *Sightseers* and applying a feminist ideological approach.

Opening paragraphs addressing the question above may look like this:

Adam's response extract

For this section I have studied *Trainspotting* (Boyle, 1996) and *Sightseers* (Wheatley, 2012). In terms of both films I think I have gained insights through the application of the ideological critical approach of feminism. A general feminist position argues that the conventional film industry is patriarchal in both its organisation and treatment of women. Both films studied have a social realist flavour but they are not strictly social realist movies with *Sightseers* emerging from the comic-horror sub-genre and *Trainspotting* having links with counter-culture drug movies.

Trainspotting is arguably a critique of contemporary Scottish society and the apathy of a drug-raddled Generation X sensibility. The main characters in the film are all male as are the majority of the production personnel. Thus, the insights gained through a feminist approach are subtle and as much to do with the absence of women or the peripheral value of the few female roles. *Sightseers*, on the other hand, is co-written by a woman, comedian Alice Lowe who also stars as a key protagonist, Tina. The film opens and closes with Tina's experience and it is perhaps significant that Lowe subsequently buoyed by the success of *Sightseers* went on to write, direct and star in an avowedly feminist horror feature called *Prevenge* (Lowe, 2017).

Feedback

This is a good response so far because the candidate immediately tells the examiner what texts they have studied. Then reference is made to key terms from the question such as 'ideological critical approach' and an approach is name-checked (feminism) and very briefly defined. In an exam it is important not to waste time defining theories but rather to devote most of your time to 'applying' them to the films.

Some knowledge is shown of the generic nature of both films as well as referencing a patriarchal industry. Then a summary of the problems and opportunities faced by applying a feminist approach to these two films is briefly discussed before the reference to Prevenge *which further anchors* Sightseers' *credentials as the more avowedly feminist text.*

What remains is now for the candidate to seek out at least three scenes from each film that lend themselves to the application of a feminist approach in particular with reference to the 'narrative resolution'. Bearing in mind that 'narrative resolution' is our focus it is still legitimate to at the very least discuss the opening scenes to show the journey of a protagonist and perhaps a pivotal scene from later in the film's development and plot which encapsulates a feminist approach and points towards the film's resolution.

AS: European film

A level: Global filmmaking perspectives

This section will help you prepare for Component 2: Global filmmaking perspectives on the A level course and Component 2: European film (AS). The focus is on the three core areas of study. This chapter will use the French/Turkish film *Mustang* (Ergüven, 2015) as a case study.

For AS

You answer one question from a choice of two and must refer to both your chosen films. You should spend 50 minutes on your response.

For A level

You will answer one 40 mark question from a choice of two, requiring reference to two global films: one European and one produced outside Europe. You should allow 60 minutes for your answer.

The specification says

Global film extends the range and diversity of narrative film by studying their distinct geographical, social, cultural world and a particular expressive use of film form.

Mustang, *the debut feature film from Deniz Gamze Ergüven, explores the lives of five orphaned girls in a remote Turkish village who are growing up in a strict environment with arranged marriages looming over them.*

5 *Mustang* (Ergüven, 2015)

Mustang is the debut feature film of Turkish-French director Deniz Gamze Ergüven, who co-wrote the screenplay with Alice Winocour. The screenplay draws on the experiences Ergüven and her cousins witnessed while growing up in Turkey and of young Turkish women more widely.

The film is set in Turkey and centres on five sisters, aged 12–16, who find their lives transformed one summer. Their parents have been dead for ten years and they live in a remote Turkish village with their uncle and grandmother. The film's exploration of gender, youth and identity met with mixed reactions, with international critics praising the film for its depiction of 'what it means to be young and female in Turkey' (Ide, 2016).

However, in Turkey the film met with criticism, as Ergüven reported,

> ... *I had some very aggressive, negative critiques there* [in Turkey], *the kind of thing I hadn't received anywhere else.* (Ide, 2016)

The criticism stemmed from Ergüven not being 'Turkish enough' (she was born in Turkey, moved to France when she was two, and spent her childhood between the two countries as dictated by her father's governmental work commitments) and by its brutal depiction of the young girls' forced marriages, sexual abuse and imprisonment. These issues will be discussed further in the social and political contexts, and the representation sections.

Although filmed in Turkey, covertly to not anger local residents, the film is a French–German–Turkish co-production, with the majority of the $1.3 million budget coming from France. As will be outlined in more detail in 'Institutional context' (page 193), co-productions are common in European cinema and give filmmakers access to funding for the distribution of films across the continent. The French film industry was supportive of the film from the outset, and submitted it as their official entry to the Academy Awards, where it was nominated for

 Independent Activity

Select a film you are studying for Global filmmaking.

- Identify at least three examples of its national cinema.
- On the surface it is about (summarise plot in one sentence) ...
- But beneath, this film is also about ...
- What genre do you think this film is?
- What do you think are the film's key messages and values?
- What function does the protagonist(s) have in the film?
- Is there a character that can be seen in opposition to them? What's their function/purpose?
- How do they contribute to the film's message and values?
- Identify a key moment in the film, which sums up the film's message and values.

British film poster

Danish film poster

the Oscar for Best Foreign Film. It also scooped-up awards at the Cannes Film Festival, the Césars (France's 'Oscars') and, despite not being in French, it won four awards at the Lumières, which honours the best in French-speaking films. It also won awards in Poland, Canada, Sweden, the UK and the USA.

Mustang's representation of young women in Turkey speaks more widely about the plight of women in some parts of the world, where women's rights are limited. The film brings to the fore issues regarding female education, employment opportunities, and the oppression and sexual abuse at the hands of older male family figures. Ergüven commented,

> I showed the film in a women's prison in France and there were women from the four corners of the world, from Africa to Eastern Europe who said they had the exact same treatment. Women from very different cultures with no intersection culturally or geographically with Turkey could completely relate to the story of the girls. (Chung, 2016)

European cinema

There are 50 countries in Europe, with five of these sharing territory with Asia, including Turkey. Just as it is hard to define what Europe is, the same can be said for European cinema. Each country will explore its own political, social, cultural past and present within its national cinema. Some may have a structured film industry producing both mainstream commercial fare, and independent art house films, while others may have little or no film industry. The films that are praised at film festivals and subsequently distributed internationally tend to be the countries' 'art house' output and not necessarily indicative of the films being watched domestically. The films' aesthetics will be governed by the institutional and cultural context in which they are produced.

The history of cinema in Europe is over 120 years old, with France considered the birthplace of 'the moving picture', when in December 1895 the Lumière Brothers gave their first paid, public screening in Paris. France has a robust film industry with national and regional governments supporting film production (both internationally, through co-productions, and nationally) and cinema exhibition. France enjoys the highest cinema attendance in Europe, 212.7 million in 2016, followed by Russia (192.1 million) and the UK (168.3 million).

The *BFI Statistical Yearbook 2017*, which examines UK film production and cinema-going in 2016 (the year *Mustang* was released in the UK), reported that there were 165 European (excluding UK) films shown in UK cinemas. These accounted for 20.1% of all films released and grossed £40 million, a 3.2% share of the box office. In comparison there were 217 American films (26.4%), accounting for 58.9% of the box office, grossing £743.1 million and 176 (21.4%) UK films, grossing £452.9 million (35.9% share).

Country of origin of films released in the UK and Republic of Ireland, 2016

Country of origin	Number of released	% of all gross (£ million)	Box office gross (£ million	Box office share (%)
USA	217	26.4	743.1	58.9
UK studio-backed*	20	2.4	359.2	28.5
UK independent	156	19.0	93.8	7.4
All UK	176	21.4	452.9	35.9
Other Europe	165	20.1	40.0	3.2
Indie		157	19.1	15.5
Rest of the world	106	12.9	10.4	0.8
Total	821	100.0	1,262.0	100.0

Source: comScore, BFI RSU analysis

Notes: Box office gross – cumulative total up to 21 February 2016. Figures/percentages may not sum to totals/ subtotals due to rounding. * 'Studio-backed' means backed by one of the major US film studios.

Mustang was released in France in June 2015, but would not open in the UK until the following May, by which point it had been enthusiastically received internationally and had been among the nominees for Best Foreign Film at the Golden Globes and Oscars. It grossed just over £300,000 at the UK box office: the highest grossing Turkish film released in the UK, beating *Once Upon a Time in Anatolia* (Ceylan, 2012), which had grossed £277,447.

Institutional context

Cinema-going and filmmaking in Turkey

Cinemas in Turkey attract significant audiences; in 2014 the European Audiovisual Observatory reported that cinema attendances in Turkey had risen by 14.8% to 50.4 million admissions. In the same year, UK admissions were 157 million (Iris, 2014).

Mustang was released in Turkey in 2015; in that year 420 films were screened in Turkey's cinemas: 134 were Turkish, 140 were from the USA and 126 were international, predominantly European.

Turkish cinema encompasses both mainstream commercial cinema (Yeşilçam) and independent art house cinema (New Turkish Cinema). In 2015 the biggest hit of the year was the comedy *Düğün Dernek 2: Sünnet* selling 5.8 million tickets and grossing Turkish lire 67.2 million (£16.38 million) at the box office. *Mustang* may have been honoured internationally but domestic audiences were small in comparison: with a limited release its audience in Turkey was 17,500.

Although made predominantly with support from the French film industry, Ergüven's film is closely aligned with the aesthetics and subject matter of a new wave of Turkish films that emerged in the 1990s. These films have garnered praise and audiences internationally, offering a social commentary on contemporary Turkey. Common themes include national and ethnic identity and religion, and gender-based issues. Directors considered part of New Turkish Cinema are Nuri Bilge Ceylan, Zeki Demirkubuz, Semih Kaplanoğlu, Yeşim Ustaoğlu, Reha Erdem and Derviş Zaimas.

European co-productions and funding

Crucial to European film production will be securing the financing; with that in mind most European countries will have film commissions, with many offering tax incentives, funding and production support. For instance, the British Film Commission (BFC) provides:

> *free tailored production support at the highest level from the earliest stages of development through to post production, including guidance on the UK's lucrative film and television tax reliefs and assistance with sourcing key crew, talent, facilities and locations.* (BFC, 2016)

Mustang is a CG Cinema production (France), co-produced with Bam Film (Turkey), Vistamar Filmproduktion (Germany), Uhlandfilm (Germany) and the Doha Film Institute (Qatar). The lead producers were CG Cinema, which was founded in 2013 by producer Charles Gillibert, with the aim of supporting films by auteur directors. The film's budget was $1.3 million, with funding received from the German–French mini-traité, Film-und Medienstiftung NRW, Eurimages and the Doha Film Institute, among others.

Once Upon a Time in Anatolia (Ceylan, 2012)

(iA) Independent Activity

Compare the poster of *Düğün Dernek 2: Sünnet* (Aydemir, 2015) with that of the English version *Mustang* (page 192). List three key differences.

Read reviews (both critics and audiences) of the two films.

What, if anything, do they say about how Turkish society is represented?

List three significant examples.

(iA) Independent Activity

Watch a film by one of the New Turkish Cinema directors mentioned on this page and compare it with *Mustang* to get a sense of New Turkish Cinema.

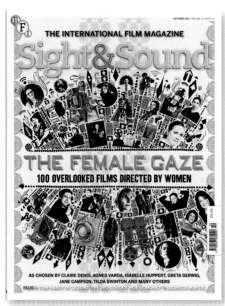

Copyright BFI. Used with permission.

Mustang was awarded the Europa Cinema's Label Award at the 2015 Cannes Film Festival. The receipt of this award is pivotal in the distribution journey of a European film, as it will help support the promotion, circulation and exhibition of a film across Europe by providing financial incentives to cinemas within their network. Europa Cinema is an integral element in the production, distribution and exhibition of European films. Via its MEDIA programme (Creative Europe), it provides operational and financial support to cinemas that commit to screening a significant number of European non-national films. In 2017, there were 2,806 cinemas in 680 cities in 43 countries in the network. In 2015, via their Eurimages programme, they supported 31 co-productions, 27 of which are feature film projects, with a total of €7,745,000. Founded in 1988, by 2015 they had provided funding to 1,685 European co-productions for a total amount of approximately €508 million. Mustang received Eurimages funding.

Women film directors

Mustang opened in the USA in November 2015, hot on the heels of significant activity, legally and socially, to investigate the lack of women working at the highest levels of filmmaking, and to raise the profile of those that were.

In 2012, film director Maria Giese, frustrated by the difficulty of getting work in Hollywood, met with the Equal Employment Opportunity Commission and the American Civil Liberties Union about sexual discrimination in the film industry. Her three-year research and campaigning reached its peak in October 2015, when it was reported that the Equal Employment Opportunity Commission had officially launched its investigation into discrimination against female film and television directors.

The same month, the Los Angeles branch of Women in Film and Television, launched the #52FilmsByWomen hashtag as part of their 'Trailblazing Women' initiative with Turner Classic Movies. They simply asked filmgoers to pledge to watch a film a week directed by a woman for a year. This campaign has helped to raise the profile of female directors, particularly global filmmakers. It has led to female-led curation at film festivals and streaming services, and the launch of the F-rating, which is awarded to films that are directed and/or written by a woman. If the film also features significant women on screen in their own right, it is TRIPLE F-rated. The rating is designed to support and promote women and redress the imbalance in the film industry. The F-rating can be seen as a complement to the Bechdel Test explored in the 'Representation' section of this book. Mustang is considered a triple F-rated film, and passes the Bechdel Test.

The October 2015 issue of the BFI's Sight & Sound magazine was subtitled 'The Female Gaze' and championed 100 female-directed hidden gems that had been forgotten or unfairly overlooked. This heightened awareness of gender inequality and representation would have helped to raise the profile of Mustang, which had a strong female creative presence both behind and in front of the camera.

Social, cultural and political context

Child marriage in Turkey

At the heart of Mustang are the arranged marriages and importance placed on the virginity of the four eldest sisters. Critics of the film railed against the depiction of Turkey that was being disseminated internationally through the success of this film, stressing that this is not the experience of all Turkish young women. However, Turkey, particularly rural Turkey, remains a patriarchal society where women are seen as the property of their fathers and then their husbands. In the absence of the parents, the patriarchal figure here is the uncle. His behaviour and the experiences of the sisters is a narrative construct: this is a fiction film and will be the experience of some young women in Turkey but not all.

However, women's behaviour in public, virginity and marriage are all common topics of conversation in Turkey. According to the website Girls Not Brides (2017), a global partnership of more than 800 civil society organisations committed to ending child marriage and enabling girls to fulfil their potential, Turkey has one of the highest rates of child marriage in Europe, with an estimated 15% of girls married before the age of 18.

The legal marriageable age is 18, but parents can apply for exemptions for 16- and 17-year-olds, there are also reports of illegal 'marriages' with girls as young as ten. The influx of desperate Syrian refugees to Turkey has seen many Syrian parents effectively selling their daughters into marriage.

 Independent Activity

Has this information on child marriage and women in Turkish society aided your understanding of the issues in *Mustang*? List five ways in which the film depicts these issues visually and within narrative.

In addition, the website Girls Not Brides (2017) indicates that Turkey's patriarchal structure is a significant factor, reporting that:

- Girls and women are expected to conform to traditional gender norms and expectations.
- Violence against women and girls is common and tolerated.
- School attendance remains low for girls, with little importance placed on their education.
- Girls are often valued for their ability to be good wives and mothers.

They add that the figures for underage marriage could be much higher as:

- Turkey has a poor birth registration system, which means that families can marry their daughters without fear of repercussion.
- Most child marriages are unregistered and take place as unofficial religious marriages.

In addition to the explicit depiction of child marriage in the film, Ergüven also incorporates controversial comments by Turkish politicians on the appropriate chaste behaviour of young women, shown in background news footage.

Independent Activity

The film focuses on the five sisters and their response to their imprisonment by their uncle and his plans to see them married.

Select at least two of the sisters and trace their journey through the film, highlighting their reactions at significant narrative points, and how this is shown through the film form.

Although the young women playing the sisters have a more liberal upbringing than on their on-screen counterparts, they too feel the pressures of Turkish gender oppression. Elit Iscan (Ece) told IndieWire,

> I'm not getting an arranged marriage, but I feel pressure from the society and political figures … In the film, there's a political figure giving a speech about how women should act in public. (Buder, 2015)

For Ergüven, the treatment of women in Turkey was central to the film. She told the *Irish Examiner*,

> There have really been some very modern peaks … but at the same time it's always been very patriarchal and quite conservative. Since 2002, we have a religious political party in power and they are trying to make Turkish society more and more conservative. While you have very free women in Turkey you also have women who are very much victims of honour crimes and arranged weddings and have all sorts of limitations to their freedom. (Barlow, 2016)

Since the film's release, there has been some success in moderating legislation linked to child marriage. In November 2016, the Turkish government withdrew a bill that would allow perpetrators of sexual assault to be exonerated if they married their victims. MPs, human rights campaigners, the public and the international community feared that the bill would legitimise rape and encourage child marriage.

Domestic violence in Turkey

Aligned with the culture of child marriage, comes one of domestic violence, as Ergüven outlines to IndieWire,

> In the newspaper every day there will be murder stories about honor killings. Even in the more liberal segments of the society, you are under pressure. When you read about a woman who has been murdered or experienced domestic violence, it doesn't feel like an [anomaly] – you feel it in your bones. You feel the violence everywhere around you. (Buder, 2015)

 Independent Activity

Do you considered *Mustang* to be an example of realist cinema? Through an examination of its film form write a 400-word essay. This should be analysis, not an evaluation of the film.

Domestic violence rates are high, in 2016 Turkey's Ministry of Family and Social Policies reported that 86% of women experienced physical or psychological violence from a partner or family member (Sheva, 2016). In 2015, 300 women died as a result of domestic violence (Hudgins, 2017), more than double the 2014 UK figure (McVeigh & Colley, 2015).

Film form in European cinema

As there are 50 countries within Europe, it is important not to make sweeping generalisations about a single European film aesthetic. The films that are, in the main, discussed within the academic study of European cinema are those of the national 'art house' cinema. The notion of an 'arthouse aesthetic' is one that David Bordwell addresses in his chapter 'The Art Cinema as a Mode of Practice' in *The European Cinema Reader* (2002), where he writes:

> … art cinema defines itself as realistic cinema. It will show us real locations (Neorealism, the New wave) and real problems (contemporary 'alienation', 'lack of communication' etc.) … Art cinema is classical in its reliance upon psychological causation; characters and their effects on one another remain central …

Mustang certainly draws on the aesthetics of the Neorealism movement through its use of real locations, observational cinematography, non-professional actors, and its exploration of the social and political issues among the working class.

Cinematography

Mustang is shot naturistically, with the shooting style being fluid and hand-held. The camera appears almost incidental, merely capturing the lives of the five young women, in an observational 'fly-on-the-wall' documentary style. This authentic approach may obscure the intentionality of the cinematography. Cinematographers David Chizallet and Ersin Gok utilise the full range of cinematography techniques to visually portray the characters and plot arcs.

Mustang was shot in colour using an Arri Alexa Plus digital camera, which is considered to provide a 'superb overall image quality … [and] efficient production workflow at low cost' (Stephen, 2015). It was used in conjunction with Zeiss Super Speed Lenses, which are praised for producing images that are 'much sharper and show a much higher contrast'.

The way the camera moves in the film mirrors the mood of the scenes. There is a freewheeling exuberance to the scene where the girls are playing in the sea and when they go to the football match. These moments of freedom are matched by the looseness of the camera. In the sea sequence, the camera is held back in a wide shot so we can see all the actors, and the interaction between them in the same way as the neighbour does. At the football match, the camera is much closer to the girls and the objective camera places us in the midst of the action. The switch to a high-angle shot looking down on them reinforces the close-knit relationship of the girls. Ergüven described the cinematographers as being, 'in orbit around the actors, like a cat, staying close' (Cooke, 2016).

 Further information

Italian Neorealist Cinema

> *In the years immediately following the Second World War, the Italian film was suddenly acclaimed by film critics all over the world … This time her reputation was based on inexpensive and homely productions which were remarkable for their sensitive presentation of ordinary people upon the screen.* (Manvell, 1951)

There is no fixed list of which films or directors contributed to the body of films known collectively as Italian neorealist. It is generally considered that the movement began with *Rome Open City* (Rossellini, 1945) and ends with *Umberto D* (De Sica, 1952). Other key films were *The Bicycle Thieves* (De Sica, 1948) and *Germany Year Zero* (Rossellini, 1948).

What is Neorealism? Is it a genre? A style? A movement? No matter the label placed on this unique body of films, it is clear that at their heart is a group of people's personal response to the war, and the distinctive way they used film as a powerful tool to deal with their memories and relate their experiences to a larger world.

Rossellini and De Sica, the most significant post-war Italian directors, took to the streets to make their films. Using real locations, hand-held cameras, non-professional actors and relying on improvisation, they produced films that seem to be completely truthful. But in fact they are not telling the truth but only a version of it, as sieved through the collective memories of the directors and actors, infused with a strong ideological and political agenda. The films blurred the lines between documentary and fiction and were greatly admired outside Italy by 'intellectual' cineasts in Britain, American and Europe.

Because the filmmakers' technical equipment was sparse, there was a freedom of visual style as well as freedom of subject matter. Their films focused on the current state of the nation and the recent past under German occupation and local resistance. Their attitude was to show the everyday reality, the life of the working classes in post-war Italy.

Independent Activity

Compare and contrast the opening sequence at school and in the sea from *Mustang* with another film you have studied, in terms of its narrative function, and the expectations they provoke in the viewer.

In the home, the scenes are more measured, and more controlled to mirror their restrictiveness and lack of freedom. There are longer takes, and the camera is held back, to allow the action to unfurl. The five girls are often framed together, which reinforces Ergüven's view shared in the *Observer* (Cooke, 2016) that,

> *They became one body with five heads: a single rebellious entity.*

Increasingly, as the girls are married off and become separated from one another, they become isolated in single close-ups or two-shots.

As Lale narrates the film, there are a number of close-ups of Lale looking at things: she is seen looking out of windows, through doorways, always looking for a way out, there are also shots from Lale's viewpoint.

The versatility of the camera can be seen in how it works in both the bright daylight scenes, and in the darker scenes in the family compound.

The lighting is naturalistic and makes great use of the daylight, with many of the interior shots back-lit to emphasise their imprisonment, by drawing focus to the brightness from which they are separated. The lighting also reflects the change in seasons, which is aligned with the five girls' emotional journey from the optimistic bright sunlight of the start of the summer holiday; through to the dimming autumn light and the realisation that their childhood dreams have ended.

Mise-en-scène

The film is set in a rural, a costal town in northern Turkey, 1,000 km from the city of Istanbul. These two key locations – the rural, coastal town and Istanbul – are used within the film to reflect the tension between the past and the future, oppression and freedom. The rural setting is depicted as a place of conformity, rooted in tradition with strict patriarchal rules. Here, the girls are being watched and judged and their innocent play with the boys in the sea is observed and reported to their grandmother and uncle. The city is represented as a place of freedom, which Lale dreams of escaping to as their plight becomes increasingly desperate.

Within the rural community, the family home becomes their prison, as the uncle, determined to bring the young women into line, imprisons them. Throughout the film, we see their freedoms being stripped away as bars are added to the windows, the walls are built up higher and gates are added, and yet they still find ways to escape.

Props are used to indicate the girls' transformations as they reach an age deemed appropriate for marriage. The grandmother removes possessions that may corrupt them (computer, televisions, phones, make-up, items of clothing) and replaces them with those required to train them in the skills required to be good wives: props linked to cooking, cleaning and sewing.

Costume is an important element of the girls' identity that is gradually stripped away from them. To reinforce Ergüven's conceit that the five girls are one character with five heads, the girls share a striking similarity, you believe they are sisters, and this is in large part due to their very long brown hair, which, in contrast to the older women in the village, is uncovered. We first see them in their school uniform of white shirt, black skirts and ties (see page 197); then in casual clothing of tight-fitting denim jeans and t-shirts (right). As their freedom is stripped away, they are forced to wear 'shapeless shit-coloured dresses' (see page 198) that have been made for them; and then, as they marry, in white wedding dresses (see page 200).

Editing

Mustang opens with Lale's narration saying,

> *Everything changed in the blink of an eye. First there was comfort, and then suddenly everything went up the creek.*

This framing device ensures that Lale remains central to the edit, with the action largely being shown from her perspective as she narrates it from some safe place in the future. The film, although told in flashback, is in the most part linear and follows conventional narrative structure. There are two temporal ellipses, both from Lale's perspective:

- As she sleeps after Ece's funeral, there is a brief memory/dream/flashback (it is not clear which) of Ece smiling.
- As she sleeps in the bus to Istanbul, again she dreams, this time of her three elder sisters in the back of Yasin's truck on the way to the football match.

Both memories are depicted as golden-moments through their soft, diffused lighting; their brief, seemingly indiscriminate, inclusion marks them as important recollections for Lale.

The editing is paced to support the scenes' emotional content, and mirrors the girls' freedom or oppression. There is a preference for long takes, offering opportunities for the viewers to absorb the interactions between characters – the nuance of the performances. As the film is told from Lale's perspective there are very few sequences of parallel action; like the girls, we are trapped with them, experiencing what they experience. A key exception is the sequence when the girls escape the family home to go to the football match in a nearby town. The sequence of them at the match is fast paced, with quick-cuts of the girls having fun; this is cut between the shots of the uncle and his friends getting ready to watch the match on TV, and their 'aunts' preparing food, with the TV on in the background, tension is being built – will the girls be spotted? The 'aunts' take decisive action and cut the power to the house, and then to the whole village. Although the village scenes are not witnessed by Lale, her narration reinforces her viewpoint by saying that she only found out later what the aunts had done.

 Independent Activity

Film theorist Annette Kuhn writes that 'mise-en-scène can be the site of extraordinarily complex and subtle meanings' (Kuhn & Westwell, 2012, page 268). With reference to a particular sequence from *Mustang*, identify how mise-en-scène can be used to demonstrate this. Write a 400-word essay.

Sound

Music plays an important role in setting the tone of a film and here Ergüven employs two styles of music.

The film's title, *Mustang*, alludes to the wild horses that roam free in North America, this is seen visually in the opening scenes where the girls run as a pack with their long hair flowing, and by their untamable nature, but it is also developed in the non-diegetic music score from Warren Ellis. Ergüven had originally considered using Turkish composers, but in the edit felt that this was not suitable. She tried a piece of Ellis's music from one of his westerns in the scene where the girls are being paraded in the village, which she felt was reminiscent of a scene from a western, and it worked, so she approached him.

Ellis has scored some of the contemporary cinema's significant contemporary westerns including *The Proposition* (Hillcoat, 2005), *The Assassination of Jesse James by the Coward Robert Ford* (Dominik, 2007) and the post-apocalyptic drama *The Road* (Hillcoat, 2009). Ellis had three weeks to score the music but Ergüven was clear about the music cues she needed and utilised some of Ellis's music from previous films with new compositions. Ellis stated in a Q&A with Milan Records that,

> *the girls actions are always dignified and I wanted the music to echo this. It needed to come from a smaller palette of sounds, rather than broad strokes on a large canvas. I chose the Alto flute as the voice of Lale and the viola as an answering voice, like a chorus in a Greek Tragedy. They both have a nobility about them and also a sadness/melancholy which resists being mawkish.* (Chamboredon, 2015)

Turkish music is also used, predominantly diegetically, in the wedding scenes, including music by Baba Zula, Selim Sesler and Ahmet (Dede) Yurt.

The diegetic sounds are naturalistic, adding authenticity to the film, Lale's non-diegetic voice-over is used intermittently to indicate significant moments, such as the last time all five sisters will be together.

A key sequence to examine is the sequence of the girls on the coach and at the football match approximately 28 minutes into the film. The heady mix of music, the girls' shouts, laughter and cheers combined with the editing and cinematography reinforce their freedom, which is juxtaposed with the quieter scenes back in the village.

iA **Independent Activity**

Watch the scene where the sisters are paraded in the village (approximately 31 minutes into the film) with the scene about Sonnay and Selma's wedding (approximately 41 minutes). Focus on the use of Ellis's score and the more traditional Turkish music. How do these affect the mood of the scene? Now try the scenes with different music. What do you notice?

iA **Independent Activity**

Write a 500-word essay on the significance of the cinematography, editing and sound in the football match sequence.

Performance

This was the debut film for four of the young girls: Günes Sensoy (Lale), Ilayda Akdogan (Sonay), Doga Zeynep Doguslu (Nur) and Tuğba Sunguroglu (Selma). Elit Iscan (Ece) had previously worked in film and television.

Ergüven discussed the casting process with the *Observer*,

> *I saw Elit, the only one who'd acted before, straight away. I found Tuğba in an airport, and then the others auditioned. I was indifferent to training, and to experience. I was looking for certain qualities. They had to be great listeners, and I had to see both the scope of their imagination, and the limits of it. I needed to know the capacity of their ability to dive into a scene, and stay in it for a long time.* (Cooke, 2016)

As a way to help shape their characters, Ergüven gave the girls film recommendations to watch. The films included Andrea Arnold's *Fish Tank* (2009), the Dardenne Brothers' *The Kid with a Bike* (2012), Ingmar Bergman's *Summer with Monika* (1953), David Lynch's *Wild at Heart* (2006), Stanley Kubrick's *Lolita* (1962) and Jean-Luc Godard's *Vivre sa vie* (1962).

Ergüven continued,

> *After they were cast, we did two boot camps: one to give them acting tools, and the other to immerse them in the story. We spoke about the backstory, about what happened between scenes, and we played games and did other exercises. It was very playful. It was about group building. And it worked. The solidarity between them was amazing, the way they protected each other.* (Cooke, 2016)

Central to the performances is authenticity, which is an indicator of a film that draws on Neorealism film techniques. To support Ergüven's perception of the five girls as a five-headed monster, their performances have an ethereal nature to them. The proximity of the five girls – the jumble of arms and legs – at times supports this.

The reviews praised their performances:

> She [Ergüven] *gets appealing and fiercely committed performances from the five young actresses at the story's center.* (Brody, n.d.)

> *A superbly acted study of suppression.* (Parkinson, 2016)

> *Ergüven's luckiest break was finding the five charismatic young women to portray these powerful and truly individual characters.* (Means, 2016)

 S&C

In an article on films starring mostly non-professional actors, Papadakis (2016) writes in 'The 30 Best Films Starring Mostly Non-Professional Actors':

> *The non-professionals' lack of training, together with their presumable real-life matching to a specific location, time period, or story, is often responsible for creating the delusion that they don't really act, which can be a perfect tool in a director's pursuance for a more realistic or documentary-like feel.*

The casting and performances of the five young women in *Mustang* was praised by critics. Read Papadakis' article on non-professional actors and watch at least one of the 30 films. Research how the films you are studying for Global filmmaking were cast and compare the acting performances of non-professional and experienced actors.

Then write a 500-word essay answering this question:

How important are casting and performance in establishing a sense of realism in the films you have studied for global filmmaking?

 Independent Activity

Watch Selma and Sonay's joint wedding (at approximately 39 minutes), and examine the performances of these two sisters, their grooms and Lale. Make notes on facial expression, body language and movements. What do you learn about the characters at this moment?

At the Lumières (French awards celebrating the best in French cinema), all five girls were jointly nominated in the Best Newcomer award, a prize which they won.

The cinematography and editing work to support the performances, by allowing time for the viewer to study the nuance of the performances, as each girl responds to their change in circumstances.

Aesthetics

In his review of *Mustang* in *Variety* (2015), Jay Weissberg comments that,

> *Visuals are maturely fluent in keeping with current arthouse aesthetics, with a particularly satisfying interplay of energetic and confined camera movements reflecting the situation inside and outside the increasingly prison-like house.*

The incremental stripping away of the girls' freedom is reflected aesthetically, reinforcing the narrative and character arcs. The hand-held camera draws us close to the action, and as the sisters find themselves trapped in the family home so too does the viewer.

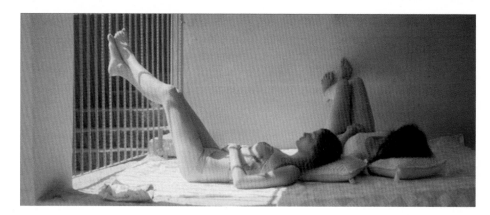

Representations

Mustang is told from the perspective of Lale reminiscing back over a period of a few months when the five girls lives 'suddenly' changed. The characters in European art house films such as *Mustang* tend to be more than mere 'characters', and serve as a prism through which to gain greater understanding of a society's beliefs and cultures, through their representation of age, gender and ethnicity.

Age

The characters' age is at the heart of the narrative, as the film explores the tension between the elder characters (uncle, grandmother and extended relations/friends) and those of the younger generation (the five girls and the local boys).

In Turkey, a traditional family unit would be under the authority of the father or oldest male, who would demand respect and obedience. In a rural community, as depicted in *Mustang*, the family would live together until the daughters married and then they all would live with her husband and in-laws. Parents would expect to be looked after by their children in old age.

Respect for elders is an expectation in Turkish culture, which is why Lale's behaviour seems so refreshing and exhilarating. As the youngest of the five sisters, she seems the most resistant to falling in line with the restrictions under which they are placed. When the neighbour, Mrs Patek, tells their grandmother about their activities in the sea, Lale, showing no respect for elders yells,

> *Do your shit-colored clothes make you everyone's judge?*

In punishment for their behaviour, the uncle imprisons them in the family home, and then proceeds to marry them off; at the end of the summer they do not return to school. The uncle and grandmother represent a generation of tradition where the supreme authority of the family rests with the father, but the household is mother-centred. In the absence of the children's parents, the grandmother has been raising the girls and running the household. When they are imprisoned in the home, Lale describes it as a 'wife factory', as their elder female relatives prepare them for married life.

When the girls are shown in smaller groupings, it is frequently paired with the eldest two, Sonay and Selma, and the younger Nur and Lale are often seen together. This leaves Ece, the middle sister, somewhat isolated. This separation from her siblings takes on a new meaning when the audience realise that Ece is the victim of abuse inflicted on her by Uncle Erol. Such exploitation often leads to people carrying a burden of secrets, which can ostracise them from others. The isolation Ece feels in this film may be a contributing factor to her sudden shocking suicide.

Gender

According to Gönül Dönmez-Colin in *Turkish Cinema: Identity, Distance and Belonging* (2008),

> *Women have been the focus of Turkish cinema since its beginnings.* (page 142)

She highlights that in

> *... the second half of the 2000s several courageous works have appeared exposing sexual taboos, particularly regarding violence against women, drawing attention to the reality that social maladies will not disappear through denial of their existence.* (page 170)

She ends her chapter on gender, by saying,

> *Turkish filmmakers' interest ... in the real issues of men and women alike, in a sincere, honest, analytical and non-judgmental way, is a feat for Turkish cinema.* (page 179)

Although made a decade later and with French financing, Ergüven's *Mustang* can clearly be seen as part of New Turkish Cinema's desire to expose and challenge societal concerns, with regards to gender and sexuality. In an article headed 'Oscar-Nominee 'Mustang' Puts Turkey in Unwanted Spotlight', in We.News, Jennifer Hattam (2016) highlights the key issue in the film – namely, child marriage. Here, she quotes Nilüfer Yılmaz, an activist with the Fethiye Free Woman and Life Association, based in southwestern Turkey, on the way many female children are seen as a family's common property:

> *From the moment they enter into adolescence, marrying them off becomes the dominant thought to protect the family's 'honor.'*

 S&C

Have a look at the websites for the BFI Film Audience Network and the UK Cinema Associations to gain an understanding of current trends in cinema exhibition.

Visit, where possible, an art house and a multiplex cinema or look at their websites.

Answer the following questions on the cinemas:

1 How far is your nearest mainstream cinema? How far is your nearest art house cinema?

2 How many screens does it have?

3 How many other cinemas are owned by the same company?

4 What price are tickets?

5 Are there any discounted ticket offers?

6 What food and drink can you get: get some comparable prices for key items, e.g. coffee, soft drink, bag of sweets?

And on its programming (for ease just select one or two weeks of programming):

1 How many films, on average, does it show each week?

2 What kind of films does it show?

3 How many foreign films are being shown?

4 Are there any special screenings, e.g. dementia friendly/parent and baby.

5 Are there any talks or education events happening?

6 How far ahead can you find detailed film information?

⊕ Further information

On 22 January 2018, the *Hurriyet Daily News* (a Turkish news source) reported on a recent survey carried out by Associate Professor Selda Sivaslıoğlu of the Women's Research Center at Gazi University in Ankara, Turkey. The survey further highlighted the problem of child marriage in Turkey (see pages 194–196), and revealed that the institutional isolation of young girls in Turkey played an important part in their subsequent forced marriage:

> *Before getting married 25 percent of the girls said they had no friends. Twenty percent said they have friends but are not permitted to meet them. Fifty percent have never gone to a cinema or theater. Sixty percent do not have access to the internet. Eleven percent say they do not share their problems with their families. The situation gets even worse after their marriage, with 66 percent saying they are left with no friends at all ...*

The survey was carried out among 600 girls, including 300 pregnant girls brought to hospital. Of these girls, 25 percent were married to relatives.

Read more on the *Hurriyet Daily News* website, 'Survey Sheds Light on Severity of Turkey's Child Marriage Problem'.

Through the five sisters, Ergüven explores a wealth of issues regarding the transition from childhood to womanhood. The catalyst for their change in circumstances is their innocent play in the sea with the boys, considered sexual by an older female neighbour. Their grandmother chastises them for their 'disgusting' and 'obscene' behaviour, and they are called whores for 'rubbing their parts on the boys'. At one end of the spectrum is Sonay who has had sex with her boyfriend 'the back way' to avoid pregnancy and breaking her hymen, therefore she is still able to pass as a 'virgin'; at the other is the pre-pubescent Lale who places apples under her shirt to give the appearance of breasts.

Although they are all forced to take part in the 'wife factory', no adult is shown talking to them about sex. The repetition of the marriage proposals with their formal phrasing, followed by the grandmother's preparations and the wedding itself, are all indicative of a cycle from one generation to the next, reinforcing women's subservient place within Turkish society. As part of the marriage preparations, the grandmother is shown taking out a worn copy of 'All About Sex', and reminiscing about her own marriage at age 14 to a man she did not know but learned to love.

Their authoritarian Uncle Erol, the patriarch, is shown as old-fashioned and judgemental. He is both fixated on ensuring their honour is upheld and secure by forcing the elder sisters to have virginity tests, but at the same time is sexually abusing at least one, if not two of them. The elder aunts and grandmother all train them for a life of marriage and servitude, but also protect them by cutting the electricity so Uncle Erol does not see them at the football match.

Serra Ciliv, director of the !f Istanbul Independent Film Festival, where the film was screened in 2015, told We.News,

> *This is a film that shows both what women are suffering and what unexpected power they can have to break through norms and take control under dire circumstances.* (Hattam, 2016)

Ethnicity

Turkey is a transcontinental Eurasian nation located between Europe and Asia. Ninety-five percent of the country is in Asia and 5% in Europe. *Mustang* is set in the Anatolia region which falls in the Asian region.

Turkey is a secular state, meaning there is no official state religion, although 99.8% of the population identify as Muslim, making it one of the most predominantly Muslim countries in the world, and the only one where religion has no place in the running of the state. Religion is strictly a private affair, as with other European countries; however, in rural communities there are still deeply held beliefs with regards to women's domestic destiny. Within rural communities it is much easier to carry out under-age marriages and withdraw children from school before the legal leaving age.

Mustang is very much rooted in this rural location, with the more ethnic diverse and enlightened city of Istanbul seen as a place of refuge. Istanbul is Europe's largest city with a population of 14.8 million (2017), compared to London's 8.7 million (2016).

Conclusion

Ergüven stated to Cineuropa film focus that her intention was:

> ... *to show what it means to be a woman, a girl, in Turkey. The project was driven by my desire to show everything I wanted to do and say when I was younger, giving my characters the courage that I never had ... I wanted something quite open and very upbeat at the beginning of the film, becoming progressively darker as the story goes on.*
> (Lemercier, 2015)

Through the five sisters, Ergüven has offered a snapshot of the lives of young women in Turkey, at a crucial time in a woman's development from child to adult. Each girl reacts differently to their 'sudden' transition from freedom and hope to oppression and despair. Although set in a specific country, Ergüven was delighted to receive comments from women from other cultures, who saw their story in *Mustang*, thereby demonstrating the universality of cinema and the importance of global filmmaking.

Independent study questions

Q The aesthetics of a film define not only the look but also the meaning of the film. How far is this true of *Mustang* or other films you have studied as part of global filmmaking?

Q How does the film convey the key social or political issues in Turkey? How are these reinforced through its film form, rather than narrative?

Q How do representations (of age, gender, ethnicity) help us identify with the characters and their roles within the film?

Q How does the film use location to explore issues of freedom and oppression?

Q To what extent do you think *Mustang* presents either clear or ambiguous messages of life in Turkey for young women today?

This section will help you to prepare for Component 2: Global filmmaking perspectives on the A level course. The focus is on the three core areas of study only. This section will use the Iranian film *Taxi Tehran* (Panahi, 2015) as a case study.

For A level

You will answer one 40-mark question from a choice of two, requiring reference to two global films: one European and one produced outside Europe. You should allow 60 minutes for your answer.

The specification says

Global film extends the range and diversity of narrative film, by studying their distinct geographical, social, cultural world and a particular expressive use of film form.

Taxi Tehran, from Iranian filmmaker Jafar Panahi, is concerned with repression. He made the film despite being banned from filmmaking in Iran – a film entirely shot from cameras installed in the taxi he drives.

Taxi Tehran (Panahi, 2015)

Taxi Tehran is presented as a found-footage documentary film, filmed entirely from a taxi being driven through the streets of Tehran by the director Jafar Panahi. From a camera on the dashboard and hidden cameras in the taxi, he films the conversations of the passengers he picks up. However, as themes emerge it becomes apparent that these are staged conversations using non-professional actors.

This film was made outside of the official Iranian commercial film industry. Jafar Panahi received a 20-year ban from making films by the Iranian government in 2010, after being charged with making propaganda against the regime.

This was the third film he made and had distributed internationally after receiving the ban. The film premiered in competition at the 65th Berlin International Film Festival in 2015, where it won the Golden Bear (the Festival's highest prize) and the FIPRESCI Prize (the International Federation of Film Critics' prize). Panahi was unable to leave Iran so his niece Hana Saied, who appears in the film, collected the award on his behalf.

The Berlin jury president, director Darren Aronofsky, said,

> *Limitations often inspire filmmakers to storytellers to make better work, but sometimes those limitations can be so suffocating they destroy a project and often damage the soul of the artist. Instead of allowing his spirit to be crushed and giving up, instead of allowing himself to be filled with anger and frustration, Jafar Panahi created a love letter to cinema. His film is filled with love for his art, his community, his country and his audience.* (*The Straits Times*, 2015)

Taxi Tehran's pared-down aesthetic, use of non-professional actors and focus on political and social issues is indicative of Panahi's work and global 'art house' cinema more widely.

 Further information

A filmmaker silenced

As will be explored further in this chapter, in 2010 Panahi had a 20-year ban on filmmaking placed on him by the Iranian government, nor is he permitted to be interviewed by the press. In the article 'Jafar Panahi Goes Through Red Lights' in *Le Monde* (Ghazal, 2015), his daughter, Solmaz Panahi, discusses her father's response to the ban and the very real threat of being sent to prison.

> *He is not scared. Cinema is the most important thing in his life, he is even ready to die for it. If he does not film, there is no difference for him between being free and being in jail.* (reprinted in New Wave Films, 2015)

⊕ Further information

Foreign-language films in UK cinemas

'For foreign-language films, you really have to have something quite exceptional to break the £1m mark', says Louisa Dent, managing director and acquisitions chief at UK art house distributor Curzon Artificial Eye.

In his article entitled 'Why Foreign-language Films are Struggling in UK Cinemas' for *Screen Daily* (2017), Charles Gant outlines some of the challenges for distributing foreign films in the UK.

The key issues he raises are:

- The UK's shared language with the US, the dominant provider of films.
- The growth in digital distribution creating a more crowded market place.
- The lack of interest from multiplex/mainstream cinemas to support foreign films.
- The disappearance of high street DVD stores, where one may come across foreign-language titles.
- Preference for talent-driven rather than high-concept films.

 S&C

Read Charles Gant's (2017) article and research five foreign-language films from the past seven years that have made more than £1 million at the UK box office. Look at the way the film was marketed, reviewed and distributed. What conclusion can you draw from these findings?

 Independent Activity

Watch at least one other contemporary Iranian film and make a note of the social and political issues raised in it. Write a 400-word essay comparing the film to *Taxi Tehran*.

Global filmmaking

Global filmmaking usually refers to films that are made outside of Hollywood but not, in your case, in the UK. You may see these films described as foreign films, foreign-language films, films not in the English language, world cinema or International films/cinema.

By exploring films from around the world, you will gain insights into different approaches to storytelling and filmmaking practices, thereby extending your knowledge of narrative film.

In the UK, we tend to see global films as those not in the English language; as a result they will generally receive a more limited cinematic release and are often found in art house cinemas and on streaming services, rather than in multiplex cinemas. The films being distributed internationally may only represent a fraction of the country's filmic output, but those selected will tend to be visually arresting and offer insights into the country's culture and political situation, past or present.

Jafar Panahi is seen as part of the New Iranian Cinema film movement (art house), whose films are in opposition to Iranian popular cinema (commercial). The films of the New Iranian Cinema and those of the Iranian New Wave, which came before it, have garnered much praise internationally. However, within Iran they have often courted controversy with their social and political messages which are at odds with the government's edicts on what is allowable.

Laura Mulvey, writing in *Sight & Sound* in 1998, said:

> *The New Iranian Cinema emerged out of comparative isolation, enforced by international politics and the post-revolutionary government's censorship of non-Islamic art and entertainment. In parallel, however, the government has actively supported home-produced films that conform to the basic rules of Islamic cultural codes. The limitations on content and images has forced directors to develop a cinema that is rigorously intellectual as well as visually striking.*

Institutional context

The Iranian film industry

The Iranian film industry has risen and fallen in line with the country's political situation. The first films shot in Persia (renamed Iran in 1935) were filmed in 1900 by the Shah's (King of Persia) official photographer, Akkas Bashi. These early films were non-fiction newsreels capturing the Shah's social and religious ceremonies. The first full-length silent fiction film, *Abi and Rabi*, was not made until 1930, by Ovanes Ohanian. The first sound film was *Lor Girl* (Sepanta, 1933). Due to World War II, no Iranian films were made between 1937 and 1947, but foreign films were screened, dubbed into Farsi. After World War II a group of new filmmakers experimented with newsreel and documentary forms, and in 1949 the National Iran Film Society was established. The Iranian film industry saw a rapid growth between 1950 and 1965, with an increase in film production and cinemas.

The 1960s was a significant turning point for Iranian cinema: in the first half of the decade approximately 25 commercial films were released a year; by the end of the decade this had increased to 65. As the 1960s progressed, alongside the state-endorsed commercial cinema there emerged a group of filmmakers who wanted to reflect the lives of ordinary Iranian people on film.

The first two films considered part of this Iranian New Wave were *Qeysar* (Kimiai, 1969) and *The Cow* (Mehrjui, 1969). The former led to a trend in gritty urban noirs, the latter to a strand of films focused on rural poverty. This tension between the rural and urban is at the heart of *Tranquility in the Presence of Others* (Taghvāī, 1972), in which an Army colonel moves from the country to the city and finds it difficult to adjust. The film was banned in Iran for its political and social messages. Abbas Kiarostami, considered the greatest Iranian filmmaker, worked on *Qeysar*, and soon began tackling issues in films that had previously been taboo such as teenage conflict (*A Wedding Suit*, 1976) and government corruption (*The Report*, 1977). These films, made by socially conscious filmmakers, only represented a small fraction of the films being produced; the vast majority were still supporting the Shah, which, although waning, was still a powerful force.

This first wave of films ended in 1979 with the Iranian Revolution. With the Shah in exile and Iran now under the leadership of Ayatollah Khomeini, the founder of the Islamic Republic of Iran, the film industry became centralised. Khomeini considered film a key propaganda tool for reinforcing the teachings of Islam and subsidised films that supported his views, while censoring and banning any views that were critical of the regime.

The Ministry of Culture and Islamic Guidance was founded in August 1984 with the responsibility for the 'promotion and enhancing the values of the Islamic Revolution based on the school of thought and political outlook of the late Imam Khomeini and the Supreme Leader of the Islamic Revolution' (Ministry of Culture & Islamic Guidance, 2017). Still in existence today, it does this by 'Promoting the moral values based on faith and piety' and 'protecting the society from influence of alien cultures' (Ministry of Culture & Islamic Guidance, 2017). With regards to film production, it oversees the 'required permission for entry and exit of audio-visual materials' and 'Directing and supporting activities of film producing centers [etc.] … issuing and revoking the license of such centers and supervising their activities based on the pertaining laws and regulations.'

This means that the Iranian government will support film activity that is aligned with its political and religious outlook, and look to marginalise and ban those that present a view of Iran that is unfavourable.

The end of the Iran–Iraq war in 1988 and the death of Khomeini in 1989 led to division and power struggles over the different visions of Islam. Out of this new political climate emerged the New Iranian Cinema film movement. Although the Ministry of Culture and Islamic Guidance was still firmly in place, changes in technology had loosened its grip over filmmakers, and these filmmakers, including Mohsen Makhmalbaf, Abbas Kiarostami and Jafar Panahi, began to enjoy critical and commercial success internationally. Female film directors also emerged, among them Rakhshan Bani-Etemad, Samira Makhmalbaf and Forugh Farrokhzad, whose films challenged women's place within society.

Conventions of New Iranian Cinema are:

- experimentation with film form and style
- ambiguity over whether what you are seeing is documentary or fiction
- open endings, leaving audiences to interpret meaning
- focus on ordinary people in contemporary Iran (rather than historical events)
- women as central characters, offering insights and commentary on their role in society
- philosophical and moral conversations on society.

 Further information

Iranian female filmmakers

In 2014 Ana Lily Amirpour's Persian-language *A Girl Walks Home Alone at Night* was released in cinemas, to great critical acclaim. Billed as 'The first Iranian Vampire Western' it was the debut feature film of Amirpour, who was born in England to Iranian parents but grew up in Miami. *A Girl Walks Home Alone at Night* draws on both traditions of New Iranian Cinema and American indie horror films. It was shot in the town of Taft in Kern County, Southern California, and its $55,000 budget was funded through Indiegogo.

Contrary to stereotyped notions of women in Iran being oppressed, Iran has a higher percentage of women directors than many Western countries; however, the difficulties of distributing and exhibiting films outside of Iran means that their names may not be as familiar as Amirpour's.

Here are five female filmmakers from Iran to look out for:

- Rakhshan Bani-Etemad
- Tahmineh Milani
- Samira Makhmalbaf
- Shirin Neshat
- Marjane Satrapi.

 Independent Activity

Watch *A Girl Walks Home Alone at Night* (Amipour, 2014) and see what influences of New Iranian Cinema you can identify.

 Independent Activity

Watch at least two other New Iranian Cinema films (i.e. 1991 to present). Identify five conventions (film form and themes) from the films that you have seen, and make a list to see where they share similarities and differences.

Technological changes

Filming on 35mm celluloid is expensive to shoot, process, edit and distribute. As a way of controlling filmmaking, the Ministry of Culture and Islamic Guidance would offer subsidies to filmmakers whose scripts endorsed their beliefs.

With the emergence of digital cameras in the late 1980s, it became possible for filmmakers to film more cheaply and swiftly. This **cinéma vérité** approach had been popular with the post-war Italian neorealist filmmakers, and those of the French New Wave in the 1960s.

In Iran, this allowed filmmakers to film more covertly, flying under the radar of government officials. Which, coupled with the rise of domestic home entertainment systems (the VCR in the 1980s and DVDs from the late 1990s) made distribution far easier.

Jafar Panahi's banned film, *Offside* (2006), was widely seen in Iran via bootleg DVDs. The importance of the 'video pirate' is discussed in *Taxi Tehran*, as Omid argues that without him access to Western cinema would be impossible, and that his work is a 'cultural activity'.

The importance of film festivals

The films of the New Iranian Cinema are held in high regard in the West, where they challenge stereotypical notions of society, particularly when it comes to women, but also reinforce the oppressive regime under which they are made, through their lack of distribution and support in Iran.

It is not the quantity of New Iranian films that makes them a significant player on the world stage, but their quality, which is measured, in part, by their performance at international film festivals.

The Cannes Film Festival has been particularly supportive of New Iranian Cinema: in 1991 it screened *In the Alleys of Love* (Sinai, 1991). The following year Abbas Kiarostami won the Palme d'Or with *Life and Nothing More* (1992); he would win again in 1997 with *Taste of Cherry*. Jafar Panahi won the Camera d'Or in 1995 for *The White Balloon* and the Prix Un Certain Regard in 2003 with *Crimson Gold*. Between 2000 and 2016, Iranian films have won 15 major awards at Cannes.

Among the dozens of other festivals that have supported Iranian filmmakers are Venice and Berlin, which have similarly awarded Iranian films on multiple occasions. These film festivals form an important part of the film's distribution and marketing, ensuring that New Iranian Cinema has stayed a central part of the global filmmaking community since its emergence in the early 1990s.

 Independent Activity

Research at least four films you are studying to see what part, if any, film festivals had in its marketing and distribution strategy?

Jafar Panahi

Social, cultural and political contexts

The Iranian Revolution of 1979 and its aftermath

In the 1960s, the Shah embarked on an extensive modernisation programme, drawing on extravagant Western ways. His party, to celebrate 2,500 years of the Persian Empire in 1971, was a public relations (PR) disaster, and the next few years saw increasing unrest among the population, which led to a series of riots, strikes and demonstrations in the late 1970s.

The Shah's excessive consumption and alignment with America and the West led to the rise of anti-Shah campaigners, including Ruholla Khomeini, a Shi'ite Muslim, known as 'Ayatollah' (the term for a leading Shia scholar). In 1962, he had been arrested for his campaign against the pro-Western regime of the Shah. His arrest made him a national hero. In 1964 he was exiled, but while living abroad he continued to urge his supporters to overthrow the government. The Shah's government collapsed in January 1979. The following month Khomeini returned and, following a national referendum, he declared Iran an Islamic republic and appointed himself Iran's political and religious leader for life. Islamic law was introduced across the country and Western influences were forbidden.

In his first speech in Iran, Khomeini spoke of using films to spread the teachings of Islam, and began restructuring the film industry to ensure that all films supported his messages, and censoring any criticism of the new regime. Between 1979 and 1985 about 100 films were released.

In September 1980, Iraq (under Saddam Hussein) invaded Iran, and for the next eight years these neighbouring countries were at war. It is estimated that a million Iranian soldiers and civilians died, and 250,000–500,000 Iraqis.

The end of the Iran–Iraq war in 1988 and the death of Khomeini in 1989 led to division and power struggles over the different visions of Islam. Out of this new political climate emerged the New Iranian Cinema film movement.

Anti-government demonstrators in Tehran confronting soldiers over the government's decision to delay the arrival of Ayatollah Khomeini during the Iranian Revolution, 1979.

The influence of Abbas Kiarostami

> *Kiarostami gave the Iranian cinema the international credibility that it has today. But his films were unfortunately not seen as much in Iran. He changed the world's cinema; he freshened it and humanised it in contrast with Hollywood's rough version.* (Pulver & Dehghan, 2016)

Abbas Kiarostami trained as a graphic designer and illustrator before beginning his filmmaking career in the 1960s in Tehran, where he made TV commercials. In the late 1960s he began working on feature films, including *Qeysar* (1969), one of the first films considered part of the Iranian New Wave. In 1969 he was one of the founding members of the Kanoon Institute for the Intellectual Development of Children and Young Adults, which showed art house and international films. This youth culture movement, set up by the Pahlavi regime (the ruling house, led by the Shah), became central to the new wave of Iranian filmmakers.

Throughout the 1970s, Kiarostami made short films with political and social messages. His first feature film was *The Report* (1977), which is about government corruption. In the 1990s, his films found audiences internationally and helped to bring about the New Iranian Cinema movement that emerged in the 1990s and is still firmly established over 25 years later. Many of his

 S&C

Despite being from two different countries, and being very different in tone and execution, *Mustang* and *Taxi Tehran* have a shared sensibility. The stories are a microcosm of their country's recent past, and their current political and social framework. The two films are linked in their depictions of 'ordinary' people living and coping with the restrictions placed upon them.

Research the cultural and political contexts of the two films you are studying for Global filmmaking. Write a 400-word essay, focusing on how these issues are reflected in the films.

Each movie has an ID or birth certificate of its own. A movie is about human beings, about humanity. All the different nations in the world, despite their differences of appearance and religion and language and way of life, still have one thing in common, and that is what's inside of all of us. If we X-rayed the insides of different human beings, we wouldn't be able to tell from those X-rays what the person's language or background or race is. Our blood circulates exactly the same way, our nervous system and our eyes work the same way, we laugh and cry the same way, we feel pain the same way. The teeth we have in our mouths – no matter what our nationality or background is – ache exactly the same way. If we want to divide cinema and the subjects of cinema, the way to do it is to talk about pain and about happiness. These are common among all countries. (cited in Sterritt, 2000)

 S&C

How far do you agree with Kiarostami's statement that a film should be considered not as part of its national cinema but how it makes us feel? Write a 400-word essay considering what the two films you have studied for Global filmmaking have in common.

(iA) Independent Activity

Watch one of these two Abbas Kiarostami films, *Taste of Cherry* or *Ten*, and note how he uses the car as a location. Compare this with *Taxi Tehran*.

obituaries hailed him as 'one of the great directors of our time'. Jean-Luc Godard, a central figure in the French New Wave film movement of the late 1950s/early 1960s, is reputed to have said, 'Film begins with DW Griffith and ends with Abbas Kiarostami.'

Kiarostami's films are visually daring and often quietly provocative; because of the changing governments they could not be overtly political. He was drawn to ordinary people in special circumstances or extraordinary people in everyday settings. He always tried to work with non-professional actors, mixing in a few professional actors.

His influence can be seen on all those who followed, including the films of Panahi. As a teenager, Jafar Panahi enrolled in the film department of the Kanoon Institute, where Kiarostami taught film. Panahi studied under him, and would later work as Kiarostami's assistant on *Through the Olive Trees* (1994). The following year, Panahi directed his first feature film, *The White Balloon* (1995), based on an original script by Kiarostami. This collaboration effectively launched Panahi's international film career.

Kiarostami claims,

> *A good film is one that has lasting power, and you start to reconstruct it right after you leave the theater.* (Jeong & Szaniawski, 2016, page 272)

The two following films of Kiarostami are a clear influence of Panahi's *Taxi Tehran*.

Taste of Cherry (1997) is a philosophical study of a man, Mr Badii, who is so tired with life that he wants to commit suicide. However, he wants to be properly looked after once he has gone, so goes in search of an accomplice to help bury him. The film focuses on his attempts to persuade three different people to help him; the three conversations take place while driving the same circular tour in a car.

Ten (2002) was shot digitally, using two static cameras on a car's dashboard, one facing the driver, the other the passenger seat. The film comprises ten car journeys, as the driver, an attractive divorcee, drives her son and occasionally strangers around Tehran. Kiarostami was not present whilst filming took place, he had to watch from a monitor and direct via an ear-piece. Many of the supporting cast were non-professional actors and, like *Taxi Tehran*, there is an element of improvisational dialogue, drawing on social problems, particularly those relating to women's place within society.

Taste of Cherry (Kiarostami, 1997)

Jafar Panahi's censorship and legal issues

Panahi came of age at a period of huge political and social change in Iran. He was 19 in 1979, when Iran saw the collapse of the dynastic royal family, and the rise of the Islamic State under Ayatollah Khomeini.

He was already engaging with filmmaking through his attendance at the Kanoon Institute, where he met and was mentored by Abbas Kiarostami. In 1980, at the outbreak of the Iran–Iraq War, he was conscripted into the Iranian military where he served for two years, producing a war documentary for Iranian television. After completing his deployment, he enrolled in the Tehran College of Cinema and Television and graduated in 1988, the year the war ended. The end of the war, combined with Khomeini's death the following year, led to a renewed alternative filmmaking community, who were keen to explore contentious issues that had been previously impossible.

The Ministry of Culture and Islamic Guidance had been founded in 1984 with the remit of providing state funding for films that supported the strict Islamic beliefs and represented their approved view of Iran to the world. They also restricted films that did not support these views.

Emerging filmmakers, keen to reflect a view that was deviant from approved subjects, shifted the focus to films with children at their centre, as these were not as heavily scrutinised. Filmmakers used them as the vehicle for telling their stories from a child's perspective. Jafar Panahi said,

> … *making children's films was a way of saying what we wanted to say in adult films. But because of the circumstances, we chose that format because it was less prone to censorship at the time.* (Saunders, 2007)

Panahi's first two films had children in the central role. His feature film debut, *The White Balloon*, based on a screenplay by Abbas Kiarostami, won four major international prizes including the Camera d'Or at the 1995 Cannes Film Festival. It was selected as Iran's entry for Best Foreign Language Film at the Academy Awards and when the Iranian government tried to withdraw the film from consideration the Academy refused. The government forbade Panahi from travelling to the USA to promote the film; neither was he allowed to hold any phone interviews. His follow-up film, *The Mirror* (1997), a blend of drama and documentary, won seven international awards.

The Circle (2000) is critical about the treatment of women under Iran's Islamist regime; it was this shift away from films about children that led to Panahi coming up against greater government interference. He had to wait a year to get an official shooting permit. The film was shot in 35 days over a 53-day period. He submitted the film to international festivals without permission, and it won the Golden Lion at the Venice Film Festival, among a number of other major awards. The Ministry later banned the film in Iran. Fearing that the film might be confiscated, he made copies and hid them around Iran.

Crimson Gold (2003) is based on real events and centres on a pizza delivery man who attempts to rob a jewellery store. Like *The Circle*, Panahi submitted it to overseas festivals where it won the Un Certain Regard at Cannes. The film was later banned in Iran.

 Further information

Jafar Panahi filmography

2015 *Taxi Tehran* (Taxi)

2013 *Closed Curtain* (Pardé)

2011 *This Is Not a Film* (In Film Nist)

2006 *Offside*

2003 *Crimson Gold* (Talaye Sorkh)

2000 *The Circle* (Dayereh)

1997 *The Mirror* (Ayneh)

1995 *The White Balloon* (Badkonake Sefid)

 S&C

Watch a second film (where possible) from the same director as a film you are studying as part of Global filmmaking, then answer the following questions:

1 What was your favourite scene of the film and why?

2 What did the film tell you about the country in which it was set?

3 What would you consider to be the main messages of the film? How did you relate and respond to these messages?

4 Could you sense any signature characteristics within this film compared with any other films of theirs you have studied?

The White Balloon (Panahi, 1995)

(+) Further information

Nasrin Sotoudeh

One of the passengers Panahi picks up in his taxi is Nasrin Sotoudeh, one of Iran's leading human-rights lawyers. She and Panahi became friends after they both received the European Union's Sakharov Prize for freedom of thought.

In 2010, Sotoudeh was arrested by the Iranian government and was jailed for six years for endangering national security and misusing her profession as a lawyer. She went on a four-week hunger strike in 2010 and a 49-day hunger strike in 2012. She was unexpectedly freed in September 2013.

In the *New York Times* (2015) she spoke about her role in the film:

> One morning, he [Panahi] just came and asked me to participate in this film ... I accepted, but I was worried that I couldn't perform my role very well. He said: 'No worries. You just need to be yourself.' (Donadio, 2015)

Sotoudeh and Panahi spent two days together working out what to include in their taxi conversation. Given their shared interest in human rights, this would be central to this section of the film. Their conversation includes prison interrogations, hunger strikes and censorship.

(Q) How does social, cultural and political information such as this about your close study film affect your response to it?

In 2003, Panahi was arrested and interrogated by the Information Ministry of Iran. They suggested that he leave Iran and make films internationally.

Offside (2006) is about the treatment of women in Iran and focuses on a group of young girls who disguise themselves as boys to watch a football match. Since 1979, women have been banned from attending sporting events. The film was partially filmed at the World Cup qualifying match between Iran and Bahrain. To obtain the licence to film he submitted a fake script to the Ministry of Culture and Islamic Guidance about young men going to the football match. They refused him permission unless he agreed to re-edit some of his earlier films. Panahi refused, and filmed without permission; using a small crew and a hand-held digital camera he went unnoticed in the football crowds. To avoid the Ministry's attention, he originally listed his assistant director as the film's director, but a newspaper article on the film shattered this pretense and the Ministry tried to shut production down. The film premiered at the 2006 Berlin Film Festival where it won the Silver Bear Jury Grand Prix. Again, it was banned, but it remains the most widely seen film of Panahi's in Iran due to the circulation of unlicensed DVDs. As the film was never officially screened in Iran, it was ineligible for Oscar consideration.

In 2009 there were reports that Panahi had been arrested, but he was quickly released and a statement issued that he had been arrested by mistake. In February 2010 he requested permission to attend the 60th Berlin Film Festival to participate in a panel discussion on 'Iranian Cinema: Present and Future. Expectations inside and outside of Iran', but his request was denied. The following month he was arrested again. There was an international campaign by leading filmmakers, critics, actors and institutions urging for Panahi's release. He had been named a member of the Cannes Film Festival jury in May, where his absence was made apparent by leaving his chair empty. The same month he was released on bail while he awaited trial.

On 20 December 2010, Panahi was convicted by Iran's Islamic republic for 'assembly and colluding with the intention to commit crimes against the country's national security and propaganda against the Islamic Republic'. He was placed under house arrest, and given a 20-year ban on writing scripts, directing films, giving interviews with Iranian or foreign media and leaving the country. In addition, he was given a six-year jail sentence that could be activated at any time. He has since been allowed to move freely in Iran, but is still not able to leave the country or legally make films.

A 20-year ban has not stopped Panahi from making films. While under house arrest, in collaboration with Iranian filmmaker Mojtaba Mirtahmasb, he made a documentary *This is Not a Film* (2001). It was shot over four days in a ten-day period in March 2011, using a digital camcorder and an iPhone. The film depicts Panahi, like a caged animal, struggling to adjust to life in his home. He is filmed making phone calls to his lawyer, watching TV, talking about his past films and the one he was in the process of making when he had been arrested the year earlier. The film was smuggled out of Iran in a cake and screened at the Cannes Film Festival in May 2011. His wife and daughter attended.

Closed Curtain (2013) saw Panahi working in collaboration with director Kambozia Partovi. The film was screened at the Berlin Film Festival where it won the Silver Bear for Best Script. Partovi and cast members Maryam Moqadam and Hadi Saeedi were in attendance but, despite pleas to the Iranian government by the Festival director, Panahi was not allowed to attend.

Taxi Tehran (which Panahi again defied the ban to make), in which he also stars, has the appearance of a found-footage film, with much of the film being captured via a camera on the car's dashboard, Omid's camera phone and his niece Hana's digital camera. There are further hidden cameras to provide coverage of Panahi and the back seat. This presentation brings into question whether he has actually 'made a film' or whether he is just offering a filmed record of him driving through the streets of Tehran talking to his passengers.

This ambiguity is reflected in the film's reviews, where there are differing views on the boundary between documentary and fiction. Richard Brody in the *New Yorker* (2015) said,

> *Panahi is driving the car, pretending to be a cab driver, encountering strangers, acquaintances, and even a relative – and filming the encounters with a dashboard-mounted camera that he passes off as a security device.*

Sarah Ward in *Metro Magazine* (2016) also comments on the techniques used and choices made,

> *He* [Panahi] *drives around the city … The filmmaker's selection of stories is canny in conveying the extent of everyday oppression.*

The impact of this on the film's realism is commented on by Jonathan Romney in the *Guardian* (2015),

> *One assumes that everything is staged; such is the feel of brisk spontaneity that it's hard to tell.*

His use of film form, combined with the absence of commentary through interviews, ensures that the extent of the film's documentary and narrative fiction parameters remain unclear. The film has no opening or closing credits, so no actors or technicians are credited. However, the themes that emerge through the conversations with the 11 people he encounters broadly fall into three key areas:

- crime
- women in society
- filmmaking.

He explores his own problems of making an 'un-distributable film' via his conversation with his young niece, Hana, who is making a short film as a school project. In order to make a distributable film, students were told they had to respect the following rules:

1. Respect for the Islamic headscarf.
2. No contact between men and women.
3. Avoid sordid realism.
4. Avoid violence.
5. Avoid the use of a tie for good guys.
6. Avoid the use of Iranian names for good guys; instead use the sacred names of the Islamic saints.
7. Avoid discussing political or economic issues.

During the course of the film, Panahi breaks all of these rules.

 Independent Activity

Read 'My Interview with Jafar Panahi' by Doug Saunders (2007) online and write a short essay on how Panahi tackles issues of censorship in the film *Taxi Tehran*.

Film Form in New Iranian Cinema

The New Iranian Cinema that emerged in the last decade of the 20th century has become a distinctive film movement very much rooted in the place and time in which it emerged. Filmmakers keen to express opinions that were in contrast to those of the post-1979 Revolutionary Islamic Republic, developed their own film form and style.

Working within budgetary constraints and utilising the developing digital technology, these filmmakers created a film form rooted in realism. Real locations, casts comprising non-professional and professional actors, long takes, limited settings/confined spaces, give these films a sense of authenticity and realism, which blurs the lines between documentary and narrative fiction filmmaking.

Cinematography

The visual style of New Iranian Cinema draws on previous cinematic film movements, most notably Italian Neorealism and cinéma vérité.

Italian Neorealism emerged in post-war Italy, where filmmakers took to the streets and, using minimal equipment, available lighting and a mix of professional and non-professional actors, told simple stories of life in Italy. Key figures in this film movement are Roberto Rossellini and Vittorio De Sica. Panahi credits *Bicycle Thieves* (De Sica, 1948) as being an influence on his work.

Cinéma vérité (sometimes called observational cinema) is a style of filmmaking that was initially used in documentary cinema, where the subject is filmed with as little interaction with the filmmakers as possible. There is limited directorial control and these films rarely use narration to guide the viewer. The filmmakers present their images and leave the audiences to interpret meaning. This naturalistic style of filmmaking was adopted by those working the French New Wave in late 1950s/early 1960s, who encompassed authentic dialogue, hand-held camera movement and filming on location to create films that looked realistic.

With the arrival of digital cameras, Iranian filmmakers were able to embody the spirit of these film movements to tell their stories. Given the low-budget, low-tech nature of New Iranian Cinema, there is a tendency for the camera to hold back and let the action unfold in relatively long static shots, or with minimal slow panning movements. There are few complex camera movements or angles, and the use of hand-held cameras brings an immediacy to the action. The shaky camera, or slight out-of-focus shots, align with the cinéma vérité observational style.

Although it may at first seem as though the cinematography in *Taxi Tehran* is limited to a single camera on the dashboard, it soon becomes clear that Panahi is introducing a number of cameras through which he can explore the nature and power of filmmaking.

The film opens with a fixed POV shot through the front windscreen (see page 219), and the audience hear passengers speaking. A male passenger notices the camera on the dashboard and assumes it is an anti-theft device (the first of two references to hidden surveillance cameras, the second being the security camera footage Panahi watches on an iPad). Panahi turns the camera to face the front-seat passenger. This is the camera we see Panahi adjusting to film through the front windscreen or into the car. About nine minutes into the film, it cuts to a shot of the driver's seat, where it is revealed that Panahi is the driver.

⊕ **Further information**

Shooting

In the article 'Jafar Panahi Goes Through Red Lights' in *Le Monde* (Golshiri, 2015), his daughter Solmaz Panahi describes how her father shot the film under convert conditions:

> *Jafar and his collaborators could not use extra lights, in order not to raise the authorities' attention. They removed the car's roof to be able to work with daylight. Afterwards, in the editing stage, they put the roof back using special effects.*
>
> *The film was shot and edited in 15 days, with Panahi editing the day's rushes in the evening.*
>
> *He had to finish the film and have it taken out of Iran as quickly as possible, before rumours started to circulate … As for his collaborators, most of them are very young and have just started their career …. Their names are kept secret. The day circumstances become favourable, their names will be published.*

(New Wave Films, 2015)

ⓘA **Independent Activity**

Create a storyboard of the sequence with the man who has been knocked down. This will give you an insight into where the cameras are, and how they are being used. Make a note of how long each shot is held and the transitions between them.

This shot is from a hidden camera. The vast majority of the shots are medium-close-ups of the front seat passenger with cutaways to Panahi.

When Panahi picks up the man, who has been knocked over, and his wife, we cut to another shot, presumably another hidden camera, and through this camera we can see action unfolding on the back seat. In this same segment, Omid (sitting in the front passenger seat) uses his phone's camera to film the dying man's will, he also uses it to film through the car windows when they arrive at the hospital.

Using her Canon digital camera, his niece Hana (Saeidi) films Panahi and shoots material for her short film for the school competition from the car. One of the acts she films is a married couple being filmed by a wedding videographer.

 Further information

Hana Saeidi

As Panahi was unable to leave Iran, his niece Hana Saeidi, who appears in this film as his niece, attended the 65th Berlin Film Festival in 2015. When the film won the Golden Bear (the Festival's highest prize) she collected the award. Her speech? 'I'm not able to say anything, I'm too moved.'

Mise-en-scène

New Iranian Cinema is rooted in realism, and this is reflected in the choice of settings where, for financial, aesthetic and socio-political reasons, real locations are prioritised over studio sets. Whether the setting is rural or urban, exterior or interior it will support the story, themes and characters.

The film's two locations are indicated in the film's title – *Taxi Tehran* – but once you have gained an understanding of the circumstances in which the film was made, and the narrative structure, this title offers alternate meanings.

The physical location is a taxi driving through the streets of Tehran, but, through the passengers that Panahi interacts with, we are shown a microcosm of life in Tehran. For instance, the juxtaposition of the poor boy collecting bottles and pocketing money that has been dropped is shown in parallel with a middle-class 'white' wedding, and Hana's insistence that he return the money so that her film does not depict 'sordid realism'. The first passengers depicted have polar-opposite political views on crime and capital punishment; while the dying man is desperate to dictate his will in order for his wife to inherit his house.

The taxi also alludes to the physical constraints placed on Panahi by the Iranian government. He is unable to leave Iran, and for some time had been placed under house arrest. The taxi offers him a certain degree of freedom and anonymity, while at the same time confinement.

There are very few props featured but those that are used support the film's themes. Phones, Hana's camera, the iPad and the pirate DVDs are all used as triggers for conversations about surveillance, films, cinema and filmmaking with the people who get into the taxi. Two other significant props are used:

- **Goldfish**: two elderly women who get in with two fish that they want to take to Ali's Spring as part of their annual birthday tradition. In Iran, goldfish represent life and traditionally Iranians incorporate goldfish into their new year festival. This festival and a young girl's desire to buy a goldfish is the central premise of Panahi's first film *The White Balloon* (1995).
- **Red roses**: human-rights lawyer Nasrin Sotoudeh gets in with a large bouquet of red roses, she addresses the dash-cam and places a rose beside it saying, 'This is for the people of cinema because the people of cinema can be relied upon. Just like you. I put it here.' This is an optimistic gesture as a red rose is a symbol of love and beauty.

Editing

There is a tendency in New Iranian Cinema to eschew conventional patterns of continuity editing, such as the shot/reverse shot, in favour of longer takes with minimal camera movements to draw focus.

Taxi Tehran appears to be edited conventionally, with no obvious shot transitions, or fragmentary editing through temporary or spatial ellipses. However, the very absence of these techniques is in itself a manipulation, as films rarely unfold in real-time.

In line with the simple cinematography, the editing appears naturalistic, and largely follows a pattern of cuts between the passenger and Panahi, or through the front windscreen. The pace of editing is leisurely, with shots held for up to three or four minutes with no edits. There are the occasional 'fade to blacks', which are used in conjunction with a POV shot through the front windscreen, and the use of non-diegetic music to mark the transition between one sequence and the next.

iA **Independent Activity**

Find three examples of where a camera is being used within the context of the film, and write 100 words on its use as both a prop and as part of the film's cinematography.

iA **Independent Activity**

Select two films you are studying for Global filmmaking. In what ways does the closing sequence of your chosen films confirm messages and values working through the film as a whole? Write a 400-word essay.

Sound

The **sound design** for *Taxi Tehran* supports the cinematic conceit of filming within a taxi. The sound is largely diegetic, as captured through the dash-cam and hidden camera's mics, and there is no additional sound recording in evidence. Consequently, there are some events that are seen but not heard, and others heard but not seen.

At times the audience witnesses activity outside the taxi, but do not hear it, such as the bride and groom, or we can hear activity in the car such as Omid taking calls in the back-passenger seat, but with the camera fixed on front-seat passenger or filming out of the front windscreen. The audience does not always know who is speaking.

The film opens with a fixed POV shot out of the front windscreen, while the car is waiting at a street crossing and is held for just over a minute. The audience sees modern Tehran pass before their eyes, as young men dressed in Western clothes and traditionally dressed Iranian women wearing hijabs walk back and forth. Motorbikes, cycles and cars are streaming from all directions. Approximately a minute and half of the car driving through the streets follows this. This shot is accompanied by non-diegetic music, which appears to be both traditional and Iranian although this is hard to verify in the absence of credits. The shot ends when a male passenger comments on the camera and the camera is turned to show a head and shoulder shot.

> Sound design: involves performing and recording new sounds and editing previously recorded audio, such as sound effects and dialogue. These are combined to create an overall soundtrack to a film.

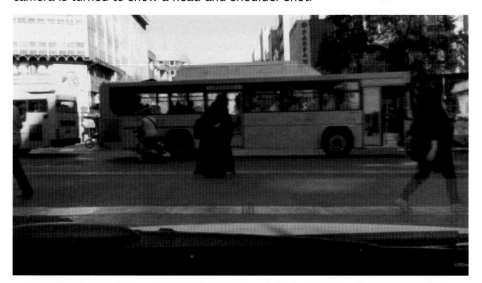

The film ends with an example of an action heard but seen. Panahi and Hana have left the car as they look for the two women at Ali's Spring. Two young men on a motorcycle pass and double back. The camera is in its fixed position out of the front window, but you can hear the glass being broken, and what sounds like rummaging through the glove compartment. As one of the men pulls the camera out of the cradle the screen goes black; however, their voices are still being recorded via the other cameras. You can hear one saying, 'He's coming!', with the other responding that he is looking for the USB, followed by the sound of the motorbike driving away. This final crime ties in with the conversations about crime and poverty that have punctuated the film, but also alludes to Panahi's punishment by the government, of having his filmmaking ripped away from him.

> **Independent Activity**
>
> Watch ten minutes of the film with the subtitles turned off. This will allow you to better focus on the juxtaposition between sound and image.
>
> Paying particular focus to the soundtrack, divide your page into two columns and in column 1 write notes on what you see, and in column 2 what you can hear.
>
> Can you always see what you are hearing?
>
> Can you always hear what you are seeing?
>
> How has the filmmaker used sound to guide your perception of the image and the action?
>
> Is the filmmaker's use of sound realistic?
>
> How have they used and/or integrated diegetic and non-diegetic sound?

The important thing is for the director to understand the strengths and weaknesses of the [child] player, and to build the character on this. At the children's filmmaking unit [The Institute for the Intellectual Development of Children and Young Adults, aka 'Kanoon'] they had a very routine manner of working with child actors. I was different. I acted out the children's roles in advance, to show what was expected of them.
(Panahi, 2009)

iA Independent Activity

The casting of non-professional actors is a convention of New Iranian Cinema, and world cinema more widely. Select two world cinema films which feature children, and research how they were cast and what was the critical and audience response.

iA Independent Activity

How do you think the film's aesthetics contribute to the social and political messages of the film?

Performance

Panahi has cast non-professional actors in this film, as he has done on previous occasions. The film has no credits, and there are no credits on the DVD or on IMDb. In the film's closing slide, Jafar Panahi explains,

> *The Ministry of Islamic Guidance approves the credits of distributable films. Despite my heartfelt wish, this film has no credits. I am indebted to everyone who helped us. This film would not exist without their support.*

Two of the actors are his niece Hana Saeid and the human rights lawyer Nasrin Sotoudeh, both of whom are essentially playing versions of themselves. The extent to which the others are playing themselves or versions of themselves is the subject of much debate both within the film and in its critical reception.

After the first couple – the mugger and teacher – exit the car, Omid the dealer of pirate DVDs recognises Panahi and is convinced that the couple were actors, as he recognised dialogue from a previous Panahi film. Panahi neither confirms nor denies they are actors or that he is making a film. Other than the mugger, Hana and Nasrin Sotoudeh, no other passenger comments on the camera or appears to be aware that they are being filmed.

Their performances are naturalistic, which is in keeping with the documentary style of the film. As Trevor Johnston wrote in his review in *Sight & Sound* (2015),

> [It] *has us wondering whether we're seeing documentary observation or the work of adeptly scripted non-professionals.*

Aesthetics

The aesthetics of New Iranian Cinema are closely aligned with both the limits and freedoms of working in a system at odds with the state-funded and supported film industry.

Stylistically the films seem to lack drama and sensationalism, which aligns them to the Italian Neorealist movement. However, much is revealed through these simply-framed, unbroken long takes. The filmmakers allow the viewer to absorb the action on screen, which, by using non-professional actors, naturalist lighting and real locations, has an air of authenticity.

These filmmakers have developed a cinematic language which combined with their thematic concerns is closely aligned with the realist film movement. A number of films, such as *Taxi Tehran,* play with documentary film conventions within a narrative fiction context.

One of the reasons that Iranian films have become so popular in the West is the perceived contradiction between such aesthetically distinctive films and the repressive conditions under which they are produced.

Representations

The filmmakers of the New Iranian Cinema are keen to reflect contemporary Iranian social and political concerns. The themes and characters they depict are at odds with the state-funded films and will therefore find themselves with limited, if any, distribution in Iran.

The characters in *Taxi Tehran* are clearly representing a cross-section of Iranian social and political perspectives: men and women; young and old; rich and poor; victim and perpetrator; filmmakers and film watchers; a human rights activist and a supporter of capital punishment; traditionalists and modernists.

Age

There are a number of ages represented *Taxi Tehran*; at one end of the spectrum are the two elderly women who are enacting their annual pilgrimage to Ali's Spring to release their current two goldfish and collect two new ones. If they do not do this by midday, they are convinced that they will die. These two women seem to represent the past, when myths and storytelling were central. At the opposite end is Hana, with her inquisitiveness and education she represents the future. However, her future is coloured by the education she is receiving under the current regime in Iran. Her future is shown in stark contrast to the young boy she chastises for not returning the money he found. Although approximately the same age, he is out working, collecting bottles for recycling rather than studying.

The present and future of filmmaking is represented in this film with Jafar Panahi as the established director passing advice and wisdom to a film student (stop reading about/watching films and make them) and to his niece.

Gender

In the style of a scripted reality TV show, the characters discuss or embody the film's three central themes: crime, filmmaking and women's place within Iranian society.

Iran is a male-dominated society, and there are written and unwritten rules about what women can and cannot do, with education being an area of discontent. However, there are many educated professional women in Iran including lawyers, doctors, teachers, engineers and filmmakers. This is reflected

in *Taxi Tehran* by the inclusion of a teacher in the opening scene, and the lawyer/human rights campaigner in the closing scene, with a budding filmmaker reflected in his niece Hana.

The teacher is shown as feisty and able to hold her own in an argument about crime and capital punishment with a man who claims to be a 'freelance mugger', clearly showing the benefits of a middle-class Iranian education. Hana is a confident and ambitious young girl, who is flourishing through education, but her education is clearly skewed towards the state's views of social and political matters, demonstrated through the list of rules she has to obey if she wants her film to be distributed.

However, the film also depicts women whose position is not as secure. The wife of the man knocked over by the car seems more agitated by the potential loss of her family home than she is her husband. Without a will, all their property will go to her husband's male relatives, leaving her penniless and homeless.

Hana also relates a story about a neighbour, a young woman, who was in love with a man from Afghanistan. When her father and brother found out, they beat him up and forbade her from seeing him again.

Human rights lawyer Nasrin Sotoudeh discusses a real case with which she was involved. British-Iranian female student Ghoncheh Ghavami was arrested in 2014 for protesting for equal access to sporting events in Iran. She was sentenced to one year in jail and had been held in solitary confinement in Evin Prison for 100 days when she went on hunger strike. She was released soon after. Panahi's film *Offside* is about young women wanting to go to a football match.

The male characters also embody a cross-section of society, with perspectives from a criminal and then later a victim of crime. This latter character, Mr Arash, is the subject of Hana and Panahi's conversation about the depiction of a 'good guy' in a film. According to the rules Hana has been given, he should not be wearing a tie (a sign of Western business practices) and should not have an Iranian name.

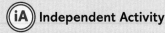 **Independent Activity**

Read Mark Hallihan's 'The 10 Best Iranian Films About Women' (2016) on the Taste of Cinema website and 'Iran's Big Woman Problem: All of the Things Iranian Women aren't Allowed to Do' by David Blair (2017) on the *Daily Telegraph*'s website.

With these articles in mind, select one of the female characters in *Taxi Tehran* and examine how she is portrayed.

Ethnicity

The films of New Iranian Cinema are rooted in their national identity. These films are set in contemporary Iran, and in the most part are focused on the lives and concerns of Iranian people. Here, Panahi explores the diversity of political, religious and social views through the prism of education, class and age.

The anecdote about the Iranian father and brothers beating the Afghan boyfriend of their daughter/sister offers an insight into the strained relationship between these neighbouring countries.

Conclusion

For over 25 years, New Iranian Cinema has dominated the global filmmaking landscape, with Jafar Panahi being a leading figure within this film movement. He made *Taxi Tehran* five years into his 20-year ban from filmmaking but when asked in 2014 if Iranian cinema had a future, he was optimistic about its future, if somewhat despondent about his place within it:

I think all movies are worth watching.

> *I'm really optimistic about the future of Iranian cinema because of all these young and talented filmmakers. Some of my colleagues are working outside of Iran. There's nothing wrong with that. They should be free to work inside or outside. But what makes me hopeful, after making this picture [Closed Curtain], is this pool of talented young filmmakers who can use the same all-digital cameras to make their own movies. There was a time when the government had a monopoly on all the filmmaking equipment. But right now, if you're a young filmmaker, you don't have to go to the government to make your films. The camera and software is available to you so you can make your movie. I myself was supposed to make a movie outside of Iran and would welcome that situation, but I would want to know that I can return.* (Panahi, cited in Kohn, 2014)

Independent study questions

Q How does Panahi use film form to bring to the fore the film's social and political messages?

Q How does Panahi employ techniques of documentary filmmaking in this film and how does this affect your response to it?

Q In what ways does knowing about the circumstances in which Panahi made the film affect your reading of the film and its themes.

Q How does the film explore the relationship between men and women?

Q Given that the Iranian government states that films should 'avoid violence', how is 'violence' depicted in *Taxi Tehran*?

Sample essay extract and feedback

With close reference to the two films you have studied, explore how either performance or editing create meaning.

For this example, we are looking at **extracts** from essays addressing *Mustang* and *Taxi Tehran*.

Jamie's response extract

Editing is used to create meaning, it does this by emphasising specific things; for example, in *Mustang*, as Lale is the film's narrator she appears in most of the scenes, or if she is not in the scene, it is shown from her point of view. There are a few exceptions, such as the reaction of the aunts when they see them on television (but the narration explains that she found out later what they did). This shows how important she is to the narrative, as she is the most impetuous of the sisters, and is the instigator of key events such as going to the football match, and her and Nur's final escape.

Although the film is told in flashback, its telling is in a conventional narrative structure outlining their experiences over a specific period. This provides the viewer with a clear presentation of their change in circumstance from joy to sadness.

Taxi Tehran is also told in a conventional narrative structure, but is presented in real-time, there is no appearance of time passing between scenes, with the focus being on what is happening in the taxi.

Here, the director, Jafar Panahi, is the central figure, and yet the editing does not dwell on him. In fact, we don't know that the director is in the film as the taxi driver for the first eight minutes of the film, as the editing focuses on the streets of Tehran and the passengers, rather than Panahi. The meaning this generates is that he is more interested in what is happening in Tehran, and what the passengers' views are, rather than his own.

In *Taxi Tehran*, the use of close-ups is part of the limitations of the camera set-up, whereas in *Mustang* they are used to portray the emotions of the characters, such as the close-ups of Lale looking longingly out of the window, or Selma's sadness in comparison to Sonay's joy at their wedding.

Feedback

This opening would have benefitted from examples of the editing techniques employed to create meaning.

Good practice to indicate the year and director's name for each film referenced.

Lale is a good example, as is the exception (football/village), the use of terms such as objective, subjective, parallel editing would have scored extra points.

Again, good point but use of terminology is needed.

Good to note that it is in edited as 'real-time' but should have made clear that these narrative structures are not considered 'conventional'.

Doesn't indicate what meaning is generated by this.

Good to note that Panahi is the central figure, and to indicate that it is some time until we discover this. A clearer comparison to Mustang *would have made this point stronger.*

Jamie has offered this meaning as 'fact', it is just one interpretation.

Jamie assumes that the close-ups are merely a technical limitation, offering no potential meanings on why Panahi might have used these.

The examples of close-ups in Mustang *are good, but would have benefitted from a conclusion.*

Quinn's response extract

It is widely considered that films are made in the edit. Editing is the only element of the production process that is unique to film.

Feedback

The examples of close-ups in Mustang *are good, but would have benefitted from a conclusion.*

Editors do more than merely place the shots in a logical order to tell the story; they can also employ a number of techniques to create additional layers of meaning. This can include the way in which they make the transition from one shot to the next (cut, dissolve, fade), the speed of the editing, and the way that time and space are presented.

The inclusion of the editing techniques that can be employed demonstrates a greater understanding of the importance of editing.

The editor can also draw attention to specific things; for example, *Mustang* (Ergüven, 2015) is told from the perspective of the youngest sister, Lale. She is the main protagonist, and appears in most of the scenes, or is seen eavesdropping and observing on others, from a mix of objective and subjective shots. As a result, the majority of the film is told as single continuous narrative around Lale's actions. There are a few examples of parallel editing such as the girls and the football match, and the scenes back in the village where the match is on TV. This builds tensions, as we wonder whether the girls are going to be found out. Lale's narration explains how she knew what happened. By placing Lale so centrally in the edit, this reinforces her dominance to the narrative, as she is the trigger for key events, but it also limits how much we know about the other sisters.

Good practice to reference director and year.

The appropriate use of terminology such as protagonists, objective and subjective, parallel editing would have all brought additional marks.

By mentioning that tension is built by juxtaposing these two actions, offers a greater understanding of the cinematic practices. Highlighting Lale is important, and it is good to reference that as a result we know less of the sisters' actions.

Mustang is told as a linear narrative, albeit in flashback, and its telling is largely conventional in presenting a pivotal period of time when the sisters went from childhood to womanhood, from freedom and fun, to oppression and sadness in a few months.

A stronger conclusion and link back to question would have gained extra marks.

Taxi Tehran (Panahi, 2015) is edited in a linear narrative form, but its presentation as a found-footage documentary unfolding in real time, is atypical of both the documentary and fiction film. There is no appearance of time passing between scenes, even when there are fades to black. This reinforces the conceit that what is happening in the taxi can be seen as indicative of what is happening in Tehran more widely.

Quinn's use of terminology and understanding of the narrative structure is good, and offers examples of what meanings this can present.

Mentioning Panahi's use of fades to black as not being not indicative of their usual practice is good.

Like Lale in *Mustang*, the director Jafar Panahi, is the central figure, and is the only consistent character in the film. But, unlike Lale, the editing does not prioritise him. It is not until approximately eight minutes into the 80-minute film that we see that the director (Panahi) is also the taxi driver. Until then we had had seen the streets of Tehran and the first pair of passengers. This could allude to his interest in hearing what the passengers' views are, rather than his own, or could be a subtle hint at the political silencing by the Iranian government, through the 20-year ban they imposed on him.

Again good use of terminology and understanding that real time is an unconventional editing structure. An indication that the film is only 80 minutes, makes the eight minutes more significant.

By offering a number of potential meanings, indicates that Quinn is aware that these meanings are not fixed, and that multiple meanings are possible.

The dominant camera angle in *Taxi Tehran* is the dashcam, this means that most of the shots are in close-ups, forcing the viewer to focus on the conversations, and, in main, Panahi's reactions. This is particularly effectively when his niece Hana is reading the rules on how to make a distributable film. In *Mustang*, the close-ups are often combined with a slow pace of editing to ensure that the viewer can study the emotions of the characters such as Lale looking longingly out of the window, or Selma's sadness in comparison to Sonay's joy at their wedding.

Quinn hasn't assumed that the close-ups are a limitation placed on the film by the camera angles. It also offers a potential meaning for their use, and an appropriate example.

By widening the close-up example from Mustang to include the pace of editing, demonstrates a greater understanding of how editing techniques are used in conjunction with one another to generate meaning.

This section will help you prepare for Component 2: Global filmmaking perspectives on the A level course. Alongside the core areas of study you will need to apply the specialist study areas of Critical Debate 2: The significance of digital technology in film and Filmmakers' theories. This section will use *Stories We Tell* (Polley, Canada, 2012) as a case study.

For A level

One question from a choice of two must be answered on the Component 2 paper. The full question is worth 20 marks and should be allocated 30 minutes.

The specification says

The documentary film in its contemporary form has become a much freer form, utilising cinematic techniques in ever more creative ways to tell 'factual' stories while problematising the divide between fact and fiction.

Stories We Tell is, on the surface, a fascinating exploration of Sarah Polley's family, including archive footage and insightful interviews with her relatives and family friends. The film initially paints a portrait of her enigmatic and charismatic late mother, actress and television personality Diane Polley, who died when Sarah was a child. The film goes on to examine Sarah's relationships with the writer and actor Michael Polley, the man who raised her as his own daughter, and film and theatre producer Harry Gulkin, who is revealed to be her biological father. The film is moving, revelatory, at times humorous and full of surprises.

Stories We Tell is also an invitation to the audience to question the authenticity of the documentary form. Spectators are encouraged to assess the reliability of personal testimony and whether or not there is such a thing as objective truth. Are the stories we tell a true portrayal of the past and, if so, why do they differ from others' recollections of the same events? Can memory ever be really relied upon? The film also exposes the constructed nature of documentary film by interspersing reconstructions with archive footage without revealing this to the audience. The film arguably misleads the spectator for a large portion of the narrative while purporting to tell the truth and, in doing so, raises interesting considerations regarding the 'true' nature of the documentary form as a representation of fact. It is for this reason that *Stories We Tell* is a useful case study for analysing this genre.

This chapter will address the core areas of study in relation to *Stories We Tell* by exploring the conventions of the documentary form and the different modes of documentary used in this film. The chapter will also examine the role digital technologies play in this genre and compare Polley's approach to those of other significant documentarians.

Documentary

Early silent films often simply recorded something real and showed it to an audience. Take as an example the famous 1895 Lumière Brothers' film *L'arrivée d'un train en gare de La Ciotat* or, as it is often referred to, *Train Pulling into a Station*. The film is entirely comprised of real-life footage of a train's arrival at a station, and therefore could be seen as an early example of the documentary genre.

L'arrivée d'un train en gare de La Ciotat (Lumière Brothers, 1895)

The documentary genre has been defined in many different ways since its inception. John Grierson, who came up with the term, referred to documentary as,

> *the creative treatment of actuality.* (cited in Eitzen, 1995, page 82)

Grierson's definition allows that there is a creativity to documentary filmmaking that suggests the filmmaker has a role to play in shaping the film and telling the story in an imaginative and compelling way. The word 'actuality' can be understood as fact, which is reflected in Bordwell and Thompson's definition, in their textbook *Film Art* (1997). They say,

> *a documentary film purports to present factual information about the world outside the film.* (page 42)

The use of the word 'purports' is interesting as it questions the reliability of the form and raises the issue of whether documentaries can ever really present an objective truth. Singleton and Conrad are very specific, defining documentaries as,

> *Film[s] of actual events; the events are documented with the real people involved, not with actors.* (2000, page 94)

This is problematised when reconstructions, a staple of many films from this genre, are taken into account. Perhaps a broader definition is more helpful, like the one from James Monaco, who describes documentary as,

> [A] *term with a wide latitude of meaning, basically used to refer to any film or program not wholly fictional in nature.* (2000, page 94)

What these definitions demonstrate is that the term documentary has multiple contested meanings. However, the genre, in its many forms, continues to fascinate audiences and has as great an impact today as in the early days of cinema when audiences allegedly ran from screenings of *L'arrivée d'un train en gare de La Ciotat* in fear of being struck by the locomotive.

Institutional context

Documentary is often regarded as a somewhat niche genre, but a quick scroll through the titles currently available on Netflix will confirm the popularity of this type of film at the present time. Consider the Academy Award-nominated exploration of race and imprisonment in the USA, *13th* (DuVernay, 2016). Contrast this with the imaginatively conceived examination of people's responses to the murder of JonBenet Ramsay, *Casting JonBenet* (Green, 2017). These films, and hugely successful documentary series such as *The Jinx* and *The Making of a Murderer*, are consistently attracting large audiences online. So much so that Netflix is getting involved in documentary production with another real crime title being a notable example: the Emmy nominated *Amanda Knox*.

Documentaries are certainly attracting audiences online and, despite the recent downturn in the genre's fortunes in the box office, the trend remains on the whole largely positive. Patricia Aufderheide in *Documentary Film: A Very Short Introduction* (2008) points to the 1990s as the turning point for the genre, with significant theatrical releases such as Michael Moore's *Roger and Me* in 1989 and a boom in television documentary, meaning the genre was considered a growth sector of the film industry. Staying with Moore, according to boxofficemojo.com (2017a) his 2004 film, *Fahrenheit 9/11*, made box office records for the genre, taking close to $120 million during its cinema release on an impressive 868 screens.

Despite this, most documentary films still tend to get limited theatrical releases and *Stories We Tell* is no exception. Even though Sarah Polley was an established name in the film industry, through both acting and directing, and the film won multiple awards, *Stories We Tell* initially opened on just two cinema screens and its widest release was 70 screens according to boxofficemojo.com (2017b). However, despite this, according to the National Film Board blog, *Stories We Tell* is one of the most successful Canadian films of all time and made the TIFF All Time Top Ten List. The film certainly achieved critical acclaim with a metascore of 91 and a rating of 'universal acclaim' on metacritic.com (n.d.). *Stories We Tell* won the 2013 New York Film Critics Circle Award for Best Non-Fiction Film and the 2013 Los Angeles Film Critics Association Award for Best Documentary. The film was also awarded the Allan King Documentary award at the 2012 Toronto Film Critics Association Awards.

Patricia Aufderheide (2008) states that there are three main sources of funding for documentary filmmakers: corporate or governmental sponsors, advertisers and users. *Stories We Tell* was produced by the first of these, specifically the National Film Board (NFB) of Canada, an organisation hugely supportive of the documentary genre. The NFB in its various guises has championed the documentary form since John Grierson's involvement in 1938, through World War II propaganda and newsreels to 1980s televised vignettes of Canadian culture.

In 2009 the Board collaborated with the Canadian Film Centre on a theatrical documentary development programme, Creative Doc Lab, which led to the production of, among other films, *Stories We Tell*. Polley's decision to work on the project with these organisations was deliberate because she wanted the freedom to experiment. Anita Lee, executive producer at Ontario Studio and NFB advisor to the Creative Doc Lab, explains on the NFB blog (2015) that,

> Stories We Tell *is a great example what can come out of Doc Lab. Sarah was able to take creative risks and to challenge traditional notions of documentary.*

More broadly, Lee argues that,

> *the documentary has always been at the core of the NFB's mission. Whether it's cinema-vérité, giant-screen IMAX non-fiction or web-docs, we've been at the forefront of documentary innovation from the get-go.* (NFB, 2015)

Social and political context

A 2012 BBC News article by Lorraine Mallinder (2012) asked 'What Does it Mean to be Canadian?' One of the points made in this article is that Canada is a diverse nation made up of over 200 ethnic groups spread over six time zones.

Mallinder quotes John Ralston Saul, who said of Canadians, 'they accept that difference is actually quite interesting'. This embracing of diversity points to a culture that is non-judgemental and open-minded: traits we can certainly see in the Polley family depicted in *Stories We Tell*.

Fahrenheit 9/11 (Moore, 2004)

 Independent Activity

Watch *Fahrenheit 9/11* and note the reasons you feel it was such a box office success.

The Polley family certainly have enlightened and progressive views. This is evident in relation to gender roles, in particular Michael's attitude to his wife's work and choices. Canada as a whole fairs well in terms of gender equality, coming 20th in the World Economic Forum's 2013 Global Gender Gap Report. This index:

> *seeks to measure one important aspect of gender equality: the relative gaps between women and men, across a large set of countries and across four key areas: health, education, economics and politics.* (page v)

Cultural context

The prevalence of 'reality' television and mockumentaries in contemporary culture may impact upon audience response to this documentary. Spectators may be more cynical and less believing now, as they are increasingly exposed to scripted 'reality' television programmes where situations are constructed for entertainment purposes.

Anita Lee addressed this on the Canadian Film Centre website (Angeletti-Szasz, 2016), saying:

> *with the proliferation of reality and factual programming and all its offshoots, the relationship between reality and the notion of truth has become obscure. I like to believe that documentary is still a realm where filmmakers are guided by the principles of seeking and reflecting some kind of truth, as they understand it.*

Approaches to storytelling and the way narratives are structured in film continue to change and become more complex in the quest to offer audiences something new and surprising. Films with plot twists have a long history of popularity among filmmakers and audiences alike. *Stories We Tell* reflects the evolution of cinema, offering something new, not a plot twist but a construction twist.

Film form in documentary

Documentary films share many conventions with fiction films, such as the range of shot types used, the use of music to create mood and tone, and clever editing to construct compelling narratives. The far from exhaustive list of documentary conventions explored here arguably includes aspects of film form seen in a range of films of all genres. Fiction films in various genres, particularly social realist films, co-opt the conventions of documentary to convey a sense of realism.

- **Hand-held camera**: it is often suggested that a hand-held camera conveys a sense of the real. It creates the sense of actually being there as it captures the camera operator's movements and changing perspectives: the image can be blurred at times through camera shake, and the frame is unfixed and often shifts erratically. Additionally, hand-held cameras can convey a sense of energy and emotion, as a result of rapid movement and/or the frame moving unevenly or fitfully. The archive footage and the reconstructions in *Stories We Tell* both use a hand-held camera with very unpredictable movements at times. The use of this technique for both these helps to contribute to the sense that all the footage is from the same source, and therefore authentic.

Blurred image caused by camera shake

- **Voice-over or narration**: occurs when a voice is heard on the soundtrack without a matching source in the image. In other words, we hear the voice speak but we cannot see the speaker utter the words. The voice often explains or comments on the visuals, presents a point of view and leads the audience towards a preferred reading. Michael Polley's voice is probably the dominant voice-over in *Stories We Tell*, but the film is unusual in the way that it includes footage of him recording it, making the filmmaking process seem transparent.

- **Talking heads**: talking heads are interviews with experts or witnesses, often filmed in their home or workplace, offering their perspectives on the events being documented. These are often shot in medium close-up or medium shot and adhere to the rule of thirds. Captions are often used to identify the participant to the audience. *Stories We Tell* makes use of this convention and all participants are framed similarly, which contributes to the sense that they play equal roles in telling this story.

- **Archive footage and photographs**: existing recordings or images that can be used to evidence that events took place. These can include stock footage, usually held by libraries or television companies, which can be used time and again for different purposes. *Stories We Tell* relies primarily on the Polley family's own archive of home movies but includes extracts from an existing documentary on Harry Gulkin too.

- **Reconstructions or re-enactments**: performances of real events that have already happened but not been recorded. They often include actors playing the parts of the real subjects. How *Stories We Tell* differs from most other documentaries in this regard is that the re-enactments included here are presented as genuine footage for the bulk of the narrative.

- Subjects are often **hyper-real** or **extraordinary**, as audiences are drawn to worlds outside of their own experiences or people different from those they know. The subjects of *Stories We Tell*, although arguably just Sarah's family members, are extraordinary in some ways. Outside of the complexity of their relationships they are renowned, accomplished, charismatic and entertaining people who are noteworthy in their own right.

 S&C

Compile a more exhaustive list of documentary conventions through your own research. For each convention find an example from *Stories We Tell* to illustrate its use. If the film does not use the particular convention find an example from the films of the other directors you are considering, i.e. two from Peter Watkins, Nick Broomfield, Kim Longinotto or Michael Moore.

Modes of documentary

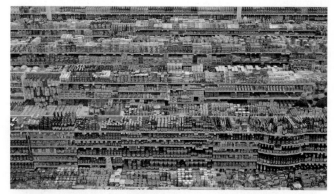

Koyaanisqatsi (Reggio, 1982)

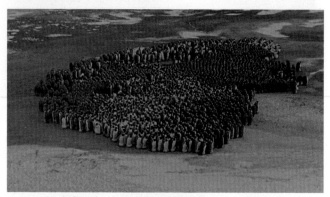

March of the Penguins (Jacquet, 2005)

Bowling for Columbine (Moore, 2002)

Être et avoir (Philibert, 2003)

Bill Nichols is an important documentary theoretician and in his seminal text, *Introduction to Documentary* (2010), he divides the documentary genre into six oft-cited 'sub-genres' or modes:

> *In documentary film and video, we can identify six modes of representation that function something like sub-genres of the documentary genre itself: poetic, expository, participatory, observational, reflexive, performative. These six modes establish a loose framework of affiliation within which individuals may work; they set up conventions that a given film may adopt; and they provide specific expectations viewers anticipate having fulfilled.*

Exploring these further is a useful way in considering the approach or approaches Polley takes in *Stories We Tell*.

- Coming to prominence in the 1920s, **poetic** documentaries are often non-linear with no clear narrative and rely instead on the juxtaposition of images and sound to create mood, tone and ultimately convey the filmmaker's message in a rather abstract way. An example is Reggio's 1982 film *Koyaanisqatsi*.

- **Expository** documentaries came to prominence around the same time but often feature an authoritative voice-over and convey a clear point of view. Consider *March of the Penguins*, Jacquet's 2005 film.

- A later development of the documentary genre, popularised in the 1960s, is the **participatory** documentary. These films include direct engagement between the filmmaker and the subject. The filmmaker is often seen on screen asking questions and expressing their perspective. An obvious example is Michael Moore who never shies away from expressing his point of view, as seen in *Bowling for Columbine* (2002).

- **Observational** documentaries, which started at a similar time, were a response to criticisms of earlier forms. Filmmakers used smaller cameras, available now due to advances in technology, and aimed to let their cameras record their subjects without intrusion. Philibert's 2003 film, *Être et avoir*, uses this technique to offer the audience access to a rural school in France.

- **Reflexive** documentaries, which evolved in the 1980s, draw attention to their own construction, often showing the process of the film being made. The intention of this can be to be transparent about the process and perhaps sidestep any questions about the ethics of the filmmaker. Nick Broomfield regularly, but not always, highlights his own involvement and the technologies of filmmaking in his work. Take as an example his 1992 documentary, *Aileen Wuornos: The Selling of a Serial Killer*. This film is as much about Broomfield securing an interview as it is about Wuornos' life and crimes.

- **Performative** documentaries tend to be very personal and often focus on subjective truths that are significant to the filmmaker him- or herself. An example of this is *Tongues Untied*, a 1989 film by Marlon Riggs who tells his own life story as a way of exploring the life of gay African-American men.

Aileen Wuornos: The Selling of a Serial Killer (Broomfield, 1992)

Stories We Tell has a number of aspects that place it within the reflexive mode of documentary, such as the shots of Polley at the mixing desk or behind the camera, but it shares traits with other sub-genres too, such as the voice-over from the expository mode. This is not unusual in documentaries, where overlap of modalities within a film is common practice.

A mode of documentary not included in Nichols' schema is that of the **personal documentary**, one that *Stories We Tell* possibly represents most coherently. These films are generally autobiographical and combine interviews and voice-overs with archive footage, photographs and artifacts to explore a person's life.

Tongues Untied (Riggs, 1989)

Polley herself has an ambivalent attitude to this mode of documentary, as she states on the NFB blogsite (2012),

> *Personal documentaries have always made me a bit squeamish. I've seen some brilliant ones, but they often push the boundaries of narcissism and can feel more like a form of therapy than actual filmmaking.*

Maybe this accounts for the fact that for a film that explores her family, and indeed her very coming into being, she at times seems like quite a peripheral participant. She is seen throughout the film but only rarely as the focus of a scene and her voice is seldom heard. In particular, her opinions and emotions are rarely explored in any depth.

What the film does uncover, though, reflects Linda Williams' view of the personal documentary. Summarised by Aufderheide (2008), Williams posits that,

> *such films challenge viewers to recognize that truths exist in a context, in relationship to lies, and are selected from other truths. Going beyond the reflexivity (that is calling attention to the fact that the film is a film), such films posit that there are important truths to be revealed and they can be revealed in spite of – or even by calling attention to – the partiality of our understanding.* (page 105)

 S&C

Watch the six films used here, or extracts from them, as examples of Nichols' modes. For each film analyse a sequence in detail, commenting on all aspects of film form.

 S&C

Research Paul Rotha's (1935) 'Traditions of Documentary' in *Documentary Film*, as an alternative way of categorising films in this genre. Summarise each 'tradition' in ten words.

Storytelling and construction of 'truth'

Documentary filmmakers usually wish to convince the audience of the authenticity of what they are representing. *Stories We Tell* challenges this, as one of the key themes of the film is how many different versions of events can be held within just one family.

As is made clear by the title and indeed the opening words, this film is about storytelling. The opening quote from novelist Margaret Atwood is, 'When you're in the middle of a story, it isn't a story at all', and the first words of Michael Polley's narration are, 'in the beginning, the end'. The audience may glean from this that what follows will not be a straightforward story, the plot may not follow a traditional structure and at times **narrative devices** may not be what they seem.

The film feels like a personal journey of discovery. There is a sense that Polley did not always know what form the film would take or how the story would be told. However, what is clear is that Polley has a very democratic approach to storytelling and strongly believes that everyone's experience and perspective are equally valid. This is expressed within the film in an email to Harry:

> *I'm just extremely uncomfortable at being involved in the telling of this story unless it includes the whole picture, which is to say my experience of it, your experience of it, as well as my family's. I wouldn't even pretend at this point to know how to tell it, beyond beginning to explore it through interviews with everyone involved, so that everyone's point of view, no matter how contradictory, is included.*

Also in communication with Harry, Polley reveals a core belief that there is no such thing as **objective truth**, as everyone's version of events will differ:

> *I'm interested in the way we tell stories about our lives, about the fact that the truth about the past is often ephemeral and difficult to pin down, and many of our stories, when we don't take proper time to do research about our pasts, which is almost always the case, end up with shifts and fictions in them, mostly unintended.*

This can be seen in Harry and Michael's conflicting memories of Diane's memorial service and in the participants' differing memories of whether Diane knew she was dying. The general consensus appears to be that she was aware of this fact, yet Michael disagrees. Perhaps it is too painful for him to imagine her confronting her imminent mortality.

Harry has a different perspective on whether accessing the truth is possible, stating,

> *you can certainly get very close to it, but you have to limit it to those who are involved in the events, directly involved and affected, and the direct witnesses to the events are only two, and one is not around.*

He adds to this,

> *the reality is, essentially, that the story with Diane, I regret to say, is only mine to tell, and I think that's a fact. Now, my recollections may be faulty at times, but I'm not gonna lie.*

So the participants in this film do not agree on how close to the facts the documentary can get or even on how best to approach seeking the truth.

Polley can be heard in the film asking participants for the 'whole story' and specifies 'in your own words'. This is crucial as it suggests she is at once

---

Narrative devices: techniques used in order to tell a story.

Objective truth: one truth that is the same for all people.

looking for the whole truth, not just edited highlights, but it also acknowledges that each account is an individual's perspective of the truth. She is expecting unique, probably somewhat conflicting, accounts. She also asks, 'what do you think of this documentary being made?', which reflects just how self-reflexive this film is, as the audience are reminded they are watching a documentary and invited to question the form as well as the content.

Bill Nichols describes such techniques thus:

> Reflexive strategies that call the very act of representation into question unsettle the assumption that documentary builds on the ability of film to capture reality. To remind viewers of the construction of the reality … undercuts the very claim to truth and authenticity on which the documentary depends. If we cannot take its images as visible evidence of the nature of a particular part of the historical world, of what can we take them? (2010, page 17)

Documentary films also raise issues of **bias** and **balance**, as the audience questions if the accounts are tainted by prejudice and whether an even-handed representation of events is being conveyed. *Stories We Tell* explores these notions in its examination of the truth.

Cinematography

Polley uses cinematography techniques from numerous different modes of documentary. The conventions of the talking heads in medium shot to medium close-up from the participatory interview are featured, moments of fly-on-the-wall filming reflect the observational documentary style and there are performed scenes, or reconstructions, as in drama documentaries. The overall effect of this range of filming techniques contributes to the reflexive documentary style: a film that does not simply explore the relationship between the director and the subject(s) but rather the director and the audience.

The film does feature real archive footage of the family, including a section made up primarily of close-ups of Diane through which the audience are at once invited to scrutinise her, although she is never fully revealed.

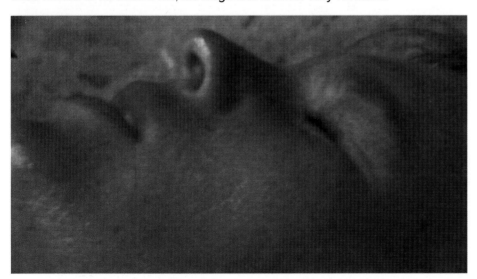

 Independent Activity

Read Sarah Polley's blog online to understand why this film was made.

 S&C

Research Michael Renov's four fundamental tendencies and note what you think the primary purpose of this film was according to his categorisations.

Bias: a concentration on one particular area or viewpoint.

Balance: different elements are treated equally.

This arguably reflects the film as a whole, as Diane remains somewhat enigmatic; a portrait made complex by differing accounts of a woman the audience does not get to meet. These close-ups are possibly used to elicit an emotional response from the spectator as they precede Sarah asking Michael to recount his memories of the day Diane died. Polley may have intended the audience to connect with Diane at this moment and perhaps therefore feel her loss more keenly.

Another emotive extreme close-up is used during the reconstructed scene of Sarah revealing to Michael that he is not her biological father. To some spectators this may lose some of its intensity as it is a scripted and performed recreation of a real moment from the past.

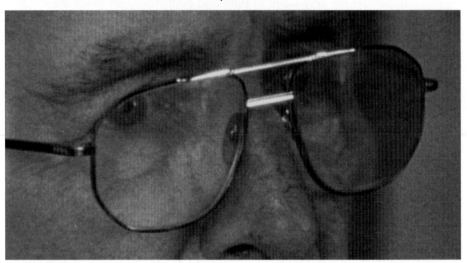

Techniques are used to encourage the audience to believe, for most of the narrative, that all the footage of the family is real. An example of this is the reconstructed footage of the play rehearsals, which are out of focus, shot with a shaky camera and have a voyeuristic feel. The audience is placed at a distance, sometimes behind props or parts of the set, like somebody filming but not wishing to interrupt.

A contrasting example, but one that also creates verisimilitude, is the way that 'Diane' breaks the fourth wall and interacts with the camera operator in an extract from a 'home movie' eight minutes into the documentary. This informality feels authentic as it is likely to resemble the natural human behaviour spectators will be familiar with from their own home movies.

Perhaps to discourage the audience from doubting the authenticity of any of the footage, the voice-over explains the importance of home movies to the family and, in particular, Michael's preoccupation with recording his family's life. In his **narration** Michael paraphrases Diane stating, 'he spent more time gripping the camera than he did holding her'.

Further evidence of this interest in home movies is seen in a photograph of Michael and Diane, which includes the Super 8 camera. These cameras and the associated film stock date back to 1965 and were most widely used for home movies. Super 8 footage has a nostalgic quality, a softness brought about by circular film grain and warmth of tone.

The inclusion of this photo contributes to the spectator potentially reading all the film's Super 8 footage as real archive home movies.

Narration: a commentary delivered to accompany a scene.

(iA) Independent Activity

The analysis of *Stories We Tell* on the Filmslie website breaks the film into three 'levels'. Read the article, called 'Analyis: Sarah Polley's Documentary' (Ignoramous, 2017), and summarise the cinematography techniques used in each 'level' of the film in less than 50 words.

The film makes use of much more contemporary digital cameras for the recent interviews, with the resulting footage being much sharper. This could be interpreted as more accurate and reliable, capturing the real without the cloudy nostalgia. To confuse matters further, Polley also uses 16mm footage for some of the more contemporary scenes, thus blurring the line between the past and the present, and contributing to the confusion. This may be instrumental in avoiding the audience spotting the deception.

Panning, alongside the aforementioned use of a hand-held camera, is an interesting example of how camera movement is used in this film. Panning is used effectively to provide insight for the spectator. An example is the pan around Michael's chaotic home, which could point to the fact that he may not be coping too well, thus revealing more to the audience than he knows.

Mise-en-scène

The mise-en-scène in this film is crucial in creating the sense that the reconstructions are real archive footage rather than re-enactments of events. Capturing the period accurately through location choices, set design, costume and styling to mislead the spectator is one central aspect of this.

Another technique is Polley's inclusion of artefacts, for example playbills and articles about Diane's roles in theatre. These are typical of documentary films and thus contribute to the sense of authenticity.

From the outset, Polley also includes the technology of filmmaking – cameras, lighting rigs and **mixing** desks – to create the impression of transparency in how the film is constructed. The audience may feel that, as she is being so open about the filmmaking techniques, she can be trusted.

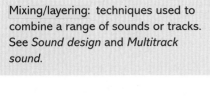

Mixing/layering: techniques used to combine a range of sounds or tracks. See *Sound design* and *Multitrack sound*.

Editing

The narrative structure of *Stories We Tell* is non-linear, as the audience are drip-fed new information throughout the film. The non-linear structure helps to create enigma by taking the audience step by step into the past. It is relatively late in the film, for example, that we learn of Diane's first marriage.

The focus of the film is not apparent from the outset either. Initially, this appears to be a film primarily about Diane, Sarah Polley's mother, but it is later revealed to be as much about her father, or fathers. The narrative has the twists and turns of a fictional film, creating suspense and intrigue but ultimately, at least partially, satisfying the audience's desire for **narrative closure**. The relationships will continue to evolve off camera but the audience has a sense that a new equilibrium has been reached, with Sarah Polley having a positive relationship with both Michael and Harry.

> Narrative closure: the feeling of finality generated when all the questions asked in a story are answered.

The complexity of the edit, mixing interviews, real archive footage and reconstructed scenes occurs from the beginning of the film, encouraging the spectators to passively accept the style and immerse themselves in the narrative. On first viewing the spectators are likely to be so caught up in the narrative that they don't pick up on hints that not all the footage they are seeing is real. Only on a second viewing, once the artifice has been revealed, is a spectator likely to fully appreciate the trickery at work. They may then question why they didn't at various moments ask themselves who was filming or indeed why a particular moment was being recorded at all. An example of this is the memorial for Diane; with hindsight clearly a reconstruction as funerals are rarely captured on film.

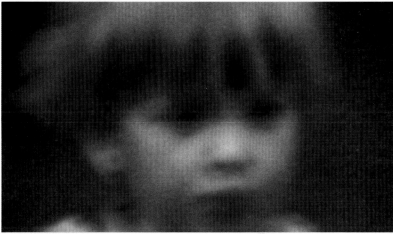

Nostalgic blurred footage of Sarah Polley as a child

The editing in *Stories We Tell* is at times used to evoke emotion. An example of this is the use of archive footage of a solemn Sarah Polley as a child, which cuts to Michael discussing with her how close he and her mother came to aborting her.

Additionally, a juxtaposition of Sarah Polley and her mother, similar both in terms of framing and facial expression, is strangely emotive as it invites the audience to consider their connection and appreciate what Sarah has lost.

On the NFB website, Polley (2012) acknowledges the agonising process of editing and how crucial it is in constructing a coherent and engaging narrative. She states,

> *I have spent five years deciding, frame by frame and word by word, how to tell this story in this film.*

Sound

The music that bookends this film is contemporary and highly emotive. 'Skinny Love' by Bon Iver and 'Demon Host' by Timber Timbre are both melancholic and ghostly. The latter immediately follows Michael recounting his last words spoken to Diane, so the song's opening line 'Death, she must have been your will', is highly pertinent and designed to provoke an emotional response. To add to this, the song is momentarily contrapuntal, as it is played over archive footage of Michael and Diane having fun at the beach. After a brief fade-out to allow Michael to continue to speak it fades back in to accompany a series of shots of long duration of the film's main participants all looking pensive as if reflecting on Diane and her death.

Music is, however, also used to humorous effect at times. The archive footage sometimes appears more comical and light due to the choice of music. Instrumental music by Abraham Lass is used sporadically throughout the film. It is taken from *Play Me a Movie: Piano Music to Accompany Silent Movie Scenes* and this link to cinema contributes to the sense of stories being told – a 'truth' being constructed.

The language use in this film is at times sophisticated, as demonstrated in a section of Michael Polley's narration:

> *From that precise moment when I was dragged out of my mother's womb into this cold world, I was complete. An amalgam of the DNA passed on to me by my mother and father, and they too had been born finished products, with their DNA handed down by their respective parents, and so back ad infinitum.*

The voice-over here includes use of Latin, complex terminology and a rather poetic turn of phrase. His **cultural capital** is clear and likely to appeal to a similarly educated audience.

Use of a Super 8 camera for the archive footage and reconstructed scenes means no sound was recorded. This arguably helps Sarah Polley blend the footage, as there is no need for voices to be mimicked. It could be argued that this makes the performed scenes less of a deception, as at least no words were being put in anyone's mouths.

In some ways Sarah Polley's voice is heard least in this film and she addressed this in the NFB blog post she wrote (Polley, 2012):

> *I declined to use a '**voice of God**' first person voice over narration because it felt false, self involved, and besides the point. But I found I could lose myself in the words of the people closest to me. I can feel and hear and see their histories, and I wanted to get lost, immerse myself in those words, and be a detective in my own life and family.*

Performance

Performance may initially seem less relevant in documentary than other film genres, as what the audience is watching is expected to be real but, as already explored in this section, *Stories We Tell* is a little different. For the sections of the film that are reconstructions it is crucial that the performances be as naturalistic as possible so as to contribute to the sense of authenticity.

The film also includes interviews and voice-overs that are performances in themselves. Consider Michael's voice-over, which is scripted and rehearsed.

Cultural capital: assets that give someone social mobility. This can involve education, personality and speech.

Voice of god: a narration technique in which the narration is given anonymously and authoritatively.

Sections are performed and sometimes repeated until 'right'. Consider also Polley's siblings, readying themselves for their interviews at the beginning of the film, considering how to sit, how they will be framed and what they want to say. They ask, 'What's my frame?' and state, 'Showtime', drawing attention to their performance and the constructed nature of documentary.

As well as a crucial aspect of film form, performance is arguably one of the key themes of this film. Michael and Diane meet while in a play together and fall in love while pretending to be other people. Michael says they were, 'playing two roles, rather than Michael and Diane'.

Aesthetics

A home movie aesthetic is created through the use of Super 8, a format the film's producer Anita Lee said is loaded as,

> *it already comes with this notion of nostalgia and the past. It's a medium of a certain time. We associate Super 8 with home movies lost in basements …* (Doucet, 2015)

This aesthetic is arguably quite romantic and there is a softness to the look of the film at times. This is not unusual for a Sarah Polley film. The image below is from the trailer for *Away From Her* (Polley, 2006) but it would not look out of place in *Stories We Tell*.

Characteristic soft focus shot in the trailer for *Away from Her* (Polley, 2006)

This is Sarah Polley's seventh film and producer Anita Lee suggests common themes running through Polley's work:

> *Her signature is to look at relationships deeply and honestly in a microscopic way, and the emotional waves these relationships have on the people around them. A deep exploration of intimate relationships at different stages was at the core of* I Shout Love, Away from Her *and* Take This Waltz, *and now* Stories We Tell *takes this territory to a new level.* (CinemaReview.com, 2017)

Polley's work is clearly linked thematically through her focus on relationships and there is a recurring visual style too: a sense of nostalgia.

Representations

It could be argued that documentaries are less likely to rely on stereotypical or archetypal representations, as the people presented are real and therefore multi-faceted, complex and changeable. However, documentary films are still constructed – still mediated – allowing the filmmaker to make decisions about what to show the audience of these people and, their lives and just as importantly, what not to show. As Krystin Arneson puts it in *Artifacts* journal (2012),

> *No matter how objectively a filmmaker approaches a topic, they will always be filtering the topic through their personal lens not just the camera's.*

Age

As the film explores families, a wide range of ages are represented. This includes Sarah and her siblings as both children and adults, Harry and Michael as middle-aged and elderly, and the youngest generation of children and grandchildren at play. Although this array of ages is represented, the film makes few comments about age, perhaps another example of Polley's democratic approach to filmmaking. A person's account of events is given no more status just because they have the wisdom of age.

One notable exception is the way that Diane is depicted. One aspect of how youthful she appears is the sad fact that she died young, so the audience don't see her age; aside from this she has a vitality and energy captured in home movies and in comments by people who knew her. Her son John describes her as, 'a really young soul'. This facet of her character could link with the irresponsibility of some of her actions and may encourage the audience to be less critical of her.

Gender

If we consider Western societies' expectations of women and consider the representation of Diane in this context, the film offers a refreshing lack of judgement of her for her transgressions. Diane is a complex individual who, unsurprisingly, adheres to some stereotypes and challenges others. Women are often represented as the homemaker and mother, something we certainly see in *Stories We Tell*. Early in the film it is established, through an interview with Joanna Polley, that gender roles were very conventional in the family home. Speaking of Diane she states,

> *She did all the cooking, all the cleaning, all the taking care of the kids.*

This is backed up by Michael Polley, the father, outlining his role thus,

> *I was a good husband in a providing way.*

The contribution of Mark Polley also confirms that Michael gave up acting for more secure employment to fulfil the role of the breadwinner. These comments are anchored through archive footage of Michael chopping wood and Diane with the children, to secure the contrasting representations in the spectators' minds. The representations are more complex though, as the audience also see Michael being very attentive to a baby, which contradicts what we hear about him leaving all parenting duties to Diane, and his closeness to Sarah after Diane's death is detailed in his voice-over.

When it comes to sex, the representations of Michael and Diane challenge social expectations because she is portrayed as being freer and uninhibited and with a higher sex drive than Michael. He is certainly modest about his own sexual prowess saying,

> a night with a dead wombat might be more exciting than a night with me.

Diane's liberal attitude to sex is central to the film's narrative and her infidelity during her marriage to Michael is presented in a very matter of fact manner with refreshingly little judgement from most of the central contributors. A notable exception is Mark's comment that she was 'out of control' but he concludes his comments with a fond smile. When the film explores Diane's adultery during her first marriage, which resulted in her losing custody of her children, the inclusion of a newspaper clipping conveys that not all of the general public were as understanding about a woman transgressing society's rules. It is mentioned in the film that this was the first time a woman lost custody of her children due to infidelity:

> Ultimately, George got custody of the kids, and that was unheard of in the '60s, and it was front-page news. And it was apparently the first time in Canada that a woman had ever lost custody of the kids, and it was because she left for another man, and she wasn't 'ladylike'.

The film also considers the role of the 'father' exploring the importance of genetics and nurture. Michael and Sarah are presented as particularly close, as they spent a lot of time together after Diane's death and this bond is unbroken by the revelations about her parentage.

 S&C

Compare the representations of Michael and Diane. What language is used to describe them? What do we see them doing? Write 400 words including an exploration of the role gender plays in these differences.

Ethnicity

David Hulchanski of the University of Toronto has argued that in recent years, after a period of greater integration, Toronto has re-segregated along income and ethnic lines (see York University, n.d.). This film is predominantly populated by well-educated, economically comfortable, white Canadians, so there is a lack of any racial diversity represented but perhaps this reflects the society and social circles the Polley family is part of.

As ethnicity also incorporates religion, the representation of Jewish culture in this film can be explored. Harry is Jewish and Sarah joins his family for the Jewish Passover festival, and mentions the fact that this is novel for her,

> I think our Passover plans are all in order. First time I've ever written that.

This sense of difference is arguably reinforced through the juxtaposed images of Sarah dining with Michael and the Polleys and the cut to images of her at the Passover dinner. The shots of Passover include traditional Jewish foods and rituals.

Alternatively, the fact that these scenes are shot using the same type of camera and similar camera movements, could be read as a suggestion that the two meals have more similarities than differences. They are just families enjoying a meal in each other's company.

The significance of digital technology in film

Robbie Pyburn wrote of Robert J. Flaherty filming the famous documentary *Nanook of the North* in 1922. Flaherty faced a long, icy journey to visit the Inuit population of Port Harrison and carried with him:

> two 'Akeley' 35mm motion picture cameras, 75,000 feet of film, a Hallberg electric light plant and a projector. (Whicker's World Foundation, n.d.)

As Pyburn points out,

> Nowadays, Flaherty would only have needed to pocket his Smartphone and be on his way. Not only would the footage have been better quality, he'd have been able to record audio as well. (Whicker's World Foundation, n.d.)

Digital technologies have had a massive impact in the film world, from the accessibility of YouTube to the expensive effects of CGI. In the world of documentary more people have the means to tell their stories because cameras are more affordable and films can be distributed immediately online. This has led to a democratisation of the form. Smaller, lighter cameras also means the camera operator is freer, more locations are within reach and the camera is less obtrusive, arguably making it less intimidating to the subject. Little of this is relevant, however, when we look at *Stories We Tell*, but this does not mean that the digital/film debate is irrelevant.

However, as this documentary uses digital and film cameras, and the sequences filmed on digital are actually the more static aspects of the film, it could be argued that in terms of flexibility and practicality the choice of digital or film had minimal impact.

Forty percent of the film is from the family's old Super 8 movies, and Super 8 cameras (Canon 1014 AZ, Canon 1014XLS and Nikon R8) are used in the reconstructions to help create the illusion of archive footage. This technique was time-consuming as it took three days to process the film. This could be seen as a challenge of working in this format but the resulting footage is all the more convincing for having been produced authentically rather than just using a filter in post-production.

The digital camera used in *Stories We Tell*, the Sony CineAlta HDW-F900R, is used for the contemporary interviews, and the crispness of the image anchors those moments in the present. It helps create the sense of distance between the family now and the events of the past. This is complicated somewhat by Polley using 16mm footage for some of the contemporary moments. This could be seen as a further method for confusing the audience and helping to pull off the narrative's deceit. In this film at least, digital is the honest form accurately capturing the real while Super 8 is romantic, nostalgic and ultimately less reliable – like memory itself.

Filmmakers' theories

In the exam you should be able to write about filmmakers' theories in relation to the film you are studying. You have to be able to write about two of the following filmmakers' approaches to the form:

- Peter Watkins
- Nick Broomfield
- Kim Longinotto
- Michael Moore.

This section will focus on Broomfield and Longinotto but there is further guidance about these filmmakers plus Watkins and Moore on the WJEC/Eduqas online resources page (http://resources.eduqas.co.uk).

Nick Broomfield

Nick Broomfield has been making documentaries since the 1970s and is arguably one of the genre's most famous names, frequently featured in the pages of film magazines and a regular on the film festival circuit. The Film Studies specification argues that,

> Broomfield, like Michael Moore, has developed a participatory, performative mode of documentary filmmaking. Broomfield is an investigative documentarist with a distinctive interview technique which he uses to expose people's real views … he keeps the filmmaking presence to a minimum, normally with a crew of no more than three.

Nick Broomfield

This is certainly true of the bulk of his work – films such as 1998s *Kurt and Courtney* and 2003's *Aileen: Life and Death of a Serial Killer* – and is the style of filmmaking he is most known for. Watching a Broomfield film, the audience expect to see him on camera, asking probing questions and trying to expose the truth about his subject. He has inspired numerous other documentary filmmakers such as Louis Theroux. This approach can be compared to aspects of *Stories We Tell*, as Polley is present on-screen and the apparatus of the documentarian can be seen but the crew members are minimal and their presence unobtrusive.

Over time, Broomfield's approach to documentary has shifted and he is either completely absent from the screen, as in the dramatised documentary *Ghosts* (2006), or only occasionally heard posing a question, as in *Whitney: Can I Be Me* (2017).

Ghosts (Broomfield, 2006)

Again, these techniques can be seen in Polley's film, which includes reconstructions of real events and Polley's voice off-camera leading her interviewees through their recollections.

 Independent Activity

Listen to the podcast 'Nick Broomfield: The Interview Technique' (2008) and note any references Broomfield makes about his technique that link in with Polley's approach to constructing *Stories We Tell*.

▶ **S&C**

Watch three films from Broomfield's back catalogue that encompass the range of styles he has used, for example *Kurt and Courtney*, *Ghosts* and *Whitney: Can I Be Me*. Note the range of techniques he is using in each, for example talking heads, archive footage or interviews, and create a Venn diagram of how the techniques used in each film overlap. Consider how *Stories We Tell* would fit into this diagram.

Kim Longinotto

Kim Longinotto has had a long and successful career, encompassing films such as *Divorce Iranian Style* (1998) and *Sisters in Law* (2005). Her films often focus on women and she explained her reasons for this to Kira Cochrane at the *Guardian* (2010) stating that she empathises with:

> the outsiders, the people struggling. If women have no rights, if they are completely powerless, then they're the ones that you're going to want to make films about.

Her championing of those without power can be linked to what she describes as her 'problem with authority' (Lacey, 2010), which includes a distrust of documentaries that strongly push the spectator towards a specific reading.

To avoid aiming for a preferred reading, Longinotto's work largely fits within the category of observational films, also known as cinéma vérité, which was popularised in the 1960s. Documentarians working within this subgenre tend to use light cameras, giving them greater freedom and access to places that may not have been seen before. They also shoot a lot of footage and construct the narrative in the editing room. These films are arguably more impartial than films featuring persuasive voice-overs and interviews. They aim to capture reality as honestly as possible and invite the spectator to interpret it however they want to. The decisions taken about what to film and how to edit the footage do, of course, mean reality is still mediated by the filmmaking process.

Longinotto has said,

> I don't think of films as documents or records of things. I try to make them as like the experience of watching a fiction film as possible, though, of course, nothing is ever set up. (Quinn, 2012, page 145)

Longinotto differs from Broomfield as she is always absent from the screen and she forgoes a lot of the techniques conventionally associated with documentaries. Her use of voice-over is minimal and she avoids captions or formal interviews. In a 2006 interview with the *Guardian*'s Helen Pidd, entitled 'The Invisible Woman', Longinotto said,

> I love the way Nick [Broomfield] *appears in his films, but I don't want you to be thinking about me, or the camera or the filming when you watch my films. I want you to feel that you're there, standing where I am and going through the emotional experience.*

This contrasts well with Polley's approach, which often reminds the audience they are watching the film. Yet Polley's film still finds a way to convey the emotions of the director and the subjects. For example, the audience hear Polley's feelings through her emails to Harry, read out late in the film and second-hand through Michael, recounting her distress when she hears that the story about her parentage is out.

Longinotto likes to leave her documentaries open, avoiding narrative closure, as she wants her films to raise questions rather than provide answers, while Polley's film does provide some answers, such as the identity of her biological father. However, as it is documenting real people's experiences made complicated by the twists and turns of life, the spectator is left with some unanswered questions. This is made very apparent by the last-minute revelation that Geoff Bowes had lied about the nature of his relationship with Diane. The biggest enigma of them all is the question of who can we really trust?

▷ S&C

Watch two of Longinotto's films alongside *Grey Gardens* (Maysles, 1975) to gain an understanding of observational documentary.

(iA) Independent Activity

1 Read the chapter on Kim Longinotto's approach to documentary from James Quinn's (2012) book, *This Much is True: 14 Directors on Documentary Filmmaking*, and summarise her observations in under 100 words.

2 Watch the interview 'Longinotto at the Encounters Festival' to learn more about her approach to documentary. It is available online.

3 Read the section about Longinotto in Jason Wood's book *Talking Movies: Contemporary World Filmmakers in Interview* (2007).

Independent study questions

(Q) What questions remain at the end of the film?

(Q) Do we hear any particular person's point of view more clearly than others?

(Q) What purpose does Sarah Polley's presence in the film serve?

(Q) What technologies were used in this film and what were there possibilities and limitations?

(Q) How does this film compare with the work of Nick Broomfield and Kim Longinotto?

Conclusion

Documentaries are inherently about truth and none more so than *Stories We Tell*.

The film starts by lulling the spectator into a false sense of security through its apparent transparency with regards to its construction but by the end the audience are left asking what is real and who can be trusted. The film doesn't answer those questions. As *Paste* magazine (2012) put it, this is a film,

> that scrutinizes the ultimate purpose of truth and comes up with a gorgeously rendered shrug.

Sample essay extracts and feedback

> How far have developments in digital technology had an impact on your chosen documentary film?

For these examples we are looking at **extracts** from essays addressing *Stories We Tell*.

Alexandra's response extract	Feedback
Stories We Tell uses lots of different types of cameras for different purposes throughout the film. Some of the scenes are blurry and look old fashioned as they were recorded in the past and used film rather than digital. These scenes from home movies show us what the Polley family was like and show the character of Diane before she died.	*Alexandra's response is not very specific. She does not name the types of cameras and uses vague descriptions such as 'old fashioned'. What does this mean? What is it about these scenes that appears outdated? A more specific analysis would be rewarded with higher grades.*
The film tricks the audience though by using the same sort of cameras to copy the home movies and show things that didn't really happen. These reconstructions are used a lot in documentaries but Polley pretends they are real for most of the film.	*Alexandra demonstrates some knowledge of the documentary genre here but as she continues to write exclusively about the use of film cameras she is not yet addressing the question. It is advisable to directly address the question from the very beginning of your response.*
Developments in digital technology include smaller, better cameras and some of this film is shot using these. The more recent interviews have clearer images and have sound. This reflects that time has passed. It makes it easier for the audience to understand when the events have taken place.	*Alexandra is now showing some understanding of the developments in digital technology and is starting to explore the impacts these have made. Her examples remain, however, and more marks would be awarded if specific moments in the film were being examined in detail.*

Aaron's response extract	Feedback
Stories We Tell (Polley, 2012) is a fascinating documentary which blends archive footage, reconstructions and contemporary talking head interviews. The mix of old home movies and crisp, professionally shot digital interviews demonstrate just how far digital technology has changed the look and sound of cinema.	*Aaron introduces the film well and his brief introduction gives some indications of the nature of the argument he intends to put forward. Essays for this module are short so there is no time for a lengthy introduction, and certainly no summary of plot, but it is advisable to identify the film, director and year.*
Starting with the most contemporary scenes, the interviews. The sharpness of the image captured is apparent to the audience as we can see details such as the wrinkles on Michael Polley's face and how they crumple further in the emotional close-ups used when he speaks of the death of his wife. The digital camera used, the Sony CineAlta, allows this level of detail to be captured and thus reflects the impact of developments in digital technology in the storytelling.	*Aaron includes detail here and shows attention to detail. He names the camera and uses a specific moment from the film to illustrate the point he is making. He also uses key terms from the question to make it very clear that he is addressing it directly.*
One of the greatest benefits of new digital cameras for documentary filmmakers was the fact that these cameras are often lighter, smaller and therefore easier to move freely. This allows documentarians to capture events in harder to reach locations and to always carry a camera and be able to film spontaneously should something interesting arise. These benefits, however, had little impact in *Stories We Tell*. Most of the digital footage is shot in the homes of the participants in organised, planned interviews with relatively little in the way of camera movement. Even the camera movements that are used, for example the enlightening pan around Michael's home, could just as easily have been captured on an old film camera.	*Aaron's argument is balanced and he uses the 'How far' aspect of the question to his advantage. In this section he talks about the ways that developments in technology have **not** made an impact on this film.*

This section will support your work on Film movements: silent cinema in Component 2 of the A level course. Alongside the core areas, you should be prepared to tackle questions on the specialist area, Critical debate 1: The realist and the expressive. The textbook offers two case studies here, *Sunrise* (Murnau, 1927) and a collection of shorts by Buster Keaton. You only need to study one option.

For A level

You will answer one 20-mark question from a choice of two on the Component 2 paper. You should allow 30 minutes for your answer.

The specification says

The silent period saw filmmakers working to develop film narrative and film form and to communicate ever more effectively through purely visual means. Film during this period is associated with the wider cultural and artistic movement of modernism. Film history identifies two key film movements: German Expressionism and Soviet Montage.

Sunrise is made by the most celebrated of German Expressionist directors, F.W. Murnau, but in Hollywood not Berlin. Learners will be required to explore critical debates about realism and the expressive within this section.

Made in Hollywood for William Fox Studio, *Sunrise: A Song of Two Humans* was directed by celebrated German director F.W. Murnau, who had established his reputation working in the German Expressionism film movement.

Murnau is regarded as one of the most gifted and inventive film directors who has worked in silent cinema. He directed 21 films, but many have now been lost. His three significant German films are *Nosferatu* (1922), *The Last Laugh* (1924) and *Faust* (1926). *Sunrise* (1927), the first film he made in Hollywood, is considered one of the greatest silent films. He died in 1931, a week before the premiere of his documentary *Tabu: A Story of the South Seas* (1931).

Filmmakers working in the German Expressionism film movement sought to present the inner life of their characters. They achieved this through their creative use of film form. They are seen in opposition to the dominant American films that aimed to represent a real world in a conventional manner. *Sunrise* combines elements of both, and therefore offers an interesting combination of American narrative cinema and German Expressionist styling.

This section will explore the German Expressionism film movement, which emerged in Germany after World War I, and, through an examination of its film form, how *Sunrise* can be seen as part of this movement. The section will be concluded by addressing the key critical debate in film history, realist versus expressive filmmaking.

Further information

F.W. Murnau (1888–1931)

Friedrich Wilhelm Murnau, formerly
Plumpe, was born in Germany in
December 1888. As a young boy
he staged short plays for his friends
and family, and was an admirer of
Ibsen and Shakespeare. He studied
philology at the University of Berlin,
and then art history and literature in
Heidelberg. It was there that he was
spotted by theatrical impresario Max
Reinhardt who invited him to join his
actor-school. During World War I he
served as a company commander
at the eastern front and then with
the Imperial German Flying Corps
undertook a mission in Northern
France. A crash landing in Switzerland
led to his arrest and internment, where
he became involved in the prison's
theatre troupe and wrote a film script.
After the war he teamed up with actor
Conrad Veidt and established his own
studio. Their first film, *The Boy in Blue*,
was released in 1919 and like most
German Expressionist films explores
notions of duality. It was his adaptation
of Bram Stoker's *Dracula*, *Nosferatu*,
in 1922 that firmly established him
as a leading filmmaker of the period.
The international success of *The Last
Laugh* (1924) led to an invitation to
Hollywood, where he made *Sunrise*.
The arrival of sound in 1927 saw a
period of upheaval, which Murnau was
still negotiating when he died in a car
crash in 1931 just before the release
of his documentary film *Tabu: A Story
of the South Seas*.

German Expressionism films

> *Expressionism in the German cinema was more than a style; it was an
> atmosphere and an ethos.* (Buscombe & White, 2002, page 74)

The German Expressionism film movement features a number of highly
regarded German films released between 1919 and 1929. For a film movement
that flourished and declined within a decade, its impact is large in cinema
history. While it never replaced the realist aesthetic that dominates cinema,
modern cinema would not be the same without these groundbreaking films.

Both Orson Welles and Alfred Hitchcock drew on many of the visual motifs to
develop the psychology of their characters.

Although made within the burgeoning Hollywood Studio System, *Sunrise*
displays many of the hallmarks of German Expressionism: a pervading sense
of dread, off-kilter camera angles, and high- and low-key lighting. It also
employs those from another popular German film genre of the 1920s: the
Kammerspielfilm (or chamber drama). This type of film explored a crisis in a
character's life in detail; the emphasis being on slow, evocative acting and
telling details, rather than extremes. They had less international impact except
for *The Last Laugh* (Murnau, 1924), which, as does *Sunrise*, integrates both
expressionist and Kammerspielfilm aesthetics.

Narrative themes and characters

The themes of expressionist cinema were often dark, drawing on the
devastation that followed World War I.

The films were not confined to contemporary settings; they could be placed
in historic or futuristic settings, thereby 'disguising' critiques on recent history
and the contemporary social and political environment.

Recurring themes:

- narrative oppositions/doubling/duality
- the known and the unknown
- temptation
- fear of death, consequences of dying
- alter-ego, other person within us, doppelgänger
- sale of oneself for material advantage
- the creation/existence of fantastical beings living within 'normal' existence
- notion of being able to control other people
- extreme situations/excessive responses
- the emotional undercurrent of human existence
- fascination with and fear of modern urban life and technology.

Characters were often:

- obsessive
- melancholic
- mad
- overwrought.
- tortured
- anti-heroic
- paranoid

As is implied by the film's sub-title, *A Song of Two Humans*, *Sunrise* is a **dialectical**
film, with doubling and oppositions central to its narrative and character arcs.

> Dialectic: two opposing or contradictory ideas or views are juxtaposed as a
> way of examining and discussing them.

- **Narrative structure**: The film is set over one day and two nights, making significant use of day/night signalled by the iconography of the sun/moon. Key sequences such as the boat journey across the lake and the tram ride are shown as they travel to and from the city. This repetition allows for clear comparisons on how the characters' relationship changes.
- **Characters**: This duality is further developed in the three central characters, where the characters are used to stand for good/bad. We see the man, from the first sunset to the second sunrise, move from bad (affair and murder attempt) to good (in love, reunited with his wife), from the path of sin (the subjective POV shot through the marshes to his mistress), to redemption (a new dawn rises). The good/bad woman is seen by the counterpoint between the angel/temptress, wife/mistress. This is discussed further in the 'Gender representation' section on page 263.

These narrative and character dialectics are further developed in the film form:

- **Sunrise/sunset**: The film is set over two days so we see two sunrises; note how different the couple are in the first (not speaking, no eye contact, the man planning the wife's murder) and the second (the mistress on her way back the city, the couple united and kissing).
- **Day/night and sun/moon**: In the first moonlit night, the man lies with his mistress imagining life in the city, and plotting his wife's murder. In the second, he has been to the city with his wife, and they are now the couple embracing, with plans for the future.
- **Country/city and rural/urban**: Here the fascination with and fear of modern urban life and technology is explored as the two simple country folk find themselves in the vibrant city. The country is where the city dwellers rush to for their summer vacation in the film's opening sequence. The version of the country depicted in the narrative present is one of darkness and betrayal. The rural idyll is shown in the maid's memory of when the couple were happy. This image is further referenced in the painted backdrop at the photography studio and in the fantasy dissolve from the cityscape when they fall in love again.
- **Blonde wife/dark-haired mistress**: The hair colouring signifies innocence and sultriness. The wife is costumed in matte whites, and the mistress in shining blacks.

Institutional context

The German film industry

World War I decimated the film industry across Europe, except in Germany. In 1911, there were 11 film companies in Germany, by 1918 there were 131. The German government, seeing the propaganda potential of cinema, encouraged film activity that supported its ideology.

In January 1917 the German government, led by General Ludendorff (Commander in Chief, 1916–1918), formed BUfA (*Bild und Filmamt*), with the intention of bringing together all Germany's film activity. The film industry benefitted from state funding of studios, equipment and distribution at a time of great financial hardship.

In 1919, the German government BUfA was renamed UfA (*Universum Film Aktiengesellschafat* [German Film Studios]), and sought to further unify the film industry, gradually taking over many small companies. The Treasury plus

 Independent Activity

Watch the two tram rides in the film and make notes on of the mise-en-scène, particularly the body codes of the man and the wife.

 Further information

Key moments in US/European cinema (1895–1927)

1895: December, in Paris the Lumière Brothers held the first public exhibition of 'moving pictures'.

1900s: Significant filmmaking activity in the USA, UK, Germany, France and Denmark. As the films were silent there was no language barrier.

1914–1918: In 1914 25% of films shown in the UK were British, by 1926 only 5%. Germany established a national filmmaking centre, and produced centrally endorsed films. The USA became the dominant filmmaking community, a situation that remains a hundred years later.

1915: William Fox founded Fox Films and opened his studio in Hollywood. Post-World War I Europe relies heavily on imported films.

1920s: German government endorsed films continued, while independent production companies made films critical of the government. US cinema continued to grow, increasingly relying on film stars, and 'star' directors.

Mid-1920s: German Expressionism has become a significant film movement attracting considerable attention from audiences and filmmakers in Europe and the USA. Soviet filmmakers working in isolation develop their political and ideological cinema, utilising montage editing and typage (casting non-professional actors in lead roles).

1926: Experimentation of films with synchronised sound. Leading this sound revolution is Warner Brothers. *The Black Pirate*, starring Douglas Fairbanks, is the first feature film shot in two-colour Technicolor. Fox Studios hire Murnau to make a 'masterpiece'.

1927: Warner Brothers release *The Jazz Singer*, the first feature film with synchronised sound, music and dialogue. *Sunrise* opened in the USA in November, with synchonised music and sound.

S&C

Make notes for a film review of one of the silent films you have studied. Use the following list as a starting point, commenting fully on the different areas, always ask yourself, 'How well does the film work?':

- Plot
- Themes
- Script
- Direction
- Cinematography
- Editing
- Sound
- Setting, costumes & make-up
- Performance

Comment on the following values for the film:

A Entertainment value

B Learning value

C Artistic value

How well did the film work overall for you?

industrial and private capital provided a third of its funding. The role of UfA was to make profitable full-length commercial and art house films. It soon embarked on international co-productions, which gave it considerable power in the worldwide film market.

A few independent film studios survived, including Decla-Bioscop, which made what is considered to be the first German Expressionist film, *The Cabinet of Dr Caligari* (Wiene, 1920), which hides its anti-government message within a crime melodrama. The studio did not have the funding to match UfA's big-budget costume dramas, so went the other way and made its world representational through its expressionist mise-en-scène. Soon other filmmakers borrowed its aesthetic, including many of UfA's most successful films.

The Cabinet of Dr Caligari (Wiene, 1920)

A year later, in 1921, UfA took over Decla-Bioscop, acquiring the Berlin-Babelsberg studios (they soon became the best-equipped studios in Europe). That year 246 films were made in Germany, more than any other European country.

For the German film industry, 1924–1929 were relatively stable years, as the German currency was under control (after a great depression), wages for skilled workers had roughly doubled, as had its industrial production. In 1929, industrial film exports were 34% higher than in 1913.

The Wall Street Crash of 1929 brought about a world economic crisis. The withdrawal of American loans to Germany led to massive unemployment and poverty, which contributed to the rapid rise of fascism.

Transition from silent to sound

Sunrise was made and released on the cusp between silent and sound films.

William Fox wanted a prestige film, and looked to Germany and Murnau to make him a 'masterpiece'. Fox had been impressed by *The Last Laugh* (Murnau, 1924), which had been an international critical and commercial success.

Murnau arrived in Hollywood in July 1926. The following month Warner Brothers released *Don Juan* (Crosland), a romantic adventure starring John

Barrymore. This was the first full-length film to be released with synchronised music and sound effects. In October 1926, Al Jolson had starred in a short film, *A Plantation Act* (Roscoe), in which he could be heard singing three of his theatrical hits. Buoyed by this success, Warner Brothers conceived a full-length film integrating songs, music and sound effects – *The Jazz Singer*.

A year later, in October 1927, *The Jazz Singer* (Fleischer & Furie), again starring Al Jolson, opened. Despite its uneasy blend of silent film (outdoor locations, fluid camera movement and inter-titles) and sound sequences (static studio shots), when Jolson ad-libbed the immortal line, 'You aint heard nothing yet', he changed movie history, as for the first time audiences heard synchronised speech, song, music and sound effects in a full-length film.

The film became a major hit, even though many cinemas had to screen it as a silent film, as they did not have the sound equipment. It grossed $3.9 million at the US box office, and became one for the top three high-grossing films of the year.

Sunrise opened in the wake of *The Jazz Singer* phenomenon, in November 1927. It had synchronised music and sound effects, but most cinemas were still running films as silent, with live music. Reviews were generally favourable, but it failed at the box office and, given its high production costs, Fox lost money. It is now widely considered one of the greatest silent film achievements.

In 1929 it won the first Academy Awards for Best Cinematography and Actress, and with *The Jazz Singer* ineligible (the Academy thought its inclusion would be unfair for the silent films), it was named Best Unique and Artistic Picture, beating competition from *Chang: A Drama of the Wilderness* (Cooper & Schoedsack, 1927) and *The Crowd* (Vidor, 1927).

Soon audiences were demanding more 'talkies' and, although silent filmmaking continued for a few more years, the popularity of silent films declined. Many were hastily re-cut and released as B movies, or new dialogue scenes/music/sound effects were crudely added.

Social, cultural and political context

Cultural context: expressionist artistic movement

Expressionism as an artistic movement extended across all the arts: music, painting, sculpture, theatre, dance, literature and film. It emerged in Germany in the early 1900s, attracting a number of creative and innovative composers (Arnold Schoenberg, Alban Berg, Anton Webern) and artists (Wassily Kandinsky, Paul Klee, Edvard Munch).

They were concerned with a visual representation of the inner soul and psychology. Using colour and shapes, artists created bizarre and outlandish images that were intended to be shocking. Expressionist music rejected the 'traditional forms of beauty' and was discordant, with extremes of volume and texture.

Given the primitive nature of film at this time, the creative output for 'live action' expressionism came from the theatrical world, most notably Max Reinhardt. Many of the film directors who are associated with expressionism obtained their grounding in the theatre (Fritz Lang) or art (F.W. Murnau).

A precursor to the German Expressionist film movement is *The Student from Prague* (Wegener, 1913); its story of a man selling his soul to the devil is one that expressionist film directors would return to, including Murnau's last German film, *Faust* (1926).

 S&C

Watch episode 1 of the documentary *Cinema Europe: The Other Hollywood, Where it All Began* (Brownlow, 1995) on YouTube. This will give you insights into the wider context of silent filmmaking across Europe.

'The Scream', Edvard Munch, 1893

Independent Activity

Watch *The Cabinet of Dr Caligari* and make notes on its film form, i.e. cinematography, mise-en-scène, editing and performance. Then watch *Sunrise* and make notes on its film form. How do they compare?

 Further information

Inter-titles

There are far fewer inter-titles in *Sunrise* that in other American films of the period. German Expressionist filmmakers were keen to rely on the visuals, rather than words, and in *The Last Laugh* (1924), Murnau had no inter-titles.

With *Sunrise*, he experimented with special effects on a significant title card 'Couldn't she get drowned?', with the text sliding down the screen and disappearing.

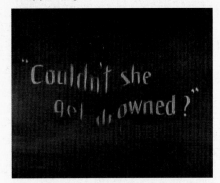

 S&C

Watch any two silent films. Write a 500-word essay on how the filmmaker has used **either** continuity/discontinuity editing **or** lighting to develop themes.

 Independent Activity

Read Pamela Hutchinson and Alex Barrett's '10 Great German Expressionist Films' (2017) on the BFI website. Annotate the ten images, noting what you can learn about the films and characters from the lighting **and** mise-en-scène.

The first film that drew together the political, philosophical and visual elements of expressionism was *The Cabinet of Dr Caligari* (Wiene, 1920). With its two central characters, Dr Caligari and Cesare, representing the government and the 'common man', the film drew clear parallels between irrational authority (authority intent on compliance through fear and pressure) and blind obedience. It was well received critically, and soon other filmmakers were integrating its aesthetic and approach to storytelling.

Social and political context: World War I and its aftermath

World War I ended in November 1918: a war that left 8.5 million dead and 21 million wounded. It had devastated Europe; leaving nations determined that this could 'never happen again'. The German people had to come to terms with emotions of guilt, despair and revolution, while living in extreme poverty. It is estimated that 700,000 Germans died of starvation between November 1918 and June 1919.

The films that emerged at this time drew on Germany's recent past, its present situation, and have been read as a warning of what was to come.

There are no explicit war films, with the German Expressionist filmmakers using subtler ways to confront the devastating experience of World War I and its aftermath. Exploring issues such as mass murders (*The Cabinet of Dr Caligari*, Wiene, 1920), sacrifice (*Nosferatu*, Murnau, 1922) and modernity (*Metropolis*, Lang, 1927).

Film form in German Expressionism

The world presented in these films is one of darkness, disillusionment, paranoia and betrayal. They used film form to show visually the state of mind of the characters who were unable to express their thoughts into words – except in the **inter-titles**.

The turmoil of the characters can be seen in the lighting design, off-kilter camera angles, exaggerated performances, slanted sets and forced perspectives that combine to give the films a distorted view of the work that corresponded with the emotional complexities of the characters.

Cinematography

Murnau's command of lighting and composition, together with fluid camera style and editing, is evident in *Sunrise*, turning it from mere melodrama to cinematic poetry. Murnau worked with the cinematographers, Charles Rosher and Karl Struss, to achieve the film's startling visual style. Rosher and Struss were rewarded with the Best Cinematography award at the first Academy Awards held in 1929.

German Expressionist filmmakers were concerned with making visual the characters' emotions and used the subjective point of view to good effect. An example of this can be seen when the man is walking to see his mistress in the marshes, approximately ten minutes into the film. This use of subjective camera is made even more striking by the way the camera moves. In Germany, Murnau had developed innovative overhead camera tracking movements, which created fluid and sophisticated moves through space, which he used in *Sunrise* to great effect in the moonlit marsh, funfair and city traffic sequences. This technique creates an unusual illusion of depth and vastness, and an apparent weightlessness. This was possible as Rosher and Struss were using an electric camera rather than hand-cranking.

The way the camera frames the shot, how far we are from the action and how the camera moves all contribute to the emotion of the scene. Key uses are:

- Extreme/oblique camera angles, to create and add an off-kilter view of the world.
- Titled angles to disorientate.
- Camera angles to distort the size of the character.
- High camera angles to create the feeling of being looked down on.
- Shifts of viewpoint.
- Violent camera movement.

A striking use of camera and shot types in *Sunrise* can be seen on the couple's first boat journey to the city when the man tries to murder his wife. High-angle shots looking down on the wife make her seem smaller and more vulnerable as her husband towers over her. The use of subjective close-ups of the husband, from the wife's POV, are an exaggeration – too close for a real POV shot – and make visual the emotions of the character, in this case – fear.

The dramatic use of lighting is an important part of the expressionist film aesthetic. Key lighting uses are:

- High contrasting blocks of light and shade (chiaroscuro).
- Low-key lighting to produce dark or semi-darkness. What is hiding in the shadow?
- Harsh lighting to produce unusual shadow effects. Making faces distorted or partly hidden in shadow.
- Back lighting to create long shadows in the foreground.
- On-screen practical light sources to draw attention to a particular character or object.

 S&C

Watch the sequence of the man walking to meet his mistress (approximately ten minutes into the film), and write a shot list comprising types of shot, camera movement and angles.

iA **Independent Activity**

Watch this walking sequence and the following montage scene, and make a note of the transitions between shots and the pace of editing in the two. How is the editing used to portray their emotions?

Expressionist filmmakers also employed a number of special effects to develop the mood and aesthetic. These effects were created in-camera and on set, many of which can also be seen in the films of Georges Méliès and Buster Keaton. Today, many of these would be achieved by CGI and/or digital editing.

- **Split-screen masking/superimposing/double exposure:** achieved by partially masking the frame and rewinding the film and shooting the unexposed part again.
- **Matte painting:** a hand-painted (usually) photorealistic image, combined with live-action footage.
- **Forced perspective:** to create an impression of depth, a combination of **matte paintings, models and miniatures** and smaller people are placed in the background, in contrast to those of normal scale in the foreground.
- **Slanted sets and props:** slanting ceilings, walls and floors means that through the camera they appear to be larger and deeper.
- **Rear projection:** as the foreground action is being shot, a previously photographed background scene is projected onto a large translucent screen from behind, or front projection.

A good example of a combination of in-camera, on-set and editing special effects is the scene following the couple's metaphorical wedding, approximately 43 minutes into the film. The vast cityscape was created using forced perspective, matte painting and models. So bound up in their new-found love, they step out into traffic as if in their own world, oblivious to the traffic (superimposed in the foreground, rear projection in the background). As they walk, the background magically changes to a country setting (a dissolve to a rear-projected image) a visual manifestation of their perfect happiness, reminiscent of the maid's memory from earlier. They are brought out of this fantasy world by the honking of horns and are now back in the city traffic.

Mise-en-scène

Fritz Lang, director of *Metropolis* (1927) and *Spione* (1928), was, like Murnau, a director renowned for his German Expressionist aesthetic.

> *An audience learns more about a character from detail and décor, in the way the light fills in a room, than from pages of dialogue.*
> (Lang cited in Frayling, 2006, page 60)

As both directors developed their style in a period where there were no 'pages of dialogue', they developed a sophisticated use of mise-en-scène to bring to the fore the emotions of the characters.

The setting is used as an emotional landscape linked to the feelings of the characters. Therefore, filmmakers used setting/props to develop these through:

- abstract sets with heavily stylised décor
- angular/jagged sets to create a sense of unease and tension
- distorted shapes created by objects, shadow or mass to signify a nightmarish world or an anxiety
- unnaturally distorted images
- extremes of composition (cluttered/bare)
- characters merging with their setting or functioning as an extension of the set
- distinctive/exaggerated hair and make-up
- frequent use of mirrors, glass and reflective surfaces.

Murnau had an entire village set built by the side of Lake Arrowhead in the San Bernardino Mountains for the country sequences and huge highly stylised sets constructed on the Fox lot for the city and fairground sequences. The city street set alone is thought to have cost $200,000 (equal to almost $3 million today) to build. For the tram ride almost a mile of track was laid by the lake with further track on the studio city set.

Even if drawing on realist traditions in their design, as with the houses in the village, the expressionist techniques of manipulating scale, using over-/under-sized props and tilting the sets or furniture are used to create an uneasy, distorted feel.

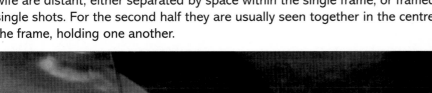

The city sets recede slightly in the distance, producing deep focus shots. This, combined with manipulation of perspective (forced perspective), creates an overwhelming vastness to the cityscapes. As a result the couple seem small, vulnerable and out of place. Technology and the city are presented as threatening and amoral.

The film's dialectical narrative structure can be seen in the composition, where the repeating of key events shows how their relationships have shifted.

In the first half of the film, body proximity and lack of contact between man and wife are distant, either separated by space within the single frame, or framed in single shots. For the second half they are usually seen together in the centre of the frame, holding one another.

S&C

Watch at least two other German Expressionist films (not studied in class). Make notes on what elements of film form they share with *Sunrise*.

iA Independent Activity

Construct a shot-by-shot analysis of one scene. Discuss in detail how the shots contribute to the continuity, pace and mood of the overall form of the film.

Editing

Although German Expressionist films are, in the main, presented in a linear form, filmmakers often employ more experimental editing techniques designed to obscure rather than express continuity.

Sunrise opens with a dissolve through the credits to a real train, and then to a model train. This is followed by a montage sequence of images of the bustling city in the summer time, and trains bringing the city folk to the peace of the coast and country. This frenetic opening sequence represents the city, and is followed by much more graceful shots of the city folk arriving at the lake. This opening highlights the different spaces through the camera movements, angles and editing. It also indicates to the audience that this is not going to be a classical Hollywood movie.

Using discontinuity of narrative to disrupt or confuse the narrative flow, such as quick cut-ins, flashbacks, flash-forwards, dreams and fantasies, offers insight into the characters' emotional and psychological states, or their histories. In *Sunrise,* discontinuity of narrative can be seen in fantasies (the man drowning his wife), cut-ins (shot of the bulrushes to show how they are playing on his mind) and flashbacks (the man selling a cow).

Although an in-camera technique at this time, double-exposure superimposing shots over one another also serves as an indirect form of narration.

iA **Independent Activity**

Watch the scene of the man the morning after he has been planning his wife's murder (approximately 20 minutes into the film). What techniques have been used to disrupt the narrative? What further meanings are being conveyed by these techniques?

Sound

Sunrise was released in 1927 with a synchronised music and sound effect track. For Murnau this was a new feature, and he uses it to great effect in key moments such as the lyrical rural idyll music juxtaposed with that of the bustling jazz of the city when the man and his mistress imagine life there.

In one of the film's most expressionistic sequences, sound in conjunction with cinematography and mise-en-scène plays a part in generating the chaotic atmosphere. When the couple first arrive at Luna Park, night has fallen and the park is illuminated by electric lights, very different from the candles and lanterns of their village. Crowds gather and stream into a tunnel, with shadows silhouetted on the wall and floor. The camera moves into the park, where miniature planes circle, huge roller-coasters thunder past, and there are water fountains and elephants.

The images are not edited as montage but as controlled extended shots, which, combined with the manipulation of scale, fuels an overwhelming sense of hedonism and confusion. This is further emphasised through the montage of diegetic and non-diegetic music and sounds; the tempo and volume increases with urgency and is interspersed with the crashing discordant bells, rings, people shouting and loud laughter.

A powerful use of a single sound can be heard when the man, fearing his wife has drowned, calls out across the lake. The score fades, and all we can hear is the plaintive sound of a French horn standing in for his calls into the darkness. A horn with an upwards inflection is used when the maid calls out that his wife has been found.

 Independent Activity

Many silent films today are released or exhibited with new scores or live accompaniment, so be careful to check whether the version you are watching has the original or new soundtrack. If you have access to the Eureka reissue of *Sunrise*, once you have watched the film with the original score composed by Hugo Riesenfeld and Ernö Rapée, watch the film again with the alternate Timothy Brock score. How does the music affect the character and narrative?

 S&C

Watch PBS's 'Crash Course Film History #7 German Expressionism' on YouTube.

Hollywood film noirs were heavily influenced by German Expressionism cinema. Watch a film noir such as *The Lady from Shanghai* (Welles, 1947) and list the similarities between the two film movements.

The Lady from Shanghai (Welles, 1947)

Sunrise: A Song of Two Humans (Murnau, 1927)

⊕ Further information

The first Academy Awards, now better known as the Oscars, were held at the Hollywood Roosevelt Hotel in Los Angeles, May 1929. They are presented by the Academy of Motion Pictures Arts and Sciences (AMPAS), which was established in 1927 by Louis B. Mayer head of Metro-Goldwyn-Mayer (MGM) as an organisation that would mediate labour disputes without going through the unions, and to improve the industry's image.

The Awards given in 1929 were for films released in 1927 and 1928. In this first year there were 12 categories including some which are no longer featured such as the Best Engineering Effects and Best Title Writer. Some of the awards were awarded for a specific film, such as the Cinematography category which Rosher and Struss won for *Sunrise*. The Best Actor and Actress awards were given for a body of work, so Janet Gaynor's win for *Sunrise* also reflected her work on *Seventh Heaven* and *Street Angel*. The Best Actor award went to Emil Jannings who had been the star of Murnau's last three films in Germany: *The Last Laugh* (1924), *Tartuffe* (1925) and *Faust* (1926), and had now made a name for himself in the US.

In this first year there were effectively two Best Picture awards: Outstanding Picture was won by the World War I epic *Wings* (Wellman, 1927) and Best Unique and Artistic Picture was awarded to *Sunrise*. This latter category was not included in any subsequent years.

Performance

In the three lead roles, Murnau cast well-known American film stars.

Janet Gaynor (wife) had her screen debut as an extra in a 1924 comedy short; three years later, she was one of Hollywood's leading ladies. She had built her reputation playing warm-hearted, fresh-faced young women. She was awarded the first Best Actress Academy Award for her roles in *Sunrise*, *Seventh Angel* (Borzage, 1927) and *Street Angel* (Borzage, 1928).

George O'Brien (man) came to Hollywood in the early 1920s, initially finding work as a cameraman before moving into acting. His star turn in John Ford's hit western *The Iron Horse* (1924) established him as a popular leading man.

Margaret Livingston's (woman from the city) screen debut was in 1916 and she made over 50 films in the silent era.

As emotions could not be portrayed through a vocal performance, attention had to be paid to all the non-verbal communication elements (as discussed in the 'Body codes' section in 'Film form performance'). Their body contact, proximity, orientation, movements, gestures, facial expressions, body posture, eye movements and general appearance all contribute to the development of character and story, the establishment of mood and to conveying emotions.

In the first half of the film, O'Brien is frequently shot from behind to emphasise his bulk, or with downcast eyes as though unable to face the world. He looms out of the darkness, or stays hidden in the shadows. His lumbering hunched-over, heavy-footed gait in the first half was created by wearing weighted shoes. In the second half, when he is happy, there are more brightly lit eye-line shots from the front, where we can see his eyes and smiling face. Only for him to return to his earlier monstrous images when his mistress comes to him after the storm (see page 264).

Gaynor's performance demonstrates how much can be done with so little. Her transformation from sorrowful downcast wife, to one filled with joy is shown through small facial expressions, gestures and body posture. The camera frequently holds her in shot for some time, allowing us to take in her nuanced performance. Her entry back into the kitchen (above left) after her husband has left to meet his lover allows us to see through body posture and facial expression that this has become a regular occurrence.

In contrast, Livingston's body gestures are larger. She strides confidentially through the village; she wiggles exotically for her lover. Her costume and styling – a slinky black satin dress and dark, bobbed hair – offer a darker sexuality and eroticism.

Aesthetics

Lotte Eisner, who wrote the first critical assessment of Murnau's work, said in *The Haunted Screen* (1969):

> In Friedrich Wilhelm Murnau, the greatest film-director the Germans have ever known, cinematic composition was never a mere attempt at decorative stylisation. He created the most overwhelming and poignant images in the whole German cinema. (page 97)

Sunrise combines elements of *Kammerspielfilm*'s realism, but exaggerates these by employing expressionistic elements to bring to the surface the emotions of the characters. With Fox's unlimited budget and vast resources available to Murnau in Hollywood, he was able to develop his strong aesthetic on a larger canvas. With *Sunrise*, he did indeed create the 'masterpiece' William Fox had sought.

Representation

The film was made in 1926/1927 but the unnamed setting and characters, allow them to stand for anywhere and anyone. The city represents the present (jazz bands, luxury fashion, electric lights and motor cars) and future (spectacular modernistic sets); the country, the past (horse-drawn carts, candles/lanterns and lack of decoration).

Within these spaces, we can explore issues of representations of gender and age and a lack of representation of any ethnicity other than white.

Age

The ages of the three central characters are not given, but the fragility and passiveness of the wife indicates that she is younger than her husband. The predatory woman from the city exudes confidence, but there is an element of 'desperation' in her pursuit of this married man, indicating that she may be a few years older than he is. The actors were 20 (Gaynor), 31 (Livingston) and 27 (O'Brien).

Gender

Critics of Murnau's films tend to praise their aesthetic, and offer criticism on their gender representation.

In the *New York Herald Tribune*'s obituary of Murnau, the columnist Richard Watts Jr commented that,

> there was that weakness of the director in handling women. In Sunrise Gaynor was unnecessarily handicapped by a clumsy headdress … [and] that character of the villainess was overstressed in the early Theda Bara manner. (Watts, 1931)

The central characters in *Sunrise* are so simple that they take on archetypal qualities. They are unnamed, referred to as only the man, the wife and the woman from the city.

Two are defined by their gender (man and woman from the city), but the third by her role (wife).

S&C

'Expressionism in the German cinema was more than a style; it was an atmosphere and an ethos.'

With this quote from 'Murnau's *Midnight* and *Sunrise*' (Wood, 1976, page 9) in mind, compare and contrast Murnau's approach to that of another German Expressionist filmmaker.

 What added interest can be found in your chosen film by placing it within the context of other work by the director or film movement or other examples of its genre? Make a list of ten examples.

Theda Bara

 Further information

Theda Bara was a silent screen star known as the Vamp, her overt 'foreign' sexuality and exoticism was seen in contrast to the wholesome American stars such as Mary Pickford and Lilian Gish.

Representation of gender and sexuality in *Nosferatu*

Murnau's first success was *Nosferatu* (1922), the first film version of Bram Stoker's 1897 novel *Dracula*. The plot concerns Nosferatu's lust for the blood of Harker and his concurrent undying love for Harker's wife Mina. Unlike *Sunrise*, where the archetype of good wife/wicked mistress are shown in two characters, here they can be seen as two sides of one woman. Mina is both the innocent wife and temptress, at the end of the film she seduces Nosferatu, tricking him into stepping into the sunlight. Her character, although crucial to the film's plot, does not have a great deal of screen time. The film concentrates mainly on the male/male relationship between Nosferatu and Harker. It has been argued that Murnau's own homosexuality has some bearing on the dominance of male/male relationships, conflicting depictions of masculinity and the downfall of a man by a woman in his films.

the love triangles in the film also lend themselves to an interpretation that brings out a more layered structure of sexual attraction and ambivalence. For instance, underlying the secret heterosexual bond between Nosferatu and Mina is the Renfield [Nosferatu's servant] – Harker – Nosferatu relation. The initial situation suggests that the film superimposes two plot lines, one heterosexual, the other developed around the homosexual relationship ... (Elsaesser, 2012)

Nosferatu (Murnau, 1922)

The dialectical of the narrative is reinforced by the two female roles whose function is both archetypes (good wife/wicked mistress) and also personification of locations. The wife belongs to the day, the past and the country. The woman in contrast reflects the night, the present/future and the city.

The wife is shot in soft, bright but diffused light, which bounces off her blonde hair, giving her a halo effect. She radiates innocence, which is emphasised in her matte, light-coloured, cotton clothing and bonnet. Her glowing brightness is a signifier of purity. In the first third, she is shown in the domestic setting, cooking and caring for her baby and husband. We see her tenderly covering the husband with a blanket even though he has been out all night with his mistress. Her role is simply one of loving 'wife', regardless of her husband's treatment towards her.

In contrast, the woman from the city exudes sexuality. She can be seen as an example of the new woman, a frequent archetype in the German culture of the period. In 1919 women had been given right to equality of education, civil service appointments and professional pay.

This new freedom and employment opportunities among single women were seen as a threat to the traditional mother/wife role. The new woman was seen as a sign of modernity and sexual liberation, and became an enduring image throughout the period, especially the mid- to late 1920s.

By having the wife triumph over the woman from the city, suggests that being a mother and wife was the desired role for women at this time.

Considering Murnau's own homosexuality, it is interesting to note how he explores sexuality and what it means to be a man in his films. In many of his films, men are not portrayed as stereotypically virile, masculine types, but instead as emotionally confused.

Whereas the duality of good/bad woman is shown through the wife/woman from the city, the male equivalent is seen in the man, who is alternately monstrous and 'normal', depending on which of the two women he is being influenced by.

Ethnicity

For contemporary audiences watching silent films, the absence of non-white actors is striking. In most Hollywood films of the period, ethnic minorities were usually depicted as racist stereotypes such as the noble savage stereotype of Native Americans, savage Arabs, Mexican bandits, Asian-American waiters and black servants or simple buffoons. This was compounded by the frequent casting of white actors in these roles, whose make-up (known as blackface/yellowface) and costuming would allude to the characteristics of the ethnic group being depicted.

Sunrise's setting is expressionistic; although, offering the illusion of reality, its styling marks it as different. All the actors are Caucasian, including those that may have traditionally have been ethnically cast such as waiters or jazz musicians.

Critical debates: realism versus expressionism

The specification says

In the 1940s, the French film critic André Bazin set in motion a major debate when he argued that both German Expressionist and Soviet Montage filmmaking went against what he saw as the 'realist' calling of cinema. This opposition between the realist and the expressive has informed thinking about film from the beginnings of cinema when the documentary realism of the Lumière Brothers was set in opposition to the fantasy films of Méliès.

The first moving films were screened in Paris 1895, when the Lumière Brothers projected their 'actualities', short one- or two-minute films depicting the real events. Soon, slightly longer (two to three minutes) narrative films emerged, including those of stage magician turned filmmaker, Georges Méliès, who employed both physical magic and early in-camera special effects to create his fantastical worlds.

Within a decade, films became longer and the craft of film language and film form developed, allowing for more complex narratives and characters. A key figure in the transition from 'primitive' early cinema to the classical period was the American director D.W. Griffith. He joined Biograph films in 1908 and over the next five years made over 450 one- and two-reel films (a reel was approximately 10–12 minutes). With these he experimented with film form, exploring how cinematography, mise-en-scène, performance and editing could be used tell a story. In their documentary on Griffith called 'D.W. Griffith: Father of Film' (1993), renowned film historian-archivists, Kevin Brownlow and David Gill, call him 'the father of film'.

His films laid the template for what has become known as 'classical Hollywood cinema', the termed was coined by Bordwell and Thompson in *Film Art* (1997), and is used to define films that follow 'a chain of events in a cause–effect relationship occurring in time and space'. The term is also used when talking about narrative films made elsewhere. These films sought a sense of **verisimilitude** through their narrative, characters and film form.

Alongside 'classical narrative cinema' emerged film movements, such as German Expressionism and Soviet Montage that utilised film form in striking ways which were anti-realist. These films defied the classical 'cause–effect' relationship through their use of montage editing and narrative discontinuity, as can be seen in *Sunrise*.

While *Sunrise* employs many techniques that support its inclusion as an example of German Expressionism through its desire to bring to the fore characters' emotions, it also employs a realist aesthetic. Its use of both special effects, montage, editing and disrupted narrative mark it as expressionist, whereas its long takes allow for greater appreciation of nuanced performance,

 S&C

Compile an annotated bibliography

Research one of the films you are studying from a variety of sources: web, books, magazines, DVD extras, podcasts.

Compile an annotated bibliography of between 6–10 of the most significant items. Each item should be appropriately referenced and be accompanied by a brief note (about four lines) explaining how each particular item is relevant/useful to your study. The bibliography should conclude with a short paragraph that identifies items which were not selected for inclusion in the bibliography and offering reasons why.

Verisimilitude: about giving the appearance of reality or truth. This does not mean that the world is presented as real, just believable within the context of the world in which the film is set. For example, we know that in the real world people do not break into song when they fall in love, but in a musical, we accept this convention, but if this happened in a gritty thriller, it would be out of place.

a style more closely aligned with the realism of the *Kammerspielfilm* and classical Hollywood cinema.

Through his seamless blend of expressionism and realism, Murnau created a film that is an enduring legacy to the silent film which by 1927 had developed into a sophisticated mode of storytelling.

Film director Peter Bogdanovich (2011) wrote that if he was:

> *teaching a master class in filmmaking, among the first things I'd assign would be a look at the pictures released in 1927/28 ... [these films] marks the end of the only dramatic art form ever presented to the masses without spoken words, a kind of universal language (needing translation only on the easily altered title-cards). For just 33 precious years, from December 1895 in Paris, to December 1928 in the entire world, publicly exhibited movies in pantomime had enthralled the planet, had the largest audience in the history of the earth, either before or after.*

Conclusion

> *I accepted the offer from Hollywood because I think one can always learn and because America gives me new opportunities to develop my artistic aims. My film* Sunrise *shows what I mean.*
> (F.W. Murnau in 1928, cited in Eisner, 1969, page 167)

Although not a financial success for Fox on its release, its success at the first Academy Awards indicates that the American filmmaking community recognised its innovative cinematography and film form.

It is now considered one of the greatest films of all time.

Once a decade the British Film Institute's *Sight & Sound* magazine asks critics to select their greatest films of all time. For their most recent poll (Christie, 2012), they received 846 top-ten lists from correspondents in 73 countries, citing 2,045 different films. *Sunrise: A Song of Two Humans* was placed 5th on the list of 'Top 50 Greatest Films of All Time'.

We will leave the final word to *The New York American*'s prescient film critic, quoted in Eisner's *The Haunted Screen* (1969), who when reviewing the film in 1927 said:

> *For years after most cinema successes of today are forgotten,* Sunrise *will be re-issued wherever movies are shown.*

Independent study questions

 How is film form used to support the dialectical oppositional of the wife and the woman from the city?

 In what ways does *Sunrise* reflect the German Expressionist aesthetic, and in what ways does it differ?

 How are special effects and editing used to disrupt the narrative, and what meanings are created by their use?

Sample essay extract and feedback

Discuss how far your chosen film or films reflect aesthetic qualities associated with a particular film movement.

For this example, we are looking at an **extract** from an essay addressing *Sunrise*.

Tegan's response extract	Feedback
Sunrise was filmed in America, and mixes German Expressionism and more traditional Hollywood storytelling.	*Tegan mentions the two different film styles, a brief summary of the similarities/differences would have led to a higher grade.*
Hollywood films were set in the real world, whereas all German Expressionism films were set in fantastical worlds.	*Tegan has confused 'real world' with realism, and made a generalisation that all expressionist films are set in fantastical worlds. Discussing* Sunrise's *setting further would have revealed this assumption false.*
Expressionist films tended to focus on plots and characters at extremes of emotion, and they use sets, performance, camera angles and lighting to tell us what the characters are thinking or feeling.	*Tegan writes about the expressionist aesthetic as a way of expressing characters' emotions. This would have benefitted from more detail, using examples of other films as well as* Sunrise *as the question is asking about* Sunrise's *relationship with other expressionist films.*
A good example of this is when the man is deciding whether to murder his wife, and we see the woman from the city whispering in his ear. This is visual way of showing us that he can't get her out of his mind.	*This is an appropriate example, but would have been stronger if Tegan had mention that the woman was superimposed.*
Expressionist filmmakers were filming in black and white, which allows for extreme use of lighting to give further meaning than just lighting the scene. In the country scenes in *Sunrise*, there are lots of candles and lanterns, making it seem like it is in the past. In the city there are electric lights, which make it seem like the modern age.	*Highlighting extremes of lighting shows an understanding of importance, but the use of technical terms such as chiaroscuro, key, back, side-lighting, etc. would have made this a stronger answer. Extra marks would have been awarded if Tegan had discussed what the use of the lighting conveyed.*
Sunrise is edited in a straightforward way, but uses flashbacks and fantasies as well. There are two montage scenes, which was unusual at this time. The first shows the people from the city going to the country. The second of a traffic jam caused by the man and wife kissing. The sudden use of montage after a normal edited sequence shows how they are shocked by finding themselves in the middle of a traffic jam.	*This section would have awarded more marks had Tegan used terminology and provided examples of flashbacks and fantasies*
This traffic jam scene is also a good use of sound. Although the film is silent, there was a score written for it, which included some sound effects in key scenes. The use of expressionistic sounds here and when they go to the fun fair adds to their confusion of being away from the country, and in the big city.	*Tegan incorporates basic analysis here, but the response would have been stronger if she had discussed sound alongside the visuals of the scene and used more terminology.*

This section will support your work on Film movements: silent cinema in Component 2 of the A level course. Alongside the core areas, you should be prepared to tackle questions on the specialist area, Critical debate 1: The realist and the expressive. The textbook offers two case studies here, *Sunrise* (Murnau, 1927) and a collection of shorts by Buster Keaton. You only need to study one option.

For A level

In the Component 2, Section D examination there are 20 marks at stake and the expected writing time for an answer is 30 minutes.

The specification says

The silent period saw filmmakers working to develop film narrative and film form and to communicate ever more effectively through purely visual means. Film during this period is associated with the wider cultural and artistic movement of modernism.

A very different contribution to modernism is represented by the work of Buster Keaton, the most surreal of the great innovative American silent comedians of the period. His work adapts vaudeville to confront the problem of living as the incongruous 'little man' in an age of accelerated change.

Learners will be required to explore critical debates about realism and the expressive within this section.

9   Buster Keaton

Buster Keaton was a true auteur of silent film comedy. Between 1920 and 1922, Keaton directed, co-wrote, edited and starred in 19 short comedy films, known as '**two-reelers**'. These films were beautifully crafted, funny and inventive. Their popularity helped cement Keaton's star persona and as a result Keaton rose to international stardom. This chapter explores four of the Buster Keaton short comedy films selected for the A level examination:

- *One Week* (Keaton & Cline, 1920): Buster Keaton attempts to build himself and his wife a flat-pack house. This film was the first two-reeler released by Buster Keaton Productions on 1 September 1920. It was an instant success and featured some dazzling special effects, including a spinning house built on a turntable.

- *The Scarecrow* (Keaton & Cline, 1920): a fast-paced comedy comprised of a number of chase sequences. The film is most famous for its ingenious set design, as objects in Keaton's house take on surreal and duel functions.

- *The 'High Sign'* (Keaton & Cline, 1921): Keaton is hired by a gang to kill a wealthy businessman while also being hired by the businessman as a bodyguard. *The 'High Sign'* was filmed in 1920 and was Keaton's first solo **two-reeler**. However, Keaton wanted the film shelved as he was unhappy with it, resulting in a delayed release in 1921.

- *Cops* (Keaton & Cline, 1922): Keaton unwittingly throws a bomb into the middle of a police parade, resulting in him being chased all over Los Angeles by the city's police force. This film is considered by critics to be Keaton's most accomplished short film.

Two-reelers: short silent films around 20 minutes long. During the 1920s, comedy two-reelers were screened in cinemas as supporting films for a feature-length film.

This collection of Keaton short films showcases his most striking work and illustrates his trademark style and themes. These films are representative of the most sophisticated and artistic American silent film comedies of the early 1920s. Film historian Kevin Brownlow, in *The Parade's Gone By* (1992), describes Keaton's style in the two-reelers as simple set-ups with flat comedy lighting and spare use of intertitles. Common themes that reoccur in these films are Keaton's relationship with machinery and modernity and heterosexual romance.

American silent film comedy

(iA) Independent Activity

Watch early examples of film comedy, including *The Gardener* (Lumière Brothers, 1895). Write 200 words on the following question:

How do Buster Keaton's two-reelers develop from early examples of film comedy?

Comedy, particularly gag-based and slapstick comedy, was a popular genre and movement of the silent era. Visual comedy was the perfect genre for silent cinema, as gags could be shown without the need for dialogue and were understood by all audiences, including immigrant populations in the USA who may not have been fluent in English. Early film pioneers exploited film's potential to create gag-based comedy. The Lumière Brothers' early film, *Le Jardinier/The Gardener* (Auguste & Louis Lumière, 1895), is one of the very first examples of film comedy. The 45-second film depicts a simple practical joke involving a boy who pranks a gardener by stepping on his hose. The gardener chases the boy, catches him and spanks him.

The Gardener (Lumière Brothers, 1895)

Film comedy emerged in the USA as a staple genre in 1912 when entrepreneur Mack Sennett founded the Keystone Company and studios. Keystone quickly gained a reputation for short, gag-based and fast-paced physical **slapstick** comedies. Keystone was the biggest producer of American comedy films in the mid-1910s. Its most popular series of films was the Keystone Cops, featuring inept, comic policemen. The trend for mocking and outwitting policemen continued in American film comedy and is exemplified by Keaton's film *Cops*, where Keaton's character is chased by the Los Angeles police.

The 1920s was the golden age of American film comedy. Buster Keaton was one of many 'classic' silent clowns, including Roscoe 'Fatty' Arbuckle, Charlie Chaplin and Harold Lloyd, who all developed their craft at Keystone. Other popular comedians included Laurel and Hardy and Charlie Chase. Roscoe 'Fatty' Arbuckle often collaborated with Keaton and the two were a major influence on each other's comedy style. Keaton was influenced by Arbuckle's character-motivated gags. Arbuckle stated that,

> *if anyone gets kicked or has a pie thrown in his face, there's going to be a reason for it.* (Koszarski, 2005, page 157)

By the 1920s, American film studios had established the **star system**. The distinct personas and comedy style of the great silent comedians were developed by the studios in which the comedians honed their craft. Many of

Slapstick: a farcical form of physical comedy, popular in early film comedy. It usually involves violent, physical action, such as pratfalls, chases and practical jokes.

Star system: the system used by Hollywood studios to create and exploit stars. Studios would publicise films using star personas as the main selling point. Publicity departments would create a public image of the star, sometimes changing their name and details about their personal life.

these silent comedians were given a great deal of control over their films. In 1919, film executive Joseph M. Schenck set up Buster Keaton Productions and gave Keaton complete creative freedom in writing, directing and acting. As a result of this creative freedom and star system, slapstick comedians of the early 1920s were more concerned with character development and star performances than in the early slapstick films.

Film scholar Charles Wolfe, in *Idols of Modernity* (2010), lists the following conventions and pleasures of American silent film:

- falls and chases played for big laughs
- stunts which thrill audiences
- star comedians with intriguing personalities
- implausible scenarios
- stories told efficiently and clearly
- evoking of dream-like states
- critiques of American society.

Buster Keaton's physical comedy developed from vaudeville, a popular form of variety entertainment in the USA from the 1880s to the early 1930s. In vaudeville shows, a variety of performers, including acrobats, singers and comedians, would perform short 'skits'. Buster Keaton himself was born into a family of performers. He performed in vaudeville with his father Joe and mother Myra as one of the 'Three Keatons'. Keaton adapted his vaudeville performance of acrobatics and comedy gags to films.

Film form in Buster Keaton short films

Cinematography

All four Buster Keaton shorts use flat lighting. Flat light has little shadow and creates an even and bright look. This type of lighting was common in silent comedy films as it enabled the audience to look around the frame and watch Keaton interact with his environment. Many of these two-reelers were shot mainly outdoors in daylight hours, therefore, Keaton could use the natural light. The entirety of *Cops* was shot outdoors, making use of outdoor studio lots and the local Los Angeles vicinity, rooting the surreal gags in real locations.

Keaton employs deep focus to provide a sense of perspective and contribute to the humour, as we can see the gag developing in the background. In *One Week*, the audience clearly sees the train in the background hurtling towards the makeshift house. In *Cops* Keaton takes a nap on the horse carriage while the city can be seen unfurling in the background. Keaton was adept at using cinematic space to build up a gag. The locomotive at the start of *The 'High Sign'* appears enormous in the frame, making Keaton look small and overpowered, then it speeds off into the background.

In these short films, Keaton's character is often placed at the centre of the frame. This gives each frame a clear symmetry and allows the audience to focus on how Keaton interacts with the world around him. The camera is straight-on at eye-level, with no **expressionist** angles used so as not to distract from what is happening in the scene.

Independent Activity

Apply Wolfe's conventions and pleasures of American silent film to one Buster Keaton short film. Give specific examples of each convention from your chosen Keaton short film.

The Three Keatons

Deep focus gives a sense of perspective in *Cops*.

Expressionist: expressionist films depict a widely distorted reality for emotional effect.

A common convention at Keystone was to shoot chase sequences in long shot. Keystone's influence on Keaton is evident in the chase sequences in *Cops*. Notice how during chase sequences in *Cops* the camera stays static in long shot as the action takes place clearly within the frame. Camera movement is used only to emphasise a gag, as seen in *One Week*, where the movement of the camera mimics the high winds and adds to the absurdity of the gag as Keaton and his wife try not to get swept away by the winds.

Mise-en-scène

These short films display Keaton's fascination for engineering and gadgets. One of Keaton's trademarks was mechanical comedy, where mechanical objects are used and may take on a dual purpose. In *The 'High Sign'*, household furniture and parts of the house take on additional functions such as the floor having a trap door. In *The Scarecrow* all the mechanical objects in the house take on dual functions, exploited for comic effect, such as the gramophone player which functions as an oven. There is a symmetry in the use of mise-en-scène as exemplified in the final sequences of *The 'High Sign'*. Here the house resembles a dolls' house, with the screen split into four in perfect symmetry, enabling the audience to witness what is happening in each room of the house simultaneously.

Objects and props in Keaton's films can function as characters and appear to take on a life of their own. This is evident in the use of the houses in *One Week*, *The 'High Sign'* and *The Scarecrow*, which all seem to come to life. The house in *One Week* seems to conspire against Keaton and his bride. The hurricane causes the house to revolve manically, a gag for which Keaton ingeniously used a giant turntable.

Objects in Keaton's short films are often imposing and appear larger than they may do in reality. Keaton utlised his small frame, appearing in front of or next to large objects. The merry-go-round and train in *The 'High Sign'* appear large and imposing. Likewise, the ever-expanding newspaper engulfs Keaton for absurd comic effect.

Editing

Editing and shots are structured around the development of the gag and edited for precise comic timing. Keaton was an intuitive editor; he described his approach to editing as,

> pacing – for fast action, you cut things closer than normal. For a dramatic scene, you lengthen them out a little bit more. (Brownlow, 1992, page 43)

Consider the scene in *The 'High Sign'* where the dog tries to eat the steak which is revealed every time Keaton rings the bell. The editing is perfectly timed to enhance the comedy through cross-cutting from Keaton stepping on the pedal to make the bell ring, to the dog outside lunging at the steak. The fast editing and cross-cutting build up the comedy as the poor dog tries repeatedly in vain to catch the steak.

In the opening of *Cops* the framing and editing create the gag. At first, the mid-shot of Keaton clinging onto the bars makes us believe he is in prison. Then, the film cuts to a long shot which reveals that Keaton is in fact behind the bars of a garden gate. This shot also demonstrates how Keaton is 'locked out' from the wealthy world his girlfriend inhabits.

In *One Week* an **iris shot** is used in conjunction with the torn calendar to signal the end of a scene and the start of each new day, suggesting the passage of time from one shot to the next.

Iris shot: the frame is partially masked in a circular frame, mimicking the iris of the eye. The iris shot may be used to begin or end a scene or draw our attention to something in the frame. Iris shots were a common convention in silent cinema.

Sound

Although these are 'silent' films, early film audiences would always experience film with live musical accompaniment, usually a piano. There is no set synchronised score, therefore the musicians in the theatres would play along to the film to heighten the emotion and emphasise the comedy. Silent films compensate for the lack of audio cues through exaggerated performances and a focus on the purely visual elements of cinema. Film historian Gerald Mast, in *The Comic Mind: Comedy and the Movies* (1979), argues that due to the lack of sound, silent films have a hypnotic quality. For Mast,

> *lacking natural sound, the silent film works on the ear solely by means of the effects of cutting and motion on the eye … The movement of physical comedy … perfectly suits the silent visual hypnosis.* (page 202)

Performance

Keaton's nickname was 'The Great Stone Face' due to his deadpan expression. Keaton learned this technique when performing in vaudeville with his family, as he noticed that when he did not emote at the end of a gag, the audience found the gag funnier. His deadpan persona differs from other silent comedians of the day such as Charlie Chaplin, who would often use a range of exaggerated facial expressions to heighten the gags.

Keaton uses his large eyes to emote. His face and eyes imply innocence, as he seems unperturbed by the hostile world around him. Keaton's more subtle style was typical of the new trend in silent cinema from 1912 for a 'verisimilar' acting style. Actors would mimic everyday human responses in a slightly more realistic fashion. This contrasted with the 'histrionic' style popular before 1912, where actors used broad and exaggerated movements that bore no relation to how people respond in real life. Keaton was a physical, agile actor, who incorporated his acrobatics into his films and performed all his own stunts. His body becomes an element of the mise-en-scène as he positions himself within the architecture and setting. A good example of this is where Keaton is being chased by the dog through a ruined building in *The Scarecrow*. Keaton leaps through the windows and across the ledges of the building with ease.

Representation

These short films foreground representational issues regarding gender, rather than age and ethnicity. Women tend to function in the narratives of these Buster Keaton shorts as devices for conflict and as Keaton's love interests. However, in *One Week* the female actress, Sybil Seely, who plays Keaton's wife, has a much stronger role. She is his equal, as the two characters pull together to build and retain their house. Seely, however, still reinforces traditional gender roles as she cooks breakfast while Keaton attempts to build the house. In *One Week*, Keaton acknowledges the voyeuristic role of the camera in the sequences where Seely takes a bath. When Seely drops her soap while bathing, a hand appears and covers the lens, as if to protect Seely's modesty. Seely breaks the fourth wall by smiling at the camera, aware she is being watched. Seely also plays Keaton's love interest in *The Scarecrow*. Here, Keaton states, 'I don't care how she votes. I'm going to marry her' – a reference to the success of women's suffrage, as most American states had granted women full voting rights by the end of 1919. Keaton's girlfriend in *Cops* is represented as snobbish and cruel, in contrast to his young sweet bride in *One Week*. She functions mainly as a plot device, as her rejection of Keaton leads him into a series of mishaps.

Sybil Seely cooks breakfast in *One Week*.

One Week (Keaton & Cline, 1920)

(iA) **Independent Activity**

Consider the following:

> Women function merely as love-interests in Buster Keaton's short films.

How far do you agree with this statement? Give examples from the four Keaton short films which support this statement and examples which oppose it.

Silent film comedians often played childlike and naive characters which, to a certain extent, defy traditional masculine roles. In *One Week*, Keaton struggles to conform to traditional masculine roles as he is unable to build a home for his wife or cope with the most basic of tasks. In these shorts, Keaton is unable to control the environment around him and often only luck gets him through. However, Keaton does possess some typical masculine traits, as he uses his physical strength and performs all his own stunts. He also demonstrates ingenuity with building and using mechanical objects. Bret Carroll in *American Masculinities: A Historical Encyclopedia* (2003) argues that definitions of masculinity in the silent era were 'body centered', typified by physical performances, as

> *through exaggerated physical movements that created dramatic and comic narratives, these male stars offered viewers compelling, albeit fictional, versions of masculinity.*

Buster Keaton and Sybil Seely in *One Week*

Aesthetics

All four of these Buster Keaton shorts share an aesthetic style that is typified by symmetry, frames, parallel lines and circular imagery. Consider the composition of the hanging salt and pepper pots in *The Scarecrow*. The characters sit at the table at each end of the frame in symmetry and the hanging pots create horizontal, vertical and diagonal patterns. Compare this to the symmetry created in *Cops* as Keaton creates a see-saw effect with a wooden plank. Film scholar Charles Wolfe in *Idols of Modernity* (Petro, 2010), places Keaton's aesthetic style within the wider cultural contexts of American art of the 1920s and 1930s, which, during a time of rising consumerism, emphasised the beauty and simplicity of everyday objects. Art in this period featured geometric shapes and reflected the flourishing industrial age and an interest in the movement of trains and ships. It was a period that celebrated the creativity of engineering and was also one of technological change, as the production line method of factory production was introduced by Ford in 1907.

▶ S&C

Search online for artist Thomas Hart Benton's 1930 mural *America Today*. Look at the 'Instruments of Power' panel of the mural. Write down the similarities between the panel and Buster Keaton's short films.

(iA) Independent Activity

Choose one sequence from *The 'High Sign'* and one sequence from *One Week*. Write down how each sequence typifies Keaton's aesthetic style. Compare the aesthetic style of the two sequences in your analysis.

Use of symmetry in *Cops*

Social, cultural and political contexts

Buster Keaton's fascination with the workings of mechanical objects bridges the end of the 19th century and beginning of the 20th century, with the rise of new industries and the expanding consumer culture. American society of the 1920s was one of increased consumerism, as advertisers began to link products to idealised lifestyles and saw the potential of film to sell products. Keaton developed the idea for *One Week* after viewing a Ford Motor Company documentary *Home Made* (1919). The documentary demonstrates how Ford workers can build their own affordable, pre-fabricated homes. In *One Week*, Keaton attempts to construct the ideal home for himself and his new bride and live an ideal married life. However, the film undercuts this notion of the idealised life, as Keaton is unable to construct a home for himself and his bride.

A Rube Goldberg illustration

The cubist house in *One Week*

These shorts depict Keaton as both confused and fascinated by the mechanical world. The house in *The Scarecrow* was a reference to the comic illustrations of American illustrator Rube Goldberg, which were published in national newspapers. Goldberg drew characters surrounded by crazy contraptions as a comment on how devices can often confuse us and complicate our lives.

Cubism was an influential artistic movement of the period. Artists such as Pablo Picasso and Georges Braque would break objects down into distinct areas or forms, creating abstract and fragmented images. Buster Keaton references cubism in *One Week* for comic effect, as the house takes on a cubist form, resembling an abstract, angular face. The roof takes on the appearance of a tiny hat, while the pickets on the front porch resemble large teeth.

Keaton was fascinated with modes of transport, reflecting a general fascination at the time with the locomotive and the motor car, such as the Ford Model T, manufactured between 1908 and 1927, opened up the possibility of motor transport to middle-class Americans. *One Week* features gags with cars and motorcycles. The climactic gag is when a steam locomotive comes hurtling through the house, while *The 'High Sign'* begins with Keaton being kicked off a locomotive. Locomotives were associated with modernity, speed, romance and danger. The locomotive, or steam train, featured heavily in silent cinema. The earliest films, including the Lumière Brothers' *L'arrivée d'un train en gare de La Ciotat* (1895) featured moving locomotives.

iA Independent Activity

Search for cubist paintings by the artists Pablo Picasso and Georges Braque. Write down three similarities between these paintings and the house in Keaton's *One Week*.

iA Independent Activity

For each Keaton short film, write two modes of transport used in it and state briefly how Keaton uses each one for comic effect.

Cultural contexts and critical debates: the realist and the expressive

The specification says:

In the 1940s, the French film critic André Bazin set in motion a major debate when he argued that both German Expressionist and Soviet Montage filmmaking went against what he saw as the 'realist' calling of cinema. This opposition between the realist and the expressive has informed thinking about film from the beginnings of cinema when the documentary realism of the Lumière Brothers was set in opposition to the fantasy films of Méliès.

Independent Activity

Watch three Lumière films and three Méliès films. Write a short essay of 300 words stating the differences between their films.

Surrealism: an international 20th-century movement of artists, writers and philosophers who valued the unconscious mind and dreams. They rejected conventional moral and artistic values. The surrealists were heavily influenced by the work of Sigmund Freud, particularly his book *The Interpretation of Dreams* (1899), which argued that our dreams reveal our unconscious motivations or desires.

 S&C

Watch Keaton's feature-length film *The General* and compare the narrative structure with the narratives of the four short films you have studied. Answer the following short-essay question: To what extent are the gags in *The General* integrated into the narrative? How does this differ to the development and function of gags in his earlier short films?

 Independent Activity

Choose one of the Buster Keaton short films. Write down three examples of surrealism in the film.

Louis & Auguste Lumière and George Méliès were key pioneers of early cinema. The Lumière Brothers used the camera as an instrument to record the world as it was. Their films are the beginnings of a realist, documentary cinema, in contrast to the magician George Méliès, who used the camera as a tool to create magic and a fantasy world. Méliès demonstrated the possibilities of the camera to create tricks and defy the laws of the real world. His most famous short film, *A Trip to the Moon* (1902), is one of the first examples of science fiction cinema and how cinema could be used to create fantasy worlds. His use of special effects, colour and constructed sets contrasts with the documentary style films of the Lumière Brothers. Keaton, like Méliès, was interested in the magical possibilities of cinema. However, Keaton uses this for comical purposes. For instance, the surreal over-sized newspaper gag in *The 'High Sign'* defies the norms of the real world and appears to open like a magic trick.

Tom Gunning, in his 1986 essay 'The Cinema of Attractions', argues that early silent film, from 1895 to around 1907, was a visual spectacle rather than a narrative cinema. It is in this early period that trick films, 'chase' films and slapstick comedy films were popular. These genres were well-suited to the new medium and modes of exhibition, as early short films were often viewed at travelling shows and fairgrounds. Early films were usually very short, anything from 30 seconds to a few minutes long. However, as film developed from around 1905 onwards, films became longer and therefore it was possible to more fully develop characters and storylines.

Buster Keaton's comedy films combine the cinema of attractions' tricks, gags and chases with a narrative cinema. Keaton referred to his gags as 'cartoon gags', ones that are surreal and function almost as magic tricks. The use of outdoor locations and natural lighting are in the realist mode, while the surreal gags and elaborate sets are more expressionistic and surrealist.

Surrealists adored silent comedy with imagery that adored the logic of the real world and anarchic gags that mocked figures. The surrealist filmmaker Luis Buñuel praised the films of Buster Keaton and Charlie Chapin as 'the finest poems that cinema has produced' (2002, page 123). **Surrealism** blends dreamlike imagery and reality, placing otherworldly images in a realistic context. Buster Keaton's shorts feature surreal gags such as the image of a man carrying a piano over his shoulder in *One Week*. Keaton's surreal gags take place in recognisable, realistic locations, such as the streets of Los Angeles in *Cops* and the fairground in *The 'High Sign'*.

The 'High Sign' lacks a cohesive narrative structure in comparison with the other short films in this study. *One Week* has a clear narrative structure, with each day revealed on the paper calendar torn away.

In Keaton's later feature-length films, such as *The General* (Keaton & Bruckman, 1926), gags are more integrated into the plot and far less surreal than those in his earlier short films. Keaton himself explained how the mode changed in feature films:

> *After we stopped making wild two-reelers and got into feature length pictures, our scenario boys had to be story-conscious. We couldn't tell any far-fetched stories, we couldn't do farce comedy, for instance … Story construction became very important to us.* (Sweeney, 2007)

Independent study questions

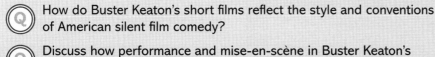

Q How do Buster Keaton's short films reflect the style and conventions of American silent film comedy?

Q Discuss how performance and mise-en-scène in Buster Keaton's short films contribute to the overall aesthetics of his films.

Q Do Buster Keaton's short films reflect the realist or expressive modes of silent cinema?

Q Discuss how far Buster Keaton's short films reflect cultural contexts associated with American silent film comedy.

Sample essay extract and feedback

Discuss how far your chosen film or films reflect cultural contexts associated with a particular film movement.

For this example, we are looking at an extract from an essay addressing the four Buster Keaton short films.

Amy's response extract	Feedback
Buster Keaton's films merge the realist style of cinema with the expressionistic style. *Cops* takes place in real locations, as Keaton shot the film on the streets of Los Angeles, yet the gags have a surreal quality. Buster Keaton's short films exemplify the use of surrealism in American silent film comedy. In *The 'High Sign'*, Keaton opens a newspaper which becomes larger and overwhelms him. In *One Week*, a surreal image of a man carrying a piano adds to the absurdity of the scene. Surrealists such as Luis Buñuel loved the comedy films of Buster Keaton and Charlie Chapin due to their dream-like gags, which merged fantasy and reality, and their mocking of authority figures. In *Cops*, policemen are figures of fun to be outwitted, a continuation of a comic tradition in American silent film comedy exemplified by the popular Keystone Cops films.	*Amy demonstrates an understanding of the surreal nature of Keaton's films. She is able to provide examples from the short films to illustrate her points.*
Keaton's films reflect silent cinema's interest in transport and the mechanical age. Steam locomotives feature heavily in his films. In the opening of *The 'High Sign'*, Keaton is kicked off a locomotive. Keaton is made to look small and insignificant in contrast to the power of the locomotive. In *One Week*, a locomotive destroys Keaton's makeshift house. Deep focus is used to enable the audience to see the locomotive hurtling towards the house from the background to the foreground.	*Amy links the use of transport in Keaton's films to silent films' repeated use of the locomotive. Amy gives specific examples from Keaton's shorts with use of film language to demonstrate how Keaton uses cinematic devices.*
The aesthetics of Keaton's films reflects artistic movement of the period. All four films feature an interest in symmetry and geometric shapes. In *The Scarecrow*, the house where mechanical objects take on a duel meaning has a clear symmetry with use of vertical, horizontal and diagonal lines. The household objects also reflect the work of cartoonist Rube Goldberg, who would depict characters grappling with everyday mechanical objects, suggesting that the modern mechanical world is confusing.	*Amy links Keaton's films to art of the period and an interest in mechanical objects. Her comparison of the house in* The Scarecrow *to Goldberg's popular cartoons is relevant and demonstrates an awareness of Keaton's influences. Amy could expand on symmetry and geometric shapes in art of the period.*

This **section** will focus on the experimental film question from the Component 2 paper Global filmmaking perspectives. This area of study is exclusive to the A level and alongside the core areas of study you will need to apply the specialist study areas of **narrative** and **auteur**. This is a single film study and our initial focus will be on the paired example of two European avant-garde films from the 1960s: the experimental art house feature, *Daisies* (Chytilová, Czechoslovakia, 1966) and the short experimental film, *Saute ma ville* (Akerman, Belgium, 1968).

For A level

In the Component 2, Section D examination there are 20 marks at stake and the expected writing time for an answer is 30 minutes.

The specification says

Alternatives to mainstream narrative film have been present throughout cinema history. The choice here is of films from 1960–2000. Over this period new waves have often challenged the mainstream.

Note: Chapters 10 and 11 offer two choices of case study for this module – only one should be studied.

Daisies
(Sedmikrásky)
A film by
Věra Chytilová

Second Run DVD

Film is an international business and even Hollywood has now woken up to the need to appeal to an international market. With US box office figures in decline, the importance of having a product that can cross borders and continents is increasingly important. However, this unit goes beyond the merely international flavour of film and looks more closely at the specifics of the film world that exist beyond mainstream Hollywood.

This unit allows the student to explore filmmaking from beyond the mainstream confines of Hollywood and Britain's fiction filmmaking. The material will challenge aesthetic and narrative expectations as well as offer philosophically charged material to disentangle and explore. The films studied here are not necessary to learn in tandem but are rather only offered to provide choice.

The analysis of *Daisies* and *Saute ma ville* will firstly look at their position in the 1960s European avant-garde, and, secondly, critique their formal and ideological experimentation.

The avant-garde

An 'avant-garde' is a military term applied to an advanced unit that literally led the way. It was used in terms of cultural analysis in the mid-1800s in France and is now synonymous with any art movement that pushes the boundaries of the form into areas that are at the very least controversial if not taboo. Avant-garde art, be it literature or music, painting or film, has the power to outrage audiences and critics, and can often lead to prohibition, censorship or even imprisonment. Since its dawn in the 1890s, film has allied itself to a number of avant-garde artistic movements such as those of Dada, surrealism and expressionism. In revolutionary Russia the constructivist art movement influenced the likes of Eisenstein and Vertov.

 S&C

Research some of the avant-garde art movements referenced on this page such as Dada, expressionism and surrealism. Consider how they may have impacted on filmmaking.

S&C

Research this period in more depth. YouTube is awash with resources on the phenomena of civil rights, gay rights, alternative lifestyles and movements in the 1960s and so on. Indeed, it is highly likely that what you discover will impact or consolidate what you have learned in other areas of the specification. For example, the films you may have studied in Component 1, New Hollywood, such as Francis Ford Coppola's *Apocalypse Now* (1979) and Miloš Forman's *One Flew Over the Cuckoo's Nest* (1975) are mainly defined by their counter-culture stance.

 Independent Activity

Research other films that arose from the radicalism of the 1960s and 1970s. Consider controversial classics such as *A Clockwork Orange* (1972) or *2001: Space Odyssey* (1968) both directed by key auteur Stanley Kubrick.

Even today, many postmodern artists have turned to filmmaking to express their artistic visions. The avant-garde is ever present but it undoubtedly reached a high water mark in the 1960s in Europe.

The mid-to-late 1950s and the 1960s was a period of enormous social, political and cultural upheaval. As a new generation of children born during or just after the calamity of World War II came of age, their interests and value systems failed to coincide with the generation that preceded them, the generation of their parents: the veterans. This new generation, the baby boomers (so called because they also represented a birth rate rise), were characterised by their attempts to reconfigure old ideologies and their distrust of mainstream authority.

It is then no surprise that the 1960s saw the development of a 'generation gap'. Into this gap numerous youth-oriented counter-ideologies and counter-movements developed. For example, there was the Campaign for Nuclear Disarmament's (CND's) response to the Cold War and later the anti-Vietnam War movement (the average age of USA conscripts was 19). There was a sexual revolution fuelled in part by the contraceptive pill and the legalisation of abortion, as well as more open attitudes to sex before marriage. Then there was the rise of global pop stars such as The Beatles and the Rolling Stones, and the first rock music festivals such as Woodstock. Additionally, the rise of counter-culture ideologies led to an increased use of recreational drugs and a rejection of societal norms; something encapsulated by the mantra of LSD (lysergic acid diethylamide) guru Timothy Leary, 'Turn on! Tune in! And drop out!' These largely youth-focused movements also coincided with significant advances in technology, leading to such events as the space race (man first walked on the moon in 1969), the dawn of computers, the growth of TV as a mass medium and increased ownership of highly aspirational mass-produced objects such as cars and household electrical goods.

Finally, there were the politically focused movements of the disenfranchised, such as the Civil Rights movement, gay rights activism, second wave feminism, ecological 'green' movements and the increased popularity of neo-Marxism. Even on a spiritual level there was a rejection of the old theocratic viewpoints enshrined in Christian dogma, and a discovery of Eastern philosophies and religions such as Buddhism and Hinduism, with their focus on such practices as yoga and meditation. Indeed, such was the tsunami of new ideologies that it was and is legitimate to talk of the era involving a 'counter-culture'.

The 1960s was a decade where the world took a dramatic U-turn, when youth-focused rebellion and the quest for personal and political freedom became paramount. The art world also responded to, if not led, this new era of freedom and non-conformity, so in filmmaking the world witnessed a number of 'new waves'.

The most famous new wave is the French New Wave, the *Nouvelle Vague*, which certainly pioneered a number of key theories and styles that have become common features of both the contemporary academic and practical film worlds. Without the contribution of the *Nouvelle Vague* to film history and theory we would not have theoretical terms such as 'auteur' or be familiar with techniques such as location shooting, improvised acting and jump-cuts. At the heart of the French New Wave lay an informality of style and a willingness to experiment with form and subject matter. Initially realist in their focus, new wave filmmakers swiftly got swept up in the maelstrom of counter-culture debate and discourse, so their sense of freedom and adventure was applied in other countries under different socio-political conditions leading to more ideologically radical work. It is against this backdrop that we must place *Daisies* and *Saute ma ville*.

The context of *Daisies*

Daisies is an unashamedly avant-garde film with a strong feminist ideology. It is experimental at virtually every level: in film form, narrative and characterisations. In brief, this is not a realist text but rather, arguably, a surrealist one. We approach this film not, then, in terms of social realism and a depiction of late 1960s Czechoslovakia but rather in terms of absurdist cinema and an oblique counter-culture critique of political authoritarianism and patriarchy. However, the film absolutely emerges from a specific socio-political context, as explored below.

Social, cultural, political contexts

The Prague Spring and the Czech New Wave

Czechoslovakia no longer exists. It fell apart as a nation and split into two countries, the Czech Republic and Slovakia, in 1993 after the collapse of the Berlin Wall and the end of the Soviet bloc. The ideology of communism led by the USSR or Soviet Union came to a relatively peaceful end in 1989. The iron curtain came down and the countries of eastern Europe, such as Poland, Hungary and Czechoslovakia, were able to dismantle their one-party communist states and set up open democracies on a western European model.

However, *Daisies* has its origins within the communist system. Overt criticism of the state was forbidden and films were banned if they were deemed anti-communist. Under such political conditions the role of the avant-garde becomes much more important than in more tolerant liberal societies, so the aesthetic experimentation of artists can have powerful effects and consequences for the spectator.

Everything came to a head in 1968 (a year also famous for student protests in Paris) in a brief period of official state relaxation of Soviet policy, called the Prague Spring. A power struggle in a time of economic crisis had led Alexander Dubček to take control of the communist party in Czechoslovakia. Dubček was a reformer who wanted to loosen the control of the communist party while still retaining one-party control. He also was keen to relax censorship laws and encourage greater press freedoms. Perhaps unsurprisingly, on 20 August 1968 Moscow used troops and tanks from the Warsaw Pact and the Soviet Union to invade Czechoslovakia and reassert Moscow's authority. The invasion led to Dubček's arrest and proved to the West that democracy was not viable for those people still living under the control of the USSR. The Prague Spring was over almost as soon as it began and the Czech New Wave ground to a halt. Chytilová found working increasingly hard and her film *Daisies* was banned.

Institutional contexts

The Czech film industry, like many non-English speaking countries, has a long history and its most famous film studio, Barrandov, which opened in 1933, remains one of Europe's major filmmaking facilities. The industry's most productive and creative era was during the period of increasingly relaxed attitudes in the mid-1960s, when the state funding of film became more

Soviet tanks crush the Prague Spring in 1968.

 S&C

Look up information on other new waves of the 1960s, including the UK wave. Examine and discuss the ending of the film *If* (Anderson, 1968) and note the parallels with Chytilová's and Akerman's work.

 Independent Activity

Read about George Orwell and take a look at the most famous film adaptations of his most popular novels, *Animal Farm* and *1984*. Consider the aspects of these texts that critique Stalinist communism.

Miloš Forman

Věra Chytilová

tolerant of films that weren't part of the prescribed Soviet model called social realism. This in turn led to critical acclaim overseas, not least in the Oscars, where two films, *The Shop on Main Street* (Kadar & Klos, 1965) and *Closely Watched Trains* (Menzel, 1967), won the award for Best Foreign Language Film. The rise of, now internationally acclaimed, auteurs in the then Eastern bloc, such as Roman Polanski from Poland and Miloš Forman from Czechoslovakia, also encouraged interest in the region. Indeed, Forman, the foremost of the Czech directors, eventually fled the repressive communist regime and ended up in Hollywood making such great films as *One Flew Over the Cuckoo's Nest* and *Amadeus* (1985). However, in the mid-1960s it seemed legitimate to start talking about a new wave of Czech filmmakers.

Many of these filmmakers like Chytilová and Forman attended the state-run film school FAMU in Prague's Film and TV Academy of Performing Arts. With the state funding their films and access to the nearby Barrandov film studio, the Czech New Wave filmmakers produced more upscale versions of film compared to the more financially threadbare films of the French *Nouvelle Vague*. There was equally a greater ideological resistance to the communist regime among this artistic Czech community than was found in the more liberal nation of France. With the collapse of the Prague Spring in 1968, the communist hierarchy re-established its ideological control over cinema and artistic culture as a whole and the bright bloom of freedom, artists such as Chytilová had briefly experienced, withered and died.

Věra Chytilová as auteur

Věra Chytilová (1928–2014), 'the first lady of Czech cinema', made her debut feature in 1963, with the experimental, *Something Different*, but she remains most famous for her work on *Daisies*. Despite falling foul of communist party censorship, she continued making feature films, shorts and documentaries until her last directorial work in 2006. Born a Catholic and originally a student of philosophy and architecture, she worked as a clapper girl at Barrandov Studios before applying to study at FAMU. Her graduation piece, *Ceiling* (1962), was widely distributed among British film societies in the 1960s and *Something Different* was shown at the 1st International Festival of Women's Films in New York in 1972. Peter Hames, in his excellent and recommended accompanying booklet to the Second Run DVD 2009 rerelease of *Daisies*, notes that,

> while she was one of the few women directors to make a major impact in the early 1960s, her work also functioned as a harbinger of developments in feminist film theory in the 1970s.

The DVD also includes an excellent hour-long documentary of Chytilová.

In a *Guardian* interview with Kate Connolly (2000) following her award for an Outstanding Contribution to World Cinema at the 35th Karlovy Vary Film Festival, it was noted that:

> she does not believe in feminism per se, but in individualism. Chytilová is quoted as saying: 'If there's something you don't like, don't keep to the rules … break them! I'm an enemy of stupidity and simple-mindedness in both men and women and I have rid my living space of these traits.'

Connolly goes on to note that Chytilová has been described as,

> choleric, diabolically crazy, aggressive, ironic, sarcastic, inflexible and arrogant – just a few of the phrases used by the Czech media to describe her after she collected her prize. Some who know her say these characteristics stem from a bitterness she shares with others of her generation, who spent the best years of their lives working under a totalitarian regime.

Chytilová's acerbic and tough qualities have also garnered her the nickname, 'the Margaret Thatcher of Czech film'. Certainly, in *Daisies* this does not come over, as her actresses are clearly having a great time and the film as a whole has a playful, whimsical lightness and charm. Věra Chytilová was a philosophically and artistically minded woman with an interest in stories about women. Her films were also adventures in formal and aesthetic experimentation. As Peter Hames, in his excellent and recommended accompanying booklet to the Second Run DVD 2009 rerelease of *Daisies*:

> … while an attack on patriarchy can to some extent be taken for granted, she was also intensely interested in film form and aesthetics.

Daisies is, then, the film that from an auteur standpoint defines her oeuvre: feminist, philosophical, experimental and aesthetically charged.

In terms of her specific authorial signature, Carmen Gray said in 2016 that Chytilová had a 'taste for visual symbolism and multi-layered associations'. She also worked regularly with her husband the cinematographer, Jaroslav Kučera. Her frequently surreal, often incisively parodic and blackly comic films drew on nature for their striking images and abstraction, and some of her opening sequences are really memorable, not least *Daisies*. Chytilová's auteur signature is then a stylistically strong one but perhaps her strongest element is the thematic treatment of material with her focus on anti-patriarchal feminist as well as more broadly her interest in artistic and aesthetic freedom. It would be a mistake to pigeonhole her as a feminist but rather a freedom fighter, an artist less concerned with labelling and more focused on unfettered expression.

The narrative of *Daisies*

Narrative construction relates to the whole film and as such *Daisies* needs to be firstly considered holistically before we engage more carefully on the themes and particular formal film aspects of the text. The film's experimentalism thus limits the utility of such notions as three-act structures and character arcs. The plotting of the film is chaotic and as such there are many ellipses and temporal duration is significantly fractured. There are no helpful framing devices to aid exposition such as voice-overs or flashbacks although some on-screen text is included but its meaning is often oblique. The dialogue is not naturalistic and there is a significant ambiguity affecting our experience of cause and effect as well as character identification (the protagonists are Marie 1 and Marie 2). However, whatever ambiguities are developed in the film's experimental approach to narrative there is little doubt that the film positions us to revel in and enjoy the antics of the two Maries. The film focuses on two teenage women: Marie 1 and Marie 2. They are not individuals (although Marie 1 is brunette and Marie 2 is blonde) but are rather interchangeable archetypes representative of modern female youth. They too describe themselves as dolls and in one early scene act like mechanical puppets with the accompanying sound design of creaking wood

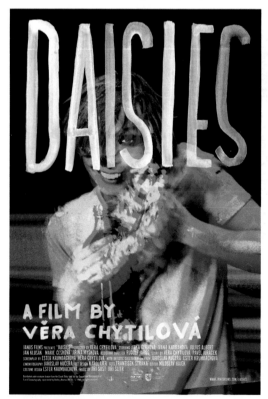

Janus (2012) DVD cover re-release of film emphasising its psychedelic nature.

S&C

(iA) Independent Activity

Consider these issues:

1 What is the distinction between censorship and classification?

2 Why might censorship be a problem for an artist or thinker?

3 Where in the world does heavily politically motivated censorship exist?

and joints. The narrative, as referenced above, is highly unconventional and very loosely plotted. Chytilová refers to the films as 'a philosophical documentary in the form of a farce' (Horton, 1991, page 98), so clearly, generically, there is a nod to the comedic but equally, underscoring the absurdity of the film, there is a philosophical message about alienation and estrangement, something key to the movement of **existentialism** that was then in vogue.

The film is open in terms of its meanings, as the cast were encouraged to improvise from the script. Chytilová notes,

> We decided to allow ourselves to be bound by nothing. Absolutely nothing. (*The Quietus*, 2014)

That said, the film starts with images of aerial warfare and ends with explosions, suggestive of a critique of militarism, the girls are often vacuous, silly and wilfully destructive, perhaps suggesting that they are examples of a vapid, depoliticised and disengaged youth. Conversely, Chytilová's husband, who was also the film's cinematographer, the highly respected Jaroslav Kučera, felt that audience identification with the girls might occur precisely because they are so wild and anarchic. Questions of their empowerment, or their coded critique of patriarchy, must then be contrasted with the idea that unfettered aesthetic experimentation can become a redundant and unhelpful exercise, and that for the world to truly change (for the bombs not to go off) something more considered is needed. The film interestingly was banned on its release for its wasteful attitude to food in a time of food shortages rather than its philosophical and social critique. Another criticism came from the leader of the Czech surrealists, who dismissed the films as 'decorative cynicism'. Some, too, have argued that male viewers may find the film less engaging then females, as the film resists simplistic and cosy female representations and men are the butt of many of the jokes.

Film form

The students of this film need to remember, however, that the aesthetic choices made by Chytilová are many and varied precisely because she does not want to be constrained by any artistic conventions such as the need to present realism through naturalistic settings or acting styles or continuity editing. If a dominant aesthetic is present then it is a surreal and experimental one: an aesthetic that rejects cinematic norms.

Cinematography

Many shots are tableaux, representing a controlled camera style in contrast to a freer use of hand-held camerawork. There is a painterly eye in much of the shot construction. A full variety of shot types are utilised and the colour palette is widely varied, ranging from garish colour to sepia and single-colour filters. The use of colour is often surreal and embedded in the construction of the mise-en-scène.

The film begins with images of stock military aerial footage from World War II, colourised with filters to create a striking contrast with a recurring imagery of the metallic grey cogs and pulleys of a moving machine. The music is sinister and powerful, largely drums and trumpet, which further adds to the militaristic and mechanistic connotations. Clearly, the world of the two Maries is violent and alienating – a machine age.

The opening credits and title sequence then cuts to the two Maries, shot in long shot, in bikinis. They are half asleep and move like dolls, discussing the fact that no one understands them and that the world is bad and so they too should be bad. This is a depiction of disaffected youth and objectified women. A further symbolic binary is developed through the juxtaposition of warfare and machines, with two young women sunbathing: the active infliction of pain and death is thus contrasted with passive and sensual pleasure.

Also of note here is the film's playful nod to early film experimentalism and the contemporaneous use of LSD. The surrealism of psychedelia is thus referenced with a fairly lengthy 'phantom train ride'.

 S&C

Explore the phantom train rides of early cinema. Also look at the experimental colour shorts made for the General Post Office in the UK in the 1930s by experimental artist and filmmaker Len Lye.

Mise-en-scène

The settings, despite their evident realism, are richly symbolic, such as the disused factory and the banquet – both towards the end of the film. The later setting, which provides the locus for the film's dénouement, is one of many scenes involving food and eating. A recurring plot device and symbolic motif involves Marie 1 and Marie 2 meeting middle-aged men at expensive restaurants, playing coquettes and conning the men out of food. Each man is presented as bemused and ridiculous but nevertheless a symbol of predatory patriarchy. Later in the film the women note that they have pulled this trick on these doting elderly men five times already. However, what is perhaps understated here is that the girls are, at the very least, offering or pretending to offer their sexual favours to elderly men in order to eat. Perhaps as a reaction to having to debase themselves, the food the women order is often excessive in quantity and quality, and Marie 2 in particular is shown in close-up deliriously gorging herself on cake. This is significant, as students of French history may know, in reference to another young, foolish and independent, Marie: Marie Antoinette.

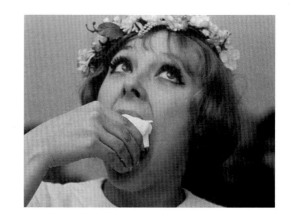

These scenes are counterpointed with two set-piece moments of anarchy where Marie 1 and Marie 2 destroy, firstly, the bourgeoisie formality of a dated and farcical cabaret, and, secondly, an equally outmoded formal banquet, which is symbolically unattended but splendidly laid out with extravagant dishes and delicacies.

The cabaret scene is purely comedic and shows them getting joyously drunk, taunting the stuffy clientele and eventually getting flung out of the venue. The banquet scene, however, demands more attention, not least because it continues the themes of food and excess.

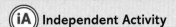

Another scene worth identifying in terms of its mise-en-scène is one of the many surreal and heavily symbolic sequences, illustrated in the screenshot on the left, which involves Marie 2's young lover, a lepidopterist (butterfly collector). The phrase is a sexual reference in Czechoslovakia to promiscuous men who seek out beautiful women. In this scene we see the film's only explicitly sexual scene involving Marie 2's nudity, something she conceals with beautiful but dead butterflies.

Later, back in the girls' apartment, the butterfly lover phones Marie 2. The two girls listen dismissively to his absurdly romantic love talk where he asserts that Marie 2 'does not belong to this century'. Like an exhibit in a display case he wants to preserve her beauty and effervescent sexuality. By containing her he hopes to control her. He is a man who clearly idealises women for what they represent, rather than what they are. As he twitters away on the phone the girls devour yet more food, but this time food that is phallic in shape such as small bread rolls, gherkins and sausages. They then chop up an egg and then a banana: two more symbolic foods. Finally, they chop up and eat pictures of food and hang up the phone. The man, a symbol of men in general, is not nourishing, like the copious amounts of food that Marie 1 and Marie 2 eat, and doesn't sate their sexual or digestive appetites.

(iA) Independent Activity

Explore the UK art house film *The Duke of Burgundy* (Strickland, 2015), which concerns, among other things, the idea of butterfly collecting and sexuality.

Editing

A riot of techniques are used with little interest in continuity, hence the frequent use of jump-cuts, match-cuts, staccato editing and so on. Discontinuity in editing is Chytilová's favoured device. This of course impacts on the spectator's narrative involvement and certainly helps develop the notion that Marie 1 and Marie 2 are interchangeable archetypes rather than separate identities.

One such use of a match-cut occurs early in the film when Marie 1 strikes Marie 2 and, as she falls, she transitions from a black and white sun deck into a vibrantly coloured meadow, swapping her bikini for a white summer dress and a garland. The meadow is dominated by daisies and is symbolic of Eden. This is anchored when both women find a tree with apples (knowledge) and a peach (pleasure). Marie 2 (the blonde) eats the peach. A further trick eye-line match occurs when Marie 1 looks off frame and asks Marie 2 a question, only for the subsequent cut to be in another location but the conversation to continue unabated. Such experimentation in terms of continuity editing quickly alerts the spectator that this film will not play by any rules, least of all those concerning editing. The film has established its playfulness with time and space, and any sense of realism has been jettisoned early on.

Sound

As with all the other aspects of film form there are realist scenes and conventionally scored scenes, but occasionally the use of non-realist juxtapositions occurs for comic effect: the ticking of clocks, the movement of puppets and so on. The mechanised and militaristic opening sequence referred to above is also particularly atmospheric in its use of non-diegetic music to unsettle and disturb the spectator.

Performance

Performances in the film are melodramatic, stylised and at times improvised. There is little focus on characterisation, back-story and arcs. Marie 1 and Marie 2 are types of people not actual people. Their intimated death at the end of the film is symbolic rather than real. The two actresses sustain non-naturalistic performances and dialogue throughout the film, never breaking character to become real characters.

Aesthetics

Chytilová is driven by the desire to experiment with film form and *Daisies* is therefore a riot of visual and audial play: play with bite but often just sheer playful exuberant fun. Thus, Marie 1 and Marie 2 in many ways seem the embodiment of Chytilová the artist, gorging herself on the medium as in the scene above where Marie 2 consumes cake.

All aspects of film form are distorted as detailed below in the section on auteur signatures but one key element that stands out is her aesthetic choices of colour. The film has a specific psychedelic quality at times (see previous screenshots) and one can't help but postulate on Chytilová's first- or secondhand experiences of LSD (arguably the definitive drug of the 1960s counter-culture). Chytilová also uses numerous light filters to colourise the entire frame. These striking colour juxtapositions are in contrast to the more conventional cinematic lighting used in shots like the one with the butterfly collector. The final shot of the two girls lying on the dinner table is tonally sepia, suggesting the colour and purpose has literally been washed out of their lives. Chytilová thus uses colour and its absence to make broader points about her culture and her protagonists, and it is this, in part, that indicates she is making aesthetic decisions.

 S&C

Watch the LSD sequence in *Easy Rider* and more contemporary drug-inflected films such as *Fear and Loathing in Las Vegas* (Gilliam, 1998) or the magic mushroom trip in Ben Wheatley's *A Field in England* (2013). What stylistic and aesthetic devices do they share with *Daisies*?

Representations in *Daisies*

Ethnicity

Ethnicity is not diversely presented in *Daisies*. The common ethnicity represented is white European and all the performers appear to be indigenous Czechoslovaks. Whether the omission of other racial identities is ideological is arguable but certainly European film was beginning to open up to the notion of representing other ethnic groups. This films white European cast is largely then in line with other works of the period. Stereotypes of white Europeans are of course hugely broad but the ones presented in this film are largely of middle class and educated dilettanti, collectors and body builders, aesthetes and gourmands and in the case of the two Maries free to have fun and seemingly unshackled by responsibility.

Gender and age

In *Daisies* gender and age are undoubtedly parodied. Marie 1 and Marie 2 are presented to us as two attractive and energetic young women who need nourishment (intellectual and physical) but seem to only find the latter in terms of their ravenous dinner dates with elderly and pathetically represented men. These guardians of patriarchy are ruthlessly parodied as foolishly lecherous and absurdly romantic, and even the younger of the men they befriend, the lepidopterist, merely wants to preserve Marie 2 as an exhibit, not as a real woman (see above). Marie 1 and Marie 2 are embodiments of a newly liberated youth, revelling in the dynamism and wonder of the world. However, the old world order re-establishes itself at the end of the film. Marie 1 and Marie 2, 'youth', pay the price for their freedom as the film ends with their supposed death beneath a falling chandelier and then the bombs start going off.

Forgive me, but life without you is torture.

Men are clearly ridiculous in these young girls' eyes and the absence of men their age suggests the desire to present men in this film as patriarchs. Even men who may be nearer their age are presented, as in the colourised composite shot on the left shows, as silly poseurs who are only interested in the girls as objects of desire.

In another scene in their apartment towards the end of the film, the girls start cutting up magazines, extracting photographs of faces and bodies, which the audience glimpse in very fast montages. They then cut each other up in a playful scissor fight (below left) that employs some clever trick photography and editing, becoming, in the process, literally disembodied representations of women.

They eventually end up 'looking for nourishment' in a disused non-specific facility or factory, where we glimpse the machine that we first saw in the opening shot of the film. They then stumble on the banquet room, which is laid out with a sumptuous feast but is otherwise symbolically deserted. Initially shot in black and white, when Marie 1 breaks a glass, the film switches to colour. A long take follows showing the girls moving from seat to seat and trying various dishes. Their messy and anarchic table manners soon descend into a food fight. They then dance on the dining table and swing on a beautiful crystal chandelier that hangs above it. Appearing to fall from the chandelier they literally end up in deep water. Calling for help they state they don't want to be bad. On-screen text notes that, 'Even if they had a chance, it would probably look like this.' There is sense then that the film is reprimanding them and that they too are contrite.

Returning to the banqueting hall with brooms, now dressed in newspapers and whispering, they proceed to tidy up their mess. 'We'll be happy if we work hard', they note. Having tidied up (not at all convincingly), they recline together (like corpses or dolls) on the dining table (see screenshot on following page). A clock ticks, an audial refrain at various times that has been used throughout the film. Perhaps connoting urgency or timeliness. Their last words are: 'We're really happy. But it doesn't matter.' Their vacillation and confusion is profound.

The chandelier falls on the girls who are lying on a table and there follows military archive footage of bombs going off. Finally, the film finishes with an aerial tracking shot over a bombed-out city, presumably from World War II.

(iA) Independent Activity

Try to find other films that mix up colour palettes. In the golden age of silent cinema this was a common practice but try to find examples from more contemporary films.

As the destruction and desolation unfurls, the sound of a machine gun shoots the words of the dedication onto the screen:

> This film is dedicated to those whose sole source of indignation is trampled-on-trifle.

This final sequence, like the film as a whole, is oblique, but clearly the work ethic beloved of communists has not given the girls happiness, as one grins like a mask while the other looks blank. The pleasures of a promiscuous sex life or the trappings of a wealthy bourgeoisie lifestyle have similarly left them unfulfilled. The film is bookended with scenes and sounds of warfare and certainly the prognosis for youth and young women in this film is not positive. That said, what remains is the effervescent comic hilarity of Marie 1 and Marie 2 and the sheer exuberance of the cinematic experimentation.

In conclusion, *Daisies* is absolutely a film of its time. Spearheading, as any avant-garde work should do, an attack on the dehumanising of the bourgeois and their political values, the film is a triumph. Gender and freedom are foregrounded as issues (something important to Chytilová) but equally the work transcends mere polemic. Yes, the targets are an outmoded patriarchy and a violent war machine that keeps on turning, but equally what is attacked is the aesthetic notion of what a film should be. By playing so drastically with the form of film, the very idea of film is undermined and challenged. The narrative is symbolic and oblique. The characters are at best stereotypes of a certain kind of man and, in terms of Marie 1 and Marie 2, interchangeable. The acting styles (particularly of Marie 1 and Marie 2) are stilted and anarchic. The use of jump-cuts, coloured filters, sped-up and slowed-down footage, staccato edits, time lapse, montage and non-sequential edits in terms of location all serve to disorientate the spectator and the art form. In *Daisies*, Marie 1 and Marie 2 are embroiled in an existential battle for their identities and so is the actual film.

Chantal Akerman

Saute ma ville

Saute ma ville (*Blow Up My Town*, 1968) was a short film produced by Belgian, Chantal Akerman (1950–2015) when she was only 18, having just left the Belgian film school Institut National Supérieur des Arts du Spectacle et des Techniques de Diffusion after one term. The film was successfully screened at the Oberhausen Short Film festival in 1971 and launched Akerman on her long film career, where she became an established figure in feminist discourse and an artist known for using long takes and filming with a minimalist slow and impassive camera style. 1968 was a politically turbulent year in France, and the film's radicalism extends out of this social context and the aesthetic context of the French New Wave. Despite this being Akerman's first film, it sets up interests pursued in her other films (most notably *Jeanne Dielman, 23, Quai du Commerce, 1080 Bruxelles* (Akerman, 1976)) with their focus on isolated women.

In this surreal and experimental short, Akerman directs and acts as the main protagonist. We ostensibly see her returning to her apartment, cooking, cleaning and then eating, before she finally commits suicide by blowing herself up. Akerman would years later take her own life, so this final scene is now infused with a tragic and unintended irony.

The film's technical formal experimentalism and radical ideology are developed in a number of ways, as we will now explore.

Narrative

The narrative expressed in this film is very experimental. On a simple level, a young woman returns to her flat to cook. However, she finds firstly the lift does not respond to her call and then, subsequently, when in her flat, her actions descend into farce. This is seen in the screenshots on the previous page where the act of cleaning her shoes and dancing become chaotic and messy.

As an experimental work the film unsurprisingly eschews conventional narrative structuring so we don't really have anything like a three-act structure and even the character arc is oblique, with action and plot largely focused on domestic activity. There is no on-screen text to guide exposition and only illegible vocalisations to further our comprehension of the character and scene. Neither is time clearly expressed with evident ellipsis between action and no concrete guide to the hours that have passed. Only the spatial treatment is dominant throughout: a recurring motif of entrapment within the domestic sphere. We are clearly aligned with this character but her eventual death is symbolic rather than emotive for the spectator. Thus, Akerman's spare poetics create an impactful scene, heavy on realism in the dreary domestic space and emphasised with a minimalist approach to camera work and editing.

Film form

Cinematography

The film is dominated by the use of hand-held cameras and a seemingly improvised cinematographic style. Akerman resists the more mainstream approach to filming a human subject by cutting in from long shot to close-up; thus much of her film is shot in long shot. This device serves to alienate the audience from the film's protagonist and is developed through the use of a long shot in a mirror. In a number of reflections in mirrors, Akerman returns her own gaze, reclaiming her identity at the same time as she paradoxically objectifies herself. Her disappointment at her reflection arguably leads to her suicide.

Mise-en-scène

The film is shot in a cramped kitchen, devoid of even a view and throughout the film Akerman's conventionally dressed young woman seems hemmed in by her domestic surroundings. Three posters on the kitchen door: a black man in close-up, a cartoon smurf saying 'Go home!' and a close-up shot of Akerman with the words, 'It's me', could all be read as symbols of her infantile alienation and segregation within the home. Women are not 'at home in the home' is one ironic interpretation.

Editing

Jump-cuts and a lack of continuity are noticeable, unhinging Akerman's work from time. The space of the kitchen is, however, treated in the opposite fashion and it is the very lack of editing that enables Akerman to develop the idea of the heart of the home and domesticity as redundant, absurd and claustrophobic space. By holding shots she bears witness to the modern-day drudgery of womankind.

Sound

There is no synchronised diegetic sound. Most sound effects are produced as Foley but they are not slickly made and actually jar the audience, destroying any sense of realism. The overall effect is vaguely comedic until the grim dénouement. Indeed, the central portion of the film is muted and the main protagonist does not speak. Instead, we are privy to what appears to be an inner monologue of discordant humming and garbled muttering. The explosion that presumably kills the protagonist is communicated only through sound and a black screen but is then followed by the protagonist humming again and Akerman herself reading the credits. The patriarchal ideology of female domestication is clearly challenged aurally. Woman have no voice.

Performance

The performance style is absurdist with little attention to characterisation, back-story or narrative arcs. The acting style is exuberant and unnatural, again a break with realism. The protagonist clumsily cleans her kitchen floor, hurriedly eats her supper, comically cleans her shoes, daubing polish all over her legs and socks, and, finally, messily applies beauty cream to her face. Much like in *Daisies*, Akerman's characterisation is that of an archetype (oppressed woman) rather than a study of an individual's psychic collapse. Her death in the film is then a symbolic death of an outmoded form of femininity and the explosion at the very end of the film presages the revolutionary end of patriarchy.

In summary, this film sits very well with *Daisies*. It is the product of another female auteur, arising out of a politicised femininity in the broad context of 1960s European avant-garde filmmaking. Both films adopt a surreal and absurdist approach (there is humour in both films) and so disdain conventional narrative. As a consequence, both films have unnamed and largely symbolic performers acting in non-realist styles. The films conclude with the female protagonists symbolically dying as they fail to make sense of the world or the world fails to make sense of them.

What distinguishes the films is their production contexts: the psychedelic and hugely ambitious feature-length *Daisies* emerging from a state-funded communist film industry with access to studio facilities and a professional crew; *Saute ma ville* emerging from an amateur background, shot in black and white on a micro-budget with a very small crew in virtually one location. Nevertheless, both films are clear examples of a broad 1960s counter-culture working together with an avant-garde aesthetic to push forwards feminist discourse. The films produced are then philosophical and ideological challenges to the status quo of patriarchy (then and now) and as such are examples of very personal films from two remarkable female auteurs.

Aesthetics

Akerman is largely known for her single-camerawork and realism, thus involving long takes. Her aesthetics are in some sense constrained by budget (hence black and white film stock and a single-camera shoot) and scale but also by her desire to depict real lives. The surrealism of at least this short film derives partly from her absurdist sound design, disorientating jump-cuts and a refusal to conform to conventional film mechanics such as using cross-dissolves to show time passing.

Representation in *Saute ma ville*

The key representations in *Saute ma ville* are, not unlike *Daisies*, the two social identities of age and gender, and like *Daisies* the experience presented from an ethnic point of view remains white, liberal and educated. Akerman's housebound protagonist is a counterpoint to the liberated young women of *Daisies*. Indeed, even their eventual fates are similar, although Akerman's is at her own hand. Some commentators have argued that the final scene in the film is an oblique reference to Akerman's Jewish decent and thus a reference to the holocaust and its horrific use of gas ovens to execute millions. Whatever the meaning, it is clear that the domestic space represented here is alienating. Where the girls in *Daisies* play and explore, Akerman's tragic figure has only kitchen utensils and cleaning products as toys. In *Daisies,* society forces Marie 1 and Marie 2 back to conform. In *Saute ma ville* society hasn't even opened-up, so the prison of Akerman's domestic space can only be defeated by the most solemn form of self-expression – suicide.

Summary of auteur signatures

Both women are central figures in their work despite their collaboration with other artists and technicians (Chytilová and her husband the cinematographer, for example). They take writing credit for both films and were also involved in the pre-production process as well as obviously directing. This level of control continued in varying degrees throughout their careers. The key thematic that links both women is that of a broadly feminist, experimental and liberal approach, with an emphasis on issues of personal, political and artistic freedom. Where they may differ is in their specific signatures: Chytilová is a maverick artist whose radical experimentation allows for a kaleidoscope of stylistic and technical features, whereas Akerman champions a more minimalist approach, evoking a higher degree of realism.

 S&C

Watch another one of Akerman's more polished features such as *Jeanne Dielman, 23, Quai du Commerce* or *1080 Bruxelles*.

This section will focus on the experimental film question from the Component 2 paper Global filmmaking perspectives. This area of study is exclusive to the A level and alongside the core areas of study you will need to apply the specialist study areas of **narrative** and **auteur**. This is a single film study and the cult postmodern experimentation of *Pulp Fiction* (Tarantino, USA, 1994) will be explored here.

For A level

In the Component 2, Section D examination there are 20 marks at stake and the expected writing time for an answer is 30 minutes.

The specification says

Alternatives to mainstream narrative film have been present throughout cinema history. The choice here is of films from 1960–2000. Over this period new waves have often challenged the mainstream.

Note: Chapters 10 and 11 offer two choices of case study for this module – only one should be studied.

Postmodern film in the 1990s

Postmodernism is a critical theory that became prominent in the 1970s. Its philosophical impetus came from a sense of distrust over the role of reason in cultural life. Modernism, with its vision of an endless process of rational progress, was flawed. The deification of reason and the idea of rationality that underpins all scientific and technological advances had lost some of its authority; as had other 'grand narratives' such as religion and the big all-explaining theories of human nature and cultural behaviour such as those of Marx and Freud. The postmodern world was one where foundationalist views were now not to be trusted. Lyotard, a key philosopher of the movement, argued that there is no reason any more, only reasons.

The essence of the postmodern text can be summarised in a few key words, which, when appearing in a film in various combinations, can suggest postmodernity:

1 **Intertextuality**: referencing other cultural products, such as films.

2 **Self-referential**: referencing the filmmaking process through such techniques as breaking the fourth wall.

3 **Randomness**: abrupt juxtapositions or non-sequiturs.

4 **Artifice or style over substance**: depth of meaning is lost beneath technique.

5 **Playfulness or surfaces over depth**: a reluctance to treat the project seriously.

6 **Fragmentation of time and space and personal identity**: people and places become transferrable or unhinged from temporality and notions of concrete identity. Thus, the film becomes ahistorical, existing almost beyond any specific cultural context. A social realist film would then become the polar opposite of such a postmodern movie.

7 **Copying, pastiche or homage**: explicit recreation of cultural products such as scenes or lines from films. At its extreme form this can result in parody.

8 **Irony**: tongue-in cheek approach to the narrative and character and theme.

This is not an exclusive list of ideas but it should be clear that a film text that employs a combination of these in a conscious way could probably be called postmodern. Tarantino's films almost universally fit this schema.

It's well known that Tarantino has lived in and around LA for much of his life and that he spent five years working as a video store clerk as well as training to act. His films are those of a cinephile who has soaked up global film culture, as well as a love for films originating in both the heart and hinterlands of Hollywood.

All of Tarantino's films (at time of writing – May 2018) can be seen as expressions of the postmodern impulse. As illustration, by just focusing on his use of homage and intertextuality we can see elements of his postmodern and auteurist credentials:

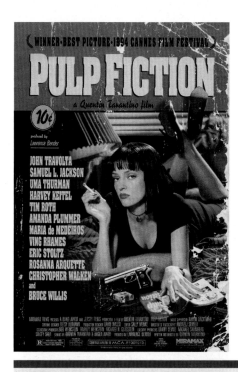

(iA) Independent Activity

Research postmodernism on YouTube, which is easy and rewarding. There are many attempts to summarise it in potted ways but it is a slippery concept that often resists precise definition. Find a definition that you like and understand and note it down.

 S&C

Be brave and try reading about Lyotard and Baudrillard, two French theorists of the postmodern. Summarise their key ideas in 100 words.

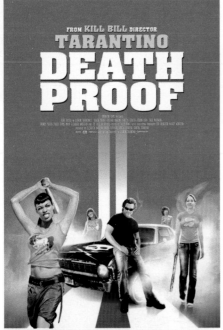

- *Jackie Brown* (1997): a homage to the Foxy Brown Blaxploitation films of the early 1970s, which starred Pam Grier as the eponymous Jackie Brown.
- *Kill Bill 1 & 2* (2003/2004): a homage to 1960s and 1970s Japanese and Chinese martial art and gangster films, featuring a cameo from legendary martial artist and film star Sonny Chiba and a very specific reference to Bruce Lee's yellow suit from *Game of Death* (Lee, 1978).
- *Death Proof* (2007): released initially as a double bill under the title *Grindhouse* with a film by Tarantino's friend and collaborator Robert Rodriguez, this film is a homage to the low-budget and often independently produced films that found their way onto the low-fi and rather scuzzy grindhouse film circuit.
- *Django Unchained* (2012): a homage to an Italian cycle of spaghetti westerns from the 1960s and 1970s, the first of which featured Franco Nero as the eponymous Django. Nero has a cameo in Tarantino's film.
- *The Hateful Eight* (2015): a homage to Sergio Leone's spaghetti western trilogy from the 1960s, scored by the same composer, the legendary Ennio Morricone.

In a 2012 *Sight & Sound* poll to select the greatest films of all time, contemporary directors were asked to select ten films of their choice. Tarantino idiosyncratically picked 12, which are listed below:

- *Apocalypse Now* (Coppola, 1979)
- *The Bad News Bears* (Ritchie, 1976)
- *Carrie* (Peirce, 2013)
- *Dazed and Confused* (Linklater, 1994)
- *The Good, the Bad and the Ugly* (Leone, 1968)
- *The Great Escape* (Sturges, 1963)
- *His Girl Friday* (Hawks, 1940)
- *Jaws* (Spielberg, 1975)
- *Pretty Maids All in a Row* (Vadim, 1971)
- *Rolling Thunder* (Flynn, 1977)
- *Sorcerer* (Friedkin, 1977)
- *Taxi Driver* (Scorsese, 2006).

What is significant from this list is firstly an absence of high-art films and a predominance of relatively low-brow crowd pleasers such as the horror films *Jaws* or *Carrie,* classic spaghetti western *The Good, the Bad and the Ugly* or the war movie *The Great Escape*. Equally, there are forgotten left-field classics such as *Sorcerer, Rolling Thunder* and *Pretty Maids all in a Row*. What is obvious is a predominance of 1970s films, which form the bulk of the films chosen. Yes, there are some established great films of the contemporary canon such as *Apocalypse Now* and *Raging Bull* but ultimately this list is a reflection of Tarantino's early teens in the mid-1970s and represents a fan's eye view of cinematic history rather than one learned at film school – somewhere Tarantino did not go.

Such was the impact of Tarantino's style, numerous copyists soon turned his early film forays into a movement, although a loose one with no oaths or allegiances as was witnessed in the ultra-realist Dogme95 Movement from Denmark. In a *Variety* interview (Debruge, 2013) it is noted that, 'Tarantino specializes in recycling' and the article cites an earlier interview in *Empire* magazine where Tarantino stated, 'I steal from every single movie ever made.' This 'cultural recycling' is yet further evidence of Tarantino's postmodernity emerging through the ideas of intertextuality and homage.

Social, political and cultural contexts

Pulp Fiction depicts a non-specific almost timeless LA. Indeed, the film's rich use of nostalgic music and mise-en-scène coupled with a highly unconventional form of narrative and cinematic realism means the film can best be located in a postmodern cultural context. As such the text has a rootless quality that does not allow for explicit social, historical and cultural analysis. On such a reading, *Pulp Fiction* is one of those cultural texts which emerged in the early 1990s that began the trend for ever increasingly postmodern play in the media as a whole and culminated most recently in the prominence of such concepts of 'post-truth' and its implied conflation of such notions as 'fact' and 'fiction'.

Institutional contexts

Pulp Fiction is arguably one of the first, and certainly the highest profile, films to be categorised as postmodern, and as such it is clear why the exam board has positioned it in a unit called 'Film Movements (experimental film 1960–2000)'. As noted earlier, the exam board refers to film as 'the epitome of postmodern' going on to note that it, 'plays with narrative and other cinematic conventions in boldly experimental ways while remaining entirely accessible'. Few would argue. Unlike the heavily symbolic and coded films discussed above, *Pulp Fiction* is in many ways a straightforward generic homage with a cool twist; it's a crime film without cops, where the central characters, various criminal types clinging to the underbelly of lowlife LA, are given ample screen time and dialogue to establish their characters and motivations. On a stylistic level there are moments of experimentation but nothing with the wild frenzy and anarchic joy of *Daisies*. The key to this film is largely in its narrative experimentation and perceived auteur status.

The latter point is illustrated by the fact that the film remains Tarantino's defining film in a body of work currently consisting of nine feature films. Its circular narrative and atypical representations of both antagonists and protagonists plus its now trademark script, make it quintessential Tarantino. He announced his postmodern styling with *Reservoir Dogs* (1992) and in his script for *True Romance* (1993), but with *Pulp Fiction* he achieved mainstream success. Of his body of work only *Inglorious Basterds* (2009) and *Django Unchained* (2012) have grossed more worldwide. Indeed, *Pulp Fiction* was the first American independent film to earn over $100 million at the US box office and heralded the arrival of Indiewood as a production phenomenon. It won the Palme d'Or at Cannes and an Oscar for Best Original Screenplay, both in 1994. Even though it was only his second film, his cinematic signature or voice was strong enough to refer to in the marketing.

The film's marketing also plays on the film's pulp (cheaply produced), B-movie, low-budget influences, if not execution, with a budget of approximately $8.5 million. Uma Thurman, in a wig, is styled as a femme fatale thus referring more to the genre of noir rather than her star status, which was at the time still in the ascendancy. Indeed, the film is actually a kind of **portmanteau film** and has no central star, as evidenced by the many Hollywood heavyweights credited, each having their cameo scenes or sequences.

 Independent Activity

To understand *Pulp Fiction* you need to know a little about the film genre it was paying homage to and revising: **film noir**. Read the film noir section on filmsite.org and summarise the key elements of the genre.

Film noir: a type of criminal film that originated in the USA in the 1930s with its origins in pulp crime fiction. It subsequently found its way onto radio and by the 1940s was a discernible sub-genre. Common tropes involved a downbeat and grizzled private detective, weak, morally compromised men, and strong, amoral and sexual femme fatales. Lighting codes were typically low-key, high contrast thus creating a gloomy sense of foreboding and mystery as well as the frequent uses of window blinds in the mise-en-scène to further create a sense of entrapment. Jazz scoring was also common as was a lurid sensationalism such as explicit sensuality and brutal violence. Contemporary noir films such as *Pulp Fiction* are often dubbed 'neo-noir'.

 S&C

In order to understand an auteur you must consider a variety of their films. Look at two more of Tarantino's films and then revisit *Pulp Fiction* and list the commonalities.

Portmanteau film: a film that consists of loosely related but largely distinct storylines. Famous examples could be the UK's seminal horror from Ealing Studios, *Dead of Night* (Cavalanati, Dearaden, Harner & Crichton, 1945) and *Four Rooms* (Tarantino, Rodriguezz, Anders & Rockwell, 1995), which featured a story called 'The Man from Hollywood' written and directed by Tarantino.

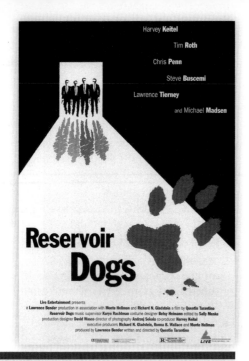

 S&C

Look at the cameos Hitchcock made in his own films; YouTube has plenty of fan-generated montages. Note their humour. Does this trait make Hitchcock postmodern?

Three-act structure: a model used in narrative that divides a story into three parts, often called the setup, the confrontation and the resolution.

Part of the contexts surrounding this film is the fact that it is Miramax's first fully funded film, their deal with Disney having gone through in 1993. The script impressed studio boss Harvey Weinstein, while being rejected by Columbia TriStar, and had been shopped around by Tarantino's producer Lawrence Bender. Bender had formed a production company with Tarantino named A Band Apart, a pun on Godard's 1964 film *Bande à Part* and Miramax gave the company $1 million for script development, which helped Tarantino (and later his co-writing partner Roger Avery) stay in Amsterdam and work on it. Elements of their 'research' entered into the opening dialogue with Jules and Vincent where Vincent talks about Europe and 'the little differences' such as mayonnaise on fries rather than ketchup and the etiquette of hash bars.

Buoyed by the critical success of *Reservoir Dogs*, Miramax and A Band Apart were able to recruit, on basic rates, fading male stars, most notably John Travolta and Bruce Willis, who both experienced career revivals courtesy of *Pulp Fiction*. The involvement of Willis in particular meant that international sales basically recouped outlay, thus ensuring the film would at least go into profit whether it succeeded or not at the box office. The supporting cast too was excellent, making household names of people such as Samuel L. Jackson and Uma Thurman, and further invigorating the career of Harvey Keitel who Tarantino had also cast in *Reservoir Dogs*. Tarantino performed cameos too, something he would do in a number of his films and something pioneered by Alfred Hitchcock.

Narrative

Beginning and endings

The film deconstructs the notion of narrative arcs and indeed the **three-act structure**, as we can see more clearly in the later section on narrative structure, is also contorted and misshapen in Tarantino's hands. However, there is the use of chapter headings and on-screen text to guide the spectator and certainly the presentation of on-screen space with its heightened sense of realism eases the viewer through the complexities of times shifts – not least the sudden death of Vincent and then his return to the diner scene that concludes the film and extends the opening sequence.

Dialogue, costume and performance are all fundamental points of interest in a Tarantino film and provide the spectator with plenty of exposition. Indeed, the heavy use of dialogue enables the spectator to align with numerous characters not least the hit men Vincent and Jules. And finally the film's use of narrative circularity enables us to perfectly seal off the narrative from disruption and play out the ending again and again – given that one of the main narrative devices used in *Pulp Fiction* is its circularity, then the close study of the opening and closing sequences is particularly worthwhile. In the opening shot we meet two small-time criminals, Pumpkin and Honey Bunny, who chat at length about the etiquette of robbery in a characteristic dialogue-heavy scene (largely shot as a low-angle two shot) before they hold up the diner they're eating in. Aside from establishing Tarantino's novel approach to screenwriting (holding scenes for a long time and building rich characterisations, even for antagonists, through whimsical dialogue), we also see the germination of characters (two psychotic lovers) which he later developed in his story material for Oliver Stone's *Natural Born Killers* (1995), itself a classic example of postmodern film.

Honey Bunny's transformation into a horrifically violent robber is immortalised in the words that she speaks. The image then freeze-frames and the iconic music that intros *Pulp Fiction* by Dick Dale and the Del Tones (a 1960s surf rock band) runs over the intentionally 'pulp styled' titles. To the right we see the two small-time crooks (a classic noir trope) holding up the diner.

In the final sequence (see right) we are back in the diner but this time from the perspective of Jules and Vincent. The last shot tracks them as they leave the diner having talked Honey Bunny and Pumpkin into making a quick getaway. The film cuts as they comically exit the building, dressed in their borrowed summer clothes (definitely not in character), walking in unison like a comic duo and holstering their guns in their shorts' waistbands. It seems like every criminal in the diner, as in the film as a whole, fails to fulfil stereotypical expectations.

Thus, the film has disturbed our notion of genre and narrative in its off-kilter characterisations and its odd circularity. The spectator gets a satisfying dénouement in that Jules and Vincent leave the scene of the crime in possession of the moral high ground. This ending is in many ways a conventional resolution to a noir-themed film: the anti-heroes get the job done and leave morally and physically intact. However, the fact that we know that Vincent will subsequently die forces the spectator to revisit the film and so search for a comforting resolution that just isn't there. It is this that makes Tarantino's masterpiece so satisfying and disconcerting at the same time. The narrative shifts beneath the spectator's feet: a very typical and now commonplace postmodern feature.

Film form

Cinematography

Aside from the opening and endings, one of the most celebrated sequences in the film is the one that introduces us to the hit men, Vincent and Jules. The sequence seen in the screenshot on the right is largely shot in a deep-focus, two-shot, close-up from within a car driven by Jules, emphasising the film's realism. As in the diner sequence that preceded this scene, the dialogue is rambling and inflected with cultural references. There are 'the little differences' between Europe and the USA. McDonald's, Wendy's and Burger King also get name-checked. The conversation continues to the next scene as they walk to do 'a hit', this time revolving around, firstly, the nature of TV pilot shows and, secondly, the etiquette of giving foot massages. This subject matter is both tender and amusing. It is amusing because we realise these killers are just like us, as much concerned with the minutiae of daily life as we are; they could as easily be discussing musical styles and hair-care products. Their conversation topics are tender because they reveal a mild social anxiety in both men and humanise them: Jules in particular is concerned about the social niceties of foot massages. Their sharp suits look similar to the suits worn by the key protagonists in Tarantino's first feature, *Reservoir Dogs*, and have a retro 1960s styling not unlike the choice of music Tarantino used to score the film. All these cinematic features (self-referential, intertextual, homage) are postmodern traits.

The now classic 'boot/trunk shot' (see right) wasn't invented by Tarantino but he did popularise the low-angle shot and has used it in a number of his films. The film has many low-angle shots, although this is the most extreme example.

The impact of this shot is to situate the spectator into the film text, forcing them to adopt the point of view of an imagined victim. Bodies in car boots is a familiar trope in crime films dating back at least to *White Heat* (Walsh, 1949) but in Tarantino's hands Jules and Vincent become ominously and terrifyingly powerful. The shot thus intimidates and victimises us in one image.

Mise-en-scène

Aside from the use of a retro-styling in all aspects of hair and clothing, the settings are all non-descript and realist – except one: the celebrated scene where Vincent and Mia Wallace visit a faux restaurant, Jack Rabbit Slims. It is full of movie and music references such as the 'Douglas Sirk steak', Marilyn Monroe and Buddy Holly waiting staff, and film posters on the wall. The dance scene that follows between Vincent and Mia is a homage to the dance scene in Godard's movie *Band à part* (1964), which was also the name of Tarantino's production company, A Band Apart (1991–2006). Marilyn Monroe (left) is paid homage to with her iconic performance from *The Seven Year Itch* (Wilder, 1955). Once again, Tarantino's magpie approach to collecting filmic references earmarks him as postmodern.

Editing

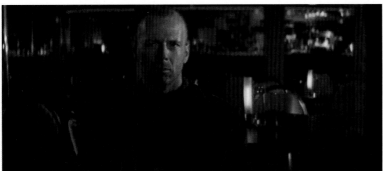

A key feature of Tarantino's work is his use of long takes. These tend to have two connotations: intensity and realism. In the example above left we get our first close-up of the film's star, Bruce Willis, playing a fading boxer, Butch, and gangland boss, Marsellus Wallace, who is telling him to take a dive in a fight. Butch barely says a word but Tarantino audaciously holds the shot for two minutes before cutting to a wider over-the-shoulder shot (see above right). Tarantino lets the script direct rather than following the conventional mechanics of shot/reverse shot. The effect is to create an unsettling intensity and builds tension and characterisation. This is certainly an auteurist trait seen frequently in his other films such as the deeply unsettling opening of *Inglorious Basterds*.

We have already noted that Tarantino loves a long take but he is not averse to using montage when the script demands it. Thus, we see Vincent cooking-up some heroin in a montage that helps to convey his 'rush', followed by Vincent's high where he appears to float, as if in a dream, against intentionally unrealistic back projection.

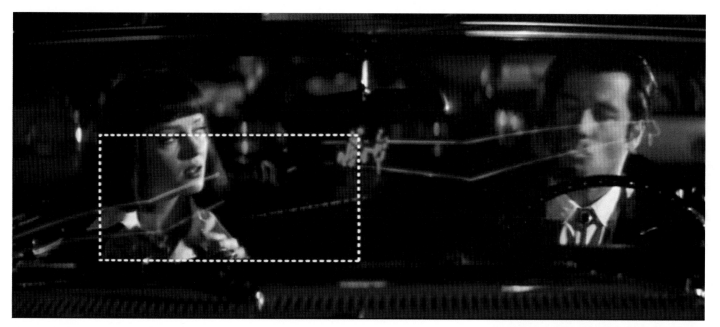

A standout moment in the film, which serves no narrative purpose and absolutely flags up the film's post-production, postmodern style, occurs in the screenshot above when Mia draws a square on the screen as she tells Vincent not to be a square. This self-conscious and self-reflexive styling is typical of Tarantino's work, as well as one of the defining features of the postmodern. It is playful and breaks the realist illusion of the film while we are reminded as spectators that we are watching a construct.

Sound

Another defining feature of Tarantino's films is his music, which often acts as the germ for his narrative creativity. This is most clearly seen from the very first scene in his first film *Reservoir Dogs* where Tarantino himself, as Mr Brown, discusses at length the sexual meaning of Madonna's pop song, *Like a Virgin*. This is an example of postmodernism's preference for pop culture referencing. Tarantino has a real ear for reenergising retro classics from the 1950s/1960s/1970s and the soundtracks of his first two films in particular became mainstream CD successes. The music also, as all good music should, embellishes character rather than merely underscoring the narrative. An example from *Pulp Fiction* is the dance-off with Mia and Vincent at Jack Rabbit Slim's where they jive to *You Never Can Tell* by Chuck Berry and start to romantically bond. The choice of music itself connotes a blossoming romance and an unexpected attraction.

Tarantino's tendency to hold shots means songs can be played for their duration or at least for much longer than the snippets often heard in many conventional Hollywood films. Sometimes the music is diegetic, as when we first meet Mia Wallace a song is playing diegetically, stopping when she takes the needle off the record. Later, after Mia and Vincent return from their night out, Mia puts on a tape recording of yet more diegetic music. This use of sound, embedding it in the context of the narrative diegetically, adds to the film's realism and increases our empathy for the main characters.

 Independent Activity

Research other fourth-wall breaks. These are moments where the audience is made aware of the fictional nature of the narrative. They could be oblique, self-referential moments in a film, such as the one above involving Mia drawing onto the film, or more explicit moments in a film when a character directly addresses the spectator. Examples of this include the final scene of *Goodfellas* (Scorsese, 1990) or numerous moments in *Fight Club* (Fincher, 1999). Watch at least three and note the possible impacts on the spectator.

Independent Activity

Watch the pivotal scenes of music and violence in Tarantino's other films such as the Candyland shootout in *Django Unchained*, or the torture scene in *Reservoir Dogs*, or the Crazy 88 battle in *Kill Bill* and make notes on how the music impacts upon your response to the scene.

Performance

Pulp Fiction resurrected the career of 1970s star John Travolta, gave cult status to actors such as Harvey Keitel and Samuel L. Jackson, and even boosted Bruce Willis' star persona, which was then in descent. The film also helped Tarantino forge a relationship with rising star Uma Thurman, casting her again in his two *Kill Bill* films. Tarantino is definitely an actor's director; his scripts are dialogue heavy, full of sub-text and he himself acts. His already noted love of the long take, which gives actors the opportunity to invest depth and detail in their characterisations, can lead to performances of great intensity. In *Pulp Fiction* we see this in numerous scenes aside from those mentioned above, including Christopher Walken's flashback comic cameo in the story of Butch's gold watch, and Samuel L. Jackson's terrifyingly intense recital of the Bible passage from Ezekiel. These scenes therefore remind us that Tarantino is a writer who loves his characters and wants them to live and breathe despite their origins as stock characters in B-movie genres.

Representations in *Pulp Fiction*

Ethnicity

Pulp Fiction is notable for its heavy use of the racist term 'nigger', something that Spike Lee in his occasional war with Tarantino has taken exception to, most recently with the furore over *Django Unchained*, which Lee felt was disrespectful and exploitative of black history. However, Alan Stone in his 1995 review of *Pulp Fiction* in the *Boston Review* reads the film as 'politically correct':

> *There is no nudity and no violence directed against women ...*
> [It] *celebrates interracial friendship and cultural diversity; there are strong women and strong black men, and the director swims against the current of class stereotype.*

Tarantino certainly is an inclusive director in that he casts black and Asian men and women in many of his films and *Pulp Fiction* is noticeable for the prominence of Jules, as well Marsellus Wallace.

Both men are interesting and charismatic criminals with a moral code. Marsellus' character is developed beyond the stereotypical gangland boss. When we first meet him talking to Butch he seems considered and calm, a man to be respected, but not an unhinged mobster. His wife is perhaps his weakness, and that we never see him and her together may indicate a rift between them. His violent jealousy over one of his henchmen giving her a foot massage suggests that beneath the cool exterior passions rage but even after being sodomised he manages to retain his aplomb.

As for Jules he is certainly the only character to go on a really transformative journey. Yes, Butch escapes a life of punch-drunk rigged boxing matches but he doesn't truly change as a person. That sense of epiphany and revelation is reserved for Jules who is presented as a rounded character, not least because he quotes passages from the Bible and gives his mother foot massages but because he feels deeply. Indeed, the final scene where Jules buys the life of Pumpkin so he doesn't have to kill him is evident of an emerging moral seriousness. As Jules says, with reference to the much quoted Biblical reading that he gives to his victims, Ezekiel 25:17,

> *Truth is you're weak. I'm the tyranny of evil men. But I'm tryin' I'm tryin' real hard to be a shepherd.*

Gender

Tarantino writes great roles for women (*Kill Bill*, *Jackie Brown*, etc.) and certainly Mia Wallace has a stand-out role in *Pulp Fiction*. However, the narrative is still largely focused on the male experience of Jules, Vincent and Butch, as it was in *Reservoir Dogs*. That said, Mia does have power and she clearly is in charge of her own destiny (despite the heroin overdose), something that Vincent is clearly not. Mia's representation is intriguing because she is not a conventional femme fatale and neither is she a stereotypical gangster's moll. Her back story as a failed actress is intriguingly developed when she tells Vincent about her role, and the fact that she is never shot in a scene with her husband Marsellus Wallace, uses cocaine heavily and is so bored that she needs her husband's henchmen to take her out as escorts. She's a thrill-seeker who is no longer thrilled. Her sudden attraction to Vincent is sweetly presented, especially in the dance scene at Jack Rabbit Slim's, but never consummated, as Tarantino pulls-the-rug on her, Vincent and the spectator, with Mia's unexpected overdose on heroin. Tarantino has his critics in terms of misogyny but his films often show women avenging themselves on either men or the minions of men, and in some oblique way, the odd and awkward date with Vincent is just that. Her transgression barely averts disaster and, shocked and traumatised, both her and Vincent are forced to pretend the evening never really happened. It was perhaps a lucky escape for both of them, as a sexually consummated affair would have lead to Vincent's death (Marsellus is a jealous husband).

Other Tarantino films that exhibit female empowerment are *Death Proof* (2007), where the antagonist, the murderous and psychotic misogynist Stuntman Mike, dies at the hands of the film's female protagonists, and in Tarantino's ultimate anthem to the oppressed, *Inglorious Basterds* (2009), where he shows the decimation of Hitler and the Nazis at the hands of a Jewish woman and a black man.

Age

Pulp Fiction isn't obviously concerned with this representational issue as there are, for example, no obvious juxtapositions between the old and young. That said, the youngest people represented, the 20-something students who Vincent and Jules kill, are shown to be clearly out of their depth in a world where innocence is crushed. The more elderly characters, such as Captain Koons and Mr Wolfe, are depicted as largely wise and dignified if not a little quirky. Wolfe, for example, is a man quintessentially equipped to fix problems in the quickest time and with the least fuss. His arrival at Jimmie's house (played by Tarantino) to clear up the carnage following the accidental killing of Marvin makes Vincent and Jules seem inept and foolish. In order to effect a spotless 'clean-up' of the situation Wolfe instructs Vincent and Jules to burn their blood-stained clothes and dress in ill-fitting and un-cool summer beach wear donated by Jimmie. The swift and comic costume change acts as a signifier both of their changing identities and their unity as members of a criminal gang. Jules is, however, the character who, it is implied, will gain maturity, electing to retire from the mob; Vincent, though, as we have already discovered, will don his dark suit again and die, unable to escape a life of immature violence and pleasure seeking.

 Independent Activity

Look at Spike Lee's film *Do the Right Thing* (1989), a film full of racist slang. Research Spike Lee's comments on Tarantino's use of racist terms to gain a better understanding of why Lee, and others, are troubled by a white director using the n word so frequently.

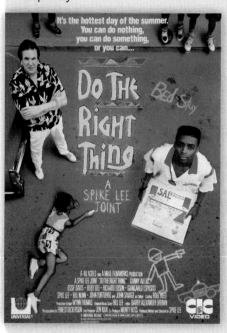

Representing violence

Aside from Tarantino's extreme use of profane language (265 uses of the F-word according to IMDb) his reverence for kinetically filmed violence is also a distinguishing feature of his work. In *Pulp Fiction* the violence is largely verbal and implied, cameras panning away at the crucial moment; something Tarantino did in his first feature *Reservoir Dogs* with the infamous ear-torture scene. In *Pulp Fiction*, seven characters die but only Vincent is a main character, his death in part triggered by his propensity to go to the toilet at the wrong moment: he was in the toilet when Mia overdosed and when Honey Bunny and Pumpkin held up the diner. Other deaths are implied rather than graphically witnessed and only Marvin's gory end is gruesomely depicted, but largely for its black comedy rather than its spectacle.

Perhaps the darkest and most blackly comic scene, with yet another of Tarantino's plot swerves, is the scene that involves Butch and Marsellus in the dungeon sex den.

Postmodern postscript –
the decontextualised theory

James Woods in the *Guardian* scathingly noted:

> *Tarantino represents the final triumph of postmodernism, which is to empty the artwork of all content ..., so entirely stripped of any politics, metaphysics, or moral interest.* (quoted in Gormley, 2005, page 25)

At first glance Woods seems correct and there are few historical/social/political insights that can be gleaned from the film other than its prominent position as a leading example of postmodern filmmaking. Postmodernism is a tricky concept but Tarantino's take on it certainly fits the profile, as we have now seen: ironic, intertextual, self-referential, full of homage and pastiche, playful and stylish. All style and no substance as Woods seems to argue. But then again is that fair? We have already noted that marginal characters of race and gender do seem to receive positive billing in many of Tarantino's films.

Indeed, it could be argued that Tarantino is a subversive who despite some postmodern playfulness does develop ideological critiques; perhaps oblique ones but ones that have some punch. He breaks the rules of genre by humanising the generic character tropes. He shows that the rules for cinematically representing and classifying people are at worst inept and at best in need of some revision. Tarantino's ability to humanise stock characters such as Vincent and Jules is important for this very reason as, no matter how amoral they are, we find ourselves empathising with them. And generic convention too, with its comforting narrative arcs and neat resolutions, is something Tarantino also challenges – thus Vincent dies an inglorious death (only to be reborn in the chronologically unhinged last sequence), Marvin is shot by accident in the car and Jules has a religious epiphany.

Tarantino's famous set pieces also subvert convention and unsettle the comfy moral universe of genre films. To argue they are merely style over substance is to miss the point. Tarantino's **humanist irony** is a moral position by which to view the world; a world where the old structures (the grand narratives) no longer apply but where moral outcomes are still achievable. So, for example, in *Pulp Fiction* (as in the more recent *Inglorious Basterds* and *Django Unchained*) Jules becomes the good shepherd rather than the avenging angel; Vincent

Humanist irony: can be conceived as an approach to art that highlights the human condition in a rather tongue-in-cheek way. Thus, in a broadly comedic sense, we explore our nature such as the need for personal identity and freedom.

saves Mia's life; Butch outwits Marsellus and runs off with Fabienne; Marsellus 'gets medieval' on the sadistic rednecks; and Butch retains his father's gold watch. All 'happy endings' by most standards.

Amiable and laconic Vincent is, however, less fortunate, and his fate suggests further room for analysis. Peter and Will Brooker (1996) note,

> In three significant moments Vincent retires to the bathroom [and] *returns to an utterly changed world where death is threatened.*

The threat increases as the narrative progresses chronologically leading to his death. The Brookers' analysis continues,

> *Through Vincent … we see the contemporary world as utterly contingent, transformed, disastrously, in the instant you are not looking.*

It is perhaps in the area of 'influence' and enduring cultural resonance that Tarantino has had the most impact. His films haven't changed the moral or political landscape but they have certainly contributed to film culture. Phil Hoad in the *Guardian* (2013) asked this very question

> *Is Quentin Tarantino the World's Most Influential Director?*

He went on to cite the *Collins Dictionary*, which had then defined the adjective 'Tarantinoesque' as referring to or reminiscent of the violence and wit of Tarantino's films. His influence remains and, according to the article above, can be found in 'any lippy thriller featuring pop culture-fried dialogue and flip violence'. Guy Ritchie and *Dead Pool* take note!

In conclusion, Tarantino is clearly an auteur in the sense that he has a vision that emerges in his control of the medium. This ranges from effective collaboration with such actors as Uma Thurman, Tim Roth and Harvey Keitel to his late editor Sally Menke. He writes, acts, produces and of course directs, and his choice of music as well as his frequent cinematic homages make his control of the medium intense.

Narrative

Structure

One of the film's most obvious postmodern traits (aside from irony, homage, intertextuality and self-referencing) is its narrative playfulness. The narrative can at best be described as episodic and circular and broadly in three acts. Equally, the appeal of the characters is worth noting, something Tarantino has worked hard to engender through his script. In terms of motivation for the characters, the normal given of monetary greed is less apparent than in many crime films and what is at stake is, rather, morality.

Below is a summary of the narrative in terms of its plotting. This may be of use to place the key narrative beats and observe the film's famous use of circularity. The bold represents chapter headings showing that the film is broadly structured around three acts with a **preface** and **coda** in the diner. The narrative strands are colour coded to aid understanding and awareness of the patterns.

Preface: a sequence in a film that sets the scene but which may not concern the dramatic focus of the film.

Coda: refers to the final narrative resolution in a film, which may not be primarily concerned with the film's main protagonist.

- Scene 1: Honey Bunny and Pumpkin hold the diner up.
- Scene 2: Vincent and Jules drive to their 'hit' – dressed in sharp, black suits. We learn that Vincent has been asked to look after his Boss's wife the following evening. They kill the young men who have cheated Marsellus Wallace (their boss) and retrieve his 'goods' in a mysterious briefcase.
- Scene 3: **Vincent Vega and Marsellus Wallace's wife**. In a bar. Marsellus Wallace tells Butch to throw a boxing match. Jules and Vincent walk in with the briefcase but oddly dressed in shorts. We learn Vincent's 'date' with Mia Wallace is the next evening. Butch and Vincent eyeball each other.
- Scene 4: Vincent scores some heroin from his friend and dealer.
- Scene 5: Vincent gets high and drives to pick Mia Wallace up.
- Scene 6: Vincent and Mia eat and dance at Jack Rabbit Slim's.
- Scene 7: Vincent and Mia return to her house. She OD's.
- Scene 8: Vincent drives Mia to Lance, his drug dealer's house and they resuscitate Mia.
- Scene 9: Vincent drives Mia home.
- Scene 10: Butch as a kid getting a visit from a soldier who knew his dead dad in a Vietnam POW camp. The man presents Butch with a family heirloom, a gold watch that his dad had hidden up his anus for five years. His dad died of dysentery and so his friend kept the watch for two further years up his own anus.
- Scene 11: **The gold watch**. Butch's fight – only heard not seen. He doesn't go down and escapes the venue in a yellow cab driven by a beautiful lady, Esmerelda. Marsellus wants him dead. Esmerelda and Butch talk about killing, as the fighter who fought against Butch has died.
- Scene 12: Butch returns to a hotel room with his girlfriend, Fabienne. He discovers his father's watch is still at their old apartment.
- Scene 13: Butch returns to get his watch and shoots Vincent as he comes out of the toilet.
- Scene 14: On his way back he meets Marsellus at a crossing, runs him down and is then concussed in a car accident. Marsellus chases Butch.
- Scene 15: Both injured men end up in a pawn shop run by sadists.
- Scene 16: Both men awaken, tied to chairs in a darkened basement used for torture. Two men seem set to torture them and the leather-clad 'Gimp' is brought out from a box. Butch escapes his bonds while Marsellus is being raped in a back room. He almost leaves the shop but decides to stay and rescue Marsellus with a samurai blade. Marsellus and Butch make their peace.
- Scene 17: Butch gets a chopper motorbike and rides off into the sunset with his girlfriend Fabienne.
- Scene 18: **The Bonnie situation.** We return to the end of scene 2. A fourth man, hiding in the bathroom, appears but doesn't successfully shoot Jules and Vincent. Jules has a religious epiphany. They decide to take the lone survivor, Marvin, to Marsellus.
- Scene 19: Vincent accidentally shoots Marvin in the car. They call a friend, Jimmy (Tarantino doing a cameo).
- Scene 20: 'Mr Fix It' – The Wolf is summoned. He arrives 'nine minutes and thirty seven seconds later …' according to on-screen text.
- Scene 21: Jules and Vincent clean the car, strip off their bloody clothes and wear some of Jimmy's summer cast-offs.
- Scene 22: They take the car and body to a breaker's yard. Mr Wolf drives off.
- Scene 23: Jules and Vincent end up at the diner where the film begins and witness the attempted robbery by Pumpkin and Honey Bunny. Jules, still feeling religious, talks them out of it. Vincent and Jules walk out of the diner.

Key:
Yellow: preface and coda in the diner
Green: Vincent and/or Jules
Blue: Marsellus and/or Butch and/or Fabienne
Red: Vincent and/or Mia
Grey: flashback to Butch's youth and the gold watch story

Aside from the film's famous circularity, what is clear from this synopsis of the plot is the unusually convoluted and experimental treatment of time. Thus, in the middle of the 'Second Act', Butch kills Vincent, who is now acting as an incidental character in Butch's story. However, in the 'Third Act', we return to the story of Vincent and Jules from earlier in 'Act 1'. This unusual plotting device was arguably behind Columbia's refusal to fund the film but it is surprisingly effective from a spectator's viewpoint. We are pleased to meet Vincent again, having met him with Jules and then seen his awkward date with Mia. The shock of his death is thus ameliorated and his amiable character given something of a mythic status.

Tarantino as auteur

Tarantino is one of the 21st century's most recognisable auteurs. Unlike a Spielberg film which may need close analysis to unearth its auteurist traits, a Tarantino film has a very strong signature. He achieves this through a number of devices and thematic treatments. On a technical level in terms of mise-en-scène there is then Tarantino's use of vibrant colour, a hyperreal approach to set design and a penchant for retro clothing. His work lends itself to merchandising precisely because it has a cool iconic look and sound. There is also his much vaunted extreme use of violence – both implied and depicted. Films such as *Kill Bill Vol. 1* and *Inglorious Basterds* feature extreme violence but something that is depicted in a comic book style – the death of Hitler, for example, at the end of the latter film. Tarantino also favours long takes in scenes, enabling the development of unbearable tension and character. His films have great action set pieces and tend to feature a love of anti-heroes. No-one in Pulp Fiction is snow white and even Django the abused slave in *Django Unchained* is a killing machine. He tends to score his films with evocative music played at length. Tarantino loves genre films, homages old films of the 60s and 70s, and even casts aging actors as a tribute to the roles they played as younger men and women – Pam Grier, the queen of 70s Blaxploitation films playing Jackie Brown, for example, in Tarantino's 1997 homage to that sub-genre. However, the key feature of Tarantino, at least for this author, is his postmodern treatment of narrative, constantly disrupting the spectator's expectations and his ironic tongue-in-cheek approach to dialogue and stock characterisation.

Sample essay extract and feedback

> Explore how far your chosen film or films are experimental in challenging conventional approaches to narrative.

For this example we are looking at an **extract** from an essay addressing *Pulp Fiction*.

Niamh's response extract

Pulp Fiction absolutely challenges conventional narrative approaches. For example, given the film's broadly noir styling, themes and characterisations, it is significant that the film almost starts and certainly ends with two arguably peripheral characters: two hitmen for a mob boss, Vincent and Jules. Such stock characters are normally expendable and have little or no back-story: Vincent and Jules are, however, presented differently by Tarantino, who not only directed and performed in the film but also co-wrote the screenplay. His postmodern auteur credentials are present throughout but no less so than when he introduces us to Vincent and Jules as they drive to a hit. The two men sport a retro-look in terms of both their 1960s styled sharp, black suits and their 1970s hair styles. The dialogue exchanged between these two men speaks volumes: Vincent, for example, likes to travel, he likes marijuana, he's a chilled-out, relaxed character and has some interesting and amusing observations to make about burger chains. Jules, who drives the car, is the leader and is agog at Vincent's tales of European liberality but later he takes the upper hand in their rambling conversation chatting about, firstly, TV pilot episodes and, secondly, the social etiquette of giving feet massages.

This eclectic series of conversations is delivered in dialogue-heavy shot/reverse shot or long 'two-shot' takes. The tone is comic and the characterisations winning despite their murderous profession. This is where Tarantino's radical experimentation with narrative form has taken the spectator. He has created characters that aren't really the heroes in his film. Indeed, one could argue that if it is anyone it is the more conventional character of Butch: a good-hearted but world weary boxer who wants to skip town with his innocent girlfriend and a ton of ill-gotten cash. This is the normal hero of a noir and that Butch is played by Bruce Willis (in 1994 still a big star) signals that trope even more clearly. But it is Jules and Vincent who steal the show in the opening first act of the film – and all they do is talk. That's what makes *Pulp Fiction* so experimental but in a way that still has fairly mainstream appeal. Tarantino (like Sergio Leone whom he much admires) has invested some time in developing anti-heroes whose quotable iconic lines give them an empathetic quality so normally missing from conventional approaches to noir narrative.

Feedback

A simplistic but technical sentence on what 'conventional narrative approaches' may be. Defining key terms in an exam question is always a good idea if done briefly.

Postmodern links need developing such as intertextuality (pilot shows), homage (1960s gangster suits), eclecticism and cultural references (their conversation topics).

More on neo-noir would be good. What elements have been revised: Marsellus Wallace's wife, Mia, for example, is not quite the traditional femme fatale.

More detail on Tarantino's other experimental narrative devices such as non-sequiturs and the scene with the gimp or plot lines crossing where Vincent is unexpectedly killed by Butch and, finally, circularity, where Vincent returns to us at the end of the film and the diner robbery scene is resolved.

PART 3 PRODUCTION

This part will help you to prepare for Component 3: Production on the A level and AS Film Studies courses. It should be noted that for AS the film production is an **extract** of 2½ to 3 minutes* in length but the AL is a **short film** of 4 to 5 minutes* in length. Written work takes a similar approach, with AS writing a screenplay extract of 1,200 to 1,400 words* and AL a full-length, short film screenplay of 1,600 to 1,800 words. The essence of your practical coursework (30% of the qualification) is to put into practice what you have learned. It is marked internally by centres and will probably be timetabled once the course is well under way.

To further focus you there is the requirement to produce an Evaluative Analysis of your creative work, which for A level must feature some narrative analysis of at least three short films featured in an anthology of texts provided by the exam board (Appendix 'A' of WJEC/Eduqas Specification published in 2017). This initial study of the short film form is intended to guide your creativity, so we'll start with it, by focusing on how to analyse short film. If taking the AS you do not need to study the short films.

*Note: these limits set by the exam board will be enforced rigorously and marks will be deducted if they are not adhered to.

Focus for AS level

Option 1: Film extract (2½–3 minutes) **or**

Option 2: Screenplay for an extract (1,200–1,400 words) and photographic storyboard (approximately 20 shots), **and**

Evaluative analysis (1,000–1,250 words) with no required focus on the set short films.

Focus for A level

Option 1: Short film (4–5 minutes) **or**

Option 2: Screenplay for a short film (1,600–1,800 words) and photographic storyboard (approximately 20 shots), **and**

Evaluative analysis (1,600–1,800 words) with reference to 80+ minutes of short film study.

The specification says

Production is a crucial and synoptic part of the specification, giving learners the opportunity to put into practice the filmmaking ideas they develop throughout their course of study.

Production skills

How to analyse short film (A level only)

Short film is a term that lacks a precise definition other than the idea of 'length', but it is a very definite error to assume that a short film is merely a slimmed-down, long film. Historically, of course, the form has been around since the dawn of film history with the work of pioneers such as the Lumière Brothers. They were absolutely short filmmakers, although due to necessity rather than aesthetics: they filmed for about a minute or so until their film ran out and they hadn't at that time developed notions of editing. However, nowadays filmmakers make 'shorts' for a whole raft of reasons but most obviously as a means of creative entry into the industry, starting at the ground floor to build a portfolio of work, develop ideas and experiment with technique before hopefully embarking on feature film length material.

So what types of short film are there? The Academy (AMPAS) in the USA, which bestows Oscars, define it as 'a film under 40 minutes in length' and it has been awarding live action shorts since the 1930s. Currently, AMPAS awards Oscars for three short film formats:

- documentary (short subject)
- short film (live action)
- short film (animated).

The latter two genres seem most relevant for A level study, as the briefs given and the case study short films all seem most suited to the discussion and development of fictional film.

> **Short film:** according to the Academy of Motion Picture and Sciences (AMPAS), a film under 40 minutes in length.

> **Independent Activity**
>
> Take a look at some of the recent winners of short film awards to gain a greater understanding of the conventions of short films.

On a practical level, short films tend to be small scale and low budget. This means that the cast, sets and plot lines, for example, tend to be discrete and limited, very often revolving around one or two characters and their reaction to a specific event in a specific location. Low-resolution endings in short films are common, as well as a more experimental treatment of non-mainstream subject matter.

AL students only must study **at least three short films** totalling a **minimum of 80 minutes in length** for this unit. One example selection would be five films:

- *La Jetèe* (Marker, France, 1962) 28 minutes
- *The Wrong Trousers* (Park, UK, 1993) 30 minutes
- *About a Girl* (Percival, UK, 2001) 9 minutes
- *High Maintenance* (Van, Germany, 2006) 9 minutes
- *The Gunfighter* (Kissack, US, 2014) 9 minutes.

All totalling 85 minutes.

The reasoning for these choices is that these films have varied production contexts, in most cases strong generic features, and both experimental and mainstream narrative structures. They therefore have a good spread of formal qualities and aesthetic choices to study. The films chosen also fall into the following categories:

- two fairly long-form shorts: the very experimental art house science fiction classic, *La Jetèe*, and the mainstream animation, *Wrong Trousers*
- a social realist film, *About a Girl*
- a high-concept postmodern comedy-western, *The Gunfighter*
- a near-future science fiction film, *High Maintenance*.

Detailed guidance on the Evaluative Analysis will follow but a good rule of thumb is that a third of it should be a narrative analysis of these films and an evaluation of their impact on your work. However, an ability to analyse film in terms of the three core areas covered earlier in this book is also essential and you would be best advised to revisit these relevant sections in this book before starting your short film study and subsequent practical work.

The **three core areas** are:

1 **The key elements of film form**: cinematography and lighting, mise-en-scène, editing, sound and performance
2 **Meaning and response**: representations and aesthetics
3 **The contexts of film**: social, cultural, political, historical and institutional

Of equal importance is your ability to revisit the knowledge and insights gained in your study of at least some of the **six specialist study areas**:

1 Spectatorship
2 Narrative
3 Ideology
4 Auteur
5 Critical debates
6 Filmmaker's theories

As we will see, 'narrative' is a major focus for the short film.

A superb analysis of *any film*, let alone a short film, would aim to include some insights into the following fundamental questions:

1 What aspects of **film form** are used and why?

2 How does the film encourage the **spectator** feel?

3 What **aesthetic** decisions have been made and why?

4 How and why is the **narrative** shaped?

5 What **genre** features are present?

6 What **institutional**, **social**, **political**, **historical and cultural contexts have** influenced the film's production and reception?

7 Has this film contributed to **critical debate**?

8 What kind of **representations** and **ideologies** are present?

9 Is there evidence of an **auteur** at work?

The exam board suggests a particular focus on these three areas for the Evaluative Analysis:

1 Narrative structure

2 Cinematic influences: the key elements of film form such as sound design, mise-en-scène and cinematography

3 Creating meaning and effect

Consequently, this section will refer to each of these areas in the following very short film analyses of three focus films: whether you are analysing your own films, or the films that have influenced you or the films in the anthology, you will need the same skills.

It is also worth remembering that all practical work follows a 'brief' supplied by the exam board. These will be changed every three years so please check on the exam board website or speak to your teacher to gain a clear understanding of the expectations for your production work.

Narrative plays a fundamental part in the practical unit, not only in terms of the product's construction but also in terms of its evaluation. You should then constantly revisit the narrative sections in this book before starting to draft a screenplay or plan a film shoot and then, of course, again when constructing your Evaluative Analysis.

Narrative theory is complex but it can be neatly summarised, as explored earlier, in terms of the formalist distinction between **plot** and **story**. This may sound odd so think of it like this:

- **Who** is the film about?
- **When** does it take place?
- **Where** does it take place?
- **What** happens?
- **Why**?
- **How** does it happen?

And then most crucially ...

- **How have I been shown** it happening?

If still struggling with the concept of narrative try answering the following questions:

- Is the plot linear or non-linear?
- Are there flashbacks or flash-forwards?
- Is the plot episodic?
- Is it circular?

- Where and when does the film start?
- Where and when does it end?
- Do various storylines interweave at critical plot points?
- Do characters move in an 'arc'?
- Does the film follow the traditional three-act structure?
- Are there ellipses?
- How do mise-en-scène, cinematography, editing and sound contribute to the development of the narrative?
- Is there repetition or a framing sequence, perhaps with an actual narrator?
- Are there very clear lines of conflict built into the film?
- Is the film ideological in terms of its narrative construction?
- Is there a twist?
- Is there an enigma in the set-up – a problem to be resolved?
- Are characters in conflict?

Questions such as these will help you navigate the theory and support your analyses but equally they will help with your planning for the production.

We can now briefly explore three of the five selected short film texts:

La Jetèe (Marker, France, 1962) 28 minutes

Contexts

This French short film by the avant-garde artist and filmmaker Chris Marker was released in 1962 and remains a favourite on film courses around the world, as its experimentation with film form and narration is strikingly original. An ultra-low budget deconstruction of the moving image, the film is also a product of the French *Nouvelle Vague*, the film movement of the late 1950s to mid-1960s that challenged conventional filmmaking tropes and techniques. Marker's film is very much in the experimental tradition of this movement. In essence, the film is almost wholly constructed from male voice of God narration and still photographs. Marker himself referred to the film as a photo novel (*un photo-roman*). It is shot in black and white using naturalistic settings despite its science fiction dystopian vision of a post-apocalyptic future where scientists are using prisoners to experiment with time travel. The film title refers to an airport jetty, observation deck or viewing platform, a location significant in terms of the narrative, as it features both at the start and the end of the film.

1 Narrative structure

The main feature of this film's narrative structure is its concern with 'time' and the effect of time travel on the nameless protagonist, a prisoner known as 'The Man'. He is compelled by scientists to go back and forth in time as well as into the future. The Man is obsessed by images from his past, in particular the killing of a strange man that he witnessed as a child on a viewing platform at Orly Airport, in Paris. The central section of the film concerns the man's romantic relationship with a woman who he also vividly remembers from the observation platform when he was a child. Returning to that moment, he discovers that the man he saw being killed, a death also witnessed by the woman he now loves, was himself from the future. Thus, the film concludes with a surprising twist.

2 Cinematic influences and key elements of film form

Marker uses grainy black and white film and a number of strikingly shot close-ups especially in the subterranean scenes involving medical experimentation. The Man's doctors are often shot in low angle, creating unease and a clear sense that he is a hapless pawn in their machinations. The mise-en-scène, fittingly for a low-budget film, is spartan in the subterranean settings and, when the man is sent back in time, contemporaneous images of Paris are used. The futuristic scenes are largely created through make-up and clothing. Marker's creation of a near future and far future is therefore sparse but utterly compelling and convincing. The rather morose narration is intended to convince the audience of the realism of the desperate times screened and the subdued mise-en-scène complements rather than derails the imagination.

A lesser director or even a director with a slightly bigger budget may well have produced an unbelievable vision of the two futuristic settings. By downplaying the future in both its forms (near and far) the past becomes the fantasy world, the playground of time. In other words, it is our past and our memory of the past that shape the present and the future. Our fascination with the past is also about our realisation that in some ways we can never escape its effect. We are therefore trapped in the past.

3 Creating meaning and effect

The film is infused with a bleak Cold War sensibility. Man has destroyed his world. Everything is broken and survivors have moved underground to conduct their fiendish experiments. Perhaps significantly, The Man's tormentors, who send him back and forth in time, whisper in a sinister way in German: a reflection on the cruel experimentation that the Germans undertook in World War II. Sound is also powerfully used to create an elegiac mood with a non-diegetic choir scoring the scenes of nuclear destruction at the start of the film as well as the final heartrending climax on the observation platform at Orly. Heartbeats too are used to raise tension and highlight the extreme medical experimentation taking place. A core idea of the film is that time cannot be escaped. Thus, the mind-melting climax where not even love saves the day.

 S&C

Research the French New Wave in more depth. YouTube has numerous video essays on the subject and many with a specific reference to auteurism. Look also at other famous experimental short films such as the surrealist masterpiece by Dali and Buñuel, *Un Chien Andalou* (France, 1929).

The Wrong Trousers (Park, UK, 1993) 30 minutes

Contexts

The maker of this animated film, Aardman Studios, has produced some of the most popular and idiosyncratic animated work to come out of the UK in the last 50 years. The mainstream success of Wallace and Gromit (the films' two protagonists) has led to a mini-franchise of three other shorts and a successful feature-length film, *The Curse of the Were Rabbit* (2005, UK). Aardman specialises in **stop-motion animation** and has been critically lauded on a global level, not least at the 1994 Oscars where *The Wrong Trousers* won an award for the best animated short. Wallace and Gromit remain a fixture at the BBC, and the TV Christmas viewing figures for some of their comic outings have been very high, reflecting their family-friendly mainstream appeal and quintessentially British character. This mainstream prowess and critical acclaim is not achieved on the cheap, however, and *The Wrong Trousers* was budgeted at £650,000.

1 Narrative structure

The Wrong Trousers is not experimental, as *La Jetèe* clearly is. *The Wrong Trousers* is primarily about the homely relationship of two characters: a middle-aged cheese enthusiast and inventor, Wallace, and his very smart, brave and capable pet dog, Gromit. The two live in a terraced Victorian house somewhere in the north of England and the majority of their adventures stem from Wallace's inventions. These are 'Heath-Robinson' styled contraptions, which run throughout the house. For example, in the opening sequence of the film we see Wallace being woken in the morning by a mechanical hand and tipped into his trousers, before disappearing through a trap door to land at the breakfast table.

In *The Wrong Trousers*, however, Wallace has appropriated some ex-NASA hardware, robotic legs called Techno-Trousers, which he reprogrammes to provide Gromit with 'walkies'. These robo-legs have suction pads on their feet,

enabling the person wearing them to walk up walls and onto ceilings. It is this ability which impresses their new lodger at the house, a mysterious Penguin, who, it transpires, is the arch-criminal, Feathers McGraw, set on stealing a huge, famous diamond from a nearby museum. Trapping Wallace in these robo-trousers (the wrong trousers, of course), the Penguin uses him to steal the jewel but is then caught by Gromit back at the house.

The narrative thus detailed is delivered in a linear way with clear exposition given to us in dialogue and through cunningly positioned pieces of mise-en-scène such as newspaper front pages.

The Penguin is silent like Gromit and all their character identity is largely communicated through expression and performance. Wallace, a bald middle-aged man, talks with a northern accent and has conventional tastes such as tea and cardigans, string vests and slippers. He is a gentle and rather hapless eccentric who often needs to be rescued by his resourceful and loyal canine friend, Gromit. *The Wrong Trousers* concludes, therefore, with the Penguin's arrest and Wallace and Gromit settling down to some tea and Wenslydale cheese. The desired impact of this characterisation on the audience is one of nostalgic whimsy. Wallace is an asexual eccentric: lovable and dopey, a child-man with an all-consuming hobby of invention. His world is pre-digital, a fondly romanticised view of 1950s UK with its gentle and homely references to teapots, biscuits, tank top jumpers, slippers and antimacassars.

2 Cinematic influences and key elements of film form

The film is replete with cinematic influence from a history of film viewing. The climatic sequence, with the chase on a toy train track through the house, is evocative of Westerns or action movies such as *James Bond*, which have all used the train as a narrative device upon which to stage action. There is also something of the kitchen-sink drama too in Wallace and Gromit: their world is a vaguely nostalgic one, a recreation of a dimly recognisable 1960s UK town. Wallace's inventions are not at all high tech and his van is clearly a dated model: if truly social, realist Wallace would be a white van man, always on his mobile phone and Gromit would be a fierce Staffordshire terrier rather than the cuddly loyal hound that he is. Chimney pots, garden gates, cars with starter motors, false teeth, cloth caps, and hair nets, etc. all clearly locate the film in the memories (cinematic or real) of Nick Park, who was born in 1958 in Lancashire. The humour, too, is largely physical and clearly derives from the era of comedy shorts produced by Hollywood throughout the silent era and into the age of sound: shorts produced by such comic legends as Laurel and Hardy and Charlie Chaplin, for example.

3 Creating meaning and effect

The effect of this film is largely comic and wistfully nostalgic. The eccentric characterisations, in particular of scatty Wallace and the icy calculating Penguin, operate brilliantly against the resourceful and resilient Gromit. Crime is shown not to pay and friendship triumphs over adversity. Even the Techno-Trousers escape from the bin that Wallace put them in, to flee into the sunset and freedom, is a trope also focused on in the first Wallace and Gromit short film, *A Grand Day Out* (1989). Equally, England is depicted as a functional but rather odd place: a harmless and rather quirky country stuck in the past.

The Gunfighter (Kissack, 2014) 9 minutes

Contexts

This short film is a postmodern whimsy, playing with the genre conventions of the western and the comical conceit of a narrator who not only can be heard by the performers but who instigates action rather than merely commenting upon it – basically, a voice of God whose honesty causes more problems than it resolves. Kissack is a film editor and emerging filmmaker, and his varied and largely comedic work, including *The Gunfighter*, can be seen on his website (www.erickissack.com). The film was shot over a weekend at a small film studio on a low budget of $25,000, with most of the money going on production design and costume. One set is used and the voice of God is performed by established comedic actor, Nick Offerman; the cast otherwise are unknown actors.

1 Narrative structure

The structuring of *The Gunfighter* begins with the eponymous gunfighter's classic entrance into a Wild West saloon. There are literally a few seconds of establishment with a dusty street scene before he enters the saloon, eyes hidden by the brim of his Stetson. Over the course of nine minutes we learn from the narrator a whole raft of private information about all the people present in the bar. These revelations eventually lead to a violent and fatal shootout for all present, despite an attempt by the gunfighter to ignore the voice and plea for peace and tolerance. Of the stock characters present, alongside the stereotypically manly gunfighter, we meet a saloon prostitute, a number of cowboys and a black barman. The prostitute is the last woman standing but the voice of God punctures her self-satisfaction with the news that she'll be killed the following day by a rabid wolf. Structurally the film has a linear delivery with a high sense of resolution and strongly delineated characterisations bordering on the stereotypical. The film's climax ('the ballet of death' referred to by the Voice) is indeed a full-blown cinematic shootout playing to the most generic of resolutions associated with the western.

2 Cinematic influences

The film is absolutely inflected by the western. The mise-en-scène, music, colour and lighting codes all pay homage to the classic western iconography: grizzled dusty gunfighters; card-playing townsfolk; trigger-happy cowboys; bounty hunters; feisty saloon girls; and tough-talking barmen. The shootout acts as a satisfying and inevitable end to the narrative and again is a homage to the many westerns of the past and present, which are concluded in a blaze of gun smoke and bullets.

3 Creating meaning and effect

The main effect of this film is comedic. By playing with the convention of a voice-over that can be heard by the entire cast, a number of intriguing opportunities arise not least the idea that the 'voice of God' can reveal aspects of people's behaviour and thinking, and so humiliate and/or enrage all present. One message may then be that brutal honesty is not always so smart and may indeed lead to disaster. Much of the humour is crude and sexual in content, and many of the men present have secret sex lives exposed to the gathering. The gunfighter himself has homoerotic thoughts about a cowboy present, who

is himself revealed to enjoy dressing up dollies. Thus, the film plays with the conventional representations of stock characters in a stock situation through the cinematic device of a mischievous narrator or 'voice of God'. Even genre conventions are mocked when Sally the whore comments on the usually non-diegetic ominous music score, which is now heard by everyone, suggesting that something bad is about to happen, something the narrator (much to the chagrin and disdain of those present) refers to as 'a ballet of death'. Despite its postmodern irony and genre-revisionism, the film does contain some problematic representations such as characters feeling and being shamed for their same-sex attraction in defiance of the normative gender roles expected of them. Racial representation is dealt with in a more progressive way through the device of the black barman but even his role becomes defined through a perceived aberrant sexuality, as it is revealed he sleeps with white women.

The production – overview

All practical work follows a brief supplied by the exam board as discussed and illustrated above. The focus of these briefs varies depending on whether the course is AS or AL but they break down into two narrative events and two characterisations (the bold is AL):

1 the opening sequence/**a narrative twist**

2 a climatic sequence/**a narrative which begins with an enigma**

3 a sequence that portrays a crisis for a single character/**a narrative that establishes and develops a single character**

4 a sequence that portrays a conflict between two central characters/**a narrative that portrays a conflict between two central characters**.

La Jetèe sets up an enigma and ends with a twist; *High Maintenance* and *The Wrong Trousers* deal with conflict between two characters, assuming Wallace and Gromit are on one side of the binary; *About a Girl* develops a single character and, finally, *The Gunfighter*, it could be argued, does all four.

 S&C

Identifying genre conventions is a great way into understanding how some films work. *The Gunfighter* relies on our prior knowledge of the western, so watch a few or at the very least look at some classic scenes such as the start of *Once Upon a Time in the West* (Leone, USA/Italy, 1968) or the end of *The Good, the Bad and the Ugly* (Leone, USA/Italy, 1966) or *High Noon* (Zinnemann, USA, 1952). Equally, acquaint yourself with revisionist film texts such as Tarantino's, *Django Unchained* or even spoof comedy westerns such as the amazing *Blazing Saddles* and the execrable *A Million Ways to Die in the West* (Macfarlane, USA, 2014).

How to write a short film screenplay

A screenplay forms the written basis for most films. Without a screenplay it is very hard to raise finance or generate interest from potential cast and crew. The purpose of the screenplay is to present character and story information in an accessible and hopefully atmospheric way. It also enables producers and key cast and crew to see what elements they need to work on in terms of their contribution to the project. Like any form of specialist writing, a screenplay has a very specific format that the exam board want all candidates to replicate.

The format favoured is called a 'master scene script' and its conventions are as follows:

- single column with wide margins
- sequential page numbering (top right)
- mf (more follows – bottom right)
- dialogue centred, with speaker's name in upper case
- slugline (see below) and sound in upper case
- character name in upper case on first appearance only
- font – courier 12 point

Each scene must be numbered and accompanied by a 'slugline', which consists of the following:

- an indication of where the action takes place – interior or exterior (INT or EXT or INT/EXT)
- location descriptor
- lighting descriptor – DAY or NIGHT or TIME
- scene/action descriptor (with succinct description of character on her/his/its first appearance)
- essential camera or edit instructions in exceptional circumstances* – in upper case – such as SLO-MO or TIME-LAPSE)
- action written in present tense.

A good 'short film' screenplay will contain some of the following elements:

- A small cast of rounded characters introduced with sharp psychological detail.
- Evocative and relevant references to atmospheres and environments.
- Convincing dialogue (beware writing in a vernacular you are unfamiliar with) and avoid lengthy monologues unless the work demands it, like in the short film *About a Girl*.
- Sensitive exposition – clunky exposition announces itself, a feature spoofed in the *Austin Powers* films by the character Basil Exposition.

Screenplays must also be accompanied by a photographic storyboard, which will be discussed below.

The best way to explore screenplays is to read some. There are many free sites online that have scripts of feature films and short films available. Often the final visualisation in film is very different from the actual screenplay as read, and discovering this is a useful thing to do. A film I have used in the past that is excellent for this task and is also on the specification is the closing sequence of *Casablanca*. This film had a number of writers and the script was being written sometimes as cameras were rolling, but it still reads beautifully and translates seamlessly to the big screen. Indeed, budding screenwriters still revere the clarity and brevity of this screenplay, regarding it as a classic of its kind.

*Screenplays do not include camera direction. A well-written screenplay will visualise the scene in the reader's mind but will not tread heavily on the toes of the technical teams who realise the screenplay on film: people such as directors, editors and cinematographers.

 Independent Activity

Convert the first page of a novel into a screenplay.

 S&C

Watch 'How to Write a Scene: *Casablanca*' on YouTube, which analyses a scene from *Casablanca* in terms of Robert McKee's idea of subtext. Then produce your own video analysis of a scene from the film.

But *Casablanca* aside, what makes a great short film script? The question is in some sense the same for any kind of creative activity involving narrative and character. Answer the following questions about your work and the work of existing filmmakers and you will come some way to at least being able to assess what a good screenplay is:

- **Are the characters sympathetic?** If not sympathetic then are they at least people the spectator will root for, an anti-hero for example? Consider *Pulp Fiction* where the two hitmen Vincent and Jules are reprehensible amoral murderers but the dialogue Tarantino writes for them and the length of time we spend with them on camera in long takes makes them accessible and engaging. Their discussions, for example, about the etiquette of giving foot massages, pilot TV shows and the 'little differences' between fast food franchises in the USA and Europe, make them seem familiar and funny, so the dialogue humanises them. Achieving this kind of connection with the spectator is certainly important for many film scripts.

  Pulp Fiction is also an episodic film, built in chapters, and actually many of the scenes could be studied as examples of short film. For example, our first meeting with Vincent and Jules is in their car on their way to a hit. They then leave the car and walk into an apartment building where they eventually knock on a door to a room. This relatively simple approach to direction, although dialogue heavy, uses the dialogue to brilliantly establish and enhance characterisation. Vincent and Jules's comedic references to the etiquette of giving foot massages – comedic because these guys are murderous hit men – also establishes something tender about them. This encourages the audience to warm to them, which is Tarantino's great gift to his otherwise stock characters.

- **Is the plot simple?** A plot that is labyrinthine will probably be unfilmable for a short film let alone a feature film (unless you're Christopher Nolan making *Inception* that is) so it is essential that the short filmmaker operates on a small scale. A successful short film is usually about a very specific and focused issue or problem, such as a man trying to stop a tap dripping or a woman looking for her keys. Yes, these sound mind numbingly bland scenarios but they could easily become psychological studies of character and, given a generic twist, could make excellent short horrors or comedies.

- **Is the dialogue essential?** One of the best screenplays this author has ever marked was a dialogue-free montage – it was basically a homage to the montage in *Up* at the start of the film, where we see how a young couple meet, age and then deal with death. If the scene setting is adequate and the description of the action engaging enough, then dialogue need not dominate like it does in Tarantino's work. It's the character that matters. Gromit the dog is silent in *The Wrong Trousers* but he has bags of character, as evidenced by his actions and mannerisms. This hints at a classic piece of filmmaking advice, 'Don't tell – show!' Don't have a character say: 'Quentin is so nervous!' Show us Quentin being nervous, pacing a room, chewing a nail, etc. Don't tell the spectator something that could be as easily shown on screen.

- **Is there an atmosphere?** The timing and setting of a scene has its own in-built atmosphere. For example, external shots of the so-called 'golden hours' of dawn and dusk are brilliant for evoking a slightly plaintive and wistful mood. Mist, rain, snow, thunder and lightning all create dramatic atmospheres. However, be careful! When these tropes are too obvious we can accuse them of committing the 'pathetic fallacy': the false belief that the natural world is affected by our psychological states. Then there are settings and sounds. What could be more evocative of natural rhythms and passing time than the sight and sound of waves crashing onto shingle? What about a ticking clock? These images will be brought to life via a filmed cutaway of a clock's second hand ticking in extreme close-up (ECU) or an extreme long shot (ELS) of waves crashing into a shoreline, but in the screenplay they need description.

- **Have you written about the mise-en-scène?** Of equal importance to the establishment of an atmosphere is an effective description of mise-en-scène. Vincent and Jules from *Pulp Fiction* both wear identical black suits and white shirts. They look like members of a gang. The retro styling evokes memories of 1960s crime dramas and this nostalgia makes them look cool and sharp dressed. They walk with relaxed swaggers and an air of supreme nonchalance. The death they are bringing with them is lost in the mise-en-scène and naturalistic dialogue, so we forget their business is murder and rather enjoy their on-screen presence. The screenplay has won us over in its control of all the elements that establish character: mise-en-scène, mannerisms and dialogue.

- **Will the spectator know when and where the film is taking place?** Using on-screen text or an establishing shot of a sign can help to situate the action in an easy and relatively simple way.

- **What resolution is on offer?** Short films have the luxury of not having to tie up loose ends. In other words, they can end on enigmas or merely the resolution of one simple plot line. The rest is left up to the spectator. Ever since the French New Wave, feature films have at times dared to end on an inconclusive freeze-frame (think of the end of *Goodfellas*) or a cut just before a crucial plot point (think of the final shot of *Inception*). Short films have this luxury in abundance and none of the briefs mentioned above suggest 'high resolution' is in order.

A final point worth making is that screenplays should be heavily drafted. (Remember that the exam board only allows one draft with teacher involvement.) Just like an editor will often fuss and worry film footage for weeks until it resembles a final product, so too must the screenplay writer expect to make many revisions to the work. Thus, a scene may be rewritten at the last moment or another scene removed. A character may be written out and dialogue freshened up to sound more realistic. A good writer knows when to stop fiddling with their work but they equally know that an excessive fondness for the first draft will probably result in something bloated and unfocused.

Following is a script extract from the opening of the classic gangster film, *Scarface* (1983, Stone). In one page we learn so much – that his father's dead, that he was an American, that Tony didn't like him, that Tony's trying to get into America, that he's poor, that he watches films, that he's angry … and so on. Atmospheric and crisp characterisation.

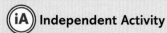 **Independent Activity**

There are numerous script sites online. Read through a few opening scenes and then watch the final result. Another thing to explore is the journey from book to script to screen: *Trainspotting* and *Fight Club* are both rewarding reads on these terms.

```
Scarface: Scene 6

By Oliver Stone

INT. OFFICE. PROCESSING HALL. AFTERNOON.

A CLOSE UP OF TONY MONTANA, the scar-faced
one, in the young angry prime of his life.
We dwell first on the scar which he likes to
scratch now and then. We move to the eyes,
pure in their fury. Finally we encompass the
face - the face of a man about to explode
- muscle, tissue, brain - a man willing to
live or die and in a moment. He is clothed
in rags crossed with holes, his shoes
broken cardboard, his hair unkempt, and his
complexion sallow from prison. Over this we
see:

                    VOICE 1
Okay so what do you call yourself?

                    VOICE 2
Como se llama?

                    MONTANA
Tony Montana ... you?

                    VOICE 1
Where'd you learn to speak English, Tony?

                    MONTANA
My old man - he was American. Sailor.
Bum. I always know, y'know, one day I
gonna come to America. I see all the movies
...

                    VOICE 1
So where's your old man now?

                    MONTANA
He's dead. He died. Somewhere ...
```

How to write a film extract (AS Production)

Many screenwriters (and the exam board) employ a rule of thumb stating that one page of the screenplay equates to one minute of screen time.

Given that the screenplay requirement asks for between 1,200 to 1,400 words for AS and 1,600 to 1,800 words for AL, and that the storyboard should approximate one and a half minutes of screen time for AS and two minutes of screen time for AL (or roughly two pages of the screenplay), then the script itself should not be far in excess of between five to ten pages long.

Extracts are, as the word implies, extracts from significantly longer imagined works. Likewise, a short film will probably have some narrative conclusion, albeit an enigmatic one.

The author's personal experience is that students like to tell stories and that those stories usually have some resolution, and even in an extract there can be a satisfying sense of conclusion.

However, if you do decide to make an extract for AS then the exam board's briefs seem in part designed to guide you to either the start or the end of the project. The initial set-up and exposition of a film can be neatly contained in the first few minutes of a project, just as the last few minutes usually give us the conclusion of character arcs and plotlines, the resolution of enigmas or conflicts and of course the swerve-ball of a 'twist ending'.

Storyboard guidance and layout

A storyboard is a visual illustration of a scene or two (it is not the entire short film!) and it must accompany the screenplay option. It would, however, be useful if it accompanied, at least informally, any film production work. So, even though the focus of this section of the textbook is the screenplay option, the principles expressed here can absolutely be applied more generally to the planning of a film shoot. For example, the website StoryboardThat is a useful and fun way to start your visualisation of a scene (see below for a ten-minute example thrown together and visit www.storyboardthat.com/storyboard-creator).

As suggested earlier, the storyboard must consist of about two minutes of screen time or two pages from the actual screenplay. This will mean the generation of approximately 20 storyboarded shots. The submitted storyboard must be digitally photographed and the generally accepted conventions of the form must be used as follows:

- Shot number and shot description such as: 'Shot 1. Close-up of protagonist's face.'
- Reference to framing such as: 'Shot 1. Close-up of protagonist's face ranged right.'
- Duration of shot. Note: even five seconds of screen time is a long time!
- Reference to detail in the mise-en-scène.
- Reference to camera movement.

- References to editing techniques such as 'CUT' or 'DISSOLVE TO'.
- References to sound design such as 'diegetic' or 'non-diegetic'.

Other requirements are as follows:

- Images are 'indicative' so there is no need to employ a 'realistic mise-en-scène'.
- Backgrounds can therefore be created with Photoshop.
- Five found shots (shots impossible to film such as an ELS of the Earth in space or an explosion) can be submitted but they must be credited.

A storyboard template is available on the Eduqas website.

Limiting the size of the shots often reduces their impact while showing the image flow on screen is encouraged by the inclusion of more than one picture – hence, this author's preference for two (or more) images. Unless black and white for aesthetic reasons, the images must be printed in colour and the industry aspect ratio should be consistently followed. That means don't shoot portrait shots on your phones. Landscape all the way.

Supporting text should be in a note form only and follow a consistent pattern of expression. No extended prose and certainly no dialogue.

It is also possible to illustrate a complex camera move by linking two shots with an arrow or even showing on-screen movement with arrows.

The biggest mistake students make when constructing storyboards is trying to cover the entire length of the film in too few shots: this leads to confusion and a collapse of image-flow. Flow, shot variety and appropriate technical detail are the key to a well-conceived storyboard.

Mark scheme for the screenplay option

A little under two-thirds (max. 25) of the 40 marks available in the practical aspect of the screenplay option are given for the following:

- Excellent knowledge and understanding of elements of film.
- Excellent ability to construct a product appropriate to the brief.
- Excellent, appropriate, meaningful and sophisticated sense of mise-en-scène through sluglines and scene descriptions.

The final third (max. 15 marks) relates specifically to:

- Excellent knowledge and understanding of screenwriting.
- Excellent and consistent use of the 'master scene script' layout.
- Purposeful and convincing dialogue.
- Excellent variety of shot types, camera angles and (if appropriate) camera movements, editing and sound design in the storyboard.
- Excellent narrative sequencing in both the screenplay and storyboard, skilfully establishing meaning in a sophisticated way.

It is clear from this rubric that for this practical option to achieve a top grade it must be cinematically sophisticated in its execution and that an effective use of film form is required along with a formal, skilful and consistent presentation of the narrative brief chosen.

S&C
Listen to a radio play. Storyboard the opening few minutes of sound design.

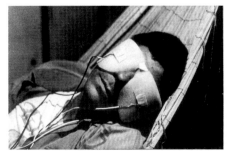

La Jetèe (Marker, 1962)

Evaluative Analysis – guidance

The Evaluative Analysis has a maximum word limit of 1,800 words for AL and 1,250 for AS. Staying in word limits is important and failure to do so is penalised as part of the mark scheme.

With a focus on AL, where the short film compilation needs referencing, the actual analysis of the short films studied should then take about 600 words.

The mark scheme is also clear on what kind of written work is expected for a very top grade:

> *An excellent, well-focussed account of the narrative features of all short films studied*
>
> *An excellent consideration of the cinematic influences on the production including the short films*
>
> *An excellent and perceptive evaluative analysis of how [screenplay] visual/audio and narrative elements are used to create meaning for spectators in relation to other professionally-produced [screenplays] films, including [screenplays for] short films*
>
> (Source: WJEC A Level Film Specification 2017)

Screenplay extracts are essential for a good Evaluative Analysis.

Page numbers should be in the top right-hand corner and a threefold footer is favoured such as:

Student name	Screenplay title	Illuminate College 2018

Font sizes should not exceed 12 points, should not be anything other than a simple font such as Arial, and film titles should always be in italics with brackets in normal case featuring (director, country of origin, if not UK or USA, and year of release) on first mention; for example, *The Wrong Trousers* (Park, 1993).

The filmmaking option

As previously discussed in the section giving an overview of the Practical work, a brief must be followed and an attention to narrative must form the core of the project. So too must you plan and prepare in terms of a study of the short film form and the production of a (non-assessed) storyboard and screenplay. But, unlike the screenplay and storyboard, which are relatively simple products to produce in terms of technology used, now there is a requirement to engage fully with filming and editing technologies.

It is also worth remembering that this project will be assessed as solo work and that all students must be in charge of the camerawork, editing and the direction of any non-assessed assistants such as sound recordists. It is also worth noting that all practical work will be authenticated and monitored by teachers through five stages before the final stage of the work being handed in:

1 Submission of initial ideas – these could be test shoots.

2 1st drafts of storyboards and/or screenplays focusing maybe on just one scene.

3 Mid-project overview – perhaps at the formal complete 1st draft stage of the screenplay or the 'rough cut' of the film.

4 Student confirms the work is theirs.

5 Directing instructions for non-assessed assistants are submitted.

6 Final work handed in.

Clearly, then, planning and authentication are key. Without either, the production will be a failure.

A final note: performances aren't marked but a canny director will cast well and try to elicit a strong performance. This may be in part down to something very simple such as not accepting the first take of a scene and allowing performers to rehearse. So even though performance isn't assessed a committed performance at least can make the project as a whole seem satisfying.

Making a film: things to do and not do

Most student filmmakers at A level have fairly generic tastes and the exam board seems happy to encourage this: 'it is recommended that learners plan genre-based extracts which do not rely on shots impossible to film …' (WJEC/ Eduqas Specification 2017).

There is good sense in this advice, as different genres beat to varied narrative rhythms. For example, the climax of a generic vampire film is usually a bloody one involving the death of the antagonist vampire; another stylised death is demanded in the generic rise and fall saga of a gangster who usually dies in a swarm of hot lead. The generic conventions of a film will include its narrative plot points and typical characterisations. That's what makes the short western film referenced above, *The Gunfighter*, so funny. It plays with the often seen trope of a lone gunman entering a bar and causing trouble for the various stock characters in the bar: saloon girls, a bar tender, cowboys playing cards and tough locals. Thus, on one level the visual iconography is largely generic. Genre revisionism occurs most obviously when the narrator's voice is overheard by everyone in the scene, a device that triggers all the action to come. An informed knowledge of the western genre has absolutely informed the production of this film. So, using a genre you know well is a brilliant way to show you can both conform to and perhaps even challenge genre expectations. One easy way to do the latter is by playing with gender and racial stereotypes. *The Gunfighter*, for example, has a black barman and makes a comedic note of the fact in the screenplay.

However, some genres come with health warnings and a degree of a caution is encouraged. Real stunts can go wrong and real weapons may kill. No guns or knives is good advice. Think again about the scene from *Pulp Fiction* when we first meet Jules and Vincent. We know they are bad. We get they're killers. But we see nothing until much later in a non-sequentially edited scene. Yes, we briefly see their guns but the use of weaponry is subtle. The key is to be smart about what you use. Accidents happen and there are often ways to imply violence rather than depict it: thus, a spinning car tyre and the Foley addition of screeching rubber evokes a chase just as effectively as depicting it.

So, genre should be your friend but so too should the following top ten filmmaking tips:

1 **Write a short script**. Without scripted dialogue, editing conversations will not work well unless shooting the whole scene in a single take, otherwise you will create awful jump-cuts. The whole crew should then read through the script before further planning takes place and your performers will obviously need time to practise their lines. As the last thing they will

probably have available to them is lots of time keep dialogue simple.

2 **Make a brief storyboard**. Planning shots will help everyone know what they're doing and aid creativity. Nowadays, there is no need to draw a storyboard unless you have the necessary speed and skills to do so, rather photograph on your phone the rough 'look' of the film and use this in your first cast and crew meeting.

3 **Shot variety**. Including a varied diet of shots will showcase your talent as a cinematographer and make the viewing experience more satisfying, certainly for a generic film where fast-paced editing is an expectation, such as a chase or a fight. Shot variety is therefore key: aim to mix up your framing and angles and camera moves. Also aim to record the same action from as many angles as possible. If you do this you will need to pay attention to continuity in the mise-en-scène as well as dialogue and framing. A famous rule to pay attention to is the 180°/30° rule which aims to maintain convincing continuity between shots and avoid jump-cuts. It is most famously explained in terms of shot/reverse shot conversations where failure to adhere to the rule can result in an error called 'crossing-the-line'. This would result in characters jumping from one side of the screen to the other and screen direction being lost, thus leaving the audience both confused and aware of the filmmaking techniques being used. Indeed, many of the best edits are invisible.

4 **Five seconds lead in and out**. This aids editing as it means you know the equipment is recording and each scene has a natural stop and start. Professional crews would use a clapperboard and identify the scene number and the take. This verbal format can be adapted and used as follows:

- Director: 'QUIET ON SET! ROLL CAMERA!'
- Camera person: Press record button. 'Camera rolling. 5, 4, 3, 2, 1 …'
- Director: 'Scene 1, Take 1 (pause 2 seconds) ACTION!'
- Director: 'CUT!'

5 **Rehearse**. 'Practice makes perfect' is a terrible cliché precisely because it's terribly true. The kind of people who are reading this textbook are probably not the kind of people who will rush a film shoot at the very last minute but those that do inevitably produce poor work. Filmmaking is both a technical and creative art form and it involves a number of people both in front of and behind the camera. As such it is something that by definition cannot be left to the last minute. **Plan. Rehearse. Plan again. Rehearse once more. Now shoot.** An ideal situation but the stress free way to do the job.

6 **Shoot cutaways**. Cutaways are really useful shots to cut to and create interest. They are great for establishing mood and atmosphere, a creepy doll just sitting there, a portrait, a flower or butterfly, a drop of water, some litter, you name it! If cutting from a scene to a cutaway and then back to the scene adds something to the spectator experience or the narration then it's time well spent.

7 **Ensure all cast/props are available for re-shoots**. Even professionals need to re-shoot but without the cast/props it is very difficult. Re-shoots are almost inevitable as there is often a scene you wish you had shot or an aspect of the narrative that seems unclear once filmed and needs focusing through the addition of another scene. A classic error is for a mate to help with your filming and then get a haircut or go on holiday and

come back with a deep tan. Also make sure clothes and props used for the shoot are kept safe and accessible until the film is complete.

8 **Mise-en-scène.** This really matters, so take the time to get it right. Dress your characters and have them operating in a world that you have at least tried to make your own through the addition of posters, cutaways, props and lighting. The films of Wallace and Gromit feature a wonderful mise-en-scène such as photographs, newspapers and so on, all of which give insights into their characters and the world they live in.

9 **Sound.** Recording sound on location is very difficult and many beautifully shot films are let down by shoddy sound recording. Avoid, if you can, windy conditions and get your performers to deliver lines with gusto and vim. Try to shoot with your sound levels visible on the camera monitor and re-shoot anything with the metre tipping into the red. Aim to shoot plenty of location Foley and be prepared to add even more in post-production. Sound too needs to be mixed carefully in the final edit, making sure your sound isn't swinging about wildly and uncomfortably in terms of volume. If it is, your audience will hate you and each sound spike will act like a visual jump-cut and remind us all we are watching a film. **Record a wild track.** Shoot a minute or two of ambient sound in whatever location you are in; this really helps smoothing over sound glitches caused by switching shots in a noisy location. An example I saw recently where this didn't happen involved firstly a two-shot of two guys talking on a station platform and then a switch to shot/reverse shot angles. The sound was different in each take, as you'd expect on a station, so sound continuity was broken.

10 **Maintenance and housekeeping.** There is a basic error that students make in terms of kit and that's not maintaining it. Batteries die. So charge them overnight. Light bulbs pop or break. Get replacements. Memory cards corrupt. Have spares. Try not to shoot everything on one card for just this reason. Back-up always. Don't leave cameras outside or in car boots: they can get wet or damp or stolen, all of which are disastrous. If looking back at footage shot before actually coming to the edit try to make a log of shots that are good and shots that are not. That way editing will become a slicker affair, as many students waste reams of time looking at every scene shot and laughing at the outtakes, thus wasting valuable edit time. Finally, let people know where you are and ask permission if filming in public spaces. It would be a courtesy to the public and the local constabulary that you tell them you're shooting a horror film in the nearby woods. Fail to do so and, as the sounds of your actor's faux screams are drowned out by a police helicopter and the red dots of a SWAT team's infra-red gun sights dance on your foreheads, you may wish you'd told someone you were making a film.

Mark scheme for the film option

A little under two-thirds (max. 25) of the maximum 40 marks available in the practical aspect of the Filmmaking option are given for the following:

- Excellent knowledge and understanding of elements of film.
- Excellent ability to construct a product appropriate to the brief.
- Excellent, appropriate, meaningful and sophisticated sense of mise-en-scène.

The final third (max. 15 marks) relates specifically to:

- Excellent knowledge and understanding of cinematography, editing and sound.

- Excellent variety of shot types and camera angles.
- Resourceful, purposeful and controlled camera movement (if appropriate).
- Editing meaningful and clear, and showing a range of continuity features.
- Excellent use of effective sound to establish mood and appropriate audience response.

It is clear from this edited rubric that for practical work to achieve a top grade it must be cinematically sophisticated in its execution and that an effective use of film form is required along with a skilful narrative focus on the chosen brief.

Summary

- Practical work 30% of total A level mark: Project 20%; Evaluative Analysis 10%.
- Two practical options: Short film or extract; Screenplay and Storyboard.
- For AL a compilation of short films must be studied and referenced (80 minutes in total from a list of text provided) in the Evaluative Analysis; part of this focus will be on cinematic influences, so watch and reference other films too.
- One of the four briefs must be chosen. These briefs are focused broadly on narrative and, more specifically, on either narrative beats and/or characterisation.
- Evidence of planning is vital for both options in terms of assessment and professionalism.
- The storyboard must be photographed (about 20 frames).
- The screenplay must use the format suggested.
- Filmmakers are responsible for their own cinematography/editing/directing.
- Performance isn't assessed.

Exemplar student film script

Here is the opening extract from an inventive and well-written screenplay by a former student of A level Film Studies for you to consider. The script's title page reads: Acts of God by Aaron Loose.

DARKNESS.

A rising roar, like the acceleration of a jet engine.

1. EXT. LIVERPOOL DOCK, LATE MORNING.

The craggy face of a Chinese Loong dragon, reptilian eyes blazing like rubies, curled lips seething with liquid fire as it bellows at an unseen opponent.

Suddenly, an uppercut thunders from below the frame, like a blur of thatch and muscle, shattering the dragon's jaw like candy cane. The dragon tumbles onto a waterfront. It lands in a plume of sea spray and stone. A hulking golem of living stone and moss looms over like a mountain. The dragon rears up. Molten gore cascades from its exposed throat. We behold the creatures in their full monstrous enormity.

The monsters are now much smaller, like action figures on a stage.

2. EXT. LIVERPOOL STREET, LATE MORNING.

A busy street, frantic with the morning commute, cacophonous with leather pounding on concrete and grumbling car engines. Stiff-lipped PEOPLE in puffy coats and polished shoes plod past, briskly but unhurriedly. The

mf

armoured Volvos look less like they're driving to Tesco than Mogadishu. A pair of DRUNKS try to keep their balance as the pavement shakes and splinters. A WOMAN wearing sunglasses skilfully sidesteps a chunk of falling masonry and enters a taxi. On the corner, AN ELDERLY MAN wears a sign. It reads "The end is ongoing."

Snippets of conversation mutter at the fringes of the soundtrack.

> COMMUTER I
> Second time this week. What are the
> council doing?

> COMMUTER II
> Keep calm and carry on, that's
> what I say.

> COMMUTER III
> Did you say semi-skimmed?

3. EXT. LIVERPOOL COASTAL ROAD, NIGHT.

MEN in yellow jackets tiredly divert traffic around a wrecked car. It's lying on its roof. Tufts of fire spit from two large dents in the undercarriage.

A man crawls out from the car. This is ANGUS, age 22. His left sleeve is badly torn and his left eye is masked by a lank fringe.

He's helped up by a yellow jacket, who looks him over, nods, and returns to work.

Angus sits on the barrier, rummages through his frayed pockets. He takes out a small plastic jar, pops off the lid, and scoops out a clear gel. He massages the mixture into his hair, begins to sculpt a quiff.

Two FF-22 raptors fly overhead.

Angus doesn't blink. Digs out his phone. It's outfitted with one of those super durable cases. Very chic. Dials a number.

mf

4. INT. SALAMANDER INSURANCE INC LONDON, MORNING.

A typical 21st century office, all spotless glass
offices and ergonomic shelving. There are no windows to
the outside.

The office belongs to ALCINA (35). She's wearing a headset
and taps rapidly on her keyboard, eyes fixed on her
computer. She's smartly dressed, although her sleeves
are rolled up. By her left side, a formidable stack of
documents.

Her headset beeps. She immediately answers.

                    ALCINA
          Good Morning, this is the
          Salamander Insurance Corp.
          My Name is Alcina, head of enquires
          for Kaiju-related accidents. How
          may I help you?

Stay close on Angus' face for the whole phone call
sequence.

                    ANGUS
          Hiya, It's Angus Falconer. I took
          out a premium policy with your
          company on January 7th when I
          purchased my E-Type from Honda's-

A sonic boom, followed by a thunderous bang. A flash of
white light illuminates Angus' face.

Alcina throws her headset off. Clutches her ear. She
grimaces and resumes the call. Angus is oblivious.

                    ANGUS (CONT'D)
          -see, I got caught up in a Kajiu
          confrontation tonight, and I'm
          afraid the losing side took his
          frustrations out on my car. I'm
          uploading my BlackBox Feed to you
          now.

Angus taps his phone. A soft beep.

A feed of information trickles into Alcina's computer
screen. It's a 3-D blueprint of his car.

mf

                         ALCINA
            I see, sir. I just heard a very
            loud explosion. Are you okay?

                         ANGUS
            Yeah. It's just the government
            arriving to break up the fight.

Another boom, another flash. There's a colossal thud.
Angus puts a stray strand of hair into place.

                     ANGUS (CONT'D)
            So, is it salvageable?

                         ALCINA
                (Slightly irritated
                but maintaining
                composure)
            No sir, that would be like giving
            a corpse a filling. But not to
            worry, your policy covers you for
            anything from Mecha collateral to
            extra-terrestrial disintegration.
            I estimate we can give you full
            compensation within 24 hours.

                         ANGUS
            Oh, really? That's great! Thank
            you.

                         ALCINA
            No problem. Is there anything else
            I can do for you?

Angus sluggishly gets to his feet. The FF-22's fly back
over the bay. Apart from the tooting of car horns, the
city is quiet.

                         ANGUS
            No, I think that's all. Thank you for
            your help.

                         ALCINA
            Not a problem. Have a nice day,
            Mr. Falconer.

Study skills

This section of the textbook is designed to help you apply the knowledge you have gained in the previous sections. As the assessment objectives of the A level suggest, Film Studies is about demonstrating **and** applying 'knowledge and understanding of elements of film'. This section will offer some study tips and use *This is England* (Meadows, 2006) to illustrate how to apply these techniques.

How to read a film

Living in a media-saturated society we have all grown up surrounded by screens. We've watched films for many reasons but often purely for entertainment and escapism. Becoming a student of film means you have to learn to look at films in a different way and this can be referred to as *reading a film*. There are whole books dedicated to this subject but here is some condensed advice on how to approach watching a film analytically.

Watching a film uninterrupted, preferably on a large screen, should always be step one. If you try to take notes, pause at key moments or rewind to revisit specific sequences, you are not experiencing the narrative as the filmmaker intended. You may miss a crucial interaction between characters, overlook an important plot development or fail to take the opportunity to get truly immersed in the beauty of visual storytelling. Fans of cinema often wish they could go back and watch a film they love for the first time again, so don't risk spoiling the experience by being distracted. Make the time to watch the films before you start studying them in class, so you can see them the way they were intended to be seen.

Once you have watched, and hopefully enjoyed, your set films then the real work begins. Watch them again, but this time, make notes as you do. Use this second viewing to really consider the narrative structure and the impact the film is having on you as a spectator. Keep a record of the key plot points, consider the significant actions the protagonist takes and the impact these have. Note the specific sequences or scenes that have an emotional impact upon you, moments in which you are shocked, moved or amused. Think also about what key messages the filmmaker is communicating and how social groups are represented. Look for patterns in the narrative such as locations that are revisited, film techniques that recur, leitmotifs and repetition in dialogue.

This is a complex set of notes to take and there are numerous ways to record this information. Some students find creating a timeline of the film useful, particularly for considering the film's narrative structure. A timeline is a visual representation of the plot with the key moments highlighted. For example, a timeline for *This is England* would start like this:

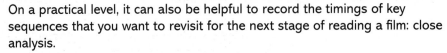

| Shaun gets bullied | Shaun meets Woody and the gang | The gang go hunting | Shaun gets a make-over | Combo arrives and creates tension |

As you can see, not every incident in the film's narrative is noted but it gives you a useful overview of the plot. It is particularly helpful for films with more complex narrative structures. This can then be built upon by adding notes on the key emotional moments of the film or aspects of narrative theory, for example the point at which the equilibrium is disrupted.

On a practical level, it can also be helpful to record the timings of key sequences that you want to revisit for the next stage of reading a film: close analysis.

The third viewing is where you start paying close attention to the Core Study areas, elements of film form in particular. You know the story now and have identified key sequences so you can now take the time to look at these moments in greater detail.

Close scene analysis

When analysing any film on the course, you need to apply the Core Study areas. These fall into three sections described in the specification as:

> *Area 1. The key elements of film form: cinematography, mise-en-scène, editing, sound and performance.*
>
> *Area 2. Meaning and response: how film functions as both a medium of representation and as an aesthetic medium.*
>
> *Area 3. The contexts of film: social, cultural, political, historical and institutional, including production.* (Eduqas, 2017, page 10)

An easy to remember acronym is CRAM SPEC, as you are trying to **cram** the contents of the **spec**ification into a simple formula.

- C – Cinematography
- R – Representation
- A – Aesthetics
- M – Mise-en-scène

- S – Sound
- P – Performance
- E – Editing
- C – Contexts

There are a number of approaches to tackling a close analysis. One approach, which can open up whole sequences, is to start with a **single frame analysis**. Simply screengrab a key frame from a scene you wish to analyse and annotate it, referring to as many aspects of the core study areas as possible. Following is an example of how a frame from *This is England* might be deconstructed.

Composition – rule of thirds can be applied to demonstrate how Shaun and the picture of his father are placed on or near the vertical lines

Cinematography – medium shot allowing the audience to see Shaun in the context of his home

Mise-en-scène – muted, subdued colours to reflect Shaun's mood

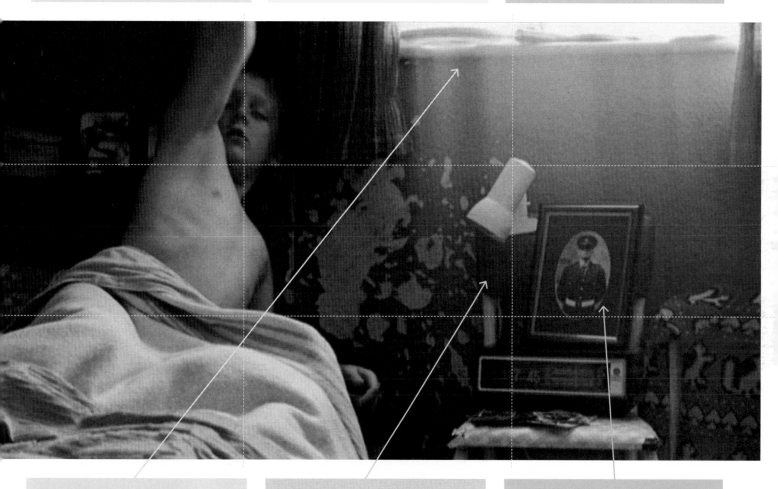

Cinematography (lighting) – natural sunlight through the window suggests social realism

Representation – chair as bedside table and chipped paintwork could imply Shaun comes from a deprived socio-economic background

Mise-en-scène – picture of father is prominent, emphasising his importance in Shaun's life and the narrative

The same technique can be used for full scenes if you just name the scene at the centre of the page and create a **mind map**.

Mind map: a visual representation of information that includes a central idea surrounded by connected branches of knowledge.

If you prefer to take a more structured approach and respond well to prompts, you may benefit from having an **analysis grid** you can use for any scene. This may look something like the one below but you can create your own so it works well for you.

This is England – Combo's speech	
Core area	**Example from the scene**
Cinematography	*Use of low-angle shots of Combo to suggest his power. Extensive use of close-ups to enable the audience to see each character's reaction to the speech and situation.*
Sound	*Use of ticking clock used to increase the tension. This has particular impact when Milky is asked whether he considers himself to be English or Jamaican, and again when he is contemplating staying and joining Combo. Music use in the scene is sparing but melancholy music is played when Shaun decides not to leave with Woody and Lol, pointing to this being a poor decision.*
Editing	*Relatively long takes, particularly as Combo progresses with his speech. He dominates screen time as he dominates the room. The audience is positioned to focus on him for prolonged periods as do the characters.*
Mise-en-scène	*Staging – all characters are seated except Banjo and Combo, which helps set up the power imbalance. Shaun's placement between Lol and Woody reflects a traditional family unit, a place of protection that Combo is jeopardising.*
Performance	*Stephen Graham's body language and facial expressions are full of barely contained rage as he vents his views about immigrants. He uses emotive and powerful language and places emphasis on the more provocative words. As his emotions get heightened he speaks louder.*
Representation	*Lol adheres to the maternal stereotype of women in her concern for Shaun stating, 'he's twelve I can't leave him here'.* *Combo refers to 'proud men' and glorifies masculinity. Minorities are demonised in Combo's speech. Shaun's youth is seen as a source of vulnerability.*
Aesthetics	*Use of hand-held camera and location shooting mean the film conforms to the social realist genre as the aesthetics of documentaries are evoked.*
Contexts	*Combo repeatedly references the political and social context of 1983 referring to high levels of unemployment and the Falklands War.*

For even closer analysis you can create specialist grids for each of the core areas of study, or even each element of film form. Remember that you wouldn't do this for a whole film, just key sequences. The specification is a useful starting point for creating one, as it breaks each element of film form down into its principal elements. For example, mise-en-scène includes:

- *setting, props, costume and make-up*
- *staging, movement and off-screen space*
- *how cinematography impacts on mise-en-scène, in particular through variation in depth of field, focus and framing.*

(Eduqas, 2017, page 11)

These would make useful subsections for a grid approach to analysing this area of film form in detail.

Another written technique that could be useful is a Film Studies take on the **Cornell note-taking system**. To do this you could split your page into three sections and complete them as suggested below (Cornell University, 2016).

Note questions that arise from watching the scene here	Note your observations about the scene here

Once you have considered your questions, write a detailed analysis of the scene here outlining how meaning is made

If you learn better through **discussion**, try explaining the techniques used in a scene to someone else. This is often a very successful way of gaining a more thorough understanding. Watch a scene and tell a friend everything you noticed. Then ask them to watch it and add anything you missed. If you are working in pairs or groups, another useful approach is writing a quiz for each other about the scene, completing it and marking each other's answers.

If you prefer working with technology you can approach close analysis a little differently by creating an **analytical commentary** for specific scenes. Write a script outlining the key points you wish to make about a sequence and record a voice-over explaining these to accompany the clip. There are free online audio editors and recorders, and most computers now come with basic editing software that is more than enough for this task. This process allows you to really get to know a scene and also provides you with a useful audio-visual revision aid for later in the course.

Alternatively, you may want to **reverse-storyboard** a scene. Screengrab each shot in a key sequence and create the storyboard including detailed notes on the shot, action, sound, shot duration and edit, and, unlike a real storyboard, write what the scene tells the audience.

For example: Shaun meets Woody and the gang:

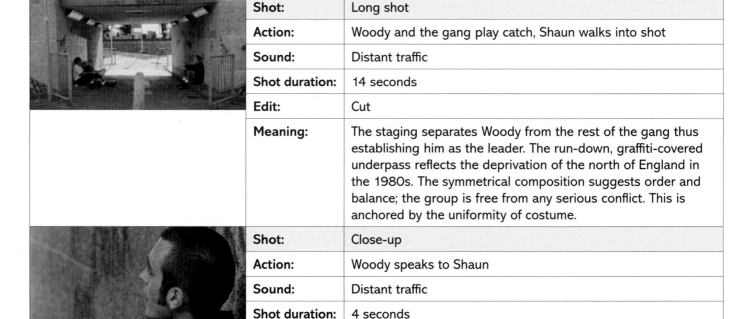

Shot:	Long shot
Action:	Woody and the gang play catch, Shaun walks into shot
Sound:	Distant traffic
Shot duration:	14 seconds
Edit:	Cut
Meaning:	The staging separates Woody from the rest of the gang thus establishing him as the leader. The run-down, graffiti-covered underpass reflects the deprivation of the north of England in the 1980s. The symmetrical composition suggests order and balance; the group is free from any serious conflict. This is anchored by the uniformity of costume.
Shot:	Close-up
Action:	Woody speaks to Shaun
Sound:	Distant traffic
Shot duration:	4 seconds
Edit:	Cut
Meaning:	The audience's attention is focused on Woody before any other member of the group, anchoring the idea of him as the leader.

Alongside the core areas of study you will also need to apply specialist study areas to certain films. These are, for A level:

- **Hollywood 1930–1990** – Auteur
- **American film since 2005** – Spectatorship and ideology
- **British film since 1995** – Narrative and ideology
- **Documentary film** – Critical debate 2 (the significance of digital technology in film) and filmmakers' theories
- **Silent cinema** – Critical debate 1 (the realist and the expressive)
- **Experimental film** – Narrative and alternative forms of narrative.

For AS level you need only study narrative in relation to **British film** and explore spectatorship through **American independent film**.

Extra sections can be added to your grids and storyboards to integrate knowledge of these areas. Your understanding of theoretical approaches will also benefit from wider reading.

Research guidance

Not knowing where to go for additional reading about films is something that students often struggle with, so here are some helpful suggestions of where to start.

A number of the films you may be studying are reasonably contemporary and consequently will have a limited range of texts published about them. The internet becomes a crucial source of information for the film student for this reason but it is easy to lose hours of valuable research time wading through fansites, reviews and opinion pieces. To help avoid this following are some suggestions on **how to do an academic internet search effectively**.

- **Google Books** (https://books.google.co.uk) is very useful, as substantial sections of useful publications are available for you to read online. These are easily searched using the find option in the edit menu to look for keywords.
- **Google Scholar** (https://scholar.google.co.uk) is similarly useful in helping you find specific journal articles relevant to your course. Alternatively, just adding pdf into your internet search often brings a lot of academic publications to the top of your results list.
- **Wikipedia** is often criticised by teachers as it can be updated by anyone so the content is not reliable. You can, however, use it wisely by using the footnotes on a film's Wikipedia page as a set of links to relevant, more reliable sources of information.

One of the keys to productive internet searching is choosing your search terms carefully. Include academic language and film terminology and you will usually return more pertinent and appropriate results.

There are some key websites that most film students find themselves returning to over and over again. Here are a few suggestions:

- **BFI.org.uk** is a great source for insight into British film. In particular, the publications in the Education and Research section offer up-to-date analysis and data (www.bfi.org.uk/education-research/film-industry-statistics-research).
- **Cineaste.com** describes itself as 'America's leading magazine on the art and politics of the cinema' and it has a lot to offer the film student, including articles relevant to the set films for this qualification.
- **Filmsite.org** helpfully categories its extensive range of information in numerous ways: by genre, by director and by decade among others.
- **IMDb.com** offers details of most film productions such as box office data and cast and crew information, alongside links to reviews.
- **RogerEbert.com**, the website of the revered film critic, is still maintained and updated, and boasts some of the best film criticism available online.
- **Sensesofcinema.com** includes an accessible and enlightening database of directors, which includes filmmakers featured on the course such as Arthur Penn, Quentin Tarantino and Sergei Eisenstein.
- **Theyshootpictures.com** is another great source for director profiles and provides key quotes on filmmakers' works from a variety of reputable sources.

Alongside online journals, it is worth visiting your school or college library as it may have hard copies of useful journals and magazines. Look out for *Screen*, *Sight & Sound* and *Media Magazine* in particular.

The **Guidance for Teaching** booklet on the WJEC/Eduqas website has an extensive bibliography with suggested reading for every film on the specification and also the core and specialist study areas. This can be accessed at: www.wjec.co.uk/qualifications/film-studies/Eduqas%20Film%20 Guidance%20for%20Teaching%20-%20A%20level.pdf?language_id=1.

You should not limit yourself to just reading about your focus films though, or indeed just reading full stop. There is a lot to be gained by **watching more films**, be they other films by the same director, films from the same genre or films from a similar period of film history. The broader your knowledge of cinema the stronger your understanding of the art of film will be. Watch, also, **documentaries** about the time periods your focus films were made or set, to aid your contextual understanding, and documentaries about filmmaking itself. Finally, make the most of the DVD or Blu-ray special features on your focus films; make notes on the featurettes and the director's commentary.

There is no specific requirement for extensive research on the course but wider reading and viewing are always beneficial. Don't be overwhelmed, though, and try to keep your tasks manageable. It is useful to set yourself challenges and limits, for example summarise an article in 50 words or less. A lot of the **Independent Activities** and **Stretch and Challenge** tasks in this book do just that. It is demanding to be so concise but is a very useful skill to develop for the exams.

How to interpret the question

Exam questions tend to be quite formulaic, as the assessment objectives are the same for a number of years. The examiners are trying to give you an opportunity to demonstrate and apply your knowledge, so don't be on the look out for trick questions, they want you to do well.

A key skill in looking at the paper is being able to work out quickly exactly what the examiners are looking for. Step one should always be underlining the key words in the question. A **key word** is often directly taken from the core or specialist areas; examples might be narrative, spectatorship or cinematography.

Once you have worked out what the focus of the question is you need to look at how the question is structured and what it is actually asking of you.

There is a range of different question types across AS and A level, ranging from 10 to 40 points. As you would anticipate, the more points the question is worth, the more detail and depth the examiner will be looking for.

Question types

Shorter exam questions often start with terms such as **explore** or **discuss**, and these questions invite you to demonstrate and apply your knowledge and understanding of elements of film. For example, 'Explore how one example of cinematography is used in one sequence from your chosen film.' This question is focused, in that it specifies cinematography as the element of film form to analyse and limits the analysis to one sequence, but it is otherwise a fairly broad question as you could look at, among other ways, how cinematography creates meaning, establishes character or contributes to the aesthetic.

'How far' questions are commonly used such as 'How far do your chosen films demonstrate the importance of visual and soundtrack cues in influencing spectator response?' These questions are quite open as they invite you to consider the aspects of film referred to but also write about the importance of other areas. In the question above, for example, although you would mainly write about visual and soundtrack cues, you could also consider additional factors that may impact upon a spectator's response to the films.

Comparative questions are rarer, as only one question on the Component 1 paper for both AS and A level asks you to demonstrate this skill. When writing about Hollywood films between 1930 and 1990 you will always be asked to compare. These questions should always directly instruct you, an example being, 'Compare how far your chosen films reflect their different production contexts.' Compare questions ask you to seek out the points of similarity between the films but also demonstrate your awareness of any points of difference.

Evaluative questions such as 'How useful has an ideological critical approach been in understanding binary oppositions in the narratives of your chosen films?' are asking you to reflect upon your own experience of the films studied. To answer this question you would need to consider your understanding of the films both before and after studying the critical approach. What does the critical approach bring to your understanding? For example, it may have challenged your initial interpretation of the film or confirmed and clarified your original response.

Questions including the phrase, **close reference**, are asking for a response rich in detail. For example, 'Explore how aesthetic effects are created in your chosen film. Illustrate your answer by close reference to at least one sequence from your chosen film', invites you to consider all elements of film form and how these combine to create aesthetic effect. You could write about a specific shot, a particular refrain from a song or an evocative lighting technique.

Bullet-pointed guidance is included in some AS level questions to help you formulate a response. Here is an example:

> *Explore how far spectators respond both actively and passively to film. Illustrate your answer by close reference to your chosen film.*
>
> *In your answer, you may consider:*
> - *What you understand by active and passive spectator responses.*
> - *How aspects of film form invite active or passive responses.*
> - *To what extent spectators respond actively or passively to the way filmmakers encourage them to respond.*

Please note that you do not have to follow the bullet-pointed guidance, it is there as a suggestion not an essay plan.

How to plan an essay

When planning an essay it can be useful to **talk** through your ideas first. This can help you formulate an argument and discover what you really think about the question. **Mind maps** can also help to organise your thoughts, turning a loose collection of thoughts into groups of similar ideas that will form paragraphs. Aim for four or five clear points or paragraphs and make sure they directly address the set question. Essay planning grids can be useful to help you organise these paragraphs into a full essay plan.

Essay title	
Introduction Key words Introduce film(s) Brief context	
Points directly addressing the question	Evidence from focus film(s)
1	
2	
3	
4	
5	
Conclusion Direct response to the question including key words	

How to write an introduction

Your introduction should include definitions of the key words from the title, so, for example, if your question mentions *spectatorship* you should **briefly** outline what the term means.

Vertigo (Hitchcock, 1958)

You should also introduce the focus film(s) concisely, ideally including the director, country (if not UK or USA) and year in brackets after the film's title, for example *This is England* (Meadows, 2006). Introducing the film does not mean recapping the plot or describing any scenes, don't waste your words, you have limited time available.

You may, however, include brief contextual knowledge such as the film's genre and social contexts. This may seem onerous but can be kept very concise, for example:

> This is England *(Meadows, 2006) is a low-budget Warp Productions film from the social realist genre. It is set in the north of England in 1983, at a time of high unemployment, race riots and social division, and was made over 20 years later when similar issues were still impacting on working-class Britain.*

Your introduction can hint at how you will tackle the question but don't outline your whole argument at this stage. Avoid starting a point in the introduction, it is there to contextualise the film(s) and start to unpick the question. It should not include close scene analysis or detailed examples from the focus film(s).

The perfect paragraph

The first sentence of each paragraph should directly addresses the question and ideally include some of the key words to establish these links clearly.

The last sentence of the paragraph should bring that point to some conclusion and link back again to the question. Ideally, this sentence should also link to the following point to try and establish a coherent sense of a developing argument.

In between these key sentences the perfect paragraph will include detailed examples from the film(s), including quotes and close analysis of elements of film form, and the contextual information established in the introduction may be revisited where relevant. References to critical approaches and specific theories will also feature in some paragraphs of course, depending on the specific question asked.

How to write a conclusion

The conclusion's main function is to answer the question. If the question asks 'How far?', state how far. If the question is asking for a comparison, summarise and account for the key similarities and differences between the films concisely.

The conclusion also offers an opportunity to demonstrate that you have not oversimplified your argument, by mentioning other perspectives that could have been taken. Finally, the conclusion should make further reference to the key words from the question to ensure it is clear that your essay has stayed focused.

Approaches to revision

A useful tactic for helping with **procrastination** is a take on the **Pomodoro technique**, which can be used for any kind of study that requires self-discipline and motivation. The key to the technique is working in 25-minute bursts separated by five-minute breaks. These timings can be adjusted to suit your own learning style but the study periods should always be significantly longer than the breaks. Ideally, you repeat this four times before allowing yourself a longer break (Cirillo, 2007).

Key to this being a success is that you set yourself a clear task before setting the timer so your study time is focused and your intention clear. You must also turn off all distractions such as mobile phones and televisions. Knowing you have a break coming up enables you to worry less about what you might be missing. The Pomodoro approach also works well in pair or group work if everyone adheres to silent working until the timer sounds.

To adapt this idea for exam preparation, a good addition is adding a ten-minute **speed write** just before the longer break in which you write down everything you can remember from your four study periods. This helps lock the information in your mind and find out which topics you are less knowledgeable about. The technique can also be adapted for analysing key sequences. Simply watch the key sequence, start the timer and write down everything you noticed. When the timer sounds, hide your notes and rewrite everything you can remember.

Past papers are always the most useful tool in preparing for an exam, so visit the exam board's website and look at the sample assessment materials (SAMs) (WJEC, 2017).

Using these past papers, plan as many responses as you can. You do not have to write full answers just a plan of what each paragraph would contain. As the course is relatively new there is not a large catalogue of past papers available but the way around this is to **write your own questions**. Look at the specification and consider all the areas that could be examined, then, using the SAMs as a guide, design a whole paper. You can then plan responses to all the questions. This is a great way to really get you thinking about all the possible questions you may have to tackle.

Knowledge organisers are incredibly useful aids for revision. Ideally, you would complete them at the end of each module and use them as a revision tool in the lead-up to the exam. Not to worry if you haven't though, as creating and completing them is in itself a great tactic for refreshing your memory about a focus film. On the next page is an example of a possible knowledge organiser grid, which you could enlarge to A3 and use. As always though, it is better to create your own grid that suits the way you work.

A possible structure for a knowledge organiser

Unit name: Exam paper: Number of questions: Points and allocated time:	Focus film (director, year): Genre: Production company:		
Core areas	**Specialist area(s)**		**Key scenes and quotes**
Notable uses of film form	e.g. Key narrative theories	e.g. Ideological perspectives	
Cinematography			
Mise-en-scène			
Editing			
Sound			
Performance			
Key representations			
Gender			
Age			
Ethnicity			
Aesthetics	**Example questions**		
Context			
Political			
Social			
Cultural			
Institutional			

Another revision aid, and one that often really helps you develop confidence, is the **personal learning checklist** (PLC) with RAG rating. This is basically a table with a list of everything you need to know for a section of a component. Creating the PLC is in itself a useful way to remind you of exactly what knowledge you need. You then judge if you feel your understanding of each area is Red (insufficient and needing extensive work), Amber (reasonable but needs some reinforcing) or Green (secure). RAG rating your knowledge helps you to focus your time and attention on the areas of study that really need further revision.

British film since 1995 – *This is England*	R	A	G
Director's name and year of production			✓
Social context		✓	
Political context			✓
Cultural context	✓		
Institutional context		✓	
Clear example of camera movement			✓
Clear example of use of music			✓
And so on …			

You can revisit the PLC after further revision to see if you can cross out some of the ticks in the red and amber columns and move them to the green one.

Using time effectively is crucial for successful revision but the best way to prepare is to give yourself **enough time** to revise everything thoroughly: **start early**. Revision should be an ongoing process and you should frequently revisit all your focus films on a regular basis.

Time management in the exam

It is useful to go into the exam knowing how long should be spent on each question.

For the two 90-minute AS exams this is quite straightforward. Each paper has two sections comprising two questions each: a shorter compulsory question and a more in-depth question selected from a choice of two. In the first section the responses are worth 20 points and 40 points, and you should allow one hour. In the second section the responses are worth 10 points and 20 points and you should allow 30 minutes. In short, allow one minute per point awarded.

For A level it is more complicated and although both papers are 150 minutes in total, the time you should allow yourself per question differs. For Component 1 all questions are equally weighted (40 points) and should be allocated 50 minutes each. For Component 2 you have four questions, the first of which is worth 40 points and should be allocated one hour, and the final three 20-point questions should take 30 minutes each.

It can be difficult to work to strict timings but having lots of experience will make it easier. Spend some time in the lead-up to the exams looking at past papers and practising writing under timed conditions. Be strict with yourself: if you run out of time on one question move onto the next. It is better to have shorter responses to all questions rather than have missed a question altogether. Remember to allow a few minutes at the beginning of each response to plan your essay. This need not be detailed, just a list of prompts will suffice, but it really is vital in helping you provide a well-structured, coherently argued essay.

Frances Ha (Baumbach, 2012)

Glossary of key definitions

Aesthetic: the style adopted by an artist (in a film's case the filmmaker) or a film movement. For example, despite the different settings of *Trainspotting* (Boyle, 1996) and *Slumdog Millionaire* (Boyle, 2009), both films share a visual look and feel created by the director's, Danny Boyle, high-energy visual style, by way of his choice of camerawork, editing and music. German Expressionism was an artistic movement that encompassed theatre, dance, architecture, painting, sculpture and film. The aesthetic shared between expressionist films included exaggeration in performance, setting, lighting and disorientating camera angles.

Aspect ratio: the shape of the image; this affects the composition of the shots. The first aspect ratio used was 4:3: the first number refers to the width of the screen and the second to the height. Therefore, for every 4 inches in width, there will be 3 in height.

Asynchronous sounds: sound effects that are not matched with a visible source of the sound on screen.

Auteur: certain directors will have a strong aesthetic; you will begin to see recurring visual styles and motifs. These directors have become known as auteurs.

Background (BG): in contrast to the FG, the depth of field is altered by the cinematographer, which can add further meaning.

Balance: different elements are treated equally.

Bias: a concentration on one particular area or viewpoint.

Binary opposition: when two characters or ideologies are set up against one another. It is an important concept of structuralism and can be used to structure representations and help create meaning.

Casting: the pre-production process for selecting a certain type of actor or extra for a particular role or part in a film.

Canted angle: when the frame is deliberately slanted to one side. This is often to portray an intoxicated or unbalanced character or to help convey a sense of unease or disorientation.

Chiaroscuro lighting: this term is borrowed from painting, and refers to the bold use of dark and light. It was a favourite for filmmakers whose work falls into film movements or styles that were filming in black and white, particularly German Expressionism and film noir. It tends to lose its dramatic impact in colour.

Cinéma vérité: a style of documentary filmmaking, also called observational cinema.

Cinematographer: responsible for the look of the film; in charge of the camera technique and translates the director's vision onto the screen, advising the director on camera angles, lighting and special effects.

Coda: refers to the final narrative resolution in a film, which may not be primarily concerned with the film's main protagonist.

Conglomerate: a company that owns and controls a diverse range of other businesses.

Cultural capital: assets that give someone social mobility. This can involve education, personality and speech.

Demographic: sector of the population.

Depth of field: the distance between the nearest and furthest objects in a scene that are in sharp focus in a shot.

Dialect: a form of language that is peculiar to a region or social group.

Dialectic: two opposing or contradictory ideas or views are juxtaposed as a way of examining and discussing them.

Existentialism: a philosophy that emphasised the existence of the individual person as a free and responsible agent.

Expressionist: expressionist films depict a widely distorted reality for emotional effect.

Expressive lighting: lighting used for emotional rather than realistic effect.

Film noir: a type of criminal film that originated in the USA in the 1930s with its origins in pulp crime fiction. It subsequently found its way onto radio and by the 1940s was a discernible sub-genre. Common tropes involved a downbeat and grizzled private detective, weak, morally compromised men, and strong, amoral and sexual femme fatales. Lighting codes were typically low-key, high contrast thus creating a gloomy sense of foreboding and mystery as well as the frequent uses of window blinds in the mise-en-scène to further create a sense of entrapment. Jazz scoring was also common as was a lurid sensationalism such as explicit sensuality and brutal violence. Contemporary noir films such as *Pulp Fiction* are often dubbed 'neo-noir'.

Film stock: the type of film used to shoot the film on.

Foreground (FG): People, objects or action closest to the camera.

Formalism: looks at a film's structure and recognises the differences between the story and how it is told through the plot. This includes a focus on the formal elements of a film.

Frames per second (fps): the frame rate, or the speed that individual frames are projected to give the illusion of movement.

French New Wave: a movement in French cinema of the late 1950s and early 1960s. Directors, such as Jacques Demy, Agnes Varda, Alain Resnais, Claude Chabrol, Jean-Luc Godard and Francois Truffaut, created stylish, energetic and self-conscious films. French New Wave films were typified by on-location shooting, naturalistic acting and ambiguous or unresolved endings. While new wave directors were inspired by Hollywood auteurs such as Hitchcock, they often broke the rules of Classical Hollywood films. For instance, in *Breathless* (1959, Godard) the opening scene lacks an establishing shot and a conversation scene breaks the 180-degree rule.

Grading: colour film always needed to be graded to make sure that colours remain consistent. Like lighting, grading affects the mood and feel of a film. Documentaries will often be 'ungraded' and appear flat and lifeless. By grading, filmmakers draw emphasis to colour themes, such as red in *Shaun of the Dead*, or visually emphasise the mood of a scene by taking out the red, to leave a scene looking blue and chilly. With digital technology it is possible to manipulate the colour palette of a scene or even a whole film.

High concept: films centred on a relatively simple scenario that can be easily pitched with a succinctly stated premise.

Humanist irony: can be conceived as an approach to art that highlights the human condition in a rather tongue-in-cheek way. Thus, in a broadly comedic sense, we explore our nature such as the need for personal identity and freedom. Intertextual: the practice of one media text paying homage to or referencing another. An example would be Sebastian in *La La Land* swinging around a lamppost like Gene Kelly's character Don in *Singin' in the Rain* (Kelly & Donen, 1952).

Iris shot: the frame is partially masked in a circular frame, mimicking the iris of the eye. The iris shot may be used to begin or end a scene or draw our attention to something in the frame. Iris shots were a common convention in silent cinema.

Juxtaposition: the positioning of two shots, characters or scenes in sequence to encourage the audience to compare and contrast them.

Leitmotif: a reoccurring piece of music that represents characters, actions or themes.

Mind map: a visual representation of information that includes a central idea surrounded by connected branches of knowledge.

Mixing/layering: techniques used to combine a range of sounds or tracks. See *Sound design* and *Multitrack sound*.

Motif: a recurring element that has symbolic significance in a narrative.

Multitrack sound: sound sources recorded at different times are blended to create a cohesive whole. This method of sound recording was developed in 1955.

Narration: a commentary delivered to accompany a scene.

Narrative closure: the feeling of finality generated when all the questions asked in a story are answered.

Narrative devices: techniques used in order to tell a story.

Non-linear editing (NLE) 'is the software, computer-based editing systems we use nowadays for editing video or audio as opposed the old systems of either cutting film and/or audio tape and sticking the pieces together manually in the required order, or in video using two or more video tape machines to transfer selected shots to a recording machine.

'NLE relies on digitised material stored on the computer's hard disc or external digital storage, which means we are effectively just joining files together (in a manner of speaking). The original material is not destroyed by any of the editing actions and shots can be placed in any order with ease and rearranged if required with no degradation.' (de la Haye, Film & Video Editor/Cameraman/Photographer, 2017)

Objective truth: one truth that is the same for all people.

Portmanteau film: a film that consists of loosely related but largely distinct storylines. Famous examples could be the UK's seminal horror from Ealing Studios, *Dead of Night* (Cavalanati, Dearaden, Harner & Crichton, 1945) and *Four Rooms* (Tarantino, Rodriguezz, Anders & Rockwell, 1995) which featured a story called 'The Man from Hollywood' written and directed by Tarantino.

Post-production: the work that is required to complete the film, after shooting, including the edit, sound mix, music composition, colour grading and computer-generated imagery (CGI) special effects.

Pre-production: the period prior to filming, where key decisions are made, including securing funding, selecting actors and creative personnel, choosing locations, building sets, designing costumes and determining the film's aesthetic, and planning the production schedule.

Preface: a sequence in a film that sets the scene but which may not concern the dramatic focus of the film.

Production: the period of actual shooting. As this is the most costly, as much planning is done in the pre-production process, with daily shooting schedules prepared to ensure that the material required in each location or with a group of actors is secured. Most films are shot out of sequence.

Rite of passage: a ceremony marking an important stage in someone's life.

Scene: may consist of one shot or a series of shots depicting a continuous event.

Second wave feminism: a period of feminist activity that began in the USA in the early 1960s and continued to the early 1980s.

Sequence: a series of scenes of shots complete in itself. A sequence may occur in a single setting or several settings, i.e. a car chase. Action should match in sequence, where it continues across several consecutive shots with straight cuts – so that is depicts the event in a continuous manner.

Short film: according to the Academy of motion Picture and Sciences (AMPAS), a film under 40 minutes in length.

Shot: used to mean different aspects of the filmmaking process.

- For the cinematographer a shot is from the moment the camera starts rolling (action) to the end (cut).
- For the editor a shot is continuous scene or sequences between two cuts or edits.
- Refers to the process of shooting a film, e.g. 'we shot four minutes of screen time today'.
- There are different types of shot, which refer to the distance between the camera and the subject.

Slapstick: a farcical form of physical comedy, popular in early film comedy. It usually involves violent, physical action, such as pratfalls, chases and practical jokes.

Socio-economic status: an individual or group's social position in relation to others, based on education, occupation and income.

Sound design: involves performing and recording new sounds and editing previously recorded audio, such as sound effects and dialogue. These are combined to create an overall soundtrack to a film.

Star system: the system used by Hollywood studios to create and exploit stars. Studios would publicise films using star personas as the main selling point. Publicity departments would create a public image of the star, sometimes changing their name and details about their personal life.

Star vehicle: films that are sold on the popularity and persona of the leading star. A role may have been written or produced for this particular star.

Stop-motion animation: where the camera is repeatedly stopped and the subject is moved incrementally to produce, once a number of separate shots have been made, the illusion of continuous movement. Claymation uses clay models and stop-motion animation, as in the work of Nick Park and Aardman. This type of animation is distinct from the other mains forms of animation such as hand drawings, CGI, rotoscoping, animatronics and motion capture.

Structuralism: the idea that films can best be understood through an examination of their underlying structure, including exploring how meaning is produced through binary oppositions.

Surrealism: an international 20th-century movement of artists, writers and philosophers who valued the unconscious mind and dreams. They rejected conventional moral and artistic values. The surrealists were heavily influenced by the work of Sigmund Freud, particularly his book *The Interpretation of Dreams* (1899), which argued that our dreams reveal our unconscious motivations or desires.

Synchronous sounds: contribute to the realism of film as the sounds heard match the actions on screen.

Tentpole: a movie with a massive budget deemed by the studio to carry less financial risk. It will be marketed heavily and given an extended saturation release. Its revenue is intended to help financially support the other films released by the studio.

Tropes: recurring or significant themes.

Two-reelers: short silent films around 20 minutes long. During the 1920s, comedy two-reelers were screened in cinemas as supporting films for a feature-length film.

Verisimilitude: about giving the appearance of reality or truth. This does not mean that the world is presented as real, just believable within the context of the world in which the film is set. For example, we know that in the real world people do not break into song when they fall in love, but in a musical, we accept this convention, but if this happened in a gritty thriller, it would be out of place.

Vertical integration: when a company controls the different stages of a product's process or construction. During the studio era, the Big Five Hollywood studios were vertically integrated, as they controlled production, distribution and exhibition.

Voice of god: a narration technique in which the narration is given anonymously and authoritatively.

References

21st Century Fox (2016) Fox Careers, www.foxcareers.com/OurCompany/Divisions/Film.

Allen, K. (2015, 8 March) 'How Long are those Oscar Coattails for Box Office Indie Films?', CNBC, www.cnbc.com/2015/03/06/how-long-are-those-oscar-coattails-for-box-office-indie-films.html?view=story&%24DEVICE%24=native-android-tablet.

Alvarado, M. & Gutch, R. (1987) *Learning the Media: Introduction to Media Teaching*, Palgrave.

Anastasia, G. & Macnow, G. (2011) *The Ultimate Book of Gangster Movies: Featuring the 100 Greatest Gangster Films of all Time*, Running Press.

Anderson, A. (2013, 22 February) '10 Lessons on Filmmaking from *Beasts of the Southern Wild*'s Benh Zeitlin', *Filmmaker Magazine*, http://filmmakermagazine.com/65614-10-lessons-on-filmmaking-from-beasts-of-the-southern-wilds-benh-zeitlin/#.Wh-pO7p2tTA/.

Angeletti-Szasz, C. (2016, 28 April) 'Anita Lee on the Evolution of the Documentary Landscape', Canadian Film Centre, http://cfccreates.com/news/627-anita-lee-on-the-evolution-of-the-documentary-landscape.

Arneson, K. (2012) 'Representation through Documentary: A Post-modern assessment', *Artifacts*, https://artifactsjournal.missouri.edu/2012/03/representation-through-documentary-a-post-modern-assessment/.

ARRI News (2017) '*Beasts of the Southern Wild*', www.arri.com/news/news/beasts-of-the-southern-wild.

Aufderheide, P. (2008) *Documentary Film: A Very Short Introduction*, Oxford University Press.

Ayers, M. (2012, 20 July) '*Beasts of the Southern Wild* Star: From Baker to Actor', CNN, http://edition.cnn.com/2012/07/20/showbiz/movies/beasts-southern-wild-actor-dwight-henry/index.html.

Baker, S. (2011) Media Studies Key Concepts: Representation, www.slideshare.net/tinkertaylor1981/representation-revision-booklet.

Barlow, H. (2016, 1 March) '*Mustang* is a Stirring Tale of Girlhood', *Irish Examiner*, www.irishexaminer.com/lifestyle/artsfilmtv/mustang-is-a-stirring-tale-of-girlhood-384801.html.

Beck, J. (2016) *Designing Sound: Audiovisual Aesthetics in 1970s American Cinema*, Rutgers University Press.

Belton, J. (2008) 'Classical Hollywood Cinema: Style', in *American Cinema/American Culture*, McGraw-Hill.

Berger, J. (2008) *Ways of Seeing*, Verso Books.

BFC (2016) British Film Commission, www.britishfilmcommission.org.uk/.

Biancolli, A. (2012, 8 October) '*Beasts of the Southern Wild* Review: Wet and Wild', SFGate, www.sfgate.com/movies/article/Beasts-of-the-Southern-Wild-review-Wet-and-wild-3686131.php.

Blair, D. (2017, 25 November) 'Iran's Big Woman Problem: All of the Things Iranian Women aren't Allowed to Do', *The Telegraph*, www.telegraph.co.uk/women/womens-life/11875128/Irans-women-problem-All-of-the-things-Iranian-women-arent-allowed.html.

Blake, H. (2010, 29 September) '*Bonnie and Clyde* Director Arthur Penn Dies', *The Daily Telegraph*, www.telegraph.co.uk/culture/film/film-news/8033875/Bonnie-and-Clyde-director-Arthur-Penn-dies.html.

Bordwell, D. & Thompson, D. (2012) *Film Art: An Introduction*, McGraw.

Bordwell, D., Staiger, J. & Thompson, K. (1988) *The Classical Hollywood Cinema: Film Style and Mode of Production to 1960*, Routledge.

Bodganovich, P. (2011, 30 January) '1928: The Last and Greatest Year of the Original Motion Picture Arat, B.S. (Before Sound)', IndieWire, www.indiewire.com/2011/01/1928-the-last-and-greatest-year-of-the-original-motion-picture-art-b-s-before-sound-131788/.

Bordwell, D. & Thompson, K. (1997) *Film Art: An Introduction*, 4th edn, McGraw-Hill.

Bordwell, D. (2002) 'The Art Cinema as a Mode of Practice', in *European Cinema Reader*, C. Fowler (ed.), Routledge.

Bouie, J. (2015, 23 August) 'Where Black Lives Matter Began', slate.com, www.slate.com/articles/news_and_politics/politics/2015/08/hurricane_katrina_10th_anniversary_how_the_black_lives_matter_movement_was.html.

Boxofficemojo.com (2016a) 2016 Domestic Grosses, www.boxofficemojo.com/yearly/chart/?yr=2016&p=.htm.

Boxofficemojo.com (2016b) Studio Market Share, www.boxofficemojo.com/studio/?view=company&view2=yearly&yr=2016&p=.htm.

Boxofficemojo.com (2017a) *Farenheit 9/11*, www.boxofficemojo.com/movies/?id=fahrenheit911.htm.

Boxofficemojo.com (2017b) *Stories We Tell*, www.boxofficemojo.com/movies/?id=storieswetell.htm.

Bradshaw, P. (2014, 25 September) '*Ida* Review – an Eerily Beautiful Road Movie', *The Guardian*, www.theguardian.com/film/2014/sep/25/ida-pawel-pawlikowski-nun-road-movie.

Bradshaw, P. (2015, 26 November) '*Carol* Review – Cate Blanchett Superb in a Five-star Tale of Forbidden Love', *The Guardian*, www.theguardian.com/film/2015/nov/26/carol-film-review-cate-blanchett-todd-haynes-rooney-mara.

Brand, N. (2013, 12 September) 'The Secret Art of the Film Soundtrack', *The Guardian*, www.theguardian.com/music/musicblog/2013/sep/12/film-soundtracks-neil-brand.

British Film Institute (BFI) (2017) *Statistical Yearbook*, www.bfi.org.uk/education-research/film-industry-statistics-research/statistical-yearbook.

Brody, R. (2015, 13 October) 'Jafar Panahi's Remarkable "Taxi"', *The New Yorker*, www.newyorker.com/culture/richard-brody/jafar-panahis-remarkable-taxi.

Brody, R. (n.d.) '*Mustang*', *The New Yorker*, www.newyorker.com/goings-on-about-town/movies/mustang.

Brooker, P. & Brooker, W. (1996) 'Pulp Modernism: Tarantino's Affirmative Action', in *Film Theory: Critical Concepts in Media and Cultural Studies*, ed. P. Simpson, A. Utterson & K.J. Shepherdson, Routledge.

Brownlow, K. (1992) *The Parade's Gone By …*, University of California Press.

Buder, E. (2015, 30 November) 'Meet France's Oscar Entry, 'Mustang,' a Controversial 5-Headed Monster of Feminity', IndieWire, www.indiewire.com/2015/11/meet-frances-oscar-entry-mustang-a-controversial-5-headed-monster-of-femininity-50271/.

Buñuel, L. (2002) *An Unspeakable Betrayal: Selected Writings of Luis Buñuel*, University of California Press.

Buscombe, E. & White, R. (2002) *British Film Institute Film Classics, Volume 1*, Routledge.

Calhoun, D. (2016, 1 September) 'La La Land', *Time Out*, www.timeout.com/sydney/film/la-la-land.

Carroll, B. (2003) *American Masculinities: A Historical Encyclopedia*, Sage.

Chamboredon, J.C. (2015, 24 November) 'Q&A with Warren Ellis – Composer of *Mustang*', Milan Records, https://milanrecords.com/qa-with-warren-ellis-composer-of-mustang/.

Chivers, S. (2011) *The Silvering Screen: Old Age and Disability in Cinema*, University of Toronto Press.

Chopra, A. (1998, 31 August) 'Lethal Connection', *India Today*, http://indiatoday.intoday.in/story/movie-review-of-dil-se-shah-rukh-khan-manisha-koirala/1/264844.html.

Christie, I. (2012) The 50 Greatest Films of All Time', *Sight & Sound*, www.bfi.org.uk/news/50-greatest-films-all-time.

Chung, N. (2016, 15 January) 'Toast Points for the Week of January 15th', *The Toast*, http://the-toast.net/2016/01/15/toast-points-week-of-jan-15th/.

CinemaReview.com (2017) *Stories We Tell*, www.cinemareview.com/production.asp?prodid=13494#.

Cirillo, F. (2007) The Pomodoro Technique, http://baomee.info/pdf/technique/1.pdf.

Cochrane, K. (2010, 12 February) 'Kim Longinotto: "Film-making Saved My Life"', *The Guardian*, www.theguardian.com/lifeandstyle/2010/feb/12/longinotto-film-making-saved-life.

Connolly, K. (2000, 11 August) 'Bohemian Rhapsodist', *Guardian* www.theguardian.com/film/2000/aug/11/culture.features2.

Cooke, R. (2016, 15 May) 'Deniz Gamze Ergüven: "For Women in Turkey it's Like the Middle Ages"', *The Observer*, www.theguardian.com/film/2016/may/15/deniz-gamze-erguven-mustang-turkey-interview-rachel-cooke.

Coplan, A. (2006) 'Catching Characters' Emotions: Emotional Contagion Responses to Narrative Fiction Film', *Film Studies*, 8, www.academia.edu/6434449/Catching_Characters_Emotions_Emotional_Contagion_Responses_to_Narrative_Fiction_Film.

Corliss, R. (2012, 26 June) '*Beasts of the Southern Wild*: A Child's Garden of Wonders', *Time*, http://entertainment.time.com/2012/06/26/beasts-of-the-southern-wild-a-childs-garden-of-wonders/.

Cornell University (2016) The Cornell Note-taking System, http://lsc.cornell.edu/wp-content/uploads/2016/10/Cornell-NoteTaking-System.pdf.

Cox, D. (2012, 28 February) Why Do Films Do Such a Bad Job of Portraying Old People?', *The Daily Telegraph*, www.theguardian.com/film/filmblog/2012/feb/28/films-bad-job-portraying-old-people.

Daily Telegraph (n.d.) 'Creating the 1950s Style for the Stars of *Carol*', www.telegraph.co.uk/film/carol/1950s_beauty_look.

Davis, D.K. & Baron, S.J. (1981) *A History of Our Understanding of Mass Communication*, Wadsworth Publishing.

Debruge, P. (2013, 7 October) 'Quentin Tarantino: The Great Recycler', http://variety.com/2013/film/markets-festivals/quentin-tarantino-the-great-recycler-1200703098/.

Deloitte (2016, September) 'Indywood: The Indian Film Industry', www2.deloitte.com/content/dam/Deloitte/in/Documents/technology-media-telecommunications/in-tmt-indywood-film-festival-noexp.pdf.

Donadio, R. (2015, 24 September) 'Jafar Panahi, Iranian Filmmaker, Persists Despite a Ban', *New York Times*, www.nytimes.com/2015/09/27/movies/jafar-panahi-iranian-filmmaker-persists-despite-a-ban.html.

Dönmez-Colin, G. (2008) *Turkish Cinema: Identity, Distance and Belonging*, Reaktion Books.

Doucet, A. (2015, 19 February) 'Ontological Narrativity and the Performativity of the *Stories We Tell Stories We Tell*', *Visual Studies*, 30 (1): 98–117, www.tandfonline.com/doi/abs/10.1080/1472586X.2015.996415?src=recsys&journalCode=rvst20.

Driscoll, C. (n.d.) *Modernism, Cinema Adolescence: Another History for Teen Film*, screeningthepast.com, www.screeningthepast.com/2011/11/modernism-cinema-adolescence-another-history-for-teen-film/

DW (2017, 1 December) 'The Musicals that Inspired *La La Land*', www.dw.com/en/the-musicals-that-inspired-la-la-land/g-37091454.

Dyer, R. (1997) *White: Essays on Race and Culture*, Routledge.

Dyer, R. (1998) *Stars*, BFI Publishing.

Earle, S. (2017, 20 January) 'The Politics of Nostalgia', *Jacobin*, www.jacobinmag.com/2017/01/donald-trump-inauguration-nationalism/.

Ebert, R. (1991, 26 May) 'It's High Tide for Black New Wave', *Roger Ebert's Journal*, www.rogerebert.com/rogers-journal/its-high-tide-for-black-new-wave.

Ebert, R. (2013, 7 July) 'Roger Ebert on the Nature of Film: "A Movie is Not a Logical Art Form"', No Film School, https://nofilmschool.com/2013/07/roger-ebert-movie-not-a-logical-art-form.

Eduqas (2017) WJEC Eduqas GCE A Level in Film Studies, www.wjec.co.uk/qualifications/film-studies/eduqas-film-studies-as-level-from-2017/eduqas-a-level-film-studies-spec-from-2017.pdf?language_id=.

Edwards, G. (2014, 20 June) 'Fight the Power: Spike Lee on "Do the Right Thing"', *Rolling Stone*, www.rollingstone.com/movies/news/fight-the-power-spike-lee-on-do-the-right-thing-20140620.

Eisenstein, S. (1937) Montage of Attractions (trans. D. Gerould, 1974), https://thecharnelhouse.org/wp-content/uploads/2015/03/sergei-eisenstein-montage-of-attractions-for-enough-stupidity-in-every-wiseman-1923.pdf.

Elsaesser, T. (2012) 'Six Degrees of Nosferatu', *Sight & Sound*.

Eisner, L.H. (1969) *The Haunted Screen: Expressionism in the German Cinema and the Influence of Max Reinhardt*, University of California Press.

Eitzen, D. (1995) 'When is a Documentary a Documentary?: Documentary as a Mode of Reception', University of Texas Press, *Cinema Journal*, www.columbia.edu/itc/film/gaines/documentary_tradition/Eitzen.pdf.

Field, S. (1979) *Screenplay: The Foundations of Screenwriting*, Delta.

Fiske, J. (2010) *Introduction to Communication Studies*, 3rd edn, Taylor & Francis.

Follows, S. (2014, 22 July) 'What Percentage of a Film Crew is Female?', https://stephenfollows.com/gender-of-film-crews/.

Frayling, C. (2006) *Mad, Bad and Dangerous? The Scientist and the Cinema*, Reaktion Books.

Freud, S. (1899) The Interpretation of Dreams.

Friedman, L.D. (ed.) (1998) *Arthur Penn's Bonnie and Clyde*, Cambridge University Press.

Friedman, L.D. (2000) *Bonnie and Clyde*, BFI Publishing.

Gant C. (2017, 1 June) 'Why Foreign-language Films are Struggling in UK Cinemas', Screen Daily, www.screendaily.com/features/why-foreign-language-films-are-struggling-in-uk-cinemas/5118664.

Gee, O. (2015, 11 May) 'The 2015 Cannes Film Festival in Numbers', The Local, www.thelocal.fr/20150511/the-2015-cannes-film-festival-in-numbers.

Geiger, J. & Rutsky, R.L. (2013) 'Casablanca', in *Film Analysis: A Norton Reader*, W.W. Norton.

Giardina, C. (2016, 19 December) 'Why *La La Land*'s Opening Number Went From Cutting-Room Floor to Curtain-Raiser', *Hollywood Reporter*, www.hollywoodreporter.com/behind-screen/why-la-la-lands-opening-number-went-cutting-room-floor-curtain-raiser-956519.

Girls Not Brides (2017) 'Turkey', www.girlsnotbrides.org/child-marriage/turkey/.

Goldstein, J.H. (1998) *Why We Watch: The Attractions of Violent Entertainment*, Oxford University Press.

Golshiri, G. (2015, 14 April) 'Jafar Panahi Goes Through Red Lights', *Le Monde*, www.newwavefilms.co.uk/assets/1143/Jafar_Panahi_goes_through_red_lights.pdf.

Gomery, D. (1998) 'Hollywood as Industry', in *The Oxford Guide to Film Studies*, ed. J. Hill & P. Gibson (eds), Oxford University Press.

Gormley, P. (2005) *The New-Brutality Film: Race and Affect in Contemporary American Cinema*, University of Chicago Press.

Grant, B.K. (2007) *Film Genre: From Iconography to Ideology*, Wallflower Press.

Gray, C. (2016, 29 November) 'Věra Chytilová for Beginners', *BFI Film Forever*, www.bfi.org.uk/news-opinion/news-bfi/features/vera-chytilova-beginners.

Gritten, D. (2012, 27 November) 'Ben Wheatley: "I'm Looking for a Happier Ending"', *The Daily Telegraph*, www.telegraph.co.uk/culture/film/filmmakersonfilm/9698727/Ben-Wheatley-lm-looking-for-a-happier-ending.html.

Grobar, M. (2017, 16 February) 'From "Boogie Nights" to "Mean Streets": *La La Land* Sound Editors on Damien Chazelle's Sonic Inspirations', Deadline, http://deadline.com/2017/02/la-la-land-oscars-ai-ling-lee-mildred-iatrou-sound-editing-interview-news-1201899086/.

Gunning, T. (1986) 'The Cinema of Attractions: Early Film, its Spectator and the Avant-Garde', *Wide Angle*, 8 (3&4).

Hall, S. (1973) *Encoding and Decoding in the Television Discourse*, Centre for Contemporary Cultural Studies.

Hallihan, M. (2016, 1 August) 'The 10 Best Iranian Films About Women', *Taste of Cinema*, www.tasteofcinema.com/2016/the-10-best-iranian-films-about-women/.

Haney, L. (2005) *Gregory Peck: A Charmed Life*, Da Capo Press.

Hardy, R. (2015, 8 March) 'Easyrig Mini is a Budget Version of One of the Most Interesting Camera Stabilizers Out There', No Film School, https://nofilmschool.com/2015/03/easyrig-mini-story-heart-video.

Harris, A. (2016, 13 December) '*La La Land*'s Many References to Classic Movies: A Guide', Slate, www.slate.com/blogs/browbeat/2016/12/13/la_la_land_s_many_references_to_classic_movies_from_singin_in_the_rain_to.html.

Hattam, J. (2016, 26 February) 'Oscar-Nominee "Mustang" Puts Turkey in Unwanted Spotlight', We.News, http://womensenews.org/2016/02/133986/.

Hauke, C. (2013) *Visible Minds: Movies, Modernity and the Unconscious*, Routledge.

Hoad, P. (2013, 15 January) 'Is Quentin Tarantino the World's Most Influential Director?', *Guardian*, www.theguardian.com/film/filmblog/2013/jan/15/quentin-tarantino-most-influential-director.

hooks, b. (2012) No Love in the World, www.newblackmaninexile.net/2012/09/bell-hooks-no-love-in-wild.html.

Horton, A. (ed.) (1991) *Comedy/Cinema/Theory*, University of California Press.

Hudgins, S. (2017) 'A Chronic Problem: Violence Against Women in Turkey', *Huffington Post*, www.huffingtonpost.com/sarabrynn-hudgins/a-chronic-problem-violenc_b_13649898.html.

Hutchinson, P. & Barrett, A. (2017) 10 Great German Expressionist Films, BFI, www.bfi.org.uk/news-opinion/news-bfi/lists/10-great-german-expressionist-films.

Hurriyet Daily News (2017) 'Survey Sheds Light on Severity of Turkey's Child Marriage Problem', www.hurriyetdailynews.com/survey-sheds-light-on-severity-of-turkeys-child-marriage-problem-126103.

Ide, W. (2016, 15 May) '*Mustang* Review – Teen Tension in Anatolia', *The Observer*, www.theguardian.com/film/2016/may/15/mustang-review-women-rural-turkey-oscar-nominated.

Ignoramous, L. (2017) 'Stories We Tell Analysis: Sarah Polley's Documentary', Filmslie, http://filmslie.com/stories-we-tell-review-sarah-polleys-documentary/.

Independent Film & Television Alliance (n.d.) 'What is an Independent?', www.ifta-online.org/what-independent.

Independent Film & Television Alliance (2013) IFTA FAQs, www.ifta-online.org/sites/default/files/FAQs_updated+Sep2013.pdf.

Iris (2014) 'The New Cinema Communication', www.obs.coe.int/documents/205595/264635/IRIS%2B_2014-1_ENcomplet.pdf/bbc3325b-379b-46ec-9664-e879e0b6b452.

Isenberg, N. (2017) *We'll Always Have Casablanca: The Life, Legend, and Afterlife of Hollywood's Most Beloved Movie*, Faber & Faber.

Jeong, S.-H. & Szaniawski, J. (2016) *The Global Auteur: The Politics of Authorship in 21st Century Cinema*, Bloomsbury.

Johnson, T. (2015, 14 December) 'Film of the Week: *Taxi Tehran*', *Sight & Sound*, www.bfi.org.uk/news-opinion/sight-sound-magazine/reviews-recommendations/film-week-taxi-tehran.

Kael, P. (1967, 21 October) 'Bonnie and Clyde', *The New Yorker*, www.newyorker.com/magazine/1967/10/21/bonnie-and-clyde.

Kenigsberg, B. (2012, 6 July) 'Beasts of the Southern Wild: A Republican Fantasy?', Time Out Chicago, www.timeout.com/chicago/film/beasts-of-the-southern-wild-a-republican-fantasy.

Kohn, E. (2014, 1 July) 'Close Curtain Director Jafar Panahi Talks About Making Movies Under House Arrest: "Put yourself in My Shoes"', www.indiewire.com/2014/07/closed-curtain-director-jafar-panahi-talks-about-making-movies-under-house-arrest-put-yourself-in-my-shoes-24727/.

Koszarski, R. (2005) Fort Lee: The Film Town, Indiana University Press.

Kuhn, A. & Westwell, G. (2012) A Dictionary of Film Studies, Oxford University Press.

Lacey, L. (2010, 6 May) Kim Longinotto: Capturing Women in Critical Transitions, www.theglobeandmail.com/arts/film/kim-longinotto-capturing-women-in-critical-transitions/article1211066/.

Laderman, D. (2002) Driving Visions: Exploring the Road Movie, University of Texas Press.

Lauzen, M.M. (2016) 'It's a Man's (Celluloid) World: Portrayals of Female Characters in the Top 100 Films of 2015', http://womenintvfilm.sdsu.edu/files/2015_Its_a_Mans_Celluloid_World_Report.pdf.

Lauzen, M.M. & Dozier, D. (2005) 'Maintaining the Double Standard: Portrayals of Age and Gender in Popular Films', Sex Roles, April, www.researchgate.net/publication/225889150_Maintaining_the_Double_Standard_Portrayals_of_Age_and_Gender_in_Popular_Films.

Lemercier, F. (2015, 6 July) 'Deniz Gamze Ergüven: Director', Cineuropa, www.cineuropa.org/it.aspx?t=interview&l=en&did=293768.

Lensflare Theory (n.d.) 'Establishing Shots: La La Land', www.lensflaretheory.com/establishing-shots-la-la-land.html.

Leonard, S. (2014) Fifty Hollywood Directors, Routledge.

Leszkiewicz, A. (2015, 27 November) 'Behind Carol: The Photographers Who Influenced Todd Haynes' Award-winning Film', The New Statesman, www.newstatesman.com/culture/art-design/2015/11/behind-carol-photographers-who-influenced-todd-haynes-award-winning-film?page=14&sa=U&ved=0ahUKEwiYrtnB2djLAhUBzR

QKHRuyDkcQpwIlJDAF&usg=AFQjCNFCTtvtgn4TXYn6tQhshqnHHH2sNQ&qt-trending=1.

Leszkiewicz, A. (2017, 6 February) 'In Defence of La La Land', New Statesman, www.newstatesman.com/culture/film/2017/02/defence-la-la-land.

Lévi-Strauss, C. (1995) Myth and Meaning: Cracking the Code of Culture, Schocken Books.

Lidz, F. (2012, December) 'How Benh Zeitlin Made Beasts of the Southern Wild', Smithsonian Magazine, www.smithsonianmag.com/arts-culture/how-benh-zeitlin-made-beasts-of-the-southern-wild-135132724/?device=iphone&no-ist=&page=4.

LoBrutto, V. (1991) Selected Takes: Film Editors on Editing, Praeger.

Lowenstein, A. (2016) 'A Cinema of Disorientation: Space, Genre, Wheatley', Critical Quarterly, 58: 5–15.

Lutz, A. (2012, 14 June) 'These 6 Corporations Control 90% of the Media in America', Business Insider UK, http://uk.businessinsider.com/these-6-corporations-control-90-of-the-media-in-america-2012-6.

Mallinder, L. (2012, 17 May) 'What Does it Mean to be Canadian?', BBC News, www.bbc.co.uk/news/world-radio-and-tv-18086952.

Manvell, R. (1951) 'Editor's Preface', in Jarratt, V. (ed.) The Italian Cinema, Falcon Press.

Mast, G. (1979) The Comic Mind: Comedy and the Movies, University of Chicago Press.

Matthau, C. (2012) 'How Tech Has Shaped Film Making: The Film Vs Digital Debate is Put to Rest', Wired, www.wired.com/insights/2015/01/how-tech-shaped-film-making/.

Mays, R. (2014, 26 December) 'Semla Reflects the #BlackLivesMatter Movement of Today', Ebony, www.ebony.com/entertainment-culture/selma-reflects-the-blacklivesmatter-moment-444#axzz506IOSBRM.

McNary, D. (2017, 4 February) 'La La Land Director Damien Chazelle Explains His Approach to Casting the Original Musical', Variety, http://variety.com/2017/film/news/damien-chazelle-la-la-land-casting-1201978332/.

McVeigh, T. & Colley, C. (2015, 8 February) 'We Record All the Killing of Women by Men. You See a Pattern', The Guardian, www.theguardian.com/society/2015/feb/08/killing-of-women-by-men-record-database-femicide.

Means, S.P. (2016, 19 January) 'Movie Review: Spirited Girls Face Religious Restrictions in Powerful Mustang', Salt Lake Tribune, http://archive.sltrib.com/article.php?id=3410725&itype=CMSID.

metacritic (n.d.) Stories We Tell: Movie Details & Credits, www.metacritic.com/movie/stories-we-tell.

Miller, G. (2014, 9 August) 'Data From a Century of Cinema Reveals How Movies Have Evolved', Wired, www.wired.com/2014/09/cinema-is-evolving/.

Miller, J. (2017a, 14 February) 'Emma Stone and Ryan Gosling's La La Land Costumes Were Inspired by These Old Hollywood Stars', Vanity Fair, www.vanityfair.com/hollywood/2017/02/emma-stone-ryan-gosling-la-la-land-costumes.

Miller, J. (2017b, 16 February) 'The Clever Tricks that Made La La Land Look Technicolor and Timeless', Vanity Fair, www.vanityfair.com/hollywood/2017/02/la-la-land-production-design.

Millman, Z. (2017, 22 February) 'Never Shined So Brightly: The Use of Color in La La Land', Film School Rejects, https://filmschoolrejects.com/color-in-la-la-land-26939a11accd/.

Ministry of Culture & Islamic Guidance (2017) Introduction of Ministry, www.farhang.gov.ir/en/profileofministry/responsibilities.

Monaco, J. (2000) The Dictionary of New Media: The New Digital World, Harbor Electronic Publishing.

Money (2017, 16 January) '5 Stocking Statistics that Show the Persistence of Racial Inequality', http://time.com/money/4632250/shocking-statistics-racial-gap-economic-inequality.

Most, M. (2013, 2 March) 'Conversation with Cinematographer Ben Richardson about his Work on Beasts of the Southern Wild, by Benh Zeitlin, AFC, www.afcinema.com/Conversation-with-cinematographer-Ben-Richardson-about-his-work-on-Beasts-of-the-Southern-Wild-by-Benh-Zeitlin.html?lang=en.

Motion Picture Association of America (2017, 19 October) 'Why Film Festivals Matter', www.mpaa.org/why-film-festivals-matter/.

Mudde, C. (2016, 15 December) 'Can We Stop the Politics of Nostalgia that Have Dominated 2016?', *Newsweek*, www.newsweek.com/1950s-1930s-racism-us-europe-nostalgia-cas-mudde-531546.

Mueller, M. (2016, 14 December) 'How Damien Chazelle Made *La La Land* for Just $30m', ScreenDaily, www.screendaily.com/features/how-damien-chazelle-made-la-la-land-for-just-30m/5112184.article.

Mulvey, L. (1998) 'Kiarostami's Uncertainty Principle', *Sight & Sound*, no. 6.

Mulvey, L. (1999) 'Visual Pleasure and Narrative Cinema', in L. Braudy & M. Cohen (eds) *Film Theory and Criticism: Introductory Readings*.

Mulvey, L. (2009) *Visual and Other Pleasures*, Palgrave Macmillan.

Murphy, M. (2016, 4 November) 'LA Transcendental: How *La La Land* Chases the Sublime', *New York Times*, www.nytimes.com/2016/11/06/movies/la-la-land-stars-ryan-gosling-emma-stone-and-los-angeles.html.

Nelmes, J. (2011) *Introduction to Film Studies*, Routledge.

Nelson, G. (2017, 6 January) 'The Unbearable Whiteness of *La La Land*', *Paste Magazine*, www.pastemagazine.com/articles/2017/01/the-unbearable-whiteness-of-la-la-land.html.

New Wave Films (2015) Tehran Taxi, www.newwavefilms.co.uk/assets/1112/Taxi_Tehran_pressbook_with_cert.pdf.

NFB (2015, 30 June) Creative Doc Lab: Non-fiction Spreads its Wings, http://blog.nfb.ca/blog/2015/06/30/creative-doc-lab-non-fiction-spreads-wings/.

Nichols, B. (2010) *Introduction to Documentary*, Indiana University Press.

Nott, G. (2014, 19 November) 'The Importance of Film Festivals', www.savageonline.co.uk/our-london/the-importance-of-film-festivals/.

O'Callaghan, P. (2014, 4 April) '*Sightseers*': Ben Wheatley, Alice Lowe and Steve Oram', BFI, www.bfi.org.uk/news/sightseers-ben-wheatley-alice-lowe-steve-oram.

O'Falt, C. (2017a, 1 February) 'How *La La Land* Cinematographer Linus Sandgren Taught His Cameras to Dance', IndieWire, www.indiewire.com/2017/02/la-la-land-cinematography-director-of-photography-linus-sandgren-1201776704/.

O'Falt, C. (2017b, 21 February) 'Why *La La Land* Was So Much Harder to Edit than *Whiplash*', IndieWire, www.indiewire.com/2017/02/la-la-land-damien-chazelle-tom-cross-editing-filmmaker-toolkit-podcast-episode-21-1201785368/.

Ordona, M. (2017, 16 February) 'Lights, Camera, Colors Give *La La Land* its Lavish Look', *Los Angeles Times*, www.latimes.com/entertainment/envelope/la-en-mn-0216-craft-la-la-look-20170216-story.html.

Ortner, S.B. (2012) 'Against Hollywood: American Independent Film as a Critical Cultural Movement', *Journal of Ethnographic Theory*, 2(2), www.haujournal.org/index.php/hau/article/view/hau2.2.002/1004.

Panahi, J. (2009, November) In Real Time: An Interview with Jafar Panahi, Off Screen, http://offscreen.com/view/interview_panahi

Papadakis, P. (2016, 13 January) The 30 Best Films Starring Mostly Non-Professional Actors, Taste of Cinema, www.tasteofcinema.com/2016/the-30-best-films-starring-mostly-non-professional-actors/#ixzz55TZqXXdl.

Parkinson, D. (2016, 13 May) '*Mustang* Review', *Empire*, www.empireonline.com/movies/mustang/review/.

Paste (2015, 8 May) The 100 Best Documentaries of All Time, www.pastemagazine.com/articles/2015/05/the-100-best-documentaries-of-all-time.html?p=4.

Patterson, J. (2017, 9 January) '*La La Land*: Why this Magical Musical Will Transport you From Trump-World', *The Guardian*, www.theguardian.com/film/2017/jan/09/why-musical-la-la-land-will-transport-you-from-trump-world.

Pawalikowski, P. (2014, 21 November) 'How We Made *Ida*: Pawel Pawlikowski on the Journey From Script to Film', *The Guardian*, www.theguardian.com/film/2014/nov/21/pawel-pawlikowski-making-of-ida-polish-film.

Petro, P. (ed.) (2010) *Idols of Modernity: Movie Stars of the 1920s*, Rutgers University Press.

Pidd, H. (2006, 14 March) 'The Invisible Woman', *The Guardian*, www.theguardian.com/film/2006/mar/14/television.

Polley, S. (2012, 29 August) '*Stories We Tell*: A Post by Sarah Polley', NFB, http://blog.nfb.ca/blog/2012/08/29/stories-we-tell-a-post-by-sarah-polley/.

Propp, V. (1928) *Morphology of the Folk Tale*, University of Texas Press.

Pulver, A. & Dehghan, S.K. (2016, 4 July) 'Abbas Kiarostami, Palme d'Or-winning Iranian Film-maker, Dies Aged 76', *The Guardian*, www.theguardian.com/film/2016/jul/04/abbas-kiarostami-palme-dor-winning-iranian-film-maker-dies.

Quinn, J. (2012) *This Much is True: 14 Directors on Documentary Filmmaking*, A&C Black.

Rea, S. (2012, 13 July) '*Beasts of the Southern Wild*: A Magical Trip to Bayou Country', *The Inquirer*, www.philly.com/philly/entertainment/movies/20120713__Beasts_of_the_Southern_Wild___A_magical_trip_to_bayou_country.html.

Romney, J. (2015, 1 November) '*Taxi Tehran* Review – Jafar Panahi's Joy Ride', *The Guardian*, www.theguardian.com/film/2015/nov/01/taxi-tehran-review-admirable-jafar-panahi-takes-to-the-streets.

Rotha, P. (1935) Traditions of Documentary Film, www.scribd.com/document/267134051/Paul-Rotha-Documentary-Film.

Saunders, D. (2007, 23 May) 'My Interview with Jafar Panahi', http://dougsaunders.net/2007/05/interview-jafar-panahi-iran/.

Schatz, T. (1998) *The Genius of the System: Hollywood Film-making in the Studio Era*, University of Texas Press.

Shadoian, J. (2003) *Dreams and Dead Ends: The American Gangster Film*, Oxford University Press.

Sheva. A. (2016, 1 April) '86% of Turkish Women Suffer Domestic Abuse', *Arutz Sheva*, www.israelnationalnews.com/News/News.aspx/210182.

Silberman, J. (2015, 26 January) '6 Lessons from *Selma* for Black Lives Matter and Other Political Movements', *Los Angeles Times*, http://beta.latimes.com/nation/la-ol-selma-black-lives-matter-20150126-story.html.

Singleton, R.S. & Conrad, J.A. (2000) *Filmmaker's Dictionary*, 2nd edn, Lone Eagle.

Siskel, G. & Ebert, R. (1989) Siskel & Ebert 1989 – Best of 1989, www.youtube.com/watch?v=XjYS8EUakgs.

Smit, D. (2012) *Ingrid Bergman: The Life, Career and Public Image*, McFarland.

Smith, D. (2011, 27 April) 'Clio Barnard: *The Arbor*', *Filmmaker Magazine*, http://filmmakermagazine.com/23471-clio-barnard-the-arbor/#.WiQ5LmTQofE.

Smith, J., Bordwell, D. & Thompson, D. (2016) *Film Art: An Introduction*, 6th edn, McGraw Hill.

Smith, S.L., Choueiti, M. & Pieper, K. (2017a) Inequality in 900 Popular Films: Examining Portrayals of Gender, Race/Ethnicity, LGBT, and Disability from 2007–2016', Annenberg Foundation, http://annenberg.usc.edu/sites/default/files/Dr_Stacy_L_Smith-Inequality_in_900_Popular_Films.pdf.

Smith, S.L., Choueiti, M. & Pieper, K. (2017b) Over Sixty, Underestimated: A Look at Aging on the 'Silver' Screen in Best Picture Nominated Films, Humana/USC Annenberg, http://annenberg.usc.edu/sites/default/files/2017/05/30/MDSCI_Over%20Sixty%20Underestimated%20Report%20Final.pdf.

Staskiewicz, K. (2012, 31 August) 'Sarah Polley: Stories We Tell Reveals Family Secret', http://ew.com/article/2012/08/31/sarah-polley-stories-we-tell/.

Stephen (2015, 17 May) A Review of the ARRI Alexa XT Professional Production Camera, http://4k.com/camera/a-review-of-the-arri-alexa-xt-4k-production-camera/.

Sterritt, D. (2000) With Borrowed Eyes: An Interview with Abbas Kiarostami, Film Comment, www.filmcomment.com/article/with-borrowed-eyes-an-interview-with-abbas-kiarostami/.

Stevens, I. (2015, 20 October) 'Rebel Charm: Benh Zeitlin on *Beasts of the Southern Wild*', *Sight & Sound*, www.bfi.org.uk/news-opinion/sight-sound-magazine/interviews/lff-blog-rebel-charm-benh-zeitlin-beasts-southern-wild.

Stevenson, B. (2017, March) From Los Angeles to *La La Land*: Mapping Whiteness in the Wake of Cinema, Senses of Cinema, http://sensesofcinema.com/2017/feature-articles/from-los-angeles-to-la-la-land/.

Stone, A.A. (1995) 'Pulp Fiction', *Boston Review*, April/May, http://bostonreview.net/archives/BR20.2/stone.html.

Summit Entertainment (2016) *La La Land* Production Notes, www.lionsgatepublicity.com/uploads/assets/LA%20LA%20LAND%20NOTES%20FINAL%209.7.16.pdf.

Sundance Institute (2018) Feature Film Program, www.sundance.org/programs/feature-film#/.

Sweeney, K.W. (2007) *Buster Keaton: Interviews*, University Press of Mississippi.

Tasker, Y. (2010) *Fifty Contemporary Film Directors*, Routledge.

The End of Cinema (2013, 8 March) On Some Objections to Auterurism, theendofcinema.blogspot.co.uk/2013/03/on-some-objections-to-auteurism.html.

The Quietus (2014, 14 March) Věra Chytilová RIP, http://thequietus.com/articles/14742-vera-chytilova-rip.

The Straits Times (2015, 15 February) 'Iranian Dissident Director Jafar Panahi Wins Berlin Film Fest Golden Bear Top Prize for *Taxi*', www.straitstimes.com/lifestyle/entertainment/iranian-dissident-director-jafar-panahi-wins-berlin-film-fest-golden-bear.

Thompson, K. (1999) *Storytelling in the New Hollywood*, Harvard University Press.

Tobias, S. (2014, 4 April) Director Jonathan Glazer on *Under the Skin*'s Complex Honesty, Dissolve, https://thedissolve.com/features/interview/496-director-jonathan-glazer-on-under-the-skins-comple/.

Todorov, T. (1966) *Theorie de la Literature*, Editions du Seuil.

Tookey, C. (2009) *Casablanca*, Movie Film Review, www.movie-film-review.com/devFilm.asp?ID=2637.

USC (2017, 31 July) Hollywood Sticks to the Script: Diversity, On Screen and Behind the Camera, Remains Elusive, https://news.usc.edu/125565/hollywood-sticks-to-the-script-films-arent-more-inclusive-despite-a-decade-of-advocacy.

Ward, S. (2016) 'Cinema of Dissent: "Taxi, Tales" and the Troubles of Modern Iran', *Metro Magazine: Media & Education Magazine*, 187, http://search.informit.com.au/documentSummary;dn=043376001314686;res=IELLCC.

Watts, Jr, R. (1931, 18 March) 'Sight and Sound', *New York Herald Tribune*.

Weissberg, J. (2015, 19 May) 'Film Review: *Mustang*', *Variety*, http://variety.com/2015/film/festivals/mustang-review-cannes-1201500486/.

Welsh, I. (1994) *Trainspotting*, Vitage.

Whicker's World Foundation (n.d.) How Emerging Technology is Shaping the Future of Documentary Filmmaking.

Wikipedia Contributors (n.d.) *Focus On: 100 Most Popular Nonlinear Narrative Films*, https://books.google.co.uk/books?id=Is5CDwAAQBAJ&pg=PP1&lpg=PP1&dq=Focus+On:+100+Most+Popular+Nonlinear+Narrative+Films&source=bl&ots=eREv5rrOjE&sig=kx9ogvSPMJrSruI5jpj-tRpZ3uY&hl=en&sa=X&ved=0ahUKEwiA15XC2rHYAhWpK8AKHX5RCHEQ6AEIKTAA#v=onepage&q=Focus%20On%3A%20100%20Most%20Popular%20Nonlinear%20Narrative%20Films&f=false.

WJEC (2017a) Film Studies AS/A Level (From 2017), http://wjec.co.uk/qualifications/film-studies/eduqas-film-studies-as-level-from-2017/.

WJEC (2017a) *Guidance for Teaching*, www.wjec.co.uk/qualifications/film-studies/Eduqas%20Film%20Guidance%20for%20Teaching%20-%20A%20level.pdf?language_id=1.

Wood, J. (2007) *Talking Movies: Contemporary World Filmmakers in Interview*, Wallflower Press.

Wood, R. (1976) 'Murnau's *Midnight* and *Sunrise*', *Film Comment*, May–June.

World Economic Forum (2013) The Global Gender Gap Report 2013, www3.weforum.org/docs/WEF_GenderGap_Report_2013.pdf.

York University (n.d.) Ethnicity & Neighbourhood, www.yorku.ca/anderson/geog2060su15/ethnicity%20and%20neighbourhood.pdf.

Young, C. (2013, 10 December) *Bonnie and Clyde* (1967), https://classichollywoodstylebook.wordpress.com/2013/12/10/bonnie-and-clyde-1967.

Young, N. (2013, 20 January) For Tribune: Ben Wheatley's *Sightseers*, www.jigsawlounge.co.uk/film/reviews/tribsightseers/.

Index